GOD AND
SEA POWER

GOD AND SEA POWER

THE INFLUENCE OF RELIGION ON ALFRED THAYER MAHAN

SUZANNE GEISSLER

NAVAL INSTITUTE PRESS
ANNAPOLIS, MARYLAND

This book has been brought to publication with the generous assistance
of Marguerite and Gerry Lenfest.

Naval Institute Press
291 Wood Road
Annapolis, MD 21402

Library of Congress Cataloging-in-Publication Data
Geissler, Suzanne.
  God and sea power : the influence of religion on Alfred Thayer Mahan / by
Suzanne Geissler.
     pages cm
  Includes bibliographical references and index.
  ISBN 978-1-61251-843-5 (alk. paper) — ISBN 978-1-61251-844-2 (ebook)
  1. Mahan, A. T. (Alfred Thayer), 1840–1914—Religious life. 2. United States.
Navy—Biography. 3. Naval historians—United States—Biography. I. Title. II.
Title: Influence of religion on Alfred Thayer Mahan.
  E182.M242G45 2015
  359.3'32092—dc23
  [B]
                              2015021200

⊚ Print editions meet the requirements of ANSI/NISO z39.48–1992
(Permanence of Paper).
Printed in the United States of America.

23 22 21 20 19 18 17 16 15   9 8 7 6 5 4 3 2 1
First printing

TO THE MEMORY OF GRAHAM

Contents

ILLUSTRATIONS

ACKNOWLEDGMENTS

This project came about because of the convergence of two of my academic interests, American religion and naval history, in the person of Alfred Thayer Mahan. Like Mahan, I am an active Episcopal layperson. When I first read about Mahan, just for my own interest, I was intrigued by his religious faith and wondered why hardly anyone paid any attention to it when it clearly played such a major role in his life and thought. And the few who did pay attention seemed to lack even the most rudimentary knowledge of the Bible, church history in general, and the Episcopal Church in particular. I put aside other projects and pursued Mahan for the next seventeen years. I was fortunate early on to connect with two distinguished naval history scholars, John B. Hattendorf, Ernest J. King Professor of Maritime History at the United States Naval War College, and Jon T. Sumida, professor of history at the University of Maryland. Both of them believed that a study of Mahan's religion was long overdue and they encouraged me to pursue it. I am happy to acknowledge my tremendous debt to them and to thank them for all the assistance they rendered along the way. John Hattendorf sent me a number of books, pamphlets, and catalogs from the Naval War College Press that got me started. Jon Sumida also read the entire first draft and gave me a detailed critique that made the revised version much better. I also thank my dear friend Ruth Richardson Ragovin, who read the first draft and made many helpful suggestions. With a doctorate in theology and many years' experience in the field of scholarly publishing, she was the ideal person to take on this task, which she graciously agreed to do.

Two other historians to whom I owe special thanks are Robert Bruce Mullin, professor of Modern Anglican Studies at General Theological Seminary and historiographer of the Episcopal Church, and Wayne Kempton, archivist of the Episcopal Diocese of New York. No one knows as much about the nineteenth-century Episcopal Church as Bruce Mullin, and he graciously answered many queries from me about Milo Mahan's career at General Theological Seminary and his mentoring of his nephew Alfred. Likewise, Wayne Kempton answered many questions from me over the years, helped me track down obscure sources, and even solved some mysteries.

It is also my pleasure to thank Evelyn Cherpak, now retired, but for many years the archivist at the Naval War College Library. Apart from assisting me in accessing the Mahan Papers, she helped me in numerous ways, including arranging the details of my trip to Newport. In later years she was always a most congenial dinner companion at the numerous naval history conferences we attended.

I can't even begin to list all the ways Adam Nettina, my editor at the Naval Institute Press, helped me. I have never worked with an editor as competent and enthusiastic as Adam. His suggestions and corrections made for a much improved manuscript. He also willingly took on many tedious jobs in readying the manuscript for production so I would not have to do them myself. Thank you, Adam, for everything.

So many people at libraries, historical societies, churches, schools, and archives lent assistance along the way. It is my pleasure to thank them now: George Maxwell, Church of the Atonement, Quogue, N.Y.; Bruce Shaw and Jordan Sleeper of the Church of St. John the Evangelist, Newport, R.I.; David Wigdor at the Library of Congress; Isaac Gewirtz and Laura Moore of the General Theological Seminary Library; Judith Sibley and Suzanne Christoff of the U.S. Military Academy Library; Marlana Cook of the U.S. Military Academy Museum; David D'Onofrio and Barbara Manvel at the U.S. Naval Academy Library; Janis Jorgensen of the U.S. Naval Institute photo archives; Scott Reilly of the Naval War College Library; Robert Doane of the Naval War College Museum; Ted Camp of St. James School, Hagerstown, Md.; Jamie Smith of St. Paul's School, Baltimore; Brig. Gen. Thomas Griess, USA (ret.), biographer of Dennis Hart Mahan; Julie Greene of the Quogue Historical Society; and the Reverend James Elliott Lindsley, Episcopal priest and historian.

I would also like to thank the Naval Institute Press, the Society for Military History, and the Historical Society of the Episcopal Church for permission to use material originally appearing in, respectively, *New Interpretations of Naval History*, the *Journal of Military History*, and *Anglican and Episcopal History*.

My colleagues in the History Department at William Paterson University also deserve my thanks for their support and encouragement during the many years I worked on this project and for asking the questions that needed to be asked. It is a privilege to be a part of such a supportive and collegial department.

My biggest debt is to my beloved husband Graham, who did not live to hold the book in his hand but did know that it was going to be published. This book is dedicated to his memory.

Note on style: All Bible quotations are from the Authorized (King James) Version of 1611, which of course is the version Mahan used.

INTRODUCTION

Those who toil in the field of naval history are usually familiar with the oft-quoted remark of Henry L. Stimson that the Navy Department inhabited "a dim religious world in which Neptune was God, Mahan his prophet, and the United States Navy the only true Church."[1] It is certainly a pithy quotation and while in its original context it referred to the Navy Department in the 1940s, it is often applied to the United States Navy and its admirers in a more general sense. Since the publication in 1890 of his *The Influence of Sea Power upon History, 1660–1783*, the name of Alfred Thayer Mahan (1840–1914) has dominated the study of not only American naval history but British as well. Indeed, one could argue that it has had an impact on the history of any nation with a navy.[2]

He was the most influential American author of the nineteenth century. Two buildings have been named after him, one at the U.S. Naval Academy in Annapolis, Maryland, and one at the U.S. Naval War College in Newport, Rhode Island. Four United States warships have been named after him, DD 102/DM 7, DD 364, DLG 11/DDG 42, and DDG 72. Three schools were named in his honor as well, the elementary and high schools at the former Naval Air Station at Keflavik, Iceland, and the mission school at Yangchow, China. Even the adjectival form of his name—Mahanian—is a fixture in the vocabulary of naval historiography.

Even though gallons of ink have been spilled analyzing his thought, as the bibliography attests, one vital aspect of his life and thought, namely his religious faith as manifested in his writings and his activities in the Episcopal Church, has been ignored or misunderstood. Mahan was a professing Christian who took his faith with the utmost seriousness, and his worldview was inherently Christian. Most scholars have overlooked this, though even a cursory familiarity with his personal papers and his public writings makes it obvious. As a result, with few exceptions, the view of Mahan is seriously incomplete. His Christianity, especially as he practiced it in the Episcopal Church, was not only central to his personal life but also influenced his writings on naval and geopolitical topics. He also wrote and spoke extensively on religious topics, a point also ignored by many historians. This is a fundamental mistake, for a deeper and more accurate understanding of Mahan as a person and as a naval theorist can be gained by an examination of his religious beliefs.

Three biographies of Mahan have been published. The first was Charles Carlisle Taylor's *The Life of Admiral Mahan*, published in 1920.[3] Taylor was British and had served as vice consul in New York City, and he made no secret of his admiration of Mahan. This admiration was largely based on the circumstances of World War I, which had only recently ended. Taylor credited Mahan's writings, both in published works and in private letters to British friends, with helping the Allied side in the Great War (even though Mahan had died shortly after the war in Europe began). The biography is essentially a long thank-you note to Mahan from a grateful British citizen. Taylor credited Mahan with three achievements: reminding Britain of the importance of its naval heritage, encouraging the pro-navy lobby in Britain to resist any downsizing of the Royal Navy, and warning Britain of the threat posed by the German naval buildup. Because of these achievements, Britain, and particularly its navy, were better able to face the German threat and ultimately prevail. Taylor even went so far as to credit Mahan with possessing a "genius" that "immeasurably contributed to save modern civilization through the mighty influence of sea power."[4] Taylor's admiration for Mahan was genuine, and, realizing this, he tried to present an accurate account of Mahan's life "resisting the while a very natural temptation to mix the colours with an over-abundance of rose-water."[5] The great value of Taylor's work is that he had the full cooperation of Mahan's family and access to his papers and correspondence. There are a number of documents in the book that are not available elsewhere. Taylor also had the advantage of being able to correspond with and interview people who knew Mahan personally. This gives the book an immediacy and personal insight that later volumes, while more thoroughly researched, do not share.[6]

The second biography was William D. Puleston's *Mahan: The Life and Work of Captain Alfred Thayer Mahan, U.S.N.*, published in 1939. Puleston was a captain in the U.S. Navy and a former director of naval intelligence. Though too young to have been a protégé of Mahan, he was clearly an admirer and something of a naval intellectual, trying in a more modest way to follow in Mahan's footsteps. If Taylor's biography was written as a thank-you after World War I, Puleston's was written as a warning to heed Mahan and prepare for the conflagration that Puleston saw coming. His book, he said, "will demonstrate that [Mahan's] message was primarily intended for the American people and his thesis is as vital today as it was to Great Britain when it was written almost a half century ago."[7] Puleston's book was more thoroughly researched than Taylor's and was based on a wider variety of sources. Puleston also had, as Taylor did, the cooperation of Mahan's surviving family and friends. He amassed a wider variety of correspondence, both American and British, and thoroughly researched Mahan's family background.[8] Puleston tried to assess Mahan fairly based on a critical study of the primary sources, and as a consequence his biographical effort is sound and thus of lasting value.

The third biography was Robert Seager II's *Alfred Thayer Mahan: The Man and His Letters*, published in 1977. Seager was an academic, but one with long service in the merchant marine and involvement with the military. At the time of publication he was a professor of history at the University of Kentucky. Previously he had, with Doris D. Maguire, edited the *Letters and Papers of Alfred Thayer Mahan*, published in three volumes by the Naval Institute Press in 1975. These papers were the raw material for his biography of Mahan.[9] Though more detailed and more thoroughly and widely researched than the previous two biographies, this work is nonetheless deeply flawed. Simply put, Seager developed such an intense, even visceral, dislike for Mahan that it colors the entire book. From birth to death Mahan does nothing right in Seager's eyes. In just about every instance, even the most trivial, Seager presents Mahan in as bad a light as possible. Though Seager uses sarcasm and mockery rather than outright attack, the result is the same. Seager, of course, is perfectly entitled to disagree with Mahan and any or all of his theories, but it is the personal attacks that render this book so suspect. No doubt Seager thought he was trying to be objective, but his *personal* dislike for Mahan seems to have contaminated his consideration of the sources. Whether intentional or not, Seager sometimes gets his facts wrong and misreads documents, but more frequently he comes to conclusions that the evidence does not warrant or in some cases actually refutes. While acknowledging that Mahan authored "perhaps the most powerful and influential book written by an American in America in the nineteenth century," he also asserts strident negatives, calling Mahan a "racist, Social Darwinist . . . social climber, [and] egoist" and labeling Mahan's philosophy as "egocentric, parochial in its Christian stridency and narrow Anglo-Americanism."[10]

Some reviewers criticized Seager on these grounds. Charles E. Neu, reviewing for the *Journal of American History*, pointed out that Seager had little interest in or sympathy "with Mahan's inner struggles" and because of his "refusal to employ psychological insights" had no way of analyzing them.[11] Richard

Turk, in an otherwise favorable review in *Military Affairs*, thought that Seager unfairly castigated Mahan for his home life. These judgments "are scarcely flattering and quite possibly unfair. Victorian attitudes and mores are an easy and irresistible target today."[12] None of those negative traits for which Seager castigates Mahan are necessarily incompatible with authoring an influential book, but are they accurate representations of the man or are they evidence of the biographer's own prejudices? It is impossible to say for certain why Seager disliked Mahan so much or why he subjected Mahan's religious beliefs to such derisive ridicule. The one substantive clue is provided by the dust jacket of Seager's book, which tells us that he was the son of Episcopal missionaries to China and went to an Episcopal high school. Possibly a rebellion against his background is the source of his animus.

Most writers on Mahan simply ignore his faith, regarding the matter as having no bearing on the work upon which his fame rests. A few see how important it was to Mahan, but view it as a negative influence on him, a pernicious trait that made him arrogant and self-righteous. That is the view of Seager as well as of Peter Karsten in his iconoclastic *The Naval Aristocracy: The Golden Age of Annapolis and the Emergence of Modern American Navalism* (1972).[13] Taylor and Puleston both acknowledged Mahan's serious practice of his Christian faith and viewed it as a positive character trait, but they did not pay it much attention, and neither made any attempt to analyze it as such. There are only two studies that show a more sophisticated understanding of Mahan's theology. One is an article, "Christianity and the Evangelist for Sea Power," by Navy chaplain Reo N. Leslie Jr., which appeared in *The Influence of History on Mahan* (1991), a collection of papers given at the Naval War College to commemorate the one hundredth anniversary of the publication of *The Influence of Sea Power upon History*. The other is Jon T. Sumida's book *Inventing Grand Strategy and Teaching Command: The Classic Works of Alfred Thayer Mahan Reconsidered* (1997).[14] Both these works contain useful insights into Mahan's Christian faith and its influence on him, but Leslie's is only an article and Sumida's book, while containing intriguing analyses of Mahan's religious writings, is not mainly about religion. The present work is the first full-length study of Mahan's religious faith. It focuses on three issues: (1) what was the content of Mahan's religious faith and how did it develop, (2) how did it influence his naval and geopolitical thinking, and (3) what role did Mahan play within the Episcopal Church.

Crucial to Mahan's development as an officer, a scholar, and a Christian were the two male role models in his early life, his father Dennis Hart Mahan, military scholar and West Point professor, and his uncle Milo Mahan, Episcopal priest and professor at General Theological Seminary, the Episcopal seminary in New York City that had been founded in 1817. Because of their importance, the lives of these two men are discussed in detail, and that is where we begin our study of Alfred.

CHAPTER 1

FAMILY

DENNIS HART MAHAN

The first Mahan to come to the United States was Alfred's grandfather John, a Roman Catholic from Ireland. Accompanied by his wife, Mary Cleary, he arrived in New York City in 1800. Their son Dennis Hart was born April 2, 1802, and baptized at St. Peter's Roman Catholic Church on April 27. Shortly thereafter the Mahans moved to Norfolk, Virginia, where, on account of war between Britain and France, the city's shipbuilding industry was thriving. John Mahan, a carpenter by trade, was attracted by the prospect of steady employment and high wages. He did quite well, expanding his business from carpentry to contracting and dabbling in real estate as well. While never becoming rich or socially prominent, John seems to have been financially comfortable and was able to provide good educations for his sons.[1]

Shortly after arriving in Norfolk, Mary Mahan died. In 1805 John married a widow, Eleanor McKim, in the Catholic church in Norfolk. Little is known about John's second wife and she died soon after their wedding.[2] John married for the third time in 1814. His bride was again a widow, Esther Moffitt, and the marriage was again performed in the Catholic church.[3] It seems most likely, though, that Esther was a Protestant. Taylor identifies her as such, and Milo's biographer, John Henry Hopkins Jr., identifies her as coming from an "old Virginia family," in which case she would almost certainly have been an Episcopalian.[4] That her son Milo was brought up as an Episcopalian would also indicate this. Esther was able to establish a good relationship with her stepson Dennis and she became the maternal figure in his life.

Little is known of Dennis' childhood, although Puleston speculates that he probably attended the Norfolk Academy. Presumably he was brought up a Roman Catholic, at least until the age of twelve, but we do not know if that affiliation was a nominal one or seriously practiced. Taylor states that he was raised

as a Protestant subsequent to his father's marriage to Esther. We also know that Dennis early on developed an antipathy for the British and an admiration for the French (a pattern that would be reversed in his son), probably due to his Irish ancestry and his childhood memories of the War of 1812.[5]

On May 24, 1819, Esther Mahan gave birth to a son Milo, Dennis' only sibling. Despite the seventeen-year age difference, the two brothers remained close all their lives. By this time the family had relocated to Suffolk, Virginia.[6]

Though it was reported in Mahan family tradition that Dennis originally thought of becoming a doctor and was studying with a Norfolk physician, Robert Archer, Puleston doubts that Dennis ever studied medicine. He did, however, know Dr. Archer and expressed to him his desire to study drawing. Dr. Archer, an Army veteran, told Dennis that West Point offered excellent instruction in drawing, and Dennis determined to go there. Through the good offices of Dr. Archer, his brother who was an Army colonel, congressman Thomas Newton, and newspaperman Thomas Broughton, Dennis secured an appointment to the Military Academy from secretary of war John C. Calhoun.[7] He entered West Point in July 1820, thus beginning a fifty-year association with that institution.

In later years Dennis told his children of his arrival at West Point (at that time accessible only by boat) on July 4, 1820. Tired and thirsty and seeing a Fourth of July party in progress, he asked a waiter for a glass of water. The waiter replied, "Water! This is the Fourth of July and no one here drinks anything but champagne."[8] An appointment to West Point did not guarantee admission; an entrance exam given on the premises still had to be passed, which Dennis negotiated easily and became a member of the class of 1824.[9]

When Dennis arrived at West Point it was under the superintendency of Brevet (i.e., Acting) Lt. Col. Sylvanus Thayer of the Corps of Engineers. Thayer is known as "the father of the Military Academy," not because he was its founder or its first superintendent—he was the fourth superintendent—but because he took over an academy that was loosely run and unsure of its purpose and turned it into a first-class military and educational institution. He instituted a number of practices and guidelines still in use today, including strict discipline, academic emphasis on mathematics and engineering, and a merit roll in which every cadet is ranked on academics, deportment, and military bearing.[10] Dennis thrived under the Thayer regime and found his true calling as a soldier-scholar.

Dennis had an extremely successful four years as a cadet. He ranked first in his class at the end of each of his four years and first overall at graduation. So great was his academic ability that at the beginning of his third class (sophomore) year he was made acting assistant professor of mathematics with the responsibility of teaching "plebe math" to fourth-class cadets. Though still a cadet himself he was a quasi-officer as well and received special privileges, extra pay, and a distinctive uniform. The extra ten dollars a month must have been welcomed since his father died in 1821 and Dennis began assisting his step-mother in providing for Milo's education.[11]

Sometime prior to his graduation Dennis experienced a religious conversion. We know almost nothing about it except that he began to study the Bible and drew comfort and spiritual sustenance from his newfound faith. In a letter to his stepmother written shortly after his graduation he told her how he tried to live his life by the Bible's teachings and urged her to instruct Milo to do the same. Referring to the Bible as "his [i.e., God's] book," he told her to "tell [Milo] above all things to stick to his book . . . tell him that his brother has done everything for himself by his book, and that he must try and do the same."[12]

The chaplain at West Point during Dennis' entire time there as a cadet was Thomas Picton, a Presbyterian. This is at variance with the oft-made assumption that West Point chaplains in the nineteenth century were exclusively Episcopalians. Academy chaplains in this period were not Army chaplains but civilian clerics hired by the academy, although it is true that Episcopalians were preferred. Joseph G. Swift, the second superintendent, wanted only Episcopalians, but it was not always possible to entice a suitable candidate to West Point, and Presbyterians seem to have been regarded as an acceptable second choice.[13] We know nothing about Picton's influence, if any, on Dennis, though certainly Dennis would have been familiar with him. Chapel attendance was made mandatory by Thayer and no alternate provision was made for non-Protestants. Dennis also would have encountered him in class since Picton taught geography, history, and ethics.[14]

Though Seager takes the cynical view and claims that Dennis' "Roman Catholic and Irish roots [had] conveniently withered somewhere along the way"—presumably because both the Irish and Catholics were looked down upon in the Protestant America of that day—there is no reason to think that Dennis' conversion was anything but genuine.[15] He professed a strong evangelical Protestant Christian faith his entire adult life, and neither Dennis nor any of the Mahans in this study practiced a lukewarm "gentleman's religion" version of Christianity.

Upon his graduation Dennis admitted to his stepmother that he was "proud, very proud" of ranking first in his class, thanked her for "the interest you take in my affairs," and expressed his sadness "that my Father could not have lived till now to enjoy my pleasure with me."[16] Dennis was then commissioned a brevet second lieutenant in the Corps of Engineers (there being more second lieutenants than there were slots for them in companies). Fortunately for him, his skill at mathematics and engineering, plus his status as Thayer's number one protégé, ensured that he would receive a prestigious assignment. He was appointed assistant professor of mathematics at the academy, though detailed for a brief summer assignment with the Corps of Engineers in New York City and Baltimore. In September he returned to West Point to begin his teaching duties and later that year the brevet was dropped from his rank and he became a full second lieutenant. Despite the disparity in their ranks, Dennis had now crossed the gulf between cadet and officer and was thus able to develop a closer relationship with his mentor Thayer, often dining with the superintendent and playing chess with him. In August 1825 Thayer appointed Dennis assistant professor of engineering, a more prestigious and demanding post.[17] Suffering from ill health in the 1825–26 academic year, Dennis requested reassignment to a warmer climate or a leave of absence. Through the intervention of Thayer and Alexander Macomb, chief of engineers, Dennis was able to wangle from the secretary of war, James Barbour, not only a leave of absence but an assignment to visit France to study aspects of civil and military engineering that might be useful to the United States. The one-year leave stretched to four, and this extended tour proved crucial to his future both professionally and personally.[18]

Dennis did little work his first year in France, but he boarded with a French family, improved his facility with the language, and made useful contacts. One of the people he met was the elderly Marquis de Lafayette, with whom he became friends. He wrote his cousin Mary Ann Charlton that "Our kind old General has contributed very much to make my trip agreeable by giving and procuring for me numberless letters of introduction to persons of the most distinction in the towns thro' which I have passed."[19] Through Thayer's influence, Dennis had already developed an admiration for the French military, especially its educational system; this admiration only increased through firsthand contact.

After travel around France as well as brief visits to England and Italy, Dennis got permission from Thayer and his superiors to extend his leave so he could enroll in the French Army's School of Application for Engineers and Artillery at Metz. At the time the French military engineers were considered the best in the world, and Dennis convinced Thayer—who probably needed little persuading—that what he learned at Metz would be of direct benefit to West Point and the U.S. Army. Though the normal course of study was two years, Dennis was allowed to stay sixteen months. This time at Metz proved valuable to Dennis. As his biographer Thomas Griess said, "it certainly broadened his professional foundation and brought him into contact with the best minds in [military engineering]."[20]

Dennis' trip to France proved significant for another reason. While there he met and formed a close friendship with Frederick Augustus Muhlenberg, a physician, hymn writer, and younger brother of William Augustus Muhlenberg, an Episcopal priest who had a profound impact on the antebellum Episcopal Church. Dennis and Frederick were the same age and their friendship continued until Frederick's untimely death in 1837. Dennis was later to name his second son after him, and it was through Frederick that Dennis was drawn into the orbit of William Muhlenberg, who was to exert a strong influence on two generations of the Mahan family. Dennis may have already become an Episcopalian by this time and this would have created a bond between him and Frederick; or, alternately, Dennis might have become an Episcopalian under Frederick's influence.[21]

Dennis returned to New York in July 1830 and proceeded directly to West Point to resume his teaching duties. Thayer was already grooming him to take over the Engineering Department, and the advancement came about sooner than anticipated because of the resignation of the incumbent. Dennis' promotion was not, however, a sure thing. Two other candidates, both lieutenants, were also being considered, but Dennis was by far the best qualified because of his study in France, and not surprisingly, he won the position. Army regulations at that time required that full professors be civilians, so on June 1, 1832 Dennis, still a second lieutenant, resigned his commission and was appointed professor of engineering (which also meant being department chairman), a position he was to hold till his death in 1871.[22]

Romance came to Dennis' life in 1830. Shortly after his return to West Point a group of teenaged schoolgirls, chaperoned by their headmistress, visited the academy to attend a "hop" (dance). The twenty-eight-year-old Dennis took a liking to fifteen-year-old Mary Helena Okill, daughter of the headmistress. It is not clear whether Dennis was aware prior to their initial meeting that the Okills were friends of the Muhlenberg brothers, but that fact contributed to the progress of the courtship, as no doubt did the young lady's Christian piety and devotion to Bible study. Despite a thirteen-year age difference they seemed entirely suited to each other, but Mary Helena's mother, at least initially, thought that Dennis was too old for her daughter. But Dennis persevered, and the Muhlenbergs might have pressed his case, and after a nine-year courtship he and Mary Helena were married in 1839.[23]

The bride's family had a distinguished lineage but also a few skeletons in the closet. Her maternal grandfather James Jay (brother of *Federalist* author and Chief Justice John Jay) and her grandmother Ann Erwin were never married "because of [Ann's] disbelief in the institution of marriage," according to Alfred's son Lyle's recollections. Their daughter Mary married John Okill, who deserted the family and left his wife with three small children, the youngest of whom was Mary Helena. In order to support herself Mrs. Okill opened a girls' school in New York City, which became "the leading girls' school of the day in the City."[24]

Dennis' career continued to prosper, and next to Thayer he became the dominant figure of nineteenth-century West Point. Of the generation that came after Thayer, Dennis was clearly the premier figure. Dennis' title changed several times, ultimately becoming professor of civil and military engineering and the science of war, and in 1838 he became the senior member of the faculty (later referred to as dean of the faculty), a position he held till his death. He published his first book, *A Treatise on Field Fortification*, in 1836 before going on to publish many of the first English-language engineering textbooks. They included *An Elementary Course of Civil Engineering* (1837), *Summary of the Course of Permanent Fortification* (1850), *An Elementary Course of Military Engineering*

Portrait of Dennis Hart Mahan by Robert Weir *(West Point Museum Collection, United States Military Academy)*

(1865), and *Industrial Drawing* (1867). His most important work went by the cumbersome name of *An Elementary Treatise on Advanced-Guard, Out-Post, and Detachment Service of Troops, and the Manner of Posting and Handling Them in Presence of an Enemy* (1853), but is better known by the short title *Outpost*. This book "still ranks as one of the foremost American contributions to the study of war."[25] *Outpost* was, in Dennis' own words, a "comprehensive survey of tactics and strategy" not just for professional soldiers alone, but also for the "use of militia and volunteers."[26] Its originality, according to William B. Skelton, lay in its adaptation of European tactics to the American situation.[27] (Skelton criticizes Dennis for not teaching or writing enough on Indian fighting, but both Griess and Ambrose dispute this and claim that he did deal with the subject adequately.[28]) In short, Dennis had quickly established himself as America's foremost authority on military engineering and tactics.

Dennis devoted himself not only to military scholarship but also to the United States Military Academy as an institution. James Morrison, historian of the early years of West Point, put it best:

> Throughout his long tenure as a professor Mahan used his brilliant intellect and facile pen to add lustre to the military academy to an extent his colleagues never matched. It was Mahan who defended West Point in the press, Mahan who acted as confidential advisor to prominent public figures and who exploited those connections to protect what he perceived to be the best interests of the academy, and it was Mahan who published articles in the leading journals of the day. It was also Mahan who by virtue of his seniority, prestige, and force of personality guided the academic board for four decades.[29]

What was Dennis Mahan like in the classroom and how did he interact with cadets? Those cadets who have left us their impressions of Professor Mahan generally mention three things. One was that he always carried an umbrella no matter what the weather. The second was that he had a chronic nasal infection and his frequently mentioned dictum to use common sense came out as "cobbon sense." Hence the cadets nicknamed him "Old Cobbon Sense."[30] The third characteristic he was noted for was his classroom demeanor, which showed no mercy to slackers. "Sloppy thinking and careless attitudes toward duty were anathema to him" was a characteristic to which many cadet reminiscences attested.[31] Morris Schaff claimed "there never was a colder eye or manner," presumably referring to Dennis' manner of staring at an unprepared cadet.[32] Tully McCrea thought Dennis "the most particular, crabbed, exacting man that I ever saw . . . always nervous and cross."[33] Even William Tecumseh Sherman, one of the few cadets for whom Dennis had a soft spot, was afraid of him and claimed that even as a general he "still shuddered when he thought of being caught unprepared by Mahan."[34] That is not to say, of course, that the cadets did not respect Dennis or appreciate his vast knowledge of military matters. Most were in awe of him, but some managed to appreciate him at an earlier stage than their classmates did. John C. Tidball thought "he was a most thorough and good instructor. His pupils believed in him and thought it impossible that any one could carry more than he knew."[35] Even if he was hard on the cadets, "a little captious and irritable . . . his severity was not designed to wound his pupils nor do them any injustice. . . . [He] was ever ready to explain [the lesson's] intricacies, and with his skillful analysis give it a new portraiture." As a military analyst he was, according to George Cullum, "an accomplished master."[36]

Dennis remained a staunch Episcopalian throughout his adult life. His interest in the Christian faith went far beyond the merely nominal, while his friendship with the Muhlenbergs continued for many years. Through William Muhlenberg he made the acquaintance of theologian Samuel Seabury III (who would later become a colleague of Milo's at General Theological Seminary). In 1831 Seabury sent Dennis the proof sheets of his new book *The Study of the Classics on Christian Principles*. Dennis thanked him and said that when the book was published he would give a copy to "a young relative of mine" (presumably Milo, then twelve). Dennis also noted that he had no objection to the expurgation of immoral "excresencies" of certain risque works, "particularly when by such means you hope to advance the great ends of morality and religion."[37] Since Seabury was then teaching at William Muhlenberg's school, Flushing Institute, this book was probably intended for the use of teenaged students.

An ongoing concern of Dennis', particularly once he had a family, was the West Point chapel. Dennis was blunt in saying that he did not want any but an Episcopal chaplain at the Military Academy. He defended his view not in terms of personal preference—which naturally would have seemed arbitrary and self-serving—but because "the great majority of the permanently settled Officers" were of that affiliation. This group's preference should be the determining factor in appointing a chaplain because unlike two other constituencies—the cadets (who were forbidden to be married) and the active duty officers (who were only there for a short rotation)—the permanent staff considered the chapel to be their regular parish church to which they brought their families. A non-Episcopal clergyman could not be "occupying the pastoral relationship to [these] families." Naturally, Episcopal parents wanted their children brought up in the Episcopal Church, and in 1850 Dennis wrote a letter to secretary of war Charles M. Conrad complaining about this very situation.[38] The chaplain in question was William T. Sprole, a Presbyterian, who had been appointed in 1847. Other

Episcopal faculty members complained as well, and even though Sprole was popular with the cadets, he was dismissed in 1856 after refusing to resign.[39]

Another facet of Dennis' complaint to Conrad was an ambiguous order recently handed down that seemed to imply that chapel attendance was mandatory for officers and staff. Dennis had no objection to mandatory chapel for cadets. He thought required attendance "produces always an impression of the most salutary and lasting character upon youth." He also thought that officers and staff should attend chapel to set a good example to the cadets. But he objected strongly to being told that he must attend when the services were not Episcopal, believing such attendance violated his conscience. He and other Episcopalians on the staff had no desire "to attend a form of worship with which they can have but little sympathy." The whole problem could be obviated, of course, by appointing only Episcopalians to the chaplaincy.[40] It is not clear how the situation was resolved, but the regulation in question does not appear to have ever been enforced, and in any case Sprole was eventually dismissed and replaced by an Episcopalian.[41] Though Dennis did not mention it in his letter, there was a recently established (1850) Episcopal parish in the village of Highland Falls (then called Buttermilk Falls) just outside the academy gate,[42] which would have provided an alternate place of worship for Episcopal staff members, but obviously not if they were ordered to attend the post chapel.

Dennis, always a stickler for proper behavior, in one notable instance (and probably many others) was horrified by the foul language used by cadets. One evening in 1852 he passed by "the room where the Cadets take their dancing lessons" and heard "swearing and such blasphemous language as I should blush to repeat." This led him to send a three-page letter to the first captain of the Cadet Corps (the highest ranking cadet), James B. McPherson. Dennis wrote, he said, "not as an officer of the Academy, but as a friend," and as one who had been a cadet himself. He understood that cadets were young, immature, isolated from civilian society, and beset by "difficulties" and "temptations," and he was prepared to "make great allowances for them." Vulgar language was bad enough, but "open irreverence and blasphemy of the Most High" (presumably using the names of God and Jesus Christ as swear words) were intolerable. Not only would such language offend civilians who might overhear it, for example, "the pure Matron, the unsullied Maiden, the Minister of religion, the hoary headed and devout Father who has a son just placed among you," but it also coarsened the cadets themselves. How could they possibly be considered gentlemen when they used "the habitual language of the lowest brothels and taprooms." Appealing to McPherson not "in its religious or moral aspect" but "as a matter of good taste," Dennis urged him to attend to the problem. Despite his denial of making a religious issue out of it, Dennis did so anyway, reminding McPherson that all "who honor God" are offended by such language and that "the sacred responsibilities of Religion and morals" required the cadets—if they wished to be considered gentlemen—to abjure these bad habits at once. McPherson's response has not survived, though surely he could not have ignored a missive from such a powerful figure at the academy. Whether the letter did any good we do not know. One suspects it probably had little effect except to impress upon cadets the need to be more circumspect when Professor Mahan was in the vicinity. If nothing else, it clearly shows Dennis' concern for the honor of God's name, and no doubt his distress was entirely genuine.[43]

Other questions regarding Dennis Mahan's role in the development of the U.S. Army, such as whether he was a Jominian (a disciple of Antoine Henri, Baron Jomini, the Swiss military strategist) or not, and to what extent his teachings influenced the decisions made by his students who fought in the Civil War, are not directly relevant to our study and are best left to military historians to debate. Dennis' role as father will be discussed further below. For now let us turn our attention to his younger brother Milo, who was also to exert a powerful influence on Alfred.

Milo Mahan

Milo was born on May 24, 1819, to John Mahan's third wife, Esther. He had the same birth date as Queen Victoria and as an adult used to joke that the British Empire celebrated his birthday. His father died in 1821, and since Dennis was already at West Point, presumably the dominant influence in his early life was his mother. When Milo reached his teens Dennis took over the direction of his education.[44]

Milo was influenced by a name familiar to the Mahan family—William Augustus Muhlenberg. Muhlenberg (1796–1877), scion of a family once prominent in American Lutheranism, was ordained in the Episcopal Church in 1817. A man of many interests including hymnody, liturgy, urban ministry, education, and ecumenism, he became a significant force in the mid-nineteenth-century Episcopal Church. Known as the Evangelical Catholic (and founding a newspaper of the same name), he was "a prophet whom no party could claim" and a priest who "combined an esteem for dignified liturgy with a deeply ecumenical outlook and a profound concern for social responsibility in the Church."[45] He was also the driving force behind the so-called Muhlenberg Memorial, a document submitted to the General Convention in 1853 proposing a plan that would make the Protestant Episcopal Church the core around which one national Protestant Church would form.[46]

Of more immediate interest to the Mahan family was Muhlenberg's founding of a high school, Flushing Institute, in Flushing, New York, in 1828, and a companion college, St. Paul's, in 1836 (In some historical accounts the high school is incorrectly referred to as St. Paul's.) Both the high school and college were personally run by Muhlenberg, and he infused them with his particular philosophy of Christian education based on the family. He perceived his schools to be a family and himself as rector as the father figure. The students as sons were "living under the same roof and eating at the same table with him."[47] The goal of education was not just academic proficiency but "the production of the highest type of individual and corporate character."[48] The cornerstone of a Flushing–St. Paul's education was the chapel and the liturgical year. Muhlenberg was particularly concerned that chapel attendance not become a rigid and stultifying experience for the students. By stressing the inherent drama of the Christian year, the boys would come to love the liturgy and find it a satisfying way of expressing their faith. The church year, he said, "is admirably suited for the young, by keeping the objects of the faith before their minds in a natural way, and without repressing the proper cheerfulness of their years."[49] Muhlenberg concerned himself with every aspect of a boy's development and knew each student personally. Classes were kept small to provide individual attention, and there was plenty of time for sports and hobbies in the afternoon. Muhlenberg even outdid the students in pranks, in one instance dumping a jug of water over a student who was pretending to sleepwalk.[50]

When Milo was fourteen Dennis arranged for his enrollment at St. Paul's, bypassing the high school and going directly to the college. The school was never authorized by the state of New York to offer degrees, so it offered diplomas instead. The lack of degrees was later rectified by St. James College in Maryland, headed by St. Paul's graduate John B. Kerfoot (later first Bishop of Pittsburgh), which conferred degrees on St. Paul's alumni. Thus Milo received a Master of Arts in 1845, a Bachelor of Divinity in 1854, and a Doctor of Divinity in 1855, all from St. James.[51]

We know little about Milo's time at St. Paul's. Muhlenberg thought him a brilliant pupil but modestly declined credit for it, observing that "intellectually, of all my pupils he owed the distinction he attained but little to his education with me. It was all in himself, and it would have come forth anywhere in one field or another."[52] Muhlenberg later commented to Kerfoot that Milo "is the first man in intellect in the Church" and "needed to serve under a bishop whom he would respect for his learning and abilities, as well as his office."[53] Puleston says that Dennis tried but failed to get Milo an appointment to West Point, although there is no evidence that Milo ever showed any interest in a military career or an engineering education and his vocation for the church seems to have already manifested itself at St. Paul's.[54]

At the age of seventeen, Milo accepted an appointment as teacher of Greek at Virginia High School, an Episcopal school in Alexandria, one of several being established all over the country based on the Muhlenberg–St. Paul's model. Milo stayed there six or seven years (it is not clear which) and while there began to acquaint himself with the writings of the Tractarians, English priests who were moving to bring back to Anglicanism elements of its Catholic heritage. Also known as the Oxford Movement, the Tractarian Movement (so called because they published a series called *Tracts for the Times*) was highly controversial, attempting to reintroduce elements into Anglicanism that had not been seen since the advent of the English Reformation. Milo was eased out or dismissed from the high school by the Bishop of Virginia, William Meade, who, though he had previously considered Milo a "prize" was shocked to see a volume of *Tracts for the Times* on his bookshelf. Meade, staunchly Low Church, was afraid the students would be adversely influenced by Milo's example.[55] Milo returned to St. Paul's and taught there for three or four years until he decided to seek ordination. He was ordained a deacon on October 27, 1845, by Bishop Thomas Brownell, and a priest on December 14, 1846, by Bishop Levi Ives. Over the next five years he served at the Church of the Annunciation in New York City, Grace Van Vorst in Jersey City, and St. Mark's in Philadelphia.[56]

In 1851 Milo was elected professor of ecclesiastical history at General Theological Seminary, the Episcopal seminary in New York City that had been founded in 1817. This was a prestigious appointment for the young man and also a controversial one. At that time new professors were elected to their positions by the incumbent professors, but it took seven ballots to elect Milo. The major objection to him was that he had made no reputation for himself as a distinguished scholar.[57] He was on the editorial staff of the *Church Journal* and had had one sermon, *Church Missions*, recently published, but as yet no scholarly output.[58] But obviously enough of his fellow professors thought he had potential. One of them, Samuel Roosevelt Johnson, described Milo as "an accomplished fellow, a beautiful writer, & an agreeable man."[59] Even Milo's biographer John Henry Hopkins admitted that he "had no special preparation to the subject of Ecclesiastical History" but compensated for it by his enthusiasm, "wrapping the warm flesh and blood of present life around the dry bones of past ages." Much as Dennis included military history and strategy in his engineering courses, Milo included other subjects in his church history courses and used to say "that his professorship gave him abundant opportunities to teach all the other departments as well."[60] The seminary still used daily recitation and memorization as the basis of classroom instruction (not unlike the Thayer system at West Point), but whereas Dennis was a staunch defender of this system, Milo found it "somewhat of a bore," though he agreed that it forced the student to do "hard work" and gave him a "solid foundation."[61] By all accounts Milo seems to have been livelier and less rigid than Dennis in the classroom, and seminarians purportedly enjoyed his introducing "more juicy" topics into his lectures.[62]

During his career at General Theological Seminary (1851–64), Milo successfully managed to counter the two criticisms most frequently leveled against him: that he was too Anglo-Catholic and that he was not an accomplished scholar. Terms such as "High Church," "Anglo-Catholic," "Tractarian," "Oxford Movement," and "Ritualist" can be confusing because they do not have a precise definition upon which all agree, and while they all overlap they do not all mean precisely the same thing. Ritualism, for instance, was a specific subcategory of the Oxford Movement that concentrated on bringing more elements of medieval Catholic worship back into the Anglican liturgy. It is interesting that Dawley describes Milo as having "considerable sympathy with the rising Ritualist movement" but does not identify him as a Ritualist as such, a subtle distinction but perhaps a significant one.[63] Despite the suspicions that his "strong Tractarian[ism]" raised in some circles, there was absolutely no danger that Milo would do what that most famous of Tractarians, John Henry Newman, had done (bolt to Rome.) For all his High Church (and this is a more accurate description of Milo than is Anglo-Catholic) sentiments, Milo was staunchly anti-Roman, or, more to the point, antipapist. His biographer credited him with preventing many an impressionable young Anglo-Catholic from converting to Roman Catholicism; "From the period we speak of to the end of his life, no one of our Clergy has been more successful than Dr. Mahan in clearing men's minds of Roman doubts, or settling their consciences firmly and intelligently upon the basis of the true catholicity of the Anglican Communion."[64] Milo wrote two antipapal works, the first *An Exercise of Faith, In Its Relation to Authority and Private Judgment*, an attack on papal absolution published in 1855. This book was also published in London under the title *The Exercise of Faith: A Book for Doubters*, which showed a growing transatlantic reputation, always good for a professor's prestige. He also wrote *The Comedy of Canonization* in 1868, a scathing satire on the doctrine of papal infallibility.[65]

Regarding his scholarly output, Milo put those doubts to rest by publishing six books as well as numerous articles and sermons. His most famous book, and the one on which his reputation as a church historian chiefly rests, was *A Church History of the First Seven Centuries to the Close of the Sixth General Council*. This work consisted ultimately of five "books," or sections. The first three were published as one unit in 1860, while the revised edition was published posthumously in 1873 and contained the fourth and fifth books, which Milo had completed but not yet published at the time of his death in 1870. The book was "intended chiefly for the use of the general reader." It also was designed to be "a help to young students and candidates for Holy Orders," but only as a supplement to Eusebius, Johann Gieseler, or Philip Schaff, three historians to whom Milo acknowledged his debt.[66] In the introduction Milo showed himself an astute historian, acknowledging that every writer brings to his work his own biases, "the worst bias being that which makes the loudest profession of being free from bias." He admitted his own preconceptions had probably crept in but said he had made "a sincere effort to state facts as they have come down to us from antiquity."[67] *Church History* was well received, was pronounced "excellent" by *North American Review*, and remained in print for many years, with the last edition published in 1900. It was a staple of many seminarians' preparation for ordination exams.[68]

Milo's busy life still allowed time for romance, and in August 1853 he married Mrs. Mary Fisher Lewis, a Philadelphia widow with five children. Milo had met her while serving at St. Mark's in Philadelphia. They lived in New York City on Twentieth Street between Ninth and Tenth Avenues.[69]

CHAPTER 2

YOUTH AND EARLY MANHOOD

CHILDHOOD

Dennis and Mary Mahan's first child was born September 27, 1840. They named him Alfred Thayer, his middle name bestowed in honor of Dennis' mentor, Sylvanus Thayer. There is a record in the West Point archives of Alfred's baptism at the cadet chapel, but unfortunately no date is given nor the names of his godparents or the officiating minister. The latter could have been either Jasper Adams or Martin Parks, both Episcopal priests. Adams left his post as chaplain in November 1840 and was succeeded the following month by Parks.[1]

The Mahans had five more children: Mary, born in 1842 (who suffered brain damage from an early illness); Helen, who was born in 1844 and died in 1846; Frederick Augustus (named after Muhlenberg), born in 1847; Dennis Jr., born in 1849; and Jane (known as Jennie), born in 1852. Alfred's younger brothers both served in the military, Frederick in the Army and Dennis in the Navy.[2]

As Alfred pointed out in his memoir, *From Sail to Steam*, West Point in his early years was still an isolated outpost. It was accessible only by boat and not at all during the winter when the Hudson River froze. There was no railroad in the vicinity until 1848 and that was on the east bank of the river. One of Alfred's earliest recollections was of "begging off from school one day, long enough to go to a part of the post distant from our house, whence I caught my first sight of a train of cars on the opposite shore."[3] Another of his early memories was of gathering with the other boys on the post to watch the return of the academy's Corps of Engineers unit, the Company of Bombardiers, Sappers, and Miners, from service in the Mexican War. "The detachment was drawn up for inspection where we boys could see it," he recalled. "One of the men had grown a full beard, a sight to me then as novel as the railroad, and I announced it at home as a most interesting fact."[4]

Mahan's boyhood home at West Point *(United States Military Academy Library)*

The Mahan children had happy childhoods at West Point. They seem to have had the run of the post, and there were plenty of interesting sites, events, and people for them to see. According to Alfred's childhood playmate William Bailey, son of Professor Jacob Bailey, he and Alfred used to scale "the steep rocks near the new dock and [search] for 'two-penny silvers' (whatever they were) among the cliffs."[5] Jane Mahan recalled exploring Revolutionary War sites with her father, and the children also got to know the famous and not-yet-famous Army personnel who were their neighbors.[6] These included the old and distinguished, such as Winfield Scott, as well as the up-and-coming, such as Robert E. Lee and George McClellan.[7]

Dennis Mahan was well-known for his exceedingly proper behavior and formal demeanor. Nor surprisingly, he taught and expected from his children punctilious attention to manners. One of his younger colleagues on the faculty commented, "His children were taught to observe scrupulous courtesy, and to avoid the use of anything approaching slang language in his presence."[8] The Mahan household was also exceedingly devout. There were family prayers every day before breakfast, and Sabbath observances were rigid in the sense that most work and recreational activities were forbidden. Even Alfred, who maintained a strict observance of the Sabbath into adulthood, felt these measures too restrictive as a child.[9]

Puleston refers to Alfred's mother as a "fundamentalist," a problematic term for several reasons. For one thing, use of the word in this context is anachronistic.[10] Neither the word nor the concept of fundamentalism existed in 1840 and Mrs. Mahan would undoubtedly have been puzzled to hear herself described as such. It is also unlikely that Alfred would have used this word to describe his mother since he was a stickler for precise theological definitions. Puleston probably meant no more than that she was a traditional, orthodox, evangelical Christian who believed in the Bible as the revealed Word of God. This hardly makes her a fundamentalist in our own day, much less hers. We do know from several sources that Mary Mahan did hope that her eldest son would become a priest, but there is no evidence that any pressure was put on young Alfred to pursue this path.[11] Yet Alfred seems to have exhibited his religious interest early on. In his earliest surviving letter, written when he was seven, he thanked his grandmother for the religious books she had sent him and told her what he learned from them; "I liked the tent on the plain Agathos or the whole armour of God, the story of Jonah teaches me that man cannot fly from God."[12]

The Mahan family had its share of tragedy with the death of Helen at age two and the illness of Mary, which left her "backward both mentally and physically."[13] Undoubtedly their strong faith helped them through these difficult times. Others suffered loss, too, and the Mahans showed deep concern for their neighbors, which was remembered years later. Alfred's playmate William Bailey lost his father, mother, and sister in 1852 when the steamboat in which they were traveling to New York City, the *Henry Clay*, caught fire. Eighty passengers died and William Bailey alone of his family survived. (Alfred's grandmother, also going to New York City, almost boarded the *Henry Clay*, but was talked out of it by Alfred because he thought Henry Clay was "a bad name.")[14] Young Bailey returned to West Point, his only home, where he lived with the Mahans. He continued to stay with them when he came home from college vacations:

> When after leaving West Point I used to return in vacations, I often stayed at the Mahans, I fear beyond reasonable limits. When I think that upon them I had no claim whatever, I wonder at their polite endurance. They never showed any annoyance, but I am quite sure I must have been a trial, and had moments, in correspondence, of sharp remorse. I owe to Mrs. Mahan very many little points of culture, sweetly indicated, against which I should otherwise have awkwardly stumbled. What an exemplary family it was, exhibiting every Christian grace and virtue.[15]

Apart from religion, Alfred's other early interest was in things military, and ultimately naval. Francis Duncan detects both these interests in Alfred's two earliest letters, which revolve around God and firepower. In addition to the letter already quoted, Alfred, still only seven, wrote to his mother (who was visiting her mother in New York City) to ask her to please bring him some fireworks in anticipation of the Fourth of July. He specified (with no punctuation) "triangles Roman candles flower pots chasers spinning wheels rockets fireballs and firecrackers."[16] It may be reading too much into this letter to see intimations of Alfred's future calling, but there is no question that from a young age he loved to read about military and naval matters. Both Puleston and Seager mention that Alfred was allowed to use the Military Academy library, but neither comments on this arrangement, although it seems unlikely that this was a privilege granted to all children on post. Was such an arrangement allowed out of deference to Professor Mahan, or had young Alfred impressed academy officials with his precocity? In any event, Alfred "spent many of those happy hours that only childhood knows poring over the back numbers of a British service periodical, which began its career in 1828, with the title *Colburn's United Service Magazine*."[17] These volumes contained numerous reminiscences by Napoleonic-era naval officers, which the boy enjoyed. His favorites, though, were the serialized stories such as "Leaves from my Log Book" by "Flexible Grommet, Passed Midshipman" and "The Order Book" by "Jonathan Oldjunk."[18] Some might consider these stories trash, but Alfred did not agree, even in old age. "Trash?" he wrote. "Upon the whole is not the trash the truest history? Perhaps not the most valuable, but the most real?" because it gave the reader the "contemporary color, contemporary atmosphere" of the subject. He also devoured the naval fiction of James Fenimore Cooper and Frederick Marryat, further turning his interest toward the Navy.[19]

As Alfred approached adolescence, the slavery issue began to dominate the national scene. Dennis Mahan, who considered himself both a Southerner and a unionist, was not at this point an abolitionist sympathizer. When Alfred was given a copy of Harriet Beecher Stowe's *Uncle Tom's Cabin* by his schoolmaster, his father "took it out of my hands, and I came to regard it much as I would a bottle labeled 'Poison.'"[20]

Up until the age of twelve Alfred attended a local school, although it is unclear whether the school was on the post or in a neighboring town. In the fall of 1852, after turning twelve, Alfred was sent to an Episcopal boarding school, St. James, in Hagerstown, Maryland. Alfred seemed to think when he wrote his memoir in 1907 that the main reason he was sent there was to expose him to a Southern environment.[21] But he either overlooked or forgot what must have been an equally significant reason, namely that the school was not only Episcopal but was modeled on Muhlenberg's St. Paul's and was attached to St. James College, both of which were headed by John Kerfoot. St. Paul's had closed by this time because of financial problems brought on by Muhlenberg's refusal to accept Episcopal Church assistance, which he felt would compromise his independence.[22] It is entirely possible that had St. Paul's still been in operation Alfred might have gone there; in either case, the next best thing was a school on the St. Paul's model run by a Muhlenberg protégé and, not coincidentally, a friend of Milo's. We do not know for certain whether Milo played any role in the selection of St. James for Alfred, but it seems likely that Dennis would have consulted his brother, who knew Kerfoot well. Southern influence aside, Dennis and Mary must have been reassured that Alfred would continue his education in a sound Episcopal environment.[23]

We know little of Alfred's time at St. James or even whether he liked it there, save for the fact that he did not complain in his writings. Alfred would have lived in a building called Kemp Hall, built in 1851, which contained a dining hall, classroom, dormitory, and instructors' apartments. Puleston says there were two hundred students there at the time, though Kerfoot's biographer Hall Harrison says there were only sixty-five, which is probably closer to the true mark.[24] Unfortunately, we have no records from St. James for this time period since they were destroyed in a later fire.[25] We do know that Alfred "remained there only two years, my father becoming dissatisfied with my progress in mathematics."[26]

In the fall of 1854 Alfred entered the freshman class at Columbia College (now University) in New York City. Columbia had two advantages. One was that Alfred would board with Uncle Milo, thus assuring his parents that even though he was in the big city with students considerably older than he was, he would still be in a protected Episcopal environment. The other was that Dennis was personal friends with Professor John Torrey, with whom he often collaborated on developing engineering curricula.[27] Again, we know little about Alfred's two years of attendance at Columbia. Records show he took courses in German and presumably he received instruction in the math and science that his father felt was lacking at St. James.[28]

During these two years Alfred lived with Milo and his family, and although we do not know the extent of the contact between Milo and Alfred before this time, this two-year period was crucial for Alfred's spiritual and emotional development, as he and Milo formed a close relationship that lasted until the latter's death in 1870. Milo provided him with "advice and information" in an atmosphere of "familiar freedom of intercourse."[29] Milo's adherence to the principles of the Oxford Movement exerted a strong impression on young Alfred. Since Alfred later referred to "men" in the plural sense who were "disciples of the Oxford Movement" who influenced him in his youth, he may well have been introduced by Milo to other Tractarian clergymen in the city or at the seminary.[30]

Life at Uncle Milo's was inspiring in another way. Alfred fell in love for the first time with Milo's stepdaughter Libbie, who was close in age to him. Their teenage romance lasted for several years.[31] Love notwithstanding, Alfred had made up his mind to become a naval officer. By the middle of his second year at Columbia he began the process of securing an appointment to the United States Naval Academy at Annapolis, Maryland. Dennis was against the idea, thinking his son "much less fit for a military than a civil profession," but he did, albeit grudgingly, use his influence to assist him.[32]

Alfred's first step was to secure a letter of recommendation from Columbia president Charles King to his congressman, Ambrose S. Murray.[33] His father also wrote several letters to his contacts in Washington, one of whom was the secretary of war, Jefferson Davis (USMA, class of 1827), a friend of Dennis'. In January 1856, fifteen-year-old Alfred journeyed by himself to the nation's capital to pursue his congressional appointment. Alfred seemed to think that his family was of no political importance and that this would hurt his chances. He did not seem to grasp that his father, while not a political figure, was well-known in the military establishment. Not everyone's father, after all, was personal friends with a member of the president's cabinet.[34]

Alfred paid a call on Congressman Murray, who was noncommittal. Secretary Davis, however, wined and dined him and personally took him to see the Secretary of the Navy, James C. Dobbin. Alfred later returned to Murray with a verbal message from Davis: If Murray would give a Naval Academy appointment to Alfred, Davis would use his influence with President Franklin Pierce to secure an at-large presidential appointment to the Military Academy for an applicant from Murray's district. "Mr. Murray replied that such a proposition was very acceptable to him, because the tendency among his constituents was much more to the army than to the navy."[35] Alfred's appointment came through in April, and he dutifully thanked Murray:

> I cannot allow this opportunity to pass without expressing to you my sincere gratitude for the kind assistance you have lent me towards obtaining the end I had in view. Your kindness has been the more appreciated, from the long & earnest desire that I have had to enter the naval profession—so much so, indeed, that it would have been a great disappointment to me to have been obliged to give it up.[36]

Alfred knew that in reality it had been Davis who had greased the wheels (presumably he thanked him too), and it amused him in later years "to believe as I do, that I owed my entrance to the United States navy [*sic*] to the interposition of the first and only President of the Southern Confederacy."[37] None of this is to imply that Alfred was unqualified, for if anything he was overqualified.

Before getting Alfred to Annapolis, one other question emerges. When was Alfred confirmed? There is no information on this question. It is virtually certain that he was confirmed before adulthood, if only because he thought confirmation an extremely important rite, as indicated by a detailed letter he wrote to his daughter Helen as she was preparing for her confirmation. He had also written a similar, though shorter, letter to his sister Jane when she was about to be confirmed at the age of fourteen.[38] Had he not been confirmed as a child, he would never have neglected to do so as an adult, and there is nothing in his voluminous correspondence to indicate an adult confirmation. It is possible that he was confirmed at the Naval Academy (the bishop of Maryland did pay a yearly visit), but we have an extensive correspondence with family and friends from these years and there are no references to a confirmation. This leaves three possibilities: he was confirmed at West Point, at St. James, or while living with Milo. The first seems unlikely since the West Point chaplain during the years Alfred would have been of confirmation age was William Sprole, a Presbyterian.[39] This remains only speculation, of course, but it is most likely that Alfred was confirmed either at St. James or while living with Milo. If he was confirmed at about the same age as his sister, then either of these places would fit that scenario.

At the Naval Academy

When Alfred entered the Naval Academy in the fall of 1856 with the rank of acting midshipman, it was still a new institution. It was founded in 1845 and in some ways, both academically and militarily, it was modeled on West Point, founded in 1802.[40] Not surprisingly, Dennis Mahan's vast network of contacts included some at the Naval Academy. The superintendent at the time of Alfred's entrance was Cdr. Louis M. Goldsborough, who had been a friend of Dennis' since they had met in France in the 1820s. Two Naval Academy professors were West Point graduates, William F. Hopkins (class of 1825) and Henry H. Lockwood (class of 1836), and both of them knew Dennis well. Even Alfred's mother had a connection to the Naval Academy, being close friends with the wife of the commandant of midshipmen, Lt. Thomas Craven, at whose house she stayed when visiting Annapolis.[41]

Although he did not realize it at the time, Alfred earned a place in naval history almost as soon as he arrived at the academy. Due to passing examinations that exempted him from first-year classes, he was able to skip his plebe year. While many since have graduated in three years due to shortened length of curriculum during wartime, Mahan remains the only person ever allowed to bypass his plebe year. Lest the reader think that Alfred was the recipient of special privilege, the reason was actually more prosaic than it might seem. The academy regulations, a copy of which was sent by Commander Goldsborough to Dennis and studied in minute detail by Alfred, permitted "an appointee to . . . enter any class for which he could pass the examinations." Alfred determined to do this and was successful. Writing about this in later life, he said he remembered nothing about the exam itself except that it was oral and that when it ended "I was by no means confident that I had cause for elation." He also expressed amazement that no other midshipmen took advantage of this provision. "There were probably in every class a dozen who could have done the same, but they accepted the prevailing custom without question" or, more likely, failed to read the regulations as carefully as Alfred had.[42]

Though Seager implies that Alfred was the beneficiary of favoritism, such was not the case. Nor was it true, as Seager claimed, that Alfred was "something of a marked man with his classmates" because he had been exempted from "plebe hazing."[43] Mahan said that his classmates showed no resentment, "[n]ot the faintest indication of discontent." More importantly, there was no plebe

Mahan at age seventeen *(U.S. Naval Institute Photo Archive)*

hazing at the Naval Academy prior to the Civil War. Charles Todorich, historian of the early years of the Naval Academy, discusses this issue at some length and concludes that hazing was not practiced at the Naval Academy until it temporarily relocated to Newport, Rhode Island, during the Civil War. Prior to that it was virtually nonexistent.[44] Mahan himself claimed that he expected to be the victim of hazing when he first arrived at the academy inasmuch as it was already practiced at West Point. He was astonished to find "the contrary state of things" at Annapolis. "Not only was hazing not practiced, but it scarcely obtained even the recognition of mention . . . it was dismissed with a turn of the nose, as something altogether beneath us."[45]

While it is true that Alfred had some problems with classmates, mostly in his first class year, Seager exaggerates the importance of these in order to magnify what he sees as Mahan's many personality flaws. Seager characterizes his academy years as "a disaster" due largely to Alfred's "ill-concealed vanity" and belief that he was "vastly superior" in all respects to his classmates.[46] Most of these episodes were silly squabbles and are more easily explained by teenage immaturity and the inevitable tensions resulting from young men being cooped up together twenty-four hours a day.

We actually know little about Alfred's first two years at the academy because only three letters survive from his second year and none from his first. It appears, though, that Alfred made a good start despite friendships and cliques having already been formed before he joined the class of 1859. Even Seager has to admit that he got along well with his roommates. He made one friend, Samuel A'Court Ashe of North Carolina, who would become his lifelong friend and confidant (though Seager characterizes Alfred's desire for Ashe's friendship as "almost pathetic").[47] In the summer of 1857 he took a summer cruise with the plebes to make up for the one he had missed the previous year, at which time he told his stepcousin Libbie Lewis how glad he was to return to the company of his classmates.[48]

Samuel Ashe resigned from the academy in September 1858 because of chronic seasickness. This was fortunate for the historian since it inaugurated a correspondence of many years' duration. Ashe, who became a lawyer, was one of the few people to whom Mahan felt comfortable revealing himself, and their letters offer insight into Mahan's personality.[49]

One thing that undoubtedly did not endear Alfred to his classmates was his view that West Point was a superior institution, both academically and militarily. Ashe recalled that "he asked me to aid him in raising the standard of the Academy and getting it more on a par with West Point." How he proposed to do this was unclear.[50] In particular, Alfred admired the West Point Honor Code, the counterpart to which did not yet exist at the Naval Academy. Lest Mahan be considered disloyal to his alma mater, it should be pointed out that this was the only area in which he explicitly stated that he thought West Point was superior. "I would not change places with them [the cadets]; but in this one respect I would rejoice to see the whole Navy imitate them."[51]

Mahan, like any young man in the military, sometimes had trouble drawing the line between friendship and duty. Though some classmates would later (in their first class year) find him too much of a martinet, this characterization, too, may have been exaggerated. In any case, Mahan was hardly the only midshipman or cadet who found himself in an awkward situation over putting friends on report. For example, in the fall of 1857 (his second class year) while serving as officer of the day (OOD), he got in trouble for refusing to identify a midshipman who had left a package for safekeeping in the OOD's office. It turned out that the package contained tobacco, a contraband item, and was confiscated by the commandant of midshipmen, Cdr. Joseph F. Green. Mahan was asked to identify who had brought the package, and, still not knowing what was in it, he refused, fearing, as he told Superintendent Capt. George Blake, "that it would involve the gentleman in trouble." Blake threatened him with dismissal and Mahan supplied the name "with the full consent of the gentleman implicated, & indeed by his request." Mahan learned from this episode that "[t]he consequences of dismissal from a *Government* institution are too heavy to be lightly encountered." Blake was satisfied with his apology and expressed his satisfaction in Mahan's "admitting that he had been entirely wrong and that nothing of the kind should ever again occur."[52]

Seager reports that Mahan was "outraged" when a "lowly fourth classman (plebe) reported him for hazing." Seager does not explain what happened, but, by silence, lets the accusation stand.[53] In fact, this episode was not an instance of hazing at all, and although Mahan "was reported the other day by a fourth classman for imposing upon him because he was a fourth classman," he told Ashe he found this "binding [i.e., galling]." What actually happened was that Mahan, as senior member of his mess table, was attempting to apportion fairly some extra toast (there not being enough for everyone to have seconds) when a rude plebe grabbed a piece from Mahan, who then ordered him to put it back.[54] To consider this hazing is highly misleading.

The most traumatic episode of Mahan's career at the Naval Academy occurred in October 1858, when a dispute he had with classmate Samuel H. Hackett split the first class into pro- and anti-Mahan factions. The midshipmen were organized into gun crews of fifteen to twenty. Mahan was first captain of the First Gun Crew and Hackett was his second captain. What happened in a general sense is known. Mahan put Hackett on report because of his (Hackett's) not reporting underclassmen who were talking in ranks. The crackdown on talking while in formation appears to have been part of Mahan's attempt to bring Naval Academy discipline up to West Point standards. But the precise details of the incident are not known. Seager admits this, but claims, on no evidence whatsoever, that "the upshot of the matter was that Sam Hackett told Alf Mahan to go straight to hell."[55] According to Mahan's account, Hackett had objected from the beginning to the antitalking crackdown, but when the actual incident occurred all Hackett said (not to Mahan directly but to others) was "that I showed a want of confidence in him by making him report when Second Captain of Crew." Mahan claimed it was all a misunderstanding that could have been set right had Hackett spoken to him directly.[56] Nonetheless, Mahan had violated the "unwritten law among the midshipmen of the first class" that they not put each other on report.[57] Some of his classmates—but, it should be noted, not *all*—stopped speaking to him.[58]

Despite being convinced he was in the right, Mahan was shaken by the incident and the loss of friendships within the class, so much so he discussed it with Ashe frequently. It was a source of great comfort to him that he had the support of his father, who sent him several reassuring letters. In an undated letter, Dennis had written, "It has been no small gratification to your Mother and myself that you have placed this whole subject on its proper basis—Christian duty. There is no other."[59] Adhering to Christian duty and behaving as a Christian gentleman were the twin hallmarks of Dennis' advice to Alfred. As to the Hackett incident, Dennis wrote, "I heartily approve your entire conduct in the difficult position in which you find yourself, and there is no man of sense who knows what is due to responsibility but will do so." As to classmates who would no longer speak to him, "do not let it trouble you for a moment. Call no man friend who expects that your friendship is to be shown in violating your duty with respect to him." He also, however, warned his son not to succumb to the temptation to use his position as first captain to retaliate. "Be careful, however, not to let your feelings enter in the slightest degree into your bearing whilst on duty; *even and blind justice to each, friend or foe* [emphasis in original]." After citing both Paul's admonition to Timothy in the Bible ("Let no man despise thy youth" [1 Tim. 4:12]) and Polonius' speech to Laertes in Shakespeare's *Hamlet*, and reassuring Alfred that his officers backed him up, Dennis concluded, "Stand up to your work bravely, My Dear Boy, and always in the tone of a high minded Christian gentleman, and then let the consequences take care of themselves."[60] This support from his father bucked Alfred up considerably, and he reported to Ashe, "Father is delighted, as you may suppose, at my conduct."[61]

Alfred's mother visited Annapolis in November, staying with the Cravens, and told Alfred that the officers "admired" his conduct.[62] The affair did not end there, however. Because ill feeling within the class continued into the spring of 1859, Dennis intervened and persuaded the superintendent, Captain Blake, to look into the matter of why so many of Alfred's classmates were shunning him. Dennis' concern seems to have been that, with graduation looming so near, Alfred would leave the academy without having been *officially* exonerated, and that, if left unresolved, this would hurt his career prospects. This "difficulty . . . has been a cause of anxiety to me" because if Alfred were not officially cleared of any wrongdoing, "it might allow persons to *infer* that there was something more serious" than what had really occurred [emphasis in original].[63] Blake did so, although when Alfred found out about it he asked the superintendent to stop the inquiry. The results were ambiguous in any case. None of the midshipmen questioned referred to the Hackett incident or said anything against Alfred other than that he was "reserved and averse to cultivating a general acquaintance among [his] classmates." Alfred himself admitted this was true, but since it could hardly be considered a military offense or even a character flaw, both he and his father were satisfied with the outcome.[64] Dennis again assured his son that "your whole conduct in this trying matter has my most hearty approval. With this and that of your own conscience you may well let the matter rest."[65] Mahan's career did not suffer as a result of the incident, and there is little evidence it harmed him in the long run. The most important things to come out of it were positive a reinforcement in the notion that duty was paramount, and an affirmation that he had the unstinting support of his father. He had, in a sense, passed an important test. Most significant for our purposes, though, was Mahan's religious development while at the Naval Academy.

The academy's religious life at this time was dominated by the Episcopal Church. Chapel services were according to the Book of Common Prayer and the chaplains were usually, though not exclusively, Episcopalian. Non-Episcopal chaplains sometimes objected—to no avail—to being forced to use the prayer book. Midshipmen attended mandatory morning prayer every weekday and had to attend a church service, either at the academy chapel or in town, on Sundays.[66] According to figures compiled by Peter Karsten, a little more than 40 percent of midshipmen in this period were Episcopalians; this at a time when Episcopalians were only about 2 percent of the nationwide population.[67]

Karsten, in his *Naval Aristocracy*, makes much of this official promulgation of Episcopalianism at the nineteenth-century Naval Academy. According to Karsten, the Episcopal Church inculcated in its members a reverence for duty and submission to authority,[68] which he explicitly connects with his thesis that "racism, authoritarianism, warmongering, navalism, and a number of other unattractive qualities" were dominant in the late nineteenth-century officer corps. There are, however, two major problems with his thesis. One is that there is no direct empirical connection between the academy's religious program and midshipmen's attitudes then or in later life, and no one knows for certain what effect it had on the midshipmen. Some were very pious but might have been so before coming to the academy. Some (like Mahan) became more devout later in life. Some were never religious at all, and some were positively irreverent. As Todorich points out, it was not unheard of for midshipmen to turn up for chapel drunk or to pass around a bottle during services.[69]

The second problem with Karsten's thesis is that he completely misunderstands the nature and composition of the Episcopal Church. Karsten views the Episcopal Church as being a totally "High Church" entity, by which he means "formal, hierarchic, [and] ritualistic."[70] While it is true that the Episcopal Church is hierarchic in that it has bishops, and ritualistic in that it has a structured liturgy as set forth in the Book of Common Prayer, neither the Episcopal Church nor its Anglican antecedent the Church of England has ever been entirely "High Church" as that term is commonly understood. Karsten contrasts the Episcopal Church (and he allies it with other liturgical churches such as Lutheran and Roman Catholic) with "Low Church" (i.e., "less ritualistic, more egalitarian") evangelical Protestant denominations. Karsten does not seem to grasp that these very distinctions (levels of formality and ritual and emphasis on different doctrines) are present within the Episcopal Church itself. He completely overlooks the fact that a High Church position was only one faction within the church. It was contrasted by an evangelical Low Church wing (and later a liberal broad church faction). More to the point, it was this Low Church view that was prevalent at the Naval Academy during Mahan's time there and throughout most of the nineteenth century. Chaplains such as George Jones and professors such as Joseph "Holy Joe" Nourse were staunch evangelicals. They may have used the Book of Common Prayer for formal worship, but their theology and predilections were entirely evangelical, a main reason why Mahan disliked them.[71] The main message Mahan and his classmates heard in chapel (as well as Sunday School, Bible study, and ethics classes) was not "Do your duty and obey your betters," but rather "Are you saved, and stop your drinking." Religion at the Naval Academy was a very different thing than religion at General Theological Seminary, as young Alfred was to find out to his dismay.

Given the strong Episcopal ethos of the Naval Academy, one would have thought that Mahan would have felt right at home. Such was not the case, however. Two years at St. James and two years at Uncle Milo's had, not surprisingly,

put Alfred firmly in the High Church camp with its emphasis on ritual, the sacraments, and the importance of the apostolic succession of bishops. The Naval
Academy brand of Anglicanism was just the opposite, staunchly Low Church
in its emphasis on simplicity of liturgy, the necessity of a conversion experience, and personal morality. Alfred—possibly going through a period of teenage rebellion anyway—was totally alienated by this approach, as his many letters
to Ashe indicated.

Naval Academy chapel, circa 1850s *(Special Collections & Archives, Nimitz Library, United
States Naval Academy)*

The chaplain during most of Mahan's time there was George Jones, called
"Slicky" by the midshipmen.[72] Jones, an evangelical, must have seemed to
Alfred the polar opposite of Uncle Milo, and there is no question that Alfred
intensely disliked him, undoubtedly because Jones' churchmanship was alien
to Alfred and much disapproved by him. There may possibly have been a
personal element as well since he once told Ashe how "bitter" he felt about
Jones, although he never mentioned any specific incident.[73] It is clear enough,
though, that Mahan despised Jones' preaching. One might say he was obsessed
with it since almost every letter to Ashe contained a negative reference to Jones.
"Jones disgusted us extremely by a sermon on Drunkenness this morning. . . .
I believe I would give a year's pay to see Old Slicky tight and limber as a rag."[74]
This seemed to have been a familiar theme of Jones' preaching. "We have lis-
tened to a delightful sermon from Old Slick on rum drinking," Mahan wrote.
"What better description of it do you need, you who have so often listened to

and been bored by a similar affliction yourself. It really is the most disagreeable thing in the world to sit quietly and listen to the rant and cant of that intolerable old poker."[75]

Mostly, though, Jones preached on the dangers of hell and the necessity of conversion. "I can't stand what looks like an effort to bully you into religion," Mahan told Ashe. "A man who is religious because he fears to go to hell is as despicable as one who remains irreligious because he fears the world's opinion."[76] Nonetheless, this was a frequent theme of Jones. "Old Slicky is getting more and more stupid every day. . . . He was ineffably tedious on the subject of conversion, revivals, et id genus omne of religious humbugging."[77] On another occasion Jones preached "*forty-five* minutes upon the text 'Almost thou persuadest me to be a Christian,' [Acts 26:28] made some eloquent allusions to conversions, mourning benches, and enquiring meetings [emphasis in original]."[78] So it was that Mahan laughed, snickered, slept, and in general made a nuisance of himself in chapel. His behavior was probably not as bad as he bragged to Ashe, inasmuch as the superintendent's wife requested that he sit with her and help her navigate through the prayer book. "I am now obliged to go through the motions in church, for Mrs. Blake told mother she wanted me to help her in making the responses, so I do so."[79]

George Jones was not, however, the bumbling, Bible-thumping boob Mahan painted him to be. Jones was a Yale graduate, a well-traveled sailor, explorer and scientist, social reformer, and author. He is also considered one of the four most influential chaplains in the nineteenth-century Navy.[80] He was clearly a man of substance, and it is hard to fathom the depth of Mahan's dislike of him aside from the fact that he did not practice the General Theological Seminary brand of churchmanship. And despite Slicky's many alleged faults, it is telling that when Mahan was given the option of attending services at St. Anne's Church in Annapolis, he did not take it, saying "I had rather go to Slicky than walk into town for nothing."[81]

Mahan also resisted all attempts to recruit him for the Bible class run by Professor Joseph "Holy Joe" Nourse. "There is a Bible Society or class here. Slicky announced it in Chapel last Sunday to my great dismay and embarrassment, for Mother was there and I could not keep from laughing. I tried to organize an opposition society to be called 'The Grand Anti-Biblical Corruption Society' [which came to nothing]."[82] He was also dismayed to find that his mother liked Jones' preaching![83] Despite prodigious efforts by Nourse to recruit him, Alfred stayed away.[84] Apart from accusing attendees of "bootlicking and hypocrisy," he also disapproved of their method of scriptural study in which each person gave his opinion on the meaning of the passage under consideration.[85]

What then are we to make of Mahan's views of religion while at the Naval Academy? He did, it appears, go through an irreligious phase, possibly brought on by teenage rebellion against a strict upbringing. Possibly it was a personal dislike of Jones, or a combination of the two. In one letter to Ashe he did use the phrase "totally irreligious" to describe himself. In a few letters he took to taking the Lord's name in vain, something that would have been unthinkable to the adult Mahan.[86] Yet at no time did he seem headed for unbelief or even doubts about the truth of Christianity. Getting behind the mask of disdain for Slicky, one sees, as Puleston points out, "his letters reveal that he gave a good part of his thoughts to theology."[87] Despite his mocking of the Bible class he did read the Bible on his own and reflect upon it. "Do you ever read the Bible?" he asked Ashe. "What a beautiful passage this is that I met the other day in a book. 'Or ever the silver cord be loosed, or the golden bowl be broken, or the pitcher be broken at the fountain, or the wheel broken at the cistern—Then shall the dust return to the earth as it was, and the spirit shall return unto God who gave it [Eccles. 12:6–7].'"[88] He also told Ashe he admired "the fortitude and courage of Job when he had lost all" and both cited and underlined the passage "the Lord gave and the Lord hath taken away; blessed be the name of the Lord [Job 1:21]."[89] He also inveighed against the scare tactics of Jones and the evangelicals, but added, "My idea of the loveliness of religion is the thought of a being who shows his love less in the physical comforts of this life, than in sympathy with our sufferings, and I believe that the great God would rather have us look on Him as a friend than as a benefactor."[90] One can see here, especially in the phrase "loveliness of religion," a certain Oxford Movement influence, probably as conveyed by Uncle Milo. One suspects that a good deal of Alfred's so-called irreligion was merely adolescent posturing.

Another characteristic that shows up is that despite an active social life with the young ladies of Annapolis, Alfred had strict views on sexual morality and believed that men as well as women should abstain from sexual relations until marriage. "In spite of all that I have heard said by young fellows to the contrary, no man should, if I were a girl, touch my hand, whose life was not pure," he wrote, in addition to believing that women should not tolerate a double standard. "If I find that women generally do not mind seeing or knowing of such vices in men, and think as much of them afterwards, I shall never marry unless I find one who does."[91] This was not an attitude shared by his classmates. Hackett, with whom Mahan had the run-in on the drill field, was rumored to have fathered a child. Mahan reported approvingly that Nannie Craven, the commandant's daughter, disliked Hackett and "was too highly principled to choose a man of that stamp for her friend."[92]

Given the high political tension of the times it is interesting there is no mention of slavery or its attendant political issues in Mahan's letters to Ashe. This was most likely a deliberate avoidance of a touchy subject so as not to jeopardize their friendship, since Ashe was a Southerner. We know from Mahan's memoirs that the subject was, in fact, a frequent topic of discussion—and argument—at the academy. He noticed a difference in the attitudes of Northern and Southern midshipmen. The Southerners, to a man, were "convinced that the justice was all on their side, that their rights as well as interests were being attacked, whereas the Northerners were divided in feeling."[93] While there were a few who were "pronounced abolitionists," most Northern midshipmen, including Mahan himself, were devoted to the Union, but "for the present counseled concession to the utmost limit, if only thereby the Union might endure." Most of the midshipmen, he admitted, had not really thought deeply about these issues but were "simply re-echo[ing] the tones of our homes."[94] Mahan himself was only becoming aware of politics for the first time and was also exposed for the first time to political opinions different from those expressed at his own home (Dennis, though a Virginian, was a staunch unionist.) Alfred was shocked when a midshipman, "the son of a N Carolina member of Congress," said to him regarding President James Buchanan's recent inauguration, "'Buchanan will be the last President of the United States.' He was entirely unmoved, simply repeating certitudes to which familiarity had reconciled him; I, to whom such talk was new, as much aghast as though I had been told my mother would die within the like term."[95] From a perspective of fifty years later, Mahan thought that the strongly expressed convictions of his Southern classmates masked "if unconsciously, the resolution of despair; of doom felt, though unacknowledged."[96] Seager claims that Mahan "was not particularly concerned with national politics at this time" and had "little interest in the heated issues" of the day. To make this claim on the basis of his correspondence with Ashe is suspect since, as Puleston suggests, Mahan was probably avoiding controversy with his closest friend. Mahan's own account refutes Seager's claim inasmuch as he was certainly aware that war was coming. In one of his last letters before graduation he told Ashe he was hoping to be assigned to a ship that would be sure to see action "in case of war that any moment may now bring on us."[97]

Mahan graduated in June 1859, standing second in his class, and was promoted to the rank of passed midshipman. Seager claims that "his career at the Naval Academy was a disaster, one that colored his attitude toward the U.S. Navy for the rest of his life." He also claims that Mahan had already discovered that "the operational navy and those who ran it bored him."[98] The evidence does not suggest this, however, as Puleston said that Mahan was happy and "on the crest of the wave." Mahan's letters support Puleston's view rather than Seager's, with Mahan telling Ashe in his last letter from the academy, "I feel damn good just at present." He was pleased with his performance in the seamanship exam, pleased with the performance of his gun crew in the howitzer competition, and looking forward to sea duty. Likewise his next letter, containing details of his postgraduation leave at West Point and his first assignment, is full of enthusiasm.[99] While Mahan had his share of ups and downs at the Naval Academy, his time there was hardly the story of travail that Seager makes it out to be.

THE CIVIL WAR

It was the custom at the time for groups of classmates to apply together to serve on a particular ship. Mahan, along with his friends Henry Claiborne and Hilary Cenas, applied to join the USS *Levant*. For some reason the plan fell through, which was fortunate since the *Levant* sailed to the Pacific and was never heard from again, "one of those mysteries of the deep," as Mahan later said.[100] The classmates were assigned to the USS *Congress* instead, due to sail from Philadelphia to the Brazil Station. Mahan was also appointed aide to Commo. Joshua Sands, commanding officer of the Brazil Squadron. "It will be a pleasant duty, I think. At quarters I have charge of the Powder Division. Fortunately, I will, by virtue of my office, be rid of the nuisance of keeping watch in port."[101]

The cruise of the *Congress* to Rio de Janeiro and Montevideo was uneventful except for Mahan "getting very drunk" on his twentieth birthday. He also fell briefly in love with a young lady from Montevideo, Clara Villegas, whom he still recalled with affection more than twenty years later. In 1884 he wrote to Ashe regarding a recent visit to Lima, "I have not got beyond my delight in a pretty face and dark Spanish eyes. . . . My eye is perhaps more critical, and no longer leads to my heart and fancy by electric wire; yet it seems that some of the beauty I once saw in Montevideo might still waken the fire in the ashes."[102] This relationship—only a brief flirtation really—came to nothing.

Despite the uncertainty of mail delivery, the crew of the *Congress* followed the deteriorating political situation as best they could; "after mail brought us increasing ill tidings of the events succeeding the election of Lincoln."[103] By the time the *Congress* anchored in Boston in August 1861 the Civil War (always called the "War of Secession" by Mahan) had begun. Four officers of the *Congress*, including Mahan's friends Claiborne and Cenas, refused to take an oath of allegiance to the Union and were imprisoned.[104]

On August 31, 1861, Mahan was promoted to lieutenant and briefly assigned to the *James Adger*. In September he wrote an interesting letter to Gustavus V. Fox, the Assistant Secretary of the Navy, in which he begged the official to "overlook what may appear like youthful presumption" and went on to propose a plan for capturing the Confederate raider CSS *Sumter*, under the command of the daring Rafael Semmes. The plan included use of a decoy, an armed ship (a "confiscated rebel vessel") disguised as an unarmed merchant vessel, which would lure the *Sumter* to her destruction. Mahan offered "to lead the enterprise" himself. He stated that "my idea may appear rash or even harebrained," but he felt little would be lost in trying and much gained in succeeding. Puleston considered Mahan's idea "a well-considered plan that might have succeeded" and a good example of the young Mahan's burgeoning grasp of tactics and wit. Unfortunately, Fox never answered the letter.[105]

After only ten days on the *James Adger*, Mahan was reassigned to the *Pocahontas* as first lieutenant (executive officer).[106] His time on the *Pocahontas* was brief—only a year—but it was nonetheless significant. He had his first and only experience of combat when the *Pocahontas* took part in a combined Army-Navy attack on Port Royal, South Carolina, in November 1861. Mahan later commented, reflecting on his youth and inexperience, "war, even in its incipiency, was new to almost all present, and the enthusiasm aroused by a great cause and approaching conflict was not balanced by that solemnizing outlook which experience gives."[107] Though the *Pocahontas* arrived late at the rendezvous point she still was able to participate in the action and took fire from the guns of the Confederacy's Fort Walker. The ship sustained some damage but no one on board was hurt. As Mahan recounted, "The *Pocahontas* passed the batteries after the main attack . . . but before the works had been abandoned; and being alone we received proportionate attention for the few moments of passage. The enemy's fire was 'good line, but high;' our mainmast was irreparably wounded, but the hull and crew escaped." After the battle "there followed the usual scene of jollification," so presumably that sense of solemnization had not yet appeared.[108] This was to be Mahan's only experience of combat in forty years of naval service.

More importantly, it was while serving on the *Pocahontas* (now patrolling the South Carolina, Georgia, and Florida coastline) that Mahan became a sudden convert to abolitionism. This episode is worth examining in detail because of its importance in his life both personally and professionally. This experience took on a quasi-religious meaning to Mahan, who even described it using religious vocabulary and was so strongly affected that he was willing to confront his father over the issue:

> My own conversion was early and sudden. The ship had made an expedition
> of some fifty miles up a South Carolina river in the course of which numerous
> negroes fled to her . . . our captain [George Blake, former USNA superintendent] was rather disconcerted, I think at having forced upon him a kind of

practical abolition, in carrying off slaves; but his duty was clear. As for me, it was my first meeting with slavery, except in the house-servants of Maryland, superficially a very different condition; and as I looked at the cowed, imbruted faces of the field hands, my early training fell away as a cloak.[109]

When his service on the *Pocahontas* ended and he returned home to West Point for a brief leave, he determined to confront his father, but was nervous, no doubt remembering the *Uncle Tom's Cabin* incident of his youth. "Knowing how strongly my father had felt, I wondered how I should break to him my instability," he wrote. But much to his amazement, "I found that he, too, had gone over. Youngster as I still was, I should have divined the truth, that in assailing the Union his best friend became his enemy, to whom abolition was good and fit as any other club." Dennis' abolitionism may have had more anti-Confederate than antislavery sentiment behind it, but he was not ashamed to bear the label "abolitionist," which he had once scorned.[110]

Seager makes much of this episode but puts a negative interpretation on it. He belittles Mahan for not having become an abolitionist sooner instead of considering it significant—not to mention praiseworthy—that he became one at all. Seager claims that the young Alfred "accepted the existence of slavery uncritically and, given his family background and training, his view of the American Negro was predictable."[111] But in fact, prior to his "conversion" he expressed no view at all on "the American Negro" or on slavery. It is possible that he did accept slavery "uncritically," but we do not know that for a fact. By his own admission his encounters with the "house-slaves of Maryland" made no impact on him, but that was the sum total of his exposure to slavery at that point. There is also no evidence to translate this into any particular view of black persons. Seager castigates Mahan for using the terms "darkies" and "nigger," conveniently overlooking the fact that millions of white Americans, in the North as well as the South, used these terms. This criticism is, in any case, unwarranted, since by Seager's own count, in all of Mahan's voluminous correspondence, he uses the word "nigger" twice, and never after 1870, and only used "darkies" once.[112] Mahan had yet to develop a coherent view of race, but he was "convinced" that slavery had to be done away with.

In September 1862 Mahan was detached from the *Pocahontas* and assigned to the faculty of the Naval Academy, which had temporarily relocated in Newport, Rhode Island. He joined the Seamanship Department, then under the chairmanship of Lt. Cdr. Stephen B. Luce. Thus began the most important professional relationship of Mahan's career, as Luce became his mentor and later made the crucial decision that changed Mahan's career and life.[113] Little is known of Mahan's time in Newport, which he referred to as "eight pleasant months," although we do know he met the widow of Capt. James Lawrence (of "Don't give up the ship" fame) while there.[114] Seager claims that Mahan "was generally disliked by the midshipmen with whom he came in contact in Newport." His only source for this is a quote by Karsten in *Naval Aristocracy* that Mahan was "'universally hated' by the midshipmen."[115]

In the long term there is no question that Mahan's meeting up with Luce was the most significant aspect of his time in Newport. But in the short term his main interest was his first serious relationship with a woman. Unfortunately, she was married. Puleston knew about this relationship and seemed to know more details about it than Mahan's few mentions of it in his correspondence with Ashe would supply. It seems likely that a family member or friend, possibly Ashe, had discussed it with him. Puleston describes the lady, whose name we never learn (Mahan called her his "Nonpareille" or "Sanspareille"), as "a belle of the summer colony of that fashionable watering place, a few years older than Mahan, and married to a man much older than herself. Mahan almost immediately succumbed to her charms. She at first appeared to be only flattered by his frank admiration, but in time partially reciprocated his devotion." This relationship had no future since "there was no desire on his part to break up a home, no thought of the lady's seeking a divorce."[116] One can only imagine the reaction this would have caused in the Mahan household. There seems no reason, however, to doubt the sincerity of Mahan's affection for her or his desire to behave with rectitude. We know that he remained in love with her for another seven years, determined to be "truly purely faithful to her."[117]

In the summer of 1863 Mahan joined the midshipmen on their summer cruise on board the USS *Macedonian*, with Lieutenant Commander Luce the commanding officer and Mahan the executive officer. They visited Britain, France, Spain, and Portugal and ran into no Confederate raiders on their voyage.[118] After returning to Newport, Mahan was assigned to the USS *Seminole* as executive officer while *Seminole* was on blockade duty in the Gulf of Mexico. The duty was boring, the food bad, and whatever news came her way was weeks old.[119] Gulf duty was so stultifying, as Mahan later said, that "I have never seen a body of intelligent men reduced so nearly to imbecility as my shipmates then were." Fortunately, the ship was "recalled in mercy to New Orleans," where a better time was had by all.[120]

One advantage of the boring duty was that Mahan had plenty of time for reflection. In 1864 we see the first sign of renewed interest in religion. This was the first step of a process involving much spiritual struggle that would culminate in a conversion experience in 1871. We know little of Mahan's interior life during the Civil War period, but it would seem that by 1864 he had gotten over his anti-Slicky prejudices and was beginning to seek God's will for his life, devote time to serious Bible study, and consider how he might best serve God in this world. We do not know for certain, but it is possible that he began to reflect more seriously on the Christian faith when he was serving under Luce on the *Macedonian*. Their five-month voyage would have given them plenty of opportunity to converse. Luce was a professing Christian and active member of the Episcopal Church who frequently introduced Christian themes into his naval writings. Luce's and Mahan's careers would become intertwined, and we know they shared many views in common including theological ones. We have no proof, but given Mahan's age and impressionability at this time, it is possible that Luce may have played a role in getting him to think more seriously about his religion.[121]

The person Mahan most relied on for religious advice was, not surprisingly, his Uncle Milo. He wrote to his uncle sometime in 1864 (the letter is now lost) asking for guidance on two specific questions: how could he be a positive influence on the men under him, especially regarding their spiritual welfare, and should the Bible be interpreted literally. Milo responded in September 1864 (by which time he had resigned from General Theological Seminary and become rector of St. Paul's Church in Baltimore). He told Alfred,

> The best influence in your position, is that of a quiet consistent life accompanied with as much courtesy, gentility and consideration in dealing with your men as the nature of the Service will allow. . . . Let punishment be administered when really needed, but till the need comes, men should be treated as if punishment never could be needed. An officer who commends his Christian character by observing this rule will find that a smile, a cheerful word, or occasionally a few words of friendly expostulation will do more in the long run, than any more ambitious or obtrusive efforts.

In other words, his most effective witness would come from his behavior toward the men rather than his preaching at them. As to the second question, that was much more difficult because interpretation of scripture was a lifetime's study. Milo cautioned Alfred not to be in a hurry nor to expect easy and quick answers. "Find a solution, if possible; but if a thoroughly satisfactory solution can not be found, *do not accept a half-solution,* rather let the matter rest . . . in short *wait* till the solution comes of itself [emphasis in original]." Seager portrays Milo as waffling on the issue and moving in an "unorthodox and rationalist" direction in his own theology, but his answer is straightforward, honest, and orthodox without dodging the difficulties of interpretation. Milo acknowledged there were "hard saying[s]" in scripture and "to admit things as true which we cannot reconcile to facts as they commonly appear" was difficult. Nonetheless, he was "of course an advocate of the closest, most exact, most *literal interpretation* of Scripture [emphasis in original]." This was not only a matter of faith but of reason as well, since it was, Milo said, eminently reasonable to trust God rather than chance. "It is certainly reasonable to refer things to God of whom I can form *some* idea, rather than to chance of which I can form *no* idea whatsoever [emphasis in original]." In short, Alfred should seek God's guidance in understanding the Bible and then "take Scripture simply as it is, without over-anxious efforts to make everything in Scripture plain."[122] Unfortunately, no more of this correspondence exists, but Alfred's later views on the Bible indicate that he followed his uncle's prescriptions fairly closely.

In February 1864 Mahan was appointed executive officer of the *James Adger*, the ship in which he had served for ten days in 1861. This entailed yet more blockade duty off the southeastern coast, boring yet preferable to gulf duty.[123] In July he was given his first command, the 4-gun steamer USS *Cimarron*. After three months he was transferred to the staff of Rear Adm. John Dahlgren, commanding officer of the South Atlantic Blockading Squadron, where Mahan worked as an ordnance officer.[124] This was much more interesting duty, and as Puleston points out, "more helpful professionally." It allowed him to be an "eye-witness to the great drama played by Sherman's army and Dahlgren's fleet which crushed the last resistance of the Confederacy," as well as observe first-hand "the truth of his father's teaching." Puleston was here referring to Dennis' book *Permanent Fortification* (1850), which "had foretold the inability of ships [alone] to conquer forts."[125]

As a member of Dahlgren's staff, Mahan was present at three significant events at the close of the war. The first was "the victorious arrival" of Sherman's army in Savannah in December 1864. Mahan went on shore to Sherman's headquarters bearing a congratulatory message from his father, recalling that "when I mentioned my name he broke into a smile—all over as they say—shook my hand forcibly, and exclaimed, 'What, the son of old Dennis?'" Sherman gave some insight into the influence of Dennis' teaching and the power of his personality when he told Alfred, after reading the letter, "that he had from it as much satisfaction as when in far-away days he had been dismissed from the blackboard with the commendation, 'Very well done, Mr. Sherman.'"[126] This also signaled the beginning of a relationship between Sherman and the younger Mahan that, while not personally close, was nonetheless professionally significant.

A less happy duty that Mahan related from this same time period involved a childhood friend of his mother's who lived in Savannah. When he called on her he found her in conversation with some Union officers who wished to use her house for quarters. "The men were perfectly respectful, but the situation was perturbing to a middle-aged lady brought for the first time into contact with the rough customs of war." Mahan introduced himself, and while she was courteous to him she was too preoccupied with her plight to pay him much attention. "It was touchingly apparent that she was trying hard to keep a stiff upper lip, and her attempted frame of mind finally betrayed itself in the words . . . 'I don't admit yet that you have beaten us.' I could scarcely contest the point, but it seemed very sad."[127]

The second event Mahan witnessed was the surrender of Charleston on February 18, 1865. The following Sunday he attended services at one of the Episcopal churches in the city, an interesting and instructive thing for a Union officer to do in a Confederate stronghold.

> The first lesson for the day, Quinquagesima [the Sunday before Lent], was from the first chapter of Lamentations, beginning, "How doth the city sit solitary, that was full of people! . . . [ellipses in original] She that was great among the nations, and princess among the provinces, how is she become tributary [Lam. 1:1]." Considering the conspicuous and leading part played by Charleston in the Southern movement . . . [these words] were strikingly and painfully applicable to her present condition.

To Mahan the relevance of the lesson was obvious, but, he noted, "the officiating clergyman saw and dodged the too evident application, reading some other chapter."[128]

The third major event at which Mahan was present was the raising of the United States flag over Fort Sumter on April 14, 1865 (four years to the day after its surrender), a highly emotional and important day for Union forces. Dennis Mahan was invited to attend but apparently he did not go, most likely because of failing health.[129] By then the war was over, as Lee had surrendered on April 9, 1865. In May Mahan was transferred back to the *James Adger*, which then sailed to the gulf to protect mail steamers from any Confederate raiders that had not yet heard that the war was over. The ship visited Haiti, and Mahan contracted malaria there. In June he was sent home on medical leave and there received notification of his promotion to lieutenant commander.[130] Seager claims, falsely, that he was promoted "only after personal agitation with the Navy Department on the subject." The letter to which Seager refers was written on July 1, while the promotion came through on June 7, and all Mahan actually did in the letter was inquire of his prospects for promotion. He wrote the chief of the Bureau of Navigation and Detail, Capt. Percival Drayton, "If it is not taking too great a liberty, may I ask you if there is any chance of my being promoted—I have stood still for some time past, and if I can I should like to know if a change is at hand." This letter, which hardly seems an example of agitation, had no bearing on his promotion, which had already occurred.[131]

DENNIS' AND MILO'S CIVIL WAR

The Civil War affected Dennis and Milo, both personally and professionally, though in different ways. Dennis Mahan was in a position that was unique. Almost certainly no one else associated with the U.S. military knew as many officers on both sides or knew them as well as Dennis did. All the West Point graduates of both sides had been either contemporaries or students of Dennis. As a teacher and a soldier Dennis must have been dismayed at the thought of his many students now trying to kill each other. But that, of course, was their profession. More dismaying to Dennis was that so many had gone over to the Confederacy. Though a proud Virginian, Dennis was first and foremost a staunch unionist. His friends who had joined the Confederacy were now his enemies, and his feelings were so strong that he even came to support abolition. He told Alfred, "I am so absorbed in seeing those fellows [the Confederates] beaten that I lose sight of the rest."[132] The defection that hit him hardest was that of Robert E. Lee. According to Puleston, who got this story from the Mahan family, "The day the telegram announcing Lee's resignation [from the U.S. Army] arrived was one of anguish for Professor Mahan. He saw [Pierre] Beauregard and others go without comment, but Lee was different. All he could say to his wife was 'Elly—Lee has gone.'"[133]

Dennis' role in the war was not just that of an observer watching from the sidelines as his former students slugged it out for four years. He made several trips to Washington during the course of the war and met frequently with secretary of war Edwin Stanton and even on occasion with President Lincoln himself. These conversations, according to Griess, did not involve strategy but rather organization and personnel. This makes sense since no one knew the strengths and weaknesses of the generals on both sides as well as Dennis did.[134]

Dennis became a strong admirer of Lincoln. Though a firm believer in the principle that military officers should be apolitical—and proud of the fact that he never voted—Dennis' sympathies prior to the war were with the Democratic Party, largely because of his admiration for Andrew Jackson.[135] That, of course, changed with the coming of the war, and Dennis became, if not exactly a Republican, at least a fervent Lincoln supporter. In a rare burst of political partisanship, not to mention a departure from his usual gentility, Dennis got into a heated argument with a fellow guest at a dinner party given by Gouverneur Kemble in September 1864.[136] The North was in the midst of a presidential campaign and

Union Maj. Gen. George B. McClellan was the Democratic nominee opposing Lincoln. McClellan was a West Point graduate and, of course, well known to Dennis. At the dinner party one of the guests, a McClellan supporter, disparaged Lincoln in harsh terms. Dennis defended the president just as strongly and the two were soon in an argument so heated that Dennis later felt obligated to apologize to his host. He explained that he was provoked by the other gentleman who had called the president "a tyrant; an imbecile; a buffoon; [and] a baboon." These insults violated "the laws of good taste" as well as the biblical injunction "not to revile the Ruler of my people [Ex. 22:28; Acts 3:25]."[137]

Dennis then went on to defend Lincoln's conduct of the war and offered the opinion that McClellan was unqualified to be president, not only because of a lack of political experience but also "a deficiency of certain cardinal moral traits." These traits were never specified, but Dennis justified his criticism on the basis of many years' acquaintance with McClellan. "Now these are not opinions hastily formed; they are not opinions hostilely formed; they are not opinions of today, or even of yesterday; but conclusions sorrowfully reached from indisputable *data* [emphasis in original]."[138]

Dennis' apology apparently was not sufficient for Kemble, who wrote back castigating him, not for his preference for Lincoln, but "for the intollerance [sic] which you displayed towards those who could not conscientiously agree with you." Dennis, no longer in an apologizing mood, replied that he had not started the argument but was merely responding to others' abuse of the president. He then launched into a diatribe against the Confederacy and its Northern sympathizers, most interesting for its expression of a providential view of history where God's justice will ultimately prevail. The war was not a political dispute that could be settled by negotiation, but a matter of "right and wrong . . . now confronted in armed opposition." The twin causes of slavery and secession were morally wrong and had to be defeated. "The slave power of the South, hate, despise and fear a free people, a free press, and free speech. . . . Can there be peace in such a state of things? Never." Finally, the war may drag on but God's purpose—a Union victory—will be accomplished. "God may allow the struggle against his immutable law of justice to prevail for a season, but the law is nonetheless immutable, and its execution sooner or later, none the less certain."[139] The correspondence seems to have ended on this less than cordial note.

Given this attitude it is not surprising that Dennis' view of his onetime friend and colleague, Robert E. Lee, hardened. Lee, whose defection had so upset Dennis, was now an enemy. Griess says that Dennis viewed Lee's action as unforgivable, but that nonetheless he "admired Lee's ability and refused to be taken for his detractor in print."[140] This is not entirely accurate. While Dennis never publicly disparaged Lee as a person, he certainly had plenty to say, most of it negative, about his military ability. Dennis thought Lee was essentially a mediocre soldier—as a cadet, a junior officer, and a field commander—who had made his way up the ranks by virtue of a pleasant personality and family connections.[141] In an interview with the *New York Times* (subsequently picked up by other Northern newspapers) shortly after Ulysses S. Grant was appointed commander of all Union forces, Dennis confidently predicted that Grant (who had graduated from West Point in 1843) would defeat Lee, and he provided a detailed analysis of why he thought so. It could be summed up simply by saying that Grant exhibited "tenacity, boldness, audacity and skill," whereas Lee was "passive" and on several occasions (for example, Second Bull Run, Antietam, Gettysburg) had inexplicably failed to press home his advantage and deliver the decisive blow. Dennis also compared Grant favorably to the Duke of Wellington in logistical skills, perhaps the ultimate compliment since it was Wellington who defeated Dennis' hero, Napoleon.[142] Griess even suggests that it might have been Dennis who urged Lincoln to appoint Grant to the top command, inasmuch as Dennis met with Lincoln in January 1864 and Grant was appointed in March.[143]

Dennis followed the war closely, viewing it "as a laboratory to improve his texts and classroom instruction."[144] He even corresponded with a number of Union generals (all West Point graduates) asking them for detailed analyses of their battles. One would think they had enough to do without being given additional homework by their old professor, but such was Dennis' stature that most complied and seemed to be flattered by the request. More revealing of the awe in which Dennis was still held by battle-hardened generals was their astonishment and pleasure at receiving letters of praise from him. We have already seen one instance of this in Sherman's remarks to Alfred. On another occasion Sherman passed on to Grant a letter he had received from Dennis praising Grant's performance at Vicksburg; "Professor Mahan's very marked encomium" was "so flattering" to Grant that Sherman offered to let him keep the letter.[145]

What influence did Dennis' classroom instruction have on the actual fighting of the Civil War? There is no consensus among military historians on this. Some, such as Stephen Ambrose, think that Dennis "was responsible for the manner in which much of the Civil War was fought," particularly his stress on the capture of strategic points rather than defeat of enemy armies in the field.[146] But others such as Griess and Russell Weigley think that Dennis' influence was not so much in the realms of tactics and strategy as it was in his emphasis on developing professional competence, especially through the study of military history.[147]

Milo's Civil War was not as successful as Dennis' and caused him considerable stress. Up until the war Milo's career had been going well. In 1859 he was a candidate for the office of bishop of New Jersey. In fact, he was Bishop George Washington Doane's personal choice for a successor. In the election Milo won large majorities in the clergy order on the first twelve ballots, but was doing poorly in the lay order. His biographer attributed this to Doane's enemies among the laity who, he says, voted against Milo for spite. Milo withdrew after the twelfth ballot and the eventual winner was William Henry Odenheimer.[148] Milo also became a trustee of the two schools founded by Bishop Doane, St. Mary's Hall and Burlington College.[149]

Milo's problems at the seminary came about when the war broke out and he, along with his colleague Samuel Seabury III, was perceived as pro-Southern and proslavery. There was less to these charges than met the eye, but in this case perception mattered more than reality. Milo was never disloyal to the Union and was a believer in the biblical injunction, the same which Dennis quoted, "Thou shalt not speak evil of the ruler of thy people."[150] On religious grounds alone he would not have defended secession. He did believe, though, that church and state were two separate realms. His expressions of this view—eccentric to be sure—were what got him labeled as pro-Southern. In 1862 he gave two speeches at the General Convention in which he opposed a pro-Union resolution. His reasoning, lost on some of his colleagues, was that political quarrels should be kept out of the church and that church and state operated in separate realms and each should not interfere in the other's province. The church cannot speak with authority on political questions; that is the job of the state. Likewise, the state cannot speak with authority on religious questions. He was also concerned about the practical matter of avoiding formal schism in the Episcopal Church, wishing to leave the door open for Southern delegates to return to the General Convention when the war was over.[151]

Undoubtedly his strangest action was to object to the American flag being flown on the seminary grounds. As Dawley suggested in his history of the seminary, "the worst possible construction was probably placed upon [this] objection."[152] While General Theological Seminary was not a hotbed of abolitionism, the prevailing sentiment was almost entirely pro-Union and antislavery. There had been only a handful of Southern students and they had left by June 1861. The ire of faculty and trustees was directed also against Professor Samuel Seabury III, who was in fact more overtly pro-Southern and proslavery than Milo was alleged to be. The two of them seemed to have been linked together, and Milo, for reasons unclear, was subject to accusations that were more accurately applied to Seabury. Professor Samuel Roosevelt Johnson wrote that "Drs. Seabury &

Mahan are rather on the Southern side in Politics (disloyal as I view the matter) and are both great friends of slavery, at least justifying it, and deeming it best."[153] Trustee George Templeton Strong considered Mahan and Seabury to be "rebel sympathizers" and was appalled that these gentlemen should be teaching at an institution that trained men for the priesthood. A seminary faculty, Strong said, "should be free from suspicion of sympathy with treason and rebellion, especially with a rebellion got up by systematic lying to support and strengthen a system of woman-flogging and children-selling and all manner of abominations."[154] On top of that, the seminary was in financial difficulties at the time and Strong was convinced that the presence of Seabury and Mahan on the faculty was hindering fund-raising. Certainly Strong's own enthusiasm as a fund-raiser was diminished. "The disloyalty of Mahan and Seabury, two of its chief teachers, chills my ardor," Strong wrote. "I cannot exert myself to raise money to support two learned and able men in influencing—unconsciously perhaps, and certainly unintentionally—the next generation of our clergymen to sympathy with rebellion and slavebreeding and to underrate the value of our national life."[155]

The proslavery charge was accurate in Seabury's case, given that he had published a defense of slavery in 1861, but why Milo's name was associated with this view is not clear.[156] In the only reference to slavery in his writings, he was very clearly against it. In an 1855 Thanksgiving Day sermon, *The Healing of the Nations*, Milo spoke negatively of slavery in ancient Rome, calling it a "withering influence" that caused the "decay" of agriculture.[157] Admittedly he was speaking about the ancient world, but this sermon—delivered when the slavery debate was raging—was full of veiled references to the contemporary political situation, as even its title suggests.

Fairly or not, Milo had nonetheless acquired a pro-Southern label. This was one, though not the only, reason he resigned his professorship in the summer of 1864 and accepted a call to be rector of St. Paul's Church in Baltimore and headmaster of its school. He also had financial concerns after the seminary, because of its poor financial condition, had cut faculty salaries.[158] As far as we know there seem to have been no problems among relationships within the Mahan family. We know Alfred was seeking spiritual advice from his uncle at this same time. Given Dennis' and Alfred's strong feelings on secession and slavery, this would seem an unlikely thing to do if Milo were truly as pro-Southern or pro-slavery as some of his colleagues had depicted him.

CHAPTER 3

CRISIS AND CONVERSION

THE *IROQUOIS* VOYAGE

T he six-year period immediately following the Civil War was a crucial one in the spiritual development of Alfred Mahan. In fact, it would not be too much to say that it was the most critical period of his life. He went through a long period of spiritual struggle and doubt, not doubt about God but doubt about his own worthiness, which culminated in a conversion experience that he later saw as the true beginning of his Christian life. This in turn enabled him to cope with family tragedies, move on to a more emotionally mature relationship culminating in marriage, and set on his life's path of service to God as Episcopal layman, naval strategist, and historian.

During the summer and fall of 1865 Mahan was home at West Point recuperating from malarial fever. During this period, judging from their later correspondence, he spent considerable time with his mother discussing spiritual matters. She became, as Puleston tells us, "his closest confidante," and he confided to her his spiritual yearnings and doubts.[1]

In November 1865 Mahan was assigned as executive officer to the USS *Muscoota*, an iron-hulled paddle steamer. This ship, which Mahan joined in Key West, Florida, patrolled the Gulf of Mexico and was supposed to keep an eye on the French presence in Mexico.[2] The duty was boring, the men were restless, and half the ship's company (though not Mahan) came down with fever. Mahan later told his mother that his orders to this ship "were the most distasteful that ever reached me" and his initial reaction was more than vindicated.[3] Seager, who examined the *Muscoota* log, characterized it as "a dreary record of desertions, fighting, disobedience of orders, neglect of duty, profanity, drunkenness, and violations of various naval regulations."[4] That Mahan found this duty trying, there is no doubt.[5] But it did give him an opportunity to demonstrate his newfound zeal to serve the Lord. He was the officer who conducted divine worship every Sunday on board ship. In the absence of a chaplain this duty would normally fall to the captain, but he could delegate it to someone else, and in this case the captain, Cdr. Thomas Pattison, was probably glad to pass it to the eager young Mahan.[6] There is no evidence, according to Seager, that Mahan's officiating at Sunday services "in any way improved the behavior of the crew, although he undertook to bring all hands speedily to God. He later boasted that he had saved two souls in the disorderly crew, a spiritual harvest so modest that it would seem to suggest that even the Creator had all but abandoned the unhappy vessel."[7] The evidence for Mahan's alleged boasting is his letter to his mother written some months after he had left the *Muscoota* in which he said he had been "the instrument in His hands of bringing two souls to confess themselves His servants."[8] But he was not boasting; in fact, he was doing just the opposite. This letter, in which he unburdened himself to his mother, was full of "doubt and uncertainty" as to the efficacy of his attempts to witness to Christ on board ship and his "dissatisfaction" with his own feeble efforts.[9]

Mahan was detached from the *Muscoota* in September 1866 and returned to West Point for a brief leave before heading to the Washington Navy Yard for "temporary ordnance duty" in October.[10] He was unhappy there. He reported that he felt "depressed" and that his feelings "are of the nature of agony while they last—the heart crying bitterly for that which it has not, nor can have."[11] Seager characterizes this depression in the conventional sense in which we use that term now: a psychological sense. He says that Mahan "felt friendless, frustrated, and lonely." This, however, is reading too much into a remark Mahan made a year and a half after the actual event, especially given that Mahan never identified the reason for his depression during the fall of 1866. Seager goes even further and claims that Mahan was having "a near nervous breakdown."[12] This, too, is exaggerated, but more importantly misses the key point. Mahan was not clinically depressed or having a nervous breakdown, but was undergoing a religious crisis, one the Puritans would have readily recognized as "preparation." This is a period of inward struggle and soul searching in which the believer who already desires to serve God and lead a Christian life is nonetheless attempting to do so by his or her own power and, consequently, failing repeatedly. This failure or falling short then brings on feelings of unworthiness and fear of God's displeasure. The individual is still attempting to earn God's approval rather than resting on the finished work of Christ. Such a crisis generally culminates in a conversion experience where the believer reaches that point of trust and rest.

Mahan's struggle followed this pattern closely. As we have seen, sometime in 1864 he expressed to his uncle a desire to serve God, study scripture, and set a good example for his men. By early 1867 he was expressing these same desires

frequently and explicitly in letters to his mother. "May God grant that I but serve
him faithfully here; I think I can truly say the outward accidents of life concern
me less than they did. But I fret at times to think of my slothfulness in spiritual
things. You will pray for me."[13] His desire was "to increase my own personal religion—and to draw nearer in Communion with God—hoping that thus I shall
be more perfectly led."[14] His quest for God continued and intensified with his
assignment in December 1866 as executive officer of the USS *Iroquois*, which
was about to embark on a three-year voyage to the Far East.[15]

Seager describes this cruise as "unhappy," and so it was in many respects.[16]
But Seager, who views Mahan's piety as symptomatic of psychological disor-
der, never sees or acknowledges that the unhappiness was a necessary stage
in Mahan's spiritual growth. The *Iroquois*, under the command of Cdr. Earl
English, departed New York in February 1867, and Mahan wrote to his mother
of his desire to serve God while also asking for her prayers.[17]

USS *Iroquois (U.S. Naval Institute Photo Archive)*

While on this voyage Mahan wrote frequently to his mother, also writing
occasionally to his father, his younger sister Jane, and to Ashe. He also wrote
to his Uncle Milo, but unfortunately these letters have not survived.[18] The most
important document we have from the *Iroquois* voyage, however, is Mahan's
diary. This was the only time in his life that he kept a diary, and the reason for
this is clear if one grasps the religious significance of it; it was the only time in his

life he needed to. A diary can serve many functions, but for Mahan it was a journal of spiritual self-examination. This was the period in his life when he needed to keep such a journal because he was undergoing the "preparation" crisis that would lead to his conversion.[19] Once his crisis was ended through a discernible conversion experience there was no longer any need for a diary.

Seager characterizes the diary as showing Mahan as a bundle of insecurities and "deathly afraid of the sea." He was "nervous, irritable, depressed, sleepless, and queasy of stomach each time the *Iroquois* left harbor."[20] This was true in a superficial sense, but Seager never seems to penetrate to the real meaning of the diary. Mahan's diary is a document that would be easily recognizable to a historian of early American religion. It is essentially a Puritan conversion narrative and bears all the hallmarks of that genre. Once one understands this, then all Mahan's fears and periods of depression are easily explained and are, as we will see, only temporary.[21]

The diary itself is not completely intact; the first part of it, begun on August 1, 1867, has been lost. The existing portion covers the period from April 26, 1868, through September 10, 1869. Seager suggests, though he has no evidence, that both Taylor and Puleston had access to the diary. He does not give a reason why he thinks this, but presumably it was because both biographers had the full cooperation of the family. "[B]ut," Seager claims, "for reasons not clear, neither author chose to make use of its insights. Perhaps in the 1920s and 1930s there were family objections to the use or publication of such personal materials."[22]

Seager contrasts Mahan's diary with that kept by Lt. Michael Gaul of the Marines, who was also serving on the *Iroquois* at the same time. The interesting thing about Gaul's diary is that it does not mention Mahan at all, and Seager makes much of this inasmuch as Gaul's diary is chatty and gossipy. Seager takes Mahan's absence from Gaul's diary to indicate that Mahan was isolated from and unpopular with his fellow officers. This might be true; Mahan, admittedly, was not the most convivial of shipmates, although he had his reasons. Mahan was going through a spiritual crisis and found his wardroom companions entirely secular in their interests. Their conversation, he said, was "entirely worldly and sometimes of a kind that I would rather not have joined."[23] Despite this, Mahan was not as unsociable as Seager makes him out to be. While he did not carouse with his fellow officers, he often participated in wardroom conversation.[24] It must also be pointed out that Gaul never showed up in Mahan's diary either. Probably the most that can be said of this is that the two men just did not bother with each other very much, as Mahan mentioned by name only those shipmates he either very much liked or very much disliked. The contrast of these two diaries is not fruitful since they were written for completely different purposes.[25]

Seager seems unaware of the diary of Dr. Samuel Pellman Boyer, surgeon on board the *Iroquois*, who spoke favorably about Mahan.[26] Nor was Mahan as unsociable as Seager likes to portray him. While in foreign ports he frequently visited the wardrooms of other ships, both American and British. He was already a staunch anglophile and enjoyed visiting British ships and socializing with British officers. He also, not surprisingly, enjoyed attending Anglican churches and chatting with Anglican clergy.[27]

What was Mahan actually trying to achieve on this voyage? His goals fell into two categories: actions and attitude. In terms of the latter, this was a constant challenge. Mahan already grasped that there was more to the Christian faith than simply going through the motions of being religious. His desire for "personal religion" and "Communion with God" would be a lifelong preoccupation. As a more mature Christian this was a theme he emphasized in his religious writings.[28]

Actions encompassed a vast arena. The areas that occupied him most included daily personal prayer, worship on Sundays and feast days, witnessing to others, studying the Bible and books on the Christian faith (especially those recommended by his uncle), and teaching himself Greek. He also found numerous faults with himself, which he endeavored to correct. These included drinking too much, unkind words and thoughts about others, wasting time in worldly pursuits, eating too much, grumbling and complaining too much, and, in general, showing too much pride and not enough humility. These were many of the same topics found in Puritan conversion narratives. The great overarching theme, aside from his fervent desire to serve God, was his great failure to do so, at least by his own lights. The failure, though he did not grasp it yet, was part of the process.

In reading the diary one thing that immediately strikes the reader is that Mahan's mode of worship, both public and private, was intimately connected to the Anglican/Episcopal liturgy and its expression in the Book of Common Prayer. Mahan followed the liturgical calendar scrupulously. All Sundays in the diary were identified by their liturgical name. For example, Sunday, May 10, 1868, was "Fourth Sunday after Easter." All feast days were also identified as such. For instance Monday, November 30, 1868, was St. Andrew's Day; Saturday, December 26, 1868, was St. Stephen's Day. This pattern was followed throughout the entire diary.[29] Mahan also attended church services as often as he could. When on shore in foreign ports he invariably located an Anglican church and attended as often as his duties allowed. On a Sunday he typically attended church twice a day, a morning prayer or communion service in the morning and evensong in the evening. For example, on Sunday, May 17, 1868, in Yokohama, Japan, he attended a service in the morning and then went again in the evening. He usually commented in the diary on his attitude during services and this day was no different. Of the morning service, he said, "my thoughts [were] either dull or wandering," but at the evening service "my attention was better and I was more devout, less wrapped in myself."[30] On feast days that occurred on weekdays he also tried to get ashore to church if at all possible. May 21, 1868, was Ascension Day (which always falls on a Thursday). He managed to get ashore to attend an afternoon service, writing, "Went to church. Congregation consisted of the clergyman, a lady & myself. Tried to remember that when two or three are gathered together in His Name, He is among them."[31]

Divine service was always held on board ship on Sundays, and when he was at sea or otherwise unable to go ashore, Mahan attended this service. Indeed, he often officiated at it. Sunday services in the Navy at the time were always conducted according to the Episcopal Book of Common Prayer. (The service was usually morning prayer unless there was an Episcopal chaplain on board who could celebrate communion.)[32] Attendance at these services was not necessarily compulsory, with that decision left to each captain. The *Iroquois's* captain, Commander English, left attendance voluntary but in one instance was tempted to change his mind. Mahan's diary entry for July 19, 1868, discussed the situation:

> The last week my mind has been very full of the slight attendance upon Divine Service, and I feared that the captain was going to institute compulsory service. Today I spoke to him and obtained permission to address a few words to them upon the matter. My timid consciousness made this a difficult task, and I did it in much trembling and fear. Let me remember that the [subsequent] larger attendance was therefore due only to God, for my words were most faint and halting.[33]

The ship's surgeon, Dr. Boyer, commented on this same episode in his diary:

> All hands to muster 10.30 A.M. Mr. Mahan, Lieut. Commander Executive Officer, addressed the crew on the importance of attending divine service. 10.45 A.M. the bell sounded for call to worship. Quite a large number of officers attending divine service—quite a contrast to the last Sabbath, for then there were only 3 or 4 parties to church. Mr. Mahan's remarks had the desired effect.[34]

On Sundays the captain appeared to be more than happy to turn over the officiating duties to Mahan.[35] On one occasion the captain ordered him to read the Articles of War as part of the service. It was within the captain's prerogative to do so, but Mahan disliked it, presumably because it introduced a secular element into the liturgy, not to mention that it was not an authorized part of the Book of Common Prayer. But Mahan obeyed and learned a lesson in humility. "I was very loath, but did so with submissiveness of heart I think. Tempted to criticise him, as I do find fault in my heart."[36]

Mahan worshiped, studied, and meditated in the privacy of his cabin every single day, but on Sundays and feast days he would usually say the daily office (morning or evening prayer) or what was called the ante-communion (the first part of the communion service) by himself if he could not go to church, or frequently even if he could.[37] Formal worship through the liturgy of the church was clearly important to him, believing as he did that it united him with the entire holy catholic (meaning universal, not Roman) church.[38] Mahan seems to have had plenty of free time on this leisurely voyage, and he determined to make good use of it for his own spiritual growth. He even attempted to teach himself Greek so he could read the New Testament in its original language. This, however, seems to have been a short-lived experiment.[39]

Mahan was a voracious reader of religious books and newspapers. As he told his mother, "I have wasted a great deal of time in my life," and he now wished to make up for it by spending his free time in edifying reading in "religious or church matters." He asked her to supply him with books and periodicals based on his uncle's advice. "I fear to buy without advice—and you can so easily get uncle's."[40] He subscribed to *Churchman*, a New York–based weekly, and *The Church Journal*, founded and edited by his uncle.[41] Mostly, though, he read the books suggested to him by his uncle, including:

Michael F. Sadler, *Emmanuel*

Edward M. Goulburn, *Thoughts on Personal Religion, Introduction to the Devotional Study of the Holy Scriptures*

Richard C. Trench, *Notes on the Parables of Our Lord*

John Henry Newman and John Keble, editors, *Remains of the Late Rev. Richard Hurrell Froude*

Joseph Butler, *Analogy of Religion, Natural and Revealed*

Jeremy Taylor, *Selected Works*

Edward Putnam, *Exposition of the Apocalypse of St. John*

Robert Leighton, *Whole Works of Robert Leighton*

Timothy Dwight, *Theology: Explained and Defended*

Ernest Renan, *The Apostles*

Henry Alford, *Meditations in Advent*

Samuel Smiles, *The Huguenots*

John Robert Seeley, *Ecce Homo*

Frederick W. Robertson, *Sermons on St. Paul's Epistles to the Corinthians*
Leopold von Ranke, *History of the Popes*
Thomas a Kempis, *Imitation of Christ*.[42]

What are we to make of this list? It can best be characterized as eclectic. It includes the Calvinist (Dwight) and the Anglo-Catholic (Sadler and Froude). It also includes some controversial skeptics/heretics (Renan and Seeley) as well as the orthodox (Trench and Butler). Assuming that all or most of these were recommended by Milo Mahan, it would appear that Milo was not afraid to recommend some controversial books to Alfred, presumably because he wanted his nephew to be aware of what was current in the field of theology and to better understand heresy so he could more ably refute it (Milo himself had recently written a response to the allegedly heretical John Colenso, bishop of Natal.[43]) Church historian Robert Bruce Mullin characterizes the list as "including some high church classics with a representation of differing religious movements of the 19th century."[44] Alfred himself did not have a lot to say about some of these books other than to comment that he read them.[45] The ones he seemed to like best were the collections of sermons or spiritual commentaries; he commented extensively, for example, on Trench's *Parables*.[46]

Seager makes much of Mahan's wrestling with various theological and scriptural issues, especially questions raised by the impact of Darwinism and "higher criticism," and he suggests that Mahan's inability to resolve these dilemmas left him "confused and uncertain of himself."[47] But Seager makes too much of both Mahan's supposed inability and his subsequent distress. Most of Mahan's dealings with these sorts of questions took place within the month of January 1869. The reason is not clear—Mahan remained a diligent student of the Bible his entire life—but it may have been related to a New Year's resolution to keep a strict rule of life, or it may simply have been related to the particular books he was reading at that time.[48] What Seager views as "agonizing" is more accurately seen as simply identifying questions and seeming discrepancies that came to his mind. Mahan was interested, for instance, in the question of Old Testament chronology (as was his uncle). He devoted a long diary entry on January 10, 1869, to discussing discrepancies about the dating of the covenant with Abraham and the Exodus, but there was no indication that he was upset about it. In fact, he stated with assurance that since all scripture is "equally inspired . . . there must be a way of reconciling the two [differing dates].[49]

Seager also suggests that Mahan was upset and threatened by the writings of Charles Darwin, claiming that Mahan had concluded that Darwin had blasted the Adam and Eve story out of the water, thus undermining the doctrine of original sin, and that "Mahan, search as he might, found no way adequately to shore it up."[50] An examination of the diary passage where Mahan discussed this issue, however, shows something quite different. Mahan raised some questions about the Genesis creation account and said that "the discoveries of science" may suggest some rethinking of "the Mosaic record of creation," but he thought this would only affect questions of chronology. He in no way thought the existence of Adam and Eve or original sin was at all affected by these "discoveries." In fact, he concluded in this same entry, "It seems beyond question by St. Paul that all the present fallen race of man are descended from one [Adam] in whom they federally fell."[51] Seager also concludes that Mahan was "[s]o confused and uncertain" that he refused to take part in wardroom discussions about science and religion. Again this is reading too much into one comment; Mahan simply related that he had spent "a great part of the afternoon listening to and at times joining in a conversation in which the attitude of science and religion towards one another was discussed. Observed that it is well to hold one's tongue under such circumstances."[52] The more obvious explanation is that he simply wanted to avoid arguments about contentious matters, not that he found the topic threatening. Indeed, his entry makes clear that he did participate in the discussion. Mahan did have many questions about the Bible, doctrine, and church history. We see these in his diary, but the questions indicate that he was thinking seriously about his reading. Unfortunately, his correspondence with his uncle is lost, but it seems clear from his reading list that Milo was providing him with a wide range of reading. Milo, always a staunch battler for orthodoxy, was not afraid of new theories, scientific or otherwise, and there is no reason to think Alfred was either.

One of Mahan's major projects, and a major source of his unhappiness during this tour, was an attempt to befriend and convert a naval surgeon named Theron Woolverton. This attempt yielded little return for all the effort Mahan expended on it, and it caused him great emotional distress. Seager makes much of this, even hinting that there might be an element of homoeroticism on Mahan's part, calling it "a consuming passion, almost unnatural in its intensity."[53] Seager uses this to reinforce his thesis that Mahan was socially retarded and a religious fanatic. The Woolverton episode, painful as it was for Mahan, is nonetheless explicable in the overall context of his spiritual struggle.

Theron Woolverton was a Canadian-born physician who had entered the U.S. Navy in 1862. At the time Mahan knew him he was serving as surgeon on board the USS *Monocacy*, a sister ship in the Asiatic Squadron.[54] Mahan first met him in Yokohama in March or April of 1868. They socialized together ashore, frequently going riding together, but no strong friendship developed. They did, however, visit each other's wardrooms several times.[55] On one of these visits to the *Monocacy* in May, Woolverton surprised Mahan by offering to lend him a volume of sermons. "I was rather astounded, but recalled that I had heard him spoken of as religiously inclined, and my heart went out to him instantly." For Mahan, desperately lonely and having little in common with his worldly ship-mates, this seemed like a lifeline. "So I thought 'I have found sympathy at last.'" Woolverton had recently been confirmed in the Anglican Church and seemed to have some interest in spiritual matters, but as he confessed to Mahan, he "was utterly at sea as to faith—and careless as to practice." Mahan was now hooked, and as he told Ashe, "he had got my affection now, and you will understand how doubly impossible it was for me to go back from him, when I found his *claim* upon my regard [emphasis in original]." Mahan believed that God had chosen him to be the instrument of Woolverton's real, not just nominal, conversion and to bring him back to the straight and narrow. "I hope it may please God to have chosen me to be of some use to him" in befriending Woolverton.[56]

Using the book of sermons as an opening, Mahan tried to talk with him about spiritual matters when the two went to the races in Yokohama. But Mahan was "surprised and grieved to find him, after having so far traveled to God as to be confirmed on this very cruise, now to have taken to rationalist reading and, as he hinted, to have forsaken prayer in great degree." Woolverton spoke freely to him, but Mahan found himself tongue-tied, then became "depressed and gloomy" over the lost opportunity.[57] The following day, a Sunday, Mahan went ashore to church and consulted the Anglican missionary, Dr. Charles Lee, "concerning the propriety or advisability of my attempting to interfere in the matter."[58] Seager states that Lee urged Mahan "to unlimber all available persua-sive and theological artillery," but in fact Mahan said nothing about what Lee had told him.[59] What Mahan did next was write Woolverton a letter. Unfortunately, the contents of it are lost, as is the reply, but we know that Mahan was nervous about how Woolverton would react to it. Mahan described himself as "nervous . . . fretful . . . excited and somewhat uncomfortable—for I am not sure in what spirit he will receive it—and I should regret an estrangement."[60] However, he received a friendly response; "I was so glad to find that he had received kindly what I had said in my own."[61] Nonetheless, Mahan quickly became "disquiet" that the relationship was not blossoming the way he had hoped. Even though they were hardly more than acquaintances, Mahan was heavily invested emotionally in what he thought would be a close relationship based on spiritual affinity.

> The human regard and affection I have [for] Woolverton, more than I have
> felt for anyone in a long, long time, my regrets at our separation, and my anx-
> iety to see him hold fast to the profession he made before many witnesses

and to which by his own confession he has not adhered; all this mixture of
human and, I trust, Christian affection makes me anxious and depressed and
morose.[62]

He did allow as to how his "spiritual pride" was bound up in this pursuit.[63] Two
days later Woolverton visited the *Iroquois*, but Mahan's reaction was "disappointment." Even though he seemed totally self-absorbed at this point in his
life, Mahan occasionally showed some insight into his own behavior, such as
when he said, "I see clearly that I had hoped to find friendship and sympathy
in Woolverton and I have been disappointed; he is less inclined to like me I
think than a month or two back."[64] Mahan used the word "sympathy" frequently
in his diary entries and he even claimed it was the "great want of my life." He
appears to have used this term to mean a close personal friendship during a
time in which he was obviously extremely lonely. There was no one in his own
wardroom who shared his spiritual interests or intensity, and one can see why he
would latch on to Woolverton and how he misread the clues.[65] His hope rose the
following day, a Sunday, when he went ashore to attend church and Woolverton
was there. After the service Mahan visited with his missionary friend, Dr. Lee,
who "cheered me somewhat by assurances that he thought I had not been altogether without influence, in my career abroad here, for good. We spoke long of
Woolverton—and will both of us continue to pray for him."[66]

Mahan wrote a letter to his mother about Woolverton and then tore it up,
trying to convince himself that he was "half indifferent" to Woolverton, though
without much success.[67] He continued to seek guidance from Lee and occasionally ran into Woolverton, though he did not seek him out. He sensed that he might
have pushed Woolverton too far, and the failure to make a close friend—and win
a convert—continued to haunt him. "My hopes of a friend are evidently dashed,
and that is wounding." He also sensed that Woolverton occasionally manipu-
lated him, being willing to spend time with him only when other engagements
fell through.[68] Mahan wrote a letter to Woolverton that caused Woolverton to
pay him a personal visit two days later. Mahan was "greatly gratified" by the visit,
"for it seemed an assurance that he had a regard for me," but Woolverton "was
very nervous and fidgety, I wonder from what cause; did he think I was cocked
and primed to lecture him at a moment's notice." Unfortunately, we know nothing of what was actually said, but Mahan continued to brood on the relationship. He did have the awareness to realize that his search for a friend may have
predominated over his desire to see Woolverton converted, which of course
was supposed to be the higher priority. The slightest show of friendliness on
Woolverton's part was magnified by Mahan, giving him "renewed hopes." They
did go to church together at Mahan's invitation on Whitsunday (Pentecost), but

afterward Woolverton went on to do something else and did not return with him.[69] And so it went, Mahan's obsession, by his own admission, distracting him from his main duty of "remembrance of Christ."[70]

Mercifully for all concerned, the *Monocacy* was ordered from Yokohama to Shanghai in June 1868. Mahan was depressed but tried to cope as best he could. He had one last go at pushing Woolverton to conversion. It is not clear whether this was done by letter or in person. "I have dared to warn him," Mahan said, "against self-deception, against the Enemy, to urge upon him the validity of his Confirmation vow, his obligations despite his doubts—and begged him to seek the help of God's Holy Spirit. What more can I do, unless he came to me? Save pray, and that I do."[71]

With Woolverton gone Mahan continued to brood on the relationship, and he showed some insight into his own false expectations. He admitted he showed "jealousy and pique when I saw my friendship prized less than that of others. . . . I was hurt by neglect on his part." But Mahan consoled himself with the thought that his desire to bring Woolverton into the kingdom of Christ was genuine. "And so I will also hope that my dear friend Woolverton may be blessed through my prayers and imperfect endeavours though God in His wisdom and care for my partaking of His holiness hath refused me to seek His fruit as my own."[72] He was also, as can be seen throughout the diary, overly hard on himself for every perceived fault. He criticized himself for trying too hard to win Woolverton as a friend, for being "pharisaic" in his criticism of Woolverton and the *Monocacy*'s wardroom—which he characterized as "hard drinking and dissipated"—and for being "harsh, overbearing and sneering to offenders, men in many cases whose faults are akin to my own." He continued to castigate himself for "my evil pride and self-conceit," but that was typical of the whole diary and not just of references to Woolverton.[73]

The Mahan-Woolverton relationship, such as it was, could not have been that much of a disaster inasmuch as Woolverton wrote to him in August 1868. But instead of taking encouragement from it, Mahan became upset because it triggered all his old emotions about it. "Received a letter from Woolverton which from pleasure and interest has upset me as I was three months ago."[74] They met up again in September in Hiogo, where there did not seem to be any hard feelings on Woolverton's part, as he came aboard the *Iroquois* several times to visit Mahan. But Mahan was "disappointed in seeing that he is, after all, running pretty much the old course." Presumably that meant a dissipated lifestyle and little interest in Christianity. They did, however, talk of religion, with Mahan now trying to appeal "more to reason than to his heart."[75]

One of the problems, as Mahan came to realize, was that Woolverton "is a terrible lady killer I have heard," a description that would never be applied to Mahan nor one he would have wanted.[76] "I am sure [Woolverton] would, and does prefer other companionship and that of a kind to me distasteful."[77] Mahan was himself intentionally embracing celibacy, both out of obedience to God and faithfulness to his unrequited love, the Nonpareille.[78]

It went on for almost another year (till July 1869), Mahan and Woolverton meeting up at shore stations, Mahan overeager for Woolverton's company, Woolverton occasionally going to church with Mahan but not taking it too seriously, Mahan praying for Woolverton, Woolverton having an active sex life, Mahan hearing about it and despairing.[79] "Much distressed and grieved about W" was a typical diary entry during this time.[80]

The relationship did not end well. Woolverton was promoted and received orders to California in July 1869. Mahan was hurt—"my sensitive jealousy took offense"—because Woolverton, claiming he had too much to do, never said goodbye. To make matters worse, Mahan found out later that Woolverton had lied to him. He had not been busy at all, but instead of visiting Mahan he had gone ashore for a "flirtation."[81] For the following month Mahan continued to think about and pray for Woolverton, but then we hear no more about him.[82] This was not the complete end of the relationship even though the two never, so far as we know, saw each other again. Woolverton did write to Mahan in 1883 congratulating him on the publication of his first book, *Gulf and Inland Waters*, and Mahan also received "a very nice letter" from him in 1894. Beyond that we know nothing of any subsequent contact between the two.[83]

What in the end are we to make of this? Were Mahan's desires toward Woolverton "almost unnatural," as Seager suggests? Or was Mahan a religious fanatic who latched onto a convenient if unsuspecting victim, as Seager also believes? The answers to these questions are suggested by the total scope of the *Iroquois* diary and Mahan's spiritual crisis. Certainly the relationship was one-sided. Woolverton, while apparently pleasant and easygoing, never showed the level of interest in Mahan that Mahan did in him. And it seems obvious that Mahan's interest in Woolverton bordered on the obsessive. Mahan agonized endlessly over every little thing Woolverton did and probed each word and action for hidden meaning. Indeed, Mahan frequently used the word "love" to describe his feelings for Woolverton.[84] No doubt Woolverton, who obviously liked a good time, felt oppressed by all this attention, and it is not surprising that he occasionally tried to avoid Mahan, especially if he was intending to indulge in activities he knew Mahan would disapprove of. For all that, though, the relationship was not as disastrous as Seager would have us believe. Indeed, its very obsessiveness fit consistently with Mahan's overall behavior as chronicled by himself. Certainly Mahan was immature, but his motives were entirely understandable given his frame of mind, and his interest in cultivating Woolverton was primarily spiritual. By Mahan's own admission, the two "have hardly a taste in common, and I think could have messed together for years, without more than ordinary chumship."[85] The only thing that attracted Mahan's attention was Woolverton's recent confirmation, which caused Mahan (mistakenly) to think he had found an Anglican soul mate. Upon realizing that Woolverton's adherence to the Christian faith was nominal at best, Mahan then made it his project to convert him to true faith. Despite all else, including his loneliness and desire for a friend, that remained Mahan's goal. "I cannot reconcile myself to the thought that he should again go back and forsake his God and separate himself from that Body to which with all my faults and sins, I hope God yet finds me bound by a living union."[86] Mahan took extremely seriously the notion of the church as the body of Christ in which all true believers were united to God and to each other. It was important to him to bring Woolverton into that body in a real, not superficial, way, which explains his interest in getting Woolverton to receive holy communion regularly. "Were he only a Communicant. If thou wouldest but had him to the Holy Table—it seems to me I might feel easier."[87] In short, Mahan's desire to win a convert was part of his overall desire to serve God and his fear that he would never do so adequately. His failure in this regard weighed on him heavily, but because we know that Woolverton did contact him in later years, their friendship could not have been as misbegotten as Seager portrays it.

Before we leave the *Iroquois* diary, several other themes need to be addressed. One was Mahan's self-perceived heavy drinking. It is impossible to gauge by any objective standard how much Mahan drank, either in absolute terms or in comparison with other officers, or even whether he was ever actually drunk. The important issue is that he felt, by his own standards, that he drank too much. This was a constant refrain throughout the diary. He was constantly vowing to cut back (although never to stop!), constantly breaking that vow, and constantly seeking the Lord's help to reform. Success was always temporary and always followed by failure, thus leading to further depression and further drinking. Seager states outright that Mahan "had a drinking problem while he was serving in the *Iroquois*. It was one that he overcame; and it seems never to have troubled him again in his career or in his life."[88] Possibly, but one has to be cautious about taking Mahan too literally when he cataloged his many flaws since he was putting himself under a microscope and scrutinizing every perceived fault, finding himself always falling short of God's standards. The first entry in his diary ("am eating and drinking more than is right or good for me") and the last ("drank and smoked too much") and many in between attest to his concern with this matter.[89] On New Year's Day 1869 he made a rule for drinking (along with other rules): "A glass of sherry before and a pint bottle at dinner." Then he frequently assessed how well he kept the vow, with some days better than others. "As for my rules: 1. Have observed them in respect of drinking." When Mahan felt guilty for berating a junior officer he asked himself, "'Would I have done so but for the ale I have drunk?'. . . I have failed and drunk too much."[90] One needs to keep his comments about his drinking in perspective. He was judging himself by a standard of absolute perfection, and he obsessed about plenty of other sins as well. He also thought he ate and smoked too much.

Sexual temptations do not seem to have troubled Mahan nearly as much as drinking or losing his temper. He does not seem to have had any sexual encounters at all on this trip, nor do we know that he had any prior. He was horrified at the thought of patronizing prostitutes, a habit in which many fellow officers indulged, and was shocked upon hearing that Woolverton had done so. "[I] have been very unhappy thinking about Woolverton's sad declension. My heart almost fails me—I dare not think of the matter scarcely for the sickness and despondency it causes." And the next day, "fearful and tearful about Woolverton; heartsick at thinking of his fault—which even now sickens me to remember."[91] Mahan also did not approve of sexual banter in the wardroom. The subject of legalizing prostitution occasionally came up, and Mahan spoke against it. "A slight discussion sprang up on the subject of legalizing prostitution, which I opposed myself." This was apparently a hot topic at the time in Yokohama, and when visiting the *Monocacy* Mahan got into an argument with members of that wardroom. "Talked some time . . . in a pretty warm argument about legalizing prostitution."[92] That may have been a legitimate topic of conversation, but generally speaking any kind of sexual talk repelled him. "At dinner conversation got upon the morals of factory girls, etc. rather an unclean topic and to be avoided."[93] He was also distressed when the subject of how to avoid venereal disease came up. "Talk . . . ran upon the sanitary precautions against syphilis etc., a style of conversation not generally either profitable or pleasant; what may be called unsavory."[94]

Although Seager maintains that "Mahan thought a great deal about women, about sex, and about marriage," he only cites eleven diary entries out of hundreds. Although occasionally "tempted to lust," "troubled with lustful thoughts," or "a tendency to soft and sensual thoughts," Mahan actually spent very little time discussing sex in his diary.[95] One aid to keeping himself pure was his still strong love for the Nonpareille and his desire to be "truly purely faithful to her—without sin or offense in His eyes."[96]

Another common theme in the diary is Mahan's irritability and impatience with others. By his own admission he did not get along well with his shipmates. For one thing, no one on board shared his spiritual interests or intensity. One does not doubt that most of the members of the wardroom thought him an unsociable prig. He was also highly critical of junior officers and the captain as well. He held his tongue with the captain and confined his disapproval to his diary, but occasionally he spoke against the captain to others, not a good trait in an executive officer. For example, in May 1868 he wrote, "The Captain was provoking as usual in great ways and small ways." Mahan "criticised and abused him," presumably not to his face but later in the wardroom, for which he then felt guilty. "I lack humility, to submit my self-will to others. . . . I feel low with mortified conceit for which I need mortification."[97] When the captain did something that disturbed him he "spoke hastily and bitterly about it, and that before subordinates."[98] On another occasion "The Captain has annoyed me, and I have felt and spoken angrily and sullenly."[99]

The diary is also full of accounts of unpleasantness in the wardroom. Though Mahan, as executive officer, was presiding officer of the wardroom, he frequently got into arguments with his juniors over many matters, some important, some trivial. He took a particular dislike to Lt. Arthur H. Fletcher. One evening at dinner Fletcher "was more than ordinarily absurd it seemed to me. I must try and make my purpose strong to bear with him."[100] Fletcher was a constant "trial" to Mahan, and he once remarked that "my feelings towards Fletcher still are those of very marked dislike."[101] Part of the reason may have been Fletcher's "swearing" and disdain for Mahan's religious beliefs. "I gave my afternoon mainly to the writing up of an argument for our faith which I intend for Fletcher." Fletcher, amazingly enough, spoke "rather complimentarily" about it, but he did not convert nor did their relationship improve.[102] The only saving grace to the situation was Mahan's acute awareness of his own guilt. He knew his habit of ridiculing and berating junior officers was "unchristian and undignified," but he seemed unable to stop no matter how hard he tried, and he did try. But improvement seemed only temporary. "My manner is very bad to subordinates, sneering and cynical. I must be very unpopular."[103]

The last topic to discuss is one that Seager makes much of, namely Mahan's alleged fear of the sea. Mahan, Seager says, "became deathly afraid of the sea. . . . And there is no evidence that he ever wholly transcended this fear."[104] Certainly there were instances where Mahan was afraid. He did not hide these; he talked about them not only in his diary, but also in letters to his mother and to Ashe. Several times he told his mother of frightening gales and said he was "almost terrified."[105] What one must remember, though, and what Mahan made explicit in his letters and diary, was that God sustained him through such trials and that he sought in them opportunities to trust and praise the Almighty. "God has been pleased to put stimulus into the wind and rain which lift one's heart up—or how could such terrors be sustained?"[106] That remark was made in a letter to his mother, but the diary contains many similar statements. At one point Mahan was so miserable over bad weather that he said, "If I could only get out of the service how glad I would be to go. . . . I can scarcely keep down my murmuring because I am so frightened." But the following day he added, "God pity my weakness and anxiety; may it lead me to closer affiance with Him."[107]

What are we to make of this fear? Seager considers it a "major dimension in any understanding of Alfred Thayer Mahan" and claims that "throughout the remainder of his career he attempted to avoid or postpone assignment to sea duty whenever that prospect reared its head."[108] Taking the last point first, Seager overlooks the far more obvious reason that Mahan, later in his career, did not want to go to sea because of his desire to write. But as to his fear of being at sea, Seager both exaggerates and misunderstands it. The fear, which Seager sees as unmanly in a naval officer, can best be understood as part of Mahan's spiritual crisis. His main fear was not bad weather, but dying in an unconverted state. His doubt, as evidenced so many times in the diary, was that he did not trust God enough. "Cowardice and lack of trust in God have been my worst tempters."[109] The entire diary is the story of his attempt to please God and win his favor, but he was never quite sure he had done enough or was pure enough. The constant doubt and frustration was what made him afraid and depressed. This is common in Puritan conversion narratives. It should not be surprising that at some point in his state of preparation he should be afraid of natural phenomena that might kill him.

Remarks by Harry S. Stout about the great eighteenth-century evangelist George Whitefield illustrate this point. Whitefield, in his preparationist phase while an undergraduate at Oxford, had a similar experience and was even thought "mad" by his tutor. Stout comments,

> In fact, Whitefield was not mad. Nor could he "act" otherwise. He was going through a powerful, renovative spiritual experience that was shaping his life and career. His personality may have dictated the extremes of abasement and anxiety, but the experience itself was common to countless saints in the Puritan mode who first had to be humbled and brought low before they could be exalted and purged. In conventional Puritan terminology, he was going through a period of "preparation" antecedent to saving grace. His spiritual experience was at once real and scripted in countless spiritual autobiographies and testimonies.[110]

This is a perfect description of Mahan's spiritual crisis on the *Iroquois* voyage, and Mahan's goal can best be summed up in the undated prayer he wrote in 1868 or 1869 while on the *Iroquois*.

> Grant unto me, O Lord, that I am here especially in Thy presence; let me pray with desire and faith, give thanks earnestly and praise Thee heartily and cheerfully. Give unto Thy servant wisdom and grace that Thy word read and preached by him may be blessed to his hearers and that he may receive the reward of a faithful minister [a reference to Mahan's officiating at services on board]. Grant that all we here assembled may join heartily in worshiping Thee, and remembering that we believe in the Communion of Saints may derive strength and comfort from the thought of the great multitude who will this day use these same words; and may the prayer and praises of Thy whole Church redound to Thy glory and the salvation of each member of the same through Jesus Christ our Lord.[111]

Happily for Mahan his various professional and personal crises would come to resolution soon.

CONVERSION AND RESOLUTION

In February 1869 the *Iroquois* captain, Cdr. Earl English, was reassigned and Mahan was given temporary command of the ship. This was his first command at sea, a huge step in the career of a naval officer. The ship returned to Nagasaki in May, and Mahan fell ill, probably with malaria, and was hospitalized before recuperating in a hotel. It was originally intended that he would take command of the *Ashuelot*, but his illness caused the order to be canceled. In mid-July, when he was fully recovered, he was ordered to Yokohama to take command of the gunboat *Aroostook*. This was only a temporary assignment until September, when the ship was to be sold. After that he received his long-awaited orders home and took six months' leave so that he could travel leisurely through Europe.[112]

After visiting Hong Kong and India, Mahan arrived in Marseilles on December 17, 1869. While there he learned that the *Sabine*—the ship on which his brother Dennis Jr., a recent Annapolis graduate, was serving—was in Nice, so he proceeded there. He had intended a brief visit with his brother and then to go to Paris, but he stayed six weeks.[113] "Why?" he rhetorically asked Ashe. "Because I have here met the woman of whom I have written you often enough before. But my dear Ashe—absence seems to have done its work on her, and it is too evident to me after this daily intimate acquaintance of a month—that the regard she now has for me is no real [remainder of letter missing]."[114] What Mahan either never mentioned, or was possibly included in the missing portion of the letter, was the startling news that the Nonpareille's husband had died. Mahan promptly proposed but she turned him down. Presumably someone, most likely Ashe, later discussed this with Puleston, as the latter seemed to know a lot about it and commented, "To his despair, the lady hesitated; she was older, perhaps wiser in such matters, and doubted that she could hold the love of her younger suitor. She refused his offer."[115] Mahan had a difficult time getting over his disappointment. He did, however, reach a point when he knew that loving her, even in a pure way from afar, was of no purpose.

> I have been a good deal harassed in my mind, owing to my meeting with and continued attachment to a person of whom I wrote to you before—a feeling as you may suppose distasteful to my relatives. I presume things of this sort are continually occurring in the histories of human life, yet to the one concerned they each seem peculiar in themselves; and I so find myself incapable of imagining any one equal to her in loveableness and fascination. The effect upon me personally is bad—for I have no occupation requiring my mind to leave what is perhaps a very morbid condition. If ever a man needed praying for, I do just now; for I am in sore straits to do right—even to know what is right. The best hope for me—humanly speaking, would be to form some stronger and more natural attachment, but is it possible? This is the only one of her sex I ever desired to possess, to call my very own.[116]

By the phrase "more natural" he may have meant someone closer to his own age, or he may have meant someone who could actually be a potential marriage partner as opposed to someone he could only worship from afar in a pure and celibate way. In any event he knew he had to move on emotionally and consign the Nonpareille to the past, and to help himself do this he took a trip to Rome. He did enjoy seeing the great works of art in the Vatican, but he did not think much of the city of Rome itself. He conceded to Ashe that he might not have appreciated all Rome had to offer because he was still preoccupied with his lost love.[117]

Following visits to Paris, London, and Spithead (to see the Royal Navy's newest battleship HMS *Captain*) he sailed from Liverpool on the steamship *Russia* headed for New York. On board was a lady from Philadelphia, Grace Evans, who it would transpire had an eligible niece.[118] He returned to his family at West Point and managed to secure additional leave. He quickly became bored but was trying his best to reassess his career prospects and his romantic prospects. "I have been living very quietly ever since my return," he told Ashe, "feeling an almost apathetic indolence and lack of interest in nearly everything that once excited it in me." He was willing to remain in the Navy but hoped for shore duty, and so far he had not met any woman to whom he was attracted or who was attracted to him.[119]

In July 1870 he went to Sharon Springs, a fashionable spa in the Adirondacks, where his doctor told him he would benefit from the sulphur baths. He was still suffering "unpleasant traces of the eastern climate."[120] While there he met up with Grace Evans, who introduced him to her nineteen-year-old niece Ellen Lyle Evans (known as Elly). She was the daughter of Mr. and Mrs. Manlius Glendower Evans, formerly of Philadelphia but recently moved to New York City. Her family regularly summered at Sharon.[121] Seager mocks Alfred and Elly's courtship, claiming it was "neither eager, rapid, nor torrid" and had "no fire and passion." "They came together by default," he says, and he even claims that Mahan married her as "an insurance policy."[122] Whether the relationship lived up to Seager's standards of passion is irrelevant, but evidence Seager himself uncovered indicates that the couple hit it off immediately. Mahan was distressed to receive orders sending him to Pittsburgh, and from the account he gave to Ashe it is clear that he did not want to leave Sharon Springs. He told his detailing officer that "I have strong personal reasons for desiring to remain in or near New York during the succeeding winter." He told Ashe that these orders gave him "such a hurt." Indeed, the courtship had already progressed to the point where he had invited Elly to visit him at West Point and she had accepted. "I was expecting my Sharon friend at the Point the first fortnight in September."[123] The visit was canceled, however, as Mahan's orders were not changed. He had barely arrived at the ordnance station at Pittsburgh when he received word of the death of his Uncle Milo.[124]

Milo Mahan had been rector of St. Paul's Church in Baltimore and headmaster of its school since the summer of 1864, when he had resigned his professorship at General Theological Seminary. Despite the murmurings against him for his supposed Southern sympathies he had been missed by some at General Theological Seminary, and in 1869 a group of professors and trustees undertook to get him back. "His friends had long felt that the General Seminary was the true field of his greatness, and that it was a grievous mistake in the Church to suffer him to be drawn away to parochial life."[125] In 1869 Milo was queried as to his interest in returning. He was in England at the time but wrote a letter declining. At a meeting in June 1869 his name was put up anyway even though some bishops on the board of trustees, including his own bishop of Maryland, William R. Whittingham, voted against him on the grounds that he was too Anglo-Catholic. Some who were present, including the bishop of New Jersey, William Henry Odenheimer, thought the strong attack on Milo by his own bishop was out of bounds, especially since Milo was not present to defend himself. After heated debate and four ballots no positive result was forthcoming, and Milo's friends decided to try again in October when Milo would have returned from England and, they hoped, would come to New York to make his own case.[126]

Although he claimed he had no interest in returning to General Theological Seminary, Milo was outraged by the charge made against him by Whittingham that his views on auricular confession were too Romanistic, an opinion based not on any writings or sermons but on an alleged private conversation. Milo responded with a "Brief for the Defense" in which he explained that his views had been "more or less distorted." He intended to have the piece published, but that proved unnecessary when Whittingham withdrew his remarks and apologized.[127] Milo attended the October board meeting, where his defense was offered and accepted and he was elected professor of systematic divinity. He declined on the grounds that he had too many projects going in Baltimore that required his attention. The professorship was left vacant for the moment, although he was re-elected the following June and he accepted. Unfortunately, he fell ill in August and died on September 3, never having made it back to New York.[128]

Alfred received permission to attend the funeral in Baltimore, the only known member of the Mahan family to attend. Milo's biographer has left us an account of his funeral; it was filled with the High Church ceremonial he so loved. Sixty priests participated in the service and a "vast crowd" attended. "Men wept like children. One great sob of grief was the farewell of the loving multitude to him whose face they should see on earth no more."[129] Even allowing for Victorian hyperbole it must have been an impressive tribute and it affected Alfred deeply. The only surviving comments we have from Alfred on his uncle's death are contained in a letter thanking Ashe for his sympathy.

> You do my uncle no more than justice, in your surmises as to the loss he has been to us and to the church. The latter is greater than the former, for during many years we have been much separated. For myself I am quite at a loss to know to whom to turn for the advice and information that I used to get from him in matters of theological, rather than religious, interest—and during my last cruise I had accumulated several points upon which I wished instruction. The loss, of course, is irreparable, for though I might find equal ability, I cannot have the same familiar freedom of intercourse. It is gratifying to our affection that two memorial windows are now to be erected to him.[130]

Alfred returned to West Point from Baltimore, where he received orders forwarded from Pittsburgh detaching him from duty there.[131] Still on leave, he remained at West Point until November after telling a detailer, Commodore

Alden, that he wished to be assigned shore duty at the Brooklyn Navy Yard.[132] He had not yet mentioned Elly Evans by name to Ashe, but he did tell Ashe that he wanted to be in New York City "that I may not find myself quite alone in my latter days." He was looking forward to "getting in love" and confessed to Ashe that he was occasionally disturbed by "that certain vague unquietness . . . due to the unnatural state that celibacy undoubtedly is." He worried that he was unsuited to family life—"I have lived so much in myself, and had so much my own way"—but felt that "a sufficiently strong affection would, I hope, enable me to struggle successfully against this trait."[133] Although Seager ridicules Mahan's "search for a wife. Almost any wife would do," that hardly seems a fair assessment. Surely the fact that Elly lived in New York City was the key reason he wanted to be stationed there (even turning down two other assignments) and as to the statement that almost any wife would do, that was clearly not the case, as his letters to his mother and Ashe indicate.[134] He was ordered to the Brooklyn Navy Yard in November, and he pursued his courtship of Elly.

Elly was a devout young girl, an Episcopalian, and these were undoubtedly high on Mahan's list of desired attributes. His earliest surviving letter to her is a note breaking a date to go to church because he had another church obligation elsewhere. "When I accepted last night your invitation to church on Sunday afternoon, I forgot that I had already promised to attend the consecration of the new seamen's Chapel at the same hour. I have therefore to ask you to excuse me. I shall certainly be in to see you very, very soon."[135] (Mahan had joined the Board of Managers of the Seamen's Church Institute in 1867 and served on it for forty-seven years.[136]) Apparently Elly did not take this amiss as the courtship proceeded successfully, and she impressed her suitor with her "sincere and practical religious principle."[137]

In February 1871 Mahan received orders to join the *Worcester*, a merchant ship chartered by the Navy to take provisions to France "for the relief of the famine supposed to be impending there" as a result of the Franco-Prussian War.[138] This required a stay of about three weeks in Boston before sailing. It was there that Mahan had the most significant experience of his life, the resolution of his spiritual crisis, his conversion experience.

The only occasion on which Mahan ever wrote about his conversion experience was in an article that is little known but hugely significant for understanding his religious development: "The Apparent Decadence of the Church's Influence," which appeared in the April 25, 1903, issue of *Churchman*. In this article, which posited the necessity of a personal relationship with Jesus Christ, Mahan told of his own conversion. This was the defining spiritual experience of his life; following it, the crisis ended. There was no need for his perfectionistic introspection and condemnation. He knew he could not gain God's favor through striving, and he put his trust in the completed work of Christ on the cross. He did not speak of this experience much in his writings or speeches, but he did make a few cryptic references to it in speeches he gave to church groups later in life. He gave two such talks in March 1899. One was given at Holy Trinity Episcopal Church in Brooklyn. The specific date is not known, but the other was given at the Church of the Holy Trinity in Middletown, Connecticut, on March 22. The speeches were not identical though they did cover similar points. What is interesting about them is Mahan's repeated references to the period of "thirty years" in which he had been a Christian. Since Mahan was fifty-nine when he gave these talks, the time frame fits perfectly. To him his real Christian life began with the experience in the Boston church. All that happened before was striving in his own "systematic effort."[139] Seager appears unaware of Mahan's conversion and the article in which Mahan's account of it appears, for it does not appear in Seager's bibliography of Mahan's works.

While the *Worcester* sailed to Europe in March 1871, Mahan wrote to Ellen Evans regularly, addressing her as "My dear Miss Elly." The letters were chatty, not particularly romantic or passionate. Seager mocks them for this but does not take into account the accepted courtship rituals of the day. If Mahan were serious about her, which he was, he would hardly write anything that would appear unseemly to her parents. The *Worcester* never did go to France, but instead visited various ports in England for about two months. Mahan took advantage of this by visiting a variety of churches, including attending Easter services at Exeter Cathedral, an experience he found "very moving."[140] The courtship must have been progressing well since he did receive letters from both Elly and her mother.[141]

The *Worcester* returned to Boston in July. Mahan paid a brief visit to his family at West Point and then proceeded to Sharon Springs to catch up with Elly. That they were an item among the spa set was apparent when a poem started making the rounds.

> Elly had a big Mahan, whose teeth were white as snow.
> Everywhere that Elly went, Mahan was sure to go.[142]

On August 15, 1871, Mahan wrote a long letter to his mother, his confidante in these matters, explaining that though before he had left West Point he had been unsure whether to propose, "a few days here with her decided me." At the time of writing the letter, a few days after his proposal, Elly had not given him a definite answer. Her mother told him "there should be as yet no engagement on the grounds that Elly was too young." Mahan suspected that his profession—requiring as it did long absences from home and not being particularly lucrative—was also an obstacle. Elly's father, being ill, was not to be told "until it is sure she will accept me." Mahan hoped that a proposed meeting of his mother and the Evanses at Long Branch, New Jersey, would work in his favor. He told his mother "above all I count upon you as rather a trump card in recommending myself to any woman." He listed Elly's many fine attributes: "her character . . . generosity, truth and loyalty . . . and above all sincere and practical religious principle, under discouragements you have already heard from me [possibly a reference to her father's illness]." Mahan closed his letter by assuring his mother that his love was genuine, mature, and based on mutual compatibility, not like his former passion for the Nonpareille. "I am not entrainé by that mad wild instinct, dignified by the name of love, which I have known of old."[143]

It is not clear whether the Long Branch trip took place. Not having a new assignment, Mahan returned to West Point in September, at which point the progress of his courtship was interrupted by the sudden death of Dennis Mahan. In April 1871 Dennis turned sixty-nine but had been in poor health for some time. It is not at all clear from what infirmity he actually suffered, but the main symptom that concerned his family and friends was some sort of mental-emotional disturbance. Evidence of depression had shown up prior to 1871, and it was thought that overwork and stress had finally brought him low. According to his two biographers, Henry Abbot and Thomas Griess, he seemed to have some awareness of an impending mental breakdown and feared he would be forced to retire.[144] He told the assistant surgeon at West Point that "his trouble was beyond the reach of the art of medicine."[145] What he feared came to pass when in 1871 the Board of Visitors recommended that he be retired. This news sent him further into despondency despite the assurance from his former pupil Ulysses S. Grant, now President of the United States, that he would not be forced to retire.[146]

In September he took a turn for the worse and was suffering from "violent nervous paroxysm" and "convulsive fits." His family urged him to visit a physician in New York City and on September 16, 1871, accompanied only by a nurse, he boarded the steamer *Mary Powell* for New York. On the way there he jumped overboard and, according to one report, was hit in the head by the paddle wheel. His body was recovered eight days later. Seager takes it as undisputed fact that Dennis "committed suicide."[147] Obviously, we can never know what was going through Dennis' mind, but given his disturbed state, it is not clear if his intention was suicide or if he even knew what he was doing. Griess, who has studied Dennis' life and career much more closely than Seager has, says that he was "seized by another of his paroxysms, and, not in control of his faculties, stepped outside his cabin and flung himself overboard."[148] Seager also claims that Alfred was subsequently worried that he had inherited a tendency toward suicide, but the letter he cites as evidence of this, one written to Ashe in 1876, does not discuss suicide, either his own or his father's. What Alfred actually said was "I used to believe that we were free from such [worry about hereditary disease] but since my father's death, and recognizing in most of us a disposition to nervous and mental excitement and worry, I have myself gone through seasons of great apprehension."[149] The context of the letter, a discussion of disease, makes clear that his concern was about inheriting a mental illness, not suicide as such.

Both Mahan's family and the Army were shocked at Dennis' death. Thanks to cadet Hugh L. Scott we have a detailed description of the funeral. "The funeral," Scott wrote to his mother, "was the most splendid thing I ever saw." The Corps of Cadets marched into the chapel and stacked their arms in the front, "then they brought in the body in a splendid coffin covered with tube roses and silver borne by soldiers and surrounded by Proffessors [sic] and his sons [Alfred, Frederick, and Dennis Jr.] followed after." After the Episcopal burial office, the cadets

> formed in front and marched off at "Reverse Arms" followed by the body carried on a caisson and wrapped in a flag[,] the caisson drawn by four big black horses. After the caisson followed the mourners [i.e., the family] and after them a long line of Officers in full dress and then friends and in front of all the Band was playing the most splendid music I ever heard[,] so solemn it almost made me cry to listen to it. After the body was buried [at the West Point cemetery] we fired three volleys over the grave and marched home again.[150]

It was a fitting tribute to a man who had given his whole adult life to West Point and had the biggest impact of any professor on the academic and professional development of the officer corps. Even though he had not been himself for the previous few years, the loss to the Army was incalculable.[151]

Though Alfred tended to confide more in his mother than in his father, the loss to him must have been great. His respect for his father bordered on awe, and in the space of a year he had lost his two most significant role models, his uncle and his father. His faith, newly fortified by his conversion experience, strengthened him and brought him through this difficult period.

Alfred was sent briefly to the Navy's Hydrographic Office at Cold Spring, New York. This allowed him to help his mother settle affairs and move to Elizabeth, New Jersey, where she moved in with her widowed sister, Jane Okill Swift. In January 1872 he was assigned to the USS *Vermont*, home ported in

New York City, a location that enabled him to resume his courtship of Elly without too much hardship.[152]

When Mr. Evans' health improved, he was told of Alfred and Elly's desire to become engaged. He had nothing against Mahan, he said, but thought that "the wife of a naval officer [was] little better than a man's widow."[153] But he soon relented and in April 1872 the couple became formally engaged. Mahan was able to get a three-month leave and then had it extended another three months. The couple were married on June 11, 1872. Unfortunately, we have no information on the wedding itself—was it held in a church or in the Evanses' home?— although we can safely assume an Episcopal priest officiated. The Mahans were eminently well-suited for each other and had a long and happy marriage.[154] With his conversion and his marriage, Mahan had matured and was now to embark on a new phase in his life.

CHAPTER 4

FAMILY MAN AND
BURGEONING AUTHOR

The newlywed Mahans stayed with Alfred's mother in Elizabeth, New Jersey (except for a brief stay at Long Branch, New Jersey), from September to December 1872. During this honeymoon period Mahan received orders to report to Washington, D.C., for examination for promotion to the rank of commander, which he successfully passed. In December he was appointed commanding officer of the USS *Wasp*, "a wooden side-wheel British steamer" on the South Atlantic Station at Montevideo, Uruguay.[1] Happily for Mahan, he was allowed to have his wife on station with him. The newlyweds, Elly now pregnant, sailed to Montevideo on a British passenger ship *Duoro*, leaving in late December and arriving in early February before Alfred took command of the *Wasp* on February 17, 1873.[2] Most of the *Wasp*'s duties involved showing the flag and protecting the interests of American businessmen.[3]

The Mahans lived on shore and appear to have socialized little apart from attending the local Anglican church. Most of Mahan's surviving correspondence from this period is of an official nature, but Elly was corresponding regularly with Alfred's mother. On August 6, 1873, Elly gave birth to a daughter, who was named Helen Evans Mahan. Mahan was nothing if not a doting father, and he "lies on the floor for her amusement and lets her pull him about, slobber over him, and do anything she wishes and does not mind it a bit."[4] Not hesitating to begin her religious education early, Mahan used to sing hymns to her, his two favorites being "Art thou weary, art thou languid, art thou sore distressed?" and "On the other side of Jordan, in the sweet fields of Eden." The Anglican vicar's wife, Mary Hoskins, found the first choice amusing.[5] For reasons unknown, Mahan wanted the baby to be baptized on St. Matthew's Day (September 21), even though he would be at sea at the time.[6]

The *Wasp* was too small a ship to rate a chaplain, so Mahan officiated at Sunday services when the ship was at sea. Most captains obliged to perform this duty no doubt clung to the safety of the Book of Common Prayer liturgy and did not extemporize on theological topics. But Mahan preached "little sermons," which were judged "very good" by his executive officer, Lt. Cdr. Charles O'Neil. Mahan also conducted services on major Anglican holy days such as Ascension Day. The crew enjoyed this if for no other reason than they had limited duty that day. O'Neil and his wife were so impressed by Mahan's faithfulness that they asked the Mahans to be godparents to their son Richard.[7]

Mahan's first effort as a historian occurred while on the *Wasp* tour. We know little about it, only that he gave a lecture on "Naval Battles" in September 1874. The lecture itself has not survived, nor do we know the audience for whom it was intended. According to his wife, however, "he has worked so much on it that it has quite upset him and he is feeling nervous and dull."[8]

In October 1874 Mahan received orders detaching him from the *Wasp*, but he did not turn over command to his successor until January 1875.[9] Given a

Mahan with daughter Helen *(Naval Historical Collection, Naval War College)*

six-month leave of absence (at reduced pay) the Mahan family sailed on the steamer *Potosi* for France, where they visited Elly's parents at Pau.[10] On the voyage over, Mahan wrote a long letter to his mother about his family—little Helen charmed both passengers and crew—and current controversies in the Episcopal Church. He caught up with ecclesiastical news by reading *Churchman*. His remarks focused on the Episcopal General Convention of 1874 and its condemnation of "any actions of adoration of or toward the Elements" and the subsequent Church Congress held in October 1874 that discussed this same topic. The General Convention action seemed on the surface to be a defeat for the Ritualist party (later referred to as Anglo-Catholics), but in some sense it was a victory since "the principle of ritual liberty" was informally established anyway.[11] Some of Mahan's remarks to his mother were cryptic, but the gist of them seemed to be that he supported the Ritualist view. He noted his mother's disapproval of some of the "recently elected bishops," but it is not clear to whom he was referring.[12]

The Mahans spent two months in Pau, where Alfred was happy to find an Anglican church of the Ritualist persuasion that offered daily services.[13] By May they were back in Elizabeth with Alfred's mother, but Elly Mahan had unfortunately suffered a miscarriage on the voyage home.[14] The Mahans were also low on money and Alfred, embarrassed, asked Ashe if he could repay money that Mahan had loaned him.[15] Ashe did pay the money back promptly and Mahan thanked him.[16]

Mahan, though a strong partisan of the Ritualist/Anglo-Catholic position of his uncle that sought to return many Catholic practices to the Anglican liturgy, was nonetheless concerned, as was his uncle, that there be a clear dividing line between Anglo-Catholicism and Roman Catholicism. Milo was, despite a high Anglican stance, adamantly opposed to Rome and the papacy. Despite some prominent defections to Rome, Alfred showed no sign of temptation toward that end, but he studied the issue carefully, no doubt with his uncle's writings still in mind. He discussed the issue with Ashe, sending him pamphlets he had picked up in England. There was a debate in print going on between prominent Catholic converts John Henry Newman and Henry Manning on one side and British statesman and sometime prime minister William Gladstone on the other. Gladstone defended the Protestant view in a pamphlet titled *Vatican Decrees and their Bearing on Civil Allegiance* (1874) followed by *Vaticanism: An Answer to Reproofs and Replies* (1875). The doctrine of papal infallibility had been declared a dogma at the First Vatican Council in 1870, and this is what precipitated (or rather reignited) the controversy over whether a Catholic could be a loyal citizen of his nation and loyal to the pope at the same time.

Mahan thought Newman the best of the Catholic defenders in that he "puts the Roman side of the question in the light least repulsive for Protestants." But he also thought that Newman was "imbued . . . with the essence of Roman error," by which Mahan meant placing others—"on earth the Pope, in heaven the Virgin"—in a role reserved for Jesus alone.[17]

Mahan's leave of absence expired in August 1875, and after hearing that there was a commander's vacancy at Boston Navy Yard, he applied for it. He received the assignment, as senior aide to Commo. Edward T. Nichols, and reported to Boston on September 1.[18] He also joined the U.S. Naval Institute, the professional organization for naval officers that had been founded in 1873.[19]

It was at Boston that Mahan first encountered political corruption affecting the Navy, and it angered him so much that he suddenly became an outspoken advocate of reform. Hitherto, he had not done anything even remotely controversial in his career. The problem was the administration of the navy yards, which instead of being professionally run by apolitical naval officers had become lucrative pork-barrel projects that supplied jobs for political hacks based on party loyalty rather than professional qualifications. Mahan put the blame squarely on the Secretary of the Navy, George M. Robeson, a Republican appointed by President Grant, and his chief collaborator, Isaiah Hanscom, chief of the Bureau of Construction and Repair. Shocked by the blatant corruption at Boston and frustrated by the powerlessness of naval officers to do anything about it, Mahan enlisted Ashe in his campaign to get Congress involved and to get rid of Robeson.[20]

Ashe was a prominent Democrat in North Carolina and a law partner of Democratic senator Augustus S. Merrimon. Ashe put Mahan and Merrimon in contact with each other, and Mahan sent detailed information to Ashe, which the latter sent on to Merrimon. In the meantime the chairman of the House Naval Committee, Democrat Washington C. Whitthorne of Tennessee, began an investigation of the Navy Department. Mahan was invited to testify in writing, which he did in the form of a long letter to Whitthorne dated March 21, 1876. In this letter he described the corruption in Boston; for example, a workman bragged to Mahan about how his pay was padded on personal orders from the secretary. He also took aim at the Navy's antiquated promotion system, which kept talented officers languishing in the lower grades, and the use of political influence to cover up misconduct and incompetence in certain officers.[21]

Mahan knew that such actions might hurt his career, but felt that conditions warranted the risk. He told Ashe that "holding such language touching the Secretary as I have here would expose me to severe punishment. That I use it may therefore prove to you how urgent I think the need is, and how deep my

conviction of the deplorable condition in which the Navy now is."[22] Nonetheless
he was shocked when his and others' testimony was made public. "To my great
astonishment the Committee have printed the answers of officers to a circular
letter which they addressed us in February last. None of us anticipated publicity,
and I expect some have opened their minds very freely."[23]

The Whitthorne Committee report was a disappointment to Mahan inasmuch as it did not turn up any hard evidence that the secretary was corrupt.[24]
One result of the investigation, though, was a severe cutback in the Navy, and
Mahan was placed first on "waiting orders" and then on "furlough" (equivalent
to a layoff). He was sure this was in retaliation for his role in the Robeson investigation. "My fears as to my position have proved too well founded."[25] Years later
he still held to this view, according to Puleston. "The Mahan family believed
they were being punished because Alfred had tried to improve conditions at the
Boston Navy Yard." But Puleston doubted this was the case, as many other officers were affected as well.[26] Although Mahan was scathing in his denunciation
of Secretary Robeson, he said nothing negative about Robeson's boss, President
Grant, who was after all one of Dennis Mahan's pupils. "I believe Grant to be
personally upright," he said, but he added that the president had an "unfortunate
habit of shutting his eyes to his friends' shortcomings."[27]

In addition to financial worries because of the furlough, the Mahans were
also trying to have a second child, thus far without success. "I can scarcely call
her [Helen] baby now being nearly three years old; it is a disappointment to
us that she is alone." They attributed the difficulty to Elly's miscarriage in May
1875, "since which we have not had hopes."[28] The Mahans left Boston in August
1876 and returned to Elizabeth to live with Alfred's mother. In October Mahan
received orders to report to the Naval Academy to sit on a Board of Examiners
that examined midshipmen for promotion to ensign. This was only a temporary
assignment, but while there he managed to convince the superintendent, Rear
Adm. Christopher R. P. Rodgers, to request his appointment to fill the vacant
position of head of the Gunnery Department. The appointment came through
in December but was rescinded within a few days.[29] Disappointed, not to say
angry, Mahan explained to Commo. Daniel Ammen of the Office of Detail
(which handled assignments) that the request had come from Admiral Rodgers
himself and that the sudden revocation would "seem to imply a serious reflection upon me, as a man, or as an officer." He wanted to know "what reasons, if
any, derogatory to me have prompted this change."[30] No doubt Mahan felt that
Secretary Robeson was behind the scuttling of his appointment, but Ammen
replied that the original order had been issued mistakenly without the secretary's approval, and that the secretary would not, in fact, approve the order.[31]

While the commotion about assignments was going on, Mahan submitted an article to the *Army and Navy Journal*. This was, as far as we know, his first attempt at publication. The article, which was turned down by the editor and does not survive, was about why staff officers (including doctors, engineers, paymasters) should not carry military rank.[32]

In an effort to economize, the Mahans returned to Pau, France, where the cost of living was lower. The good news, though, was that Elly was pregnant again. She gave birth to another daughter, named Ellen Kuhn Mahan, on July 10, 1877. Presumably she was baptized in the Ritualist Anglican Church the Mahans attended when in Pau.[33]

While in Pau, Mahan traveled to "Carcassonne, Albi, Toulouse and several other small towns" and developed an interest in the history of French cathedrals. He also spent time in the Pau City Library and "formed the idea of writing a couple of articles, afterward a small book, for which I collected a number of photographs as illustrations." He submitted the manuscript to *Harper's Magazine*, which rejected it on the grounds that it would not appeal to American readers. They did offer to print it if he paid the expenses, but that was out of the question given his financial situation.[34] Puleston tells us "the failure discouraged him, but Mrs. Mahan was convinced he could write and continually urged him to try again."[35]

Another piece of good news reached Mahan the day after his daughter's birth. He received orders to report to the Naval Academy on September 1 to head the Gunnery Department, which had just come under the command of the new Rutherford B. Hayes administration and Richard W. Thompson's Navy Department. The family moved into "a large and fairly commodious house" on the Academy grounds.[36] Mahan reported that his duties were not too onerous, however. "I have charge of the Gunnery both in instruction and drill. The former I find is left entirely in my hands, the drills however are run by the Supt. [Rodgers] and the Commandant of Midn [Silas W. Terry], so much so that I have nearly washed my hands of any concern in them, finding that I could do nothing."[37]

The most significant occurrence of this tour of duty was the achievement of his first publication, an essay submitted for a contest sponsored by the U.S. Naval Institute. The Naval Institute "was growing feeble," he said, and "we determined as a last resort to offer a money prize for an Essay on the subject of Naval Education." Ten competitors entered, and while Mahan did not win the money prize, he came in third, which was good enough to get his essay published in what is now known as *Proceedings*, then called *The Record*.[38] Even Seager admits this was "a creditable piece of work."[39]

The essay is interesting for several reasons beyond its being his first publication. First, it shows that Mahan was already interested in determining
what attributes make for a successful naval officer. This interest would show
up later in works such as *Admiral Farragut* (1892), *Life of Nelson* (1897), and
Types of Naval Officers (1901). In Mahan's view a naval officer should possess
three qualities above all: first, "moral power," which he defined as "strength
to control self and others; fearlessness in responsibility and in danger; self
reliance; promptitude in action; readiness of resource; calmness amid excitement." Second was "physical vigor" and third was "intellectual equipment [or]
acquired knowledge."[40] Mahan would later conclude that these virtues had
their greatest embodiment in Lord Nelson. Interestingly, Mahan also thought
that the academic standard of admission to the Naval Academy should be low.
This may sound surprising, but Mahan made two good points in defending
this unusual view. One was that the taxpayers were funding an Annapolis education and it should be equally accessible to candidates from all areas of the
country, including those less settled areas that did not have good educational
facilities. His other reason was that, once admitted, those boys that had "force
of character and perseverance" would rise to the top regardless of their lack of
academic attainments.[41]

Most of the essay is devoted to criticizing the current Naval Academy curriculum and offering suggestions for improvement. Seager misinterprets what
Mahan said in this essay, claiming that Mahan wanted to strengthen the technical
and scientific areas of the curriculum. "Technical knowledge of this kind," says
Seager speaking for Mahan, "could only produce better combat naval officers."[42]
But Mahan actually said just the opposite. "The knowledge that is necessary to
a naval line officer is simply and solely that which enables him to discharge his
many duties intelligently and thoroughly. Any information that goes beyond
this point is after all simply culture, which, however desirable in itself, must not
be confused with essentials."[43] Mahan was worried that the curriculum would be
too cluttered up with technical subjects that, however important to specialists
(who should be staff officers, not line officers), would not foster those attributes
of character he deemed essential to a line officer who aspired to command.

Mahan concluded his essay with a brief section on the education of enlisted
men, asserting that technical training could always be picked up on the job or in
training establishments. Mahan was more concerned with "moral tone," the lack
of which resulted in what he saw as the two greatest conduct problems of the
lower deck: desertion and drunkenness. He advocated an "apprentice system"
for boys aged fourteen to sixteen that would not only teach them their trade
but good personal habits as well. He understood that their greatest difficulty

was being away from home and family: "The seaman lives without the constant solace and restraint of family life." Therefore anything that attended to that need, even if not perfect, should be encouraged. He advocated, for instance, classes in cooking, dancing, and music, as well as sports, games, and any "means for healthfully occupying the mind." He was not sure how realistic it was, but he hoped to stimulate in at least some sailors an interest in "naval biography and history," which he thought would inculcate "high aims and enthusiasm" in what was, after all, "a noble profession."[44]

Most important, though, was the religious component. "So I think any scheme of education is defective that makes no effort to teach the learner to believe in and depend upon God." He does not mention anything about Christianity specifically—possibly he took that as a given—but instead ties religious education, at least in the military context, to the concept of duty. Those who take duty seriously, even when no one is watching, walk a difficult road, "find little sympathy," and are often too hard on themselves. But to know and trust God is to find the companionship, encouragement, and strength that one needs. Mahan concluded his essay with the admonition that mere lip service paid to religion will not do the job. Men will see through the "cant" and "lack of conviction" right away. Only real believers can convey their faith persuasively to others. Mahan urged "the necessity, even as a matter of policy," that such believers have a role in naval education.[45]

While on duty at the Naval Academy, Mahan made the acquaintance of Tasuka Serata, one of four Japanese midshipmen who were attending the academy under an agreement between Japan and the United States. Because he had been to Japan, Mahan often invited the midshipmen to his home. He was friendly with all of them but formed a special bond with Serata, who was a Christian. Many years later Mahan would write the introduction to Lieutenant Commander K. Asami's biography of Vice Admiral Serata.[46]

Because his position offered him a good deal of leisure time, he had time to read in the academy library. This reading was important to Mahan's development as a military and naval thinker. He regularly studied the British *Journal of the Royal United Service Institution* and the French *Revue maritime et coloniale*. He also participated in the monthly meetings of the Naval Institute, where he met fellow reform-minded officers and the most creative Navy thinkers. These included Stephen B. Luce, now a captain and frequent contributor to *Proceedings*, and Cdr. William T. Sampson, a friend of Mahan's since midshipman days and now head of the Department of Chemistry and Physics.[47]

In June 1880, toward the end of Mahan's tour at Annapolis, his younger daughter Ellen ("Nelly") "was taken dangerously ill with malarial fever and prostration from the excessive heat." The temperature was ninety-five degrees and the doctor told her parents they had to move her to a cooler area. Fortunately, the Mahans were able to get to Bar Harbor, Maine, and the child recovered. When Ellen was seven, her father wrote her a long letter describing her illness and how she had recovered. Referring to himself in the third person, he said "that was the happiest night of his life."[48]

At the end of his three-year tour Mahan faced some uncertainty about his next assignment, or if he would even get one. He did not want to go back to half pay, especially as his wife was expecting another baby. The new superintendent George Balch wanted him to stay on but did not let the bureaucracy know of his desire. "Seeing then that his sluggishness would let all go by default, I went to Washington to see if I could find some occupation [i.e., assignment]." Hearing that there was a suitable vacancy at the Brooklyn Navy Yard he applied for it and got it. The position was navigation officer of the yard.[49]

Mahan welcomed being back in New York and enjoyed his new duty. "I like the change in most ways but as I have no house am much worse off pecu-niarily."[50] The family rented a house on Eleventh Street near Fifth Avenue. Unfortunately, this meant a long commute each way, but apart from that the location and rent were good. Elly Mahan's father had recently died and her mother returned from France to live in New York City on East Fifteenth Street at the Hotel Hanover.[51]

Lyle Evans Mahan was born February 12, 1881.[52] He was baptized at Trinity Church, Broadway and Wall Street. It is not clear why he was baptized at Trinity since the Mahans at the time attended St. George's on East Sixteenth Street. We know there was a connection to Trinity through Mahan's friendship with Trinity's famous and powerful rector, the Reverend Dr. Morgan Dix. We don't know the origin of the friendship—possibly a connection with Milo Mahan—but it was close enough that Dix was godfather to the Mahan's elder daughter Helen, though he had been represented by proxy at her baptism in Montevideo. Dix, however, did not officiate at Lyle's baptism. The Reverend George William Douglas did. This was the first time Douglas and Mahan met, although they went on to become friends. Years later Douglas would write a tribute to Mahan in Churchman. As Douglas recalled this first meeting, "I was a young clergyman then, and I had the idea that most army and navy men are irreligious, or at any rate not 'churchly.' But now I found myself face to face with a naval officer whose whole demeanor indicated that he was a Churchman to the core."[53]

One of the works Mahan read had a profound impact on him in stimulating his interest in military history. It was Sir William Napier's History of the War in the Peninsula and in the South of France (6 vols., 1828–40).[54] Prior to this Mahan had not shown much interest in military history, though he undoubtedly knew of his father's interest in Napoleon, but Napier's massive work sparked something in him. "During my last tour of shore duty I had read carefully Napier's *Peninsular War,* and had found myself in a new world of thought, keenly interested and appreciative, less of the brilliant narrative—though that few can fail to enjoy—than of the military sequence of cause and effect." In words almost (but not quite!) as though he were describing a religious conversion, this book was "like the sun breaking through a cloud" and "aroused an emotion as joyful as the luminary himself to a navigator doubtful of his position."[55]

Another significant factor in Mahan's development as a historian began to take shape during this tour in New York. He began to prepare lessons for his children, first in religion and then in history. The whole project started because he did not trust the abilities or training of the average Sunday school teacher. Mahan took seriously the religious education of his children and looked on Sunday school teachers as amateurs, well meaning, but amateurs all the same. "We were never sent to Sunday School," said Ellen, "as my father greatly distrusted the ability of the average teacher. But he took great pains to see that we knew and understood the catechism and wrote my confirmation instructions himself." This was echoed by his son Lyle, who said, "Not content with the catechism, my father himself got up what might be called a supplementary catechism explaining various things and the meanings of certain words, used frequently in the church service, but which would be entirely unfamiliar to children."[56]

Possibly inspired by his newfound interest in history, Mahan told Ashe, "I have undertaken to teach my eldest child history after my return in the eve." Helen was nine at the time and apparently did not go to school but had a private tutor. Mahan prepared lessons for her in notebooks in question-and-answer form written at a child's level. The notebooks have not survived, though Puleston saw some of them and commended Mahan for writing "in language easy for a child to understand" and for making the lessons "interesting." "His account of the War of the Roses is concise, clear, and at the same time omits no essential element, foreign or domestic. His description of Joan of Arc is spirited and doubtless held Helen's attention." Puleston considers these lessons significant, not for their content, which was based on standard textbooks of the day, but for his "selection of the important factors and the method of condensation." Puleston thinks the preparation of these lessons honed Mahan's skills and were a harbinger of things to come, though entirely unanticipated at the time. "Teaching his children was excellent preparation for his later work and may partly account for his subsequent ability to point out the controlling factors in a long and complicated war."[57]

The children's religious education consisted of more than catechism lessons, of course. It started at birth when he "used to sing us to sleep with hymns." As soon as practicable the children were taught prayers, which they recited to him. Once Ellen had a mental blank and forgot the words to the Lord's Prayer. Her father, she said, "was struggling to keep his face straight." Lyle was still a baby but the girls were regularly taken to church. Ellen recalled it as one of her earliest memories: "my father and I are in Church and I still feel the prickle of the lingerie ruffle on my cap as I knelt with my forehead pressed against the pew in front." Mahan himself routinely went to church three times on Sunday, an early communion followed by morning prayer and then an afternoon evening prayer or evensong service. When the children were very small they were taken to the afternoon service, "staying until we were tired." They were also "expected to read our Bibles regularly and to pray night and morning and what he expected of us he did himself. It was his custom to read the Bible to my mother every morning; immediately after breakfast, he had family prayers which lasted exactly five minutes." In addition to prayer Mahan tithed and taught his children to do so as well "with what money we received." He also tried to instill in them an interest in supporting missions, with Ellen recalling, "He would tell us all about the poor little Indian or Chinese until we longed to help; the rest was easy."[58]

The most significant development, professionally and intellectually, of the Brooklyn Navy Yard tour was the writing of Mahan's first book, *The Gulf and Inland Waters*.[59] Charles Scribner's Sons wrote to him in December 1882 and asked him to write a volume on naval operations in the Gulf of Mexico and on the Mississippi River for their series, the Navy in the Civil War. They wanted it by April 10. Mahan accepted the offer but protested the date and after much dickering got an extension until May 12. He accepted mainly because "I wanted the money" ($600) but had "great misgivings as to whether I could do justice to the subject."[60] It is not known how Scribner's got Mahan's name, though Puleston suggested it was either from Stephen B. Luce or Daniel Ammen, both now commodores. Ammen was Mahan's old detailer from the Bureau of Navigation and "had himself written a volume [*The Atlantic Coast*] for this series."[61]

Karsten criticizes *Gulf and Inland Waters*, calling it "unimaginative" and "mundane."[62] But that misses the point of why *Gulf and Inland Waters* is important. True, there is nothing in it that is a precursor of a theory of sea power, but it does show that Mahan was already developing research and writing techniques that would make him a good historian. *Gulf and Inland Waters* is a highly creditable account of naval operations that showed careful research and thoughtful analysis, and in reading both the book itself and Mahan's correspondence about it, we see the makings of a historian. Unlike the lessons for his children, which were based entirely on secondary sources, Mahan understood that a book of this nature would have to be based on primary research. He used official reports but recognized that these sorts of documents "are liable to errors of statement and especially to the omission of facts." He supplemented these by getting written accounts from "surviving witnesses . . . both Union and Confederate."[63] Most of the people he contacted were glad to help him.[64] Mahan was also particular about including maps and making sure they were accurate.[65] We also see Mahan beginning to grapple with issues of fairness and objectivity. He understood, as many historians of the day did not, that he could not be 100 percent objective, but at the same time he tried to be fair. "Of course I don't pretend to believe that I have no bias; I only claim that I did my utmost to speak the truth."[66] He also did not pretend to be neutral between the Union and the Confederacy, as the point of view of the book was from the side of the Union, and he did not hesitate to refer to the Confederacy as "the enemy."[67] As far as tactical operations went, he was fair, criticizing and praising both sides when warranted, and he made sure to include differing points of view on controversial operational decisions.[68]

While the book contains no hint of a thesis on sea power, it does show that Mahan was beginning, for the first time as far as we know, to think about the importance of a navy in the larger military scheme of things. Mahan clearly grasped, and just as clearly conveyed to the reader, that in this particular theater of operations the Union, through its navy, had to do two things: sever the Confederacy by taking control of the Mississippi River, and blockade the Gulf Coast to prevent the Confederacy from trading with foreign countries.[69]

The book was well-received by veterans of both sides, currently serving officers, and the press. It was only out a few weeks when Mahan proudly reported to Ashe, "I have received three very cordial letters from Union officers and two from Confederates."[70] Classmate Samuel Dana Greene wrote, "You have told your story wonderfully well, and I believe that its success is assured, and that such will be the verdict of all fair-minded men. As my classmate, I congratulate you most sincerely." Greene was also perceptive in noting in this book a trait that would distinguish Mahan's greater works. "You are most fortunate, in condensing so big a story into such a small space and yet in having said all that was necessary, to give a clear and distinct idea of the work that your book covers."[71] Loyall Farragut, son of the great Union admiral David Farragut, wrote, "I have read your book with much pleasure and consider that you have been fair with all hands."[72] The *Chicago Tribune* praised him for being "simple and direct" and "conscientiously" researching both sides.[73] The *Army and Navy Journal* also praised his "conscientious industry of preparation," his "grasp of the subject," and his "frankness and general fairness of criticism." In addition, "his narrative is throughout picturesque and instructive."[74]

Two letters in particular must have given him great pleasure, one for personal and one for professional reasons. He heard from the former object of his missionary efforts, Theron Woolverton, now stationed in Philadelphia, who said, "I admire your deliberative style very much." He also received high praise from James Russell Soley, former head of the Department of English, History and Law at the Naval Academy and an author himself of a volume in the Scribner Civil War series. Now librarian of the Navy Department, Soley said that "everybody here speaks highly of it and seems to be thoroughly pleased with it."[75] Most importantly, Commo. Stephen Luce liked the book. Mahan may not have realized it yet, but he had found his calling.

In the meantime, though, his tour at New York was coming to an end, and in August 1883 he was assigned to command the USS *Wachusett* in the Pacific Squadron. This required leaving his wife and children for the first time. He journeyed to Callao, Peru, where the ship was based and took command on September 9.[76]

During Mahan's time aboard the *Wachusett* his family lived with Elly Mahan's mother at the Hotel Hanover on East Fifteenth Street, where they continued to attend St. George's Church.[77] One of Mahan's main concerns at the time was the preparation of his eldest daughter Helen for confirmation. During his time on the *Wachusett* he received numerous letters from Helen about her progress and the ups and downs of the various confirmation classes she attended. It must have been frustrating for Mahan to be away from home and not be able to direct her preparation himself. Helen must have known how important this was to him as she wrote him detailed letters about church and confirmation classes from August 1883 until she was finally confirmed in April 1885. Helen duly reported that she read the Bible every evening, studied the catechism with her tutor Mr. Chetwood (whom she liked), and attended a children's service on Saturday mornings. She told her father "the clergyman speaks to the children, what I mean is he always preaches a sort of a little sermon, but he explains it to them. This morning he told us about the Bible being God's letter to us and said that if we had a father in South America and that we were here he thought we would like to get a letter from him. It was very much like me, wasn't it?"[78]

January 1884 began a long series of letters on Helen's adventures in confirmation class. Mahan had indicated around this time that she should be confirmed or at least begin classes to prepare for it. Judging from Helen's letters, a lot of leeway had been left to Mrs. Mahan to direct the operation.[79] The confirmation class at St. George's was conducted by the rector, the Reverend William

Rainsford, with whom Mahan had a checkered relationship. The class lasted only from February to April 1884 and on at least one occasion Rainsford didn't show up, a fact duly reported by Helen. This could hardly have pleased Mahan.[80] For reasons unknown, Helen was not confirmed that year, possibly because of conflict with Rainsford or possibly because her parents thought she was not ready. One suspects, however, that given Mahan's tutelage, she was probably far more ready than the other children.

In any case, Helen continued to study the Bible and church history as directed by her father. He advised her not to merely read a daily portion of scripture but to think about it for ten minutes. She reported back that she tried this "but I found it was too much time because I read very slowly and carefully."[81] Helen's letters included some church gossip, which she no doubt thought would interest her father. "There was a man in church today who has two wives and is divorced from his first one and he handed the [collection] plate." Her letters also revealed that the Mahan children in addition to their birthdays also celebrated their baptismal days and received presents.[82] By November she had a new tutor, Miss Wiltsie, after Mr. Chetwood left for other endeavors. Mahan and his wife did not seem overly concerned about their daughters' education as far as formal schooling went, but felt that as long as they read extensively they would educate themselves. Mahan wrote to Helen, "Mamma and I do not wish to burden you with much study, but by your reading you may without hard work live as it were with those who talk well and think nobly."[83]

By March 1885 Helen was in confirmation class at St. George's again. She received from her father a lengthy letter explaining why the rite was so important. This letter—really an instructional sermon—illustrates among other things how theologically knowledgeable Mahan was, how seriously he took his faith, and how concerned he was to pass it on to his children. The theme of this letter, which could compete with anything written by a clergyman, was the importance of growing spiritually. Confirmation was a means to that end that God had graciously provided. Mahan well knew that many children viewed this ritual as a rite of passage and went through it simply because their parents wanted them to. He did not want Helen to have that attitude. "I wish you to have a right idea about Confirmation." The most important aspect of it, even more important than confirming the promises made by godparents at baptism, was receiving the gift of the Holy Spirit. This "is by far and away the most important, for man is weak and often will fail in his most honest efforts; but God is All-mighty, 'able to save to the uttermost them that so come to Him [Heb. 7:25].'" He then explained that even though Helen was young, it was the proper time, not because of her own strength, but because of the reliability of God's promise. Confirmation was ultimately a gift from God that her parents wanted her to have. "You are not too young to receive His blessing; and we may be very sure that if we kept you back from those manifold gifts of grace, Satan would not think you too young for the work of his evil spirits." Confirmation would strengthen her and help her grow spiritually. He also cautioned that she should not be afraid to promise to lead a Christian life because she might fail. Falls would be inevitable—God knew that—but the key was to renounce evil, not worry about specific failures.[84] The letter certainly shows Mahan's careful thought and his devoted effort to explain theological concepts in a way his eleven-year-old daughter could understand.

Helen was confirmed on Easter Eve (April 4), 1885, but, in a last-minute change, at Trinity Church rather than St. George's. The reason for this is not clear but it may have been related to Elly Mahan's dissatisfaction with Rainsford. Possibly it stemmed from a polite reprimand from Rainsford when Helen missed a class because her mother took her to a concert. "Momma considers the concert part of my education," Helen told her father. Three weeks later she reported the change of location. "Momma first went to see Mr. Rainsford about it and then she went to see Dr. Dix [rector of Trinity]."[85] More will be said about Rainsford below, but it is interesting to note that this was the second important ceremony (the other being Lyle's baptism) that was held at Trinity rather than at St. George's. That Dix was Helen's godfather may also have influenced this decision.

Despite Mahan's sincere happiness at Helen's confirmation, he was nonetheless mostly unhappy being aboard the *Wachusett*. Undoubtedly the most important reason was the lengthy separation from his family for what would probably be a three-year tour. Even Puleston admits he had "several spells of depression."[86] This is indicated by one very strange letter written to his son Lyle (who was only three at the time) dissuading him from a military career! That Lyle had serious career aspirations at this point seems improbable. That he could even read the letter seems more improbable. The letter shows that Mahan was lonely and bored and felt he had nothing useful to accomplish on this ship, which only exacerbated his loneliness.

> Do you think soldiers have nothing to do but to put on fine clothes and march round with the music. When you get bigger papa will tell you how soldiers in our country have to live far away from home—leave their dear mammas and lead such very idle useless lives. And sailors, too, much the same way no useful thing to do. Do you think it nice to be like papa, when he is away from mamma and Helen and Nellie and the Major [Lyle's nickname] and can never see them. When he is all alone and has nothing to do fit for a man to do.[87]

One should note that Mahan wrote this letter shortly after Christmas (December 29), and spending the holiday away from his family doubtless contributed to his misery. Certainly this letter is peculiar given the tender age of its recipient, but it would be wrong to read too much into it when its author was clearly at a melancholy postholiday low point.

The other galling feature of command of the *Wachusett* was that it was a ship in terrible shape and the appointment was beneath what an officer of Mahan's rank and experience should have received. He even wrote to Secretary of the Navy William C. Whitney that "the *Wachusett* is probably the worst commander's command in the service, while I am the next to the senior commander. While not deluding myself with the idea that this is a terrible grievance, I think that the Department will recognize that some mortification is natural."[88]

Mahan was, in fact, about to get a new assignment, a totally unexpected one that would change his life forever. It resulted in a professional conversion experience almost as dramatic as his spiritual one.

Separated from his family and his career seemingly going nowhere, "at forty-five I was drifting on the lines of simple respectability as aimlessly as one very well could." Then he received the letter that not only changed the direction of his career, but provided him with "my special call."[89] On September 4, 1884, when the *Wachusett* put in at Guayaquil, Ecuador, Mahan received a letter dated July 22 from his mentor, now a rear admiral, Stephen B. Luce, offering him a position teaching naval tactics and history at the new Naval War College.[90]

The Naval War College was the brainchild of Luce, who had long believed that naval officers, especially as they assumed higher ranks, needed to think about their profession in a wider, more intellectual and analytical way. Luce wanted to teach officers "the science of their own profession, the Science of War."[91] Luce, according to Puleston, "insisted that the art of war was the vital subject for naval officers, and if they lacked familiarity with this subject, knowledge of all other subjects was inadequate."[92] A key component of this was the study of history.[93] A significant intellectual pedigree presents itself here; Luce's ideas came from many sources, but one of the most important was Gen. William T. Sherman, whom Luce, then a lieutenant commander, first met in 1865 during the siege of Charleston. "I will cut her communications and Charleston will fall into your hands like a ripe pear," Sherman told Luce. And Luce related years later, "that is just what actually came to pass."[94] Sherman, of course, had studied under Dennis Mahan at West Point. "So," as Puleston points out, "the development of naval science in the United States can be traced from Dennis Mahan to Sherman to Luce to Alfred Mahan."[95] Another link between Dennis Mahan and the Naval War College was Brig. Gen. Emory Upton, another former pupil of the senior Mahan. When Luce met him in 1877, Upton was commanding officer of the Artillery School at Fort Monroe, Virginia, which was then considered "America's model institution of higher military learning." Luce was hugely impressed by Upton and forwarded a copy of the Artillery School curriculum to the Secretary of the Navy with a recommendation that the Navy establish something similar. Upton and Luce remained in contact with each other and Upton encouraged Luce's efforts.[96]

Ironically, given Mahan's later fame, he was not Luce's first choice for the position. Luce originally offered the job to Lt. Cdr. Caspar F. Goodrich, but he had just been assigned to Washington, D.C., and did not want to move.[97] (Up to that point Mahan had no involvement with the Naval War College at all whereas Goodrich had been a member of the board appointed by the Secretary of the Navy in 1884 to consider the feasibility of a war college.)[98] Mahan did not know this and was happy, flattered, and a little nervous to accept Luce's offer. "I was as much pleased as surprised by the offer you make me and, though the unusual delay in getting the mail has cut short my time for reflection, I am ready to give a clear reply; though not a direct yes or no." What Mahan meant was that he wanted the position, but only if Luce really thought he was the right man for it. Mahan worried that despite the success of *Gulf and Inland Waters*, he was not well-qualified for the position. "I fear you give me credit for knowing more than I do, and having given a special attention to the subject which I have not." On the plus side Mahan believed he had "the capacity and perhaps some inherited aptitude for the particular study."[99] Years later in his autobiography Mahan reiterated these points.

> I felt, therefore, that I should bring interest and understanding to my task, and hoped that the deficits of knowledge, which I clearly realized, would be overcome. I recalled also that at the Military Academy my father, though professor only of engineering, military and civil, had of his own motion introduced a course of strategy and grand tactics, which had commended itself to observers. I trusted, therefore, that heredity, too, might come to my aid.[100]

Despite his reservations, Mahan clearly wanted the job and told Luce he would begin to prepare himself "as though the matter were settled." He also asked Luce's help in getting off the *Wachusett* and back home as soon as possible.[101] Luce answered in the affirmative, but getting Mahan off the *Wachusett* was not so easy and it would be another full year before Mahan was relieved of his command and assigned to the Naval War College.[102]

Frustrated that his departure was delayed, Mahan nonetheless tried to pre-pare for his new position as best he could. In November 1884 the *Wachusett* was at Callao, Peru, and Mahan was able to get some leave time and spend a month in Lima, about an hour away, using the library of what he referred to as the "English Club" (actually the Phoenix Club). It was there that he read Theodor Mommsen's *History of Rome* written in 1870, which Mahan credited for putting into his mind the idea of sea power. But the real origin of the concept came to him from God. "He who seeks finds, if he does not lose heart; and to me, continuously seeking, came from within the suggestion that control of the sea was an historic factor which had never been systematically appreciated and expounded."[103]

It was Mommsen's discussion of Hannibal's campaign in Italy during the Second Punic War that jump-started Mahan's thinking process: "It suddenly struck me . . . how different things might have been could Hannibal have invaded Italy by sea, as the Romans often had Africa, instead of by the long land route; or could he, after arrival, have been in free communication with Carthage by water. This clew, once laid hold of, I followed up in the particular instance."[104]

Suddenly grasping the larger implication, Mahan said, "My plan was formed by the time I reached home in September, 1885. I would investigate coincidently the general history and naval history of the past two centuries, with a view to demonstrating the influence of the events of the one upon the other."[105] He also wrote to Luce laying out his idea of what the naval history course would cover. He was so excited about what he had found that, in case the Naval War College assignment fell through, he intended to write a book on the topic anyway.[106] The gist of it would be "a general consideration of the sea as a highway for commerce and also for hostile attacks upon countries bordering on it."[107]

Mahan did not get back to the United States until August 1885 and was finally reunited with his family in September. In October he was in Washington, D.C., to take the exam for promotion to captain, which he passed.[108] He then paid a visit to Newport, where the infant war college was located. Because of delays in decommissioning the *Wachusett* he was too late to join the faculty that academic year, and he was not yet prepared in any case. Luce agreed that he should spend a year reading and preparing lectures and begin at the college the following September. So Mahan, happy with this arrangement, returned to New York City, rented an apartment at 2 East Fifteenth Street (in the same building as his mother-in-law), and set about studying at the Astor Library and the New York Lyceum.[109] He was glad to be back in the city "amid surroundings wholly familiar, which will necessitate no planning and where I can get to my work without worry." He told Luce, "I look forward to my work very hopefully, trust-ing in a quiet engrossment of mind to find my best medium."[110]

Mahan settled into a pleasant routine working at libraries in the morn-ing and at home in the afternoon. His readings were both in general history (mainly European) and military-naval history "of the past two centuries."[111] Admitting that he did not have a particularly good background in history—he underrated himself here—he confessed to Ashe to being "somewhat fearful of failure" but nonetheless enjoyed the work especially as he began to make con-nections between events and theories. "Every faculty I possessed was alive and jumping."[112] The books he read and the ideas he gleaned from them have always been a topic of interest to Mahan scholars; they were discussed in *Sail to Steam* as well as in Puleston's and Seager's works.[113] Three authors Mahan found use-ful were Léonard Lapeyrousse-Bonfils, a French navy lieutenant whose *History of the French Navy* was published in 1845; John Campbell, author of *Lives of the British Admirals* (1742 and many later editions); and Henri Martin, author of *A Popular History of France from the First Revolution to the Present Time* (1877–82).[114]

Most important of all were the writings of Swiss military historian Antoine Henri, Baron de Jomini. Jomini's writings also provided an intellectual link between Dennis Mahan and his son. The elder Mahan was a keen student of Jomini and used his principles in teaching the "Art of War" to West Point cadets. One of Dennis Mahan's greatest pupils on the battlefield, William T. Sherman, thought that his knowledge of Jomini, as studied in Mahan's classroom, was a key feature of his tactical success. Indeed, he instructed his officers to "Learn the art of war (Mahan and Jomini)."[115] Alfred Mahan must have known of his father's interest in Jomini and must have seen Jomini's books in the house, but he appears never to have read him until this time. In any case Jomini's two clas-sic works, *Critical and Military History of the Campaigns of the Revolution* (1819–24) and *The Summary of the Art of War* (1836) had a profound impact on him.[116] Most importantly they gave him a lens through which his study of endless naval battles suddenly made sense.

> The authority of Jomini chiefly set me to study in this fashion the many naval histories before me. From him I learned the few, very few, leading consider-ations in military combination; and in these I found the key by which, using the record of sailing navies and the actions of naval leaders, I could elicit, from the naval history on which I looked despondingly, instruction still pertinent.[117]

Mahan also learned from Jomini two additional principles: "that the organized forces of the enemy are ever the chief objective" and that "the thoughtlessly accepted maxim that the statesman and the general occupy unrelated fields [was untrue]."[118]

While working at his studies Mahan kept in regular touch with Luce, report-ing what books he was reading and the preliminary organization of his lectures.[119] He also spent considerable time in the spring of 1886 visiting his mother and aunt in Elizabeth, New Jersey. His youngest sister Jane had the unenviable task of serving as companion and caretaker for the two widows. Mrs. Mahan was having difficulties collecting her widow's pension from the Army, and Mahan sought the help of Sam Ashe. Mahan's younger brother Frederick was a captain in the Army stationed in Washington, D.C., and was also trying to straighten out the matter. Mahan asked Ashe to use his influence with William Cowles, a member of the House of Representatives from North Carolina and a member of the Committee on Pensions. "I would be glad if you can word the letter so as to obtain for my brother a cordial reception, instead of a merely formal one, from Mr. Cowles."[120] After spending the summer in Bar Harbor, Maine, where he continued to work on his lectures, Mahan reported to the Naval War College in late August, his family returning to New York to arrange their move to Newport in October.[121]

CHAPTER 5

PROVIDENCE AND SEA POWER:
OUR JOMINI IS HERE

Mahan had originally thought he was going to Newport as a professor, but in June 1886 Luce was given command of the North Atlantic Squadron. Mahan became the college president "by default, without special orders."[1] He arrived at the college, located on Coasters Harbor Island in Newport, at the end of August 1886. The college was housed in the former Newport Almshouse, which, while still undergoing renovation, housed lecture halls, a library Mahan rated as "very respectable," and "two as yet uncompleted suites of quarters." The only other permanently assigned faculty member was 1st Lt. Tasker H. Bliss, U.S. Army. Bliss had quarters in town, so when Mahan arrived he found himself the only occupant of the building. "As I walked round the lonely halls and stairways, I might have parodied Louis XIV, and said, "Le Collège, c'est moi."[2] There was only one lamp operational and Mahan carried it with him from room to room. It gave him the feeling, he said, of "camping out." Conditions were not entirely primitive, though, as he had a steward who prepared his meals and made his bed.[3] He had about a month before classes began, and he used the time to prepare maps to accompany his lectures, assisted in this by retired Navy lieutenant William McCarty Little. These maps were the origin of the war-gaming exercises for which the college became famous.[4]

The two-and-a-half-month term began on September 6 with a class of twenty-one officers, nineteen from the Navy and two from the Marine Corps.[5] The opening lecture was given by Luce and was titled "On the Study of Naval Warfare as a Science," a revision of the lecture he had given the previous year and which was later published in the USNI *Proceedings*. For our purposes the most significant part of the address was its conclusion. After stressing the importance of studying history Luce said, "[L]et us confidently look for that master mind who will lay the foundations of that science [naval history] and do for it what Jomini has done for the military science."[6]

Mahan's family joined him in October. Renovations were still under way and the family had to vacate their living quarters every morning so that the rooms could be used for lectures. Ellen recalled that in the early days there was no hot water in the house, "but my father had some rubber tubing attached to the valve in the radiator and cut the right length to lie in the bath tub. I can hear the comforting gurgle of the steam as it kindly heated the water to a comfortable temperature for my shivering body." Despite the primitive conditions the children enjoyed themselves. Indeed, Ellen was rapturous about it. "After the very first, I knew it as the one place in all the world that was most like Heaven and felt, in some strange way, that no period in my life would ever quite equal it."

Lyle Mahan age nine *(Naval Historical Collection, Naval War College)*

The children appear to have had the run of the base, such as it was, the only rule being to take care that no damage was done to "Uncle Sam's property."[7]

Elly Mahan bought a second-hand typewriter and began typing all her husband's lectures. One of Lyle's earliest memories was of "my mother pounding away on the typewriter."[8] It was at Newport that the Mahans acquired a bull terrier puppy they named Jomini. Ellen recalled, "Jomini became a member of the family at once and so much was this the case that friends of mine said he *looked* like my father. I can see what they meant, the dog intent on his own thoughts, as the man was on his."[9]

Mahan's beloved dog Jomini *(Naval Historical Collection, Naval War College)*

The Mahans attended St. John the Evangelist Episcopal Church, which was near the college (in 1894 the parish was renamed the Zabriskie Memorial Church of St. John the Evangelist). The rector was the Reverend Samuel W. Moran. The parish was Anglo-Catholic and celebrated the Eucharist every Sunday, an unusual practice at that time, and was also racially integrated. These features may have inclined Mahan to prefer St. John's over Newport's other Episcopal parish, Trinity, but according to Ellen the family always attended the parish nearest their home regardless of whether it was High or Low Church. Mahan was elected to the vestry (the lay governing body of Episcopal parishes) in 1888 and served a one-year term. This would indicate a high level of involvement in parish life and is the first instance of Mahan serving on a vestry.[10]

Though Mahan and Bliss were the only officers assigned full-time to the college, seven other officers were on temporary or part-time duty as faculty. Some of the officer-students questioned why they had to sit through lectures given by an Army officer, and a junior one at that. Mahan explained that the utility was twofold. One was the more practical reason, to learn about "conducting such expeditions as may be feasible with forces landed from a fleet alone." Mahan had already touched on this theme in *Gulf and Inland Waters*. The second reason was more philosophical. He and Luce wanted the students to begin to think about warfare as a whole and look for principles from land operations that could be applied to naval warfare. Mahan thought this was particularly important, as ship and weapon technology was changing so quickly and opinion was so divided over it. Recent military history, he thought, could aid the naval officer in adjusting, tactically and strategically, to these changes.[11] Luce, aboard his flagship *Tennessee*, stayed in Newport for the first term. After hearing Mahan's final lecture of the term, Luce addressed the class and reminding them of what he had stated on opening day: that naval history needed its own Jomini. He said, "He is here; his name is Mahan."[12] Thus Luce made his prophecy and Mahan found his calling.

When the fall 1886 session ended it was generally deemed a success. Mahan wrote that it "surpassed expectation."[13] But the college had powerful enemies in Washington and its survival was by no means assured. Luce and Mahan spent much of their time over the next three years, in addition to their regular duties, lobbying for the continued existence of and necessary appropriations for the college.[14]

In the meantime Mahan was revising and polishing his lectures in naval history. He was asked by the Naval Institute to submit some of his lectures for publication in *Proceedings*. He was not a fan of *Proceedings* at the time and believed it had become a journal totally consumed by technical issues or, as he put it, "mechanical and physical problems." He refused to submit any lectures, telling the secretary of the institute that any article he wrote would be "swamped" by the technical articles and "receive rare and desultory attention." More to the point, he said that publication of his lectures—at least in this venue—would take away any incentive for officers to come to the college to hear the lectures in person. The "art of war" was the topic of these lectures and the Naval War College was the proper venue for them.[15]

Through the initiative of Luce, Mahan met for the first time a young naval historian whose future career would intersect his, Theodore Roosevelt. Luce, a friend of Roosevelt's father, was favorably impressed with the young Roosevelt's *The Naval War of 1812*, which had been published in 1882. In 1888 Luce arranged for Roosevelt, then aged thirty, to give a lecture at the college and make the acquaintance of Mahan.[16]

Mahan was now giving thought to getting his lectures published as a book, and he contacted his old publisher, Scribner's. "While lecturing at this institution during the past two years I have accumulated the text for a work, whose general scope is the bearing of naval power upon the general course of History in Western Europe and America between the years 1660 and 1783." The purpose of the book was not to provide "an exhaustive account of all that happened, but rather a selection of such campaigns and battles as have a tactical and strategic value, and so afford an opportunity for pointing a lesson."[17] Scribner's rejected it on the grounds that it was too specialized to appeal to a general audience.[18]

The effort to find a publisher was put on hold as the college suffered a setback and Mahan was given another assignment. In January 1889 the lame-duck Secretary of the Navy, William C. Whitney, no friend of the college, ordered the college moved to Goat Island (also in Newport) and combined with the Torpedo Station, all under the command of Cdr. Caspar Goodrich. Goodrich said that he knew Whitney's "evident purpose in this move was to kill the college," but the secretary seemed unaware of or indifferent to the fact that Goodrich was a known supporter of the college.[19] In the meantime Mahan was appointed chairman of a commission to select a site for a navy yard on the northwest coast.[20]

The college's fortunes improved when Benjamin Harrison and a new Secretary of the Navy, Benjamin F. Tracy, took office in March 1889. The college was returned to Coasters Harbor Island and funds were appropriated for a new building, while Mahan returned to the college staff and resumed his lectures. The college was temporarily shut down and Mahan was allowed to go to Bar Harbor and then Elizabeth to continue his research and writing, noting "the college slumbered and I worked."[21]

He continued to look for a publisher without success. His wife and Luce remained his principal encouragers. Fearing he would never get a commercial publisher, Mahan tried to find means to publish the book privately, even "offering to surrender all property in the work myself" if a wealthy backer would step forward. J. Pierpont Morgan, whom Mahan knew as a fellow parishioner at St. George's in New York City, offered $200 but would not bankroll the entire project. Mahan was discouraged, but his wife would not let him give up. Said their son Lyle, "She had the utmost confidence in my father's ability . . . and she knew that my father had a message for the naval world that ought to be published."[22]

A publisher was finally found through the intervention of Mahan's longtime friend, James Russell Soley, former Naval Academy professor and librarian of the Navy Department, and currently lecturer in international law at the War College. Soley had a friend, James W. McIntyre, who worked for Little, Brown, and Company of Boston. McIntyre thought the work significant and recommended it to John Murray Brown, owner of Little, Brown. Mahan went to Boston to sell the idea in person. "By Soley's advice I dwelt upon the fact that it was *popular* and *critical*, both of which are very true [emphasis in original]."[23] Brown agreed with McIntyre's assessment and the deal was signed in October 1889, a happy Mahan reported to Luce. As he pointed out, that 250 copies were sold even before Brown's acceptance could not have hurt. (The War Department wanted 100 copies and the Navy Department wanted 150—50 for ships' libraries and 100 for the War College).[24]

The result was *The Influence of Sea Power upon History, 1660–1783*, which came out in May 1890. The book's impact was nothing short of phenomenal. It turned Mahan from "old Dennis's boy" into the Prophet of Sea Power, not to mention the Jomini that Luce had been looking for. It revolutionized the study of naval history, moving beyond battle tactics to strategy and international diplomacy. McIntyre and Brown had judged well, even better than they could have grasped at the time they made their decision. The book went through numerous editions and has never been out of print, a remarkable achievement for a specialized book more than one hundred years old. Within a few years of its initial publication it was translated into Russian, German, Japanese, French, Spanish, and Swedish.[25] The book's popularity was not entirely attributable to Mahan's own wisdom and skill. As Sumida has pointed out, "external factors" were clearly at work: "His prolific output coincided with a quarter century of rapid naval growth at home and abroad, during which time naval questions became much more significant in world politics."[26] Nonetheless, the book owed much to Mahan's analytical skills and thoughtful, careful prose.

The book has been dissected, analyzed, and even "deconstructed," as might be said today in certain intellectual circles. *The Influence of Sea Power upon History* is probably the most analyzed naval book ever; a look at the bibliography of this book attests to that. It is a tribute to Mahan that his book still generates such discussion and debate more than one hundred years later. The purpose here is not to attempt yet one more analysis, but rather to examine the book to see how, if at all, Mahan's religious views are pertinent to his overall argument.

The gist of the book is the concept of sea power and the notion that control of the sea—which Mahan thought was like "a great highway; or better, perhaps . . . a wide common"[27]—was essential to a nation (that is, a nation with a significant coastline), both for military and economic reasons. In fact, no nation (unless it was solely a land power) could become a great power without it. He intended to illustrate this through the example of Britain in the seventeenth and eighteenth centuries, rising to world power by defeating at sea the Dutch, Spanish, and most crucially the French, its main rival for world supremacy. As John Hattendorf put it, through this book Mahan converted the study of naval history from "largely a record of battles" to "a subject which related activity at sea to foreign policy and the general activity of nation-states."[28]

In Chapter I, Mahan listed six conditions "affecting the sea power of nations." These were:

1. Geographic Position
2. Physical Conformation
3. Extent of Territory
4. Number of Population
5. Character of the People
6. Character of the Government.[29]

Character of the People and Character of the Government are the most interesting. While it should be pointed out that Mahan rarely spoke directly about religion in his historical writings, his worldview was nonetheless based on certain biblical principles. The most important was divine sovereignty, that is, the belief that God ruled the universe, was active in human history, and was leading human history to its divinely ordained goal. The study of history, he said some years later, was the study of the "plan of Providence." Every aspect of history thus becomes a part of "the great mosaic which the history of the race is gradually fashioning under the Divine overruling."[30] Though these comments were made twelve years after the publication of *The Influence of Sea Power*, there is no reason to think he had not already held such views since his twenties and possibly even before. The second key theological principle he held was that of original sin, the doctrine that claims that because of Adam and Eve's disobedience in the Garden of Eden the entire human race (with the sole exception of Jesus Christ) has an inborn predisposition to sin.[31] These two Christian doctrines are the twin pillars of his worldview. We see these as subtle underlying assumptions in his discussion of national character and character of government.

Of course any human traits could be seen as the expression of divine providence, more so traits peculiar to certain peoples. Mahan saw this in the "tendency to trade," which he believed was "the national characteristic most important to the development of sea power."[32] To some extent this was a human characteristic in that "[a]ll men seek gain and, more or less, love money," but there were good and bad ways to do that, good and bad in both a moral and financial sense.

The Spaniards and the Portuguese, for instance, sought wealth in such a way that "not only brought a blot upon the national character, but was also fatal to the growth of a healthy commerce." Their mistake was to succumb to "fierce avarice" and seek to acquire only gold and silver. They neglected the development of commerce and industry and were dependent on other nations to supply them with the products they needed. By viewing their colonies solely as a source of precious metals they invested no human capital in them as places to live.[33]

The French, though an "industrious people," never made a huge success as a sea power, a topic to which Mahan would frequently return in his historical writings. In this section on national character what he singles out as debilitating is that "the temper of the French people leads them to seek it [wealth] by thrift, economy, hoarding." The French, in other words, lack "the adventurous spirit" that not only creates wealth for their nation, but "conquers worlds for commerce." Likewise the French were not successful colonizers because instead of seeing their colonies as places to live in which their futures were invested, they "were ever longingly looking back to the delights of their pleasant land."[34]

The Dutch, while better than the Spanish, Portuguese, or French, still had a handicap compared to the English. They had a "placid satisfaction with gain alone, unaccompanied by political ambition." Thus, even though their nation was not a "despotism [like] France and Spain," their colonies did not grow naturally, but remained "mere commercial dependencies upon the mother country."[35]

The English, according to Mahan, had the best national character for sea power, not only an "adventurous spirit" that was willing to take risks to create wealth, but also "the capacity for planting *healthy* colonies [emphasis added]." The English colonies were successful because of two traits in the national character. First, the English colonist quickly identified with the "interest" of his new home; that is, he saw it as an actual home and not just a way station to make money. Second, the English colonist sought to "develop the resources of the new country in the broadest sense," thus ensuring its long-term growth.[36]

Mahan closed this section by asking "how far the national character of Americans is fitted to develop a great sea power, should other circumstances become favorable." His answer, though not developed in any detail, was a yes because of America's "inherited aptitude for self-government and independent growth." The key word is *inherited*, by which he meant inherited from the English.[37] Self-government is another key concept that leads into the next section, Character of the Government.

This section is more complex. The gist of it is that a government should be in "full accord with the natural bias of the people" and "successfully advance its growth." In other words, a seafaring people should be led by a government that has "intelligent direction" and is "fully imbued with the spirit of the people and conscious of its true general bent." The best government should represent "the will of the people" and those people should have "some large share in making it." Mahan concedes that a "despotic power" might "at times" create a strong sea power but that it generally does not last after the death of the despot.[38] Nothing in these two sections directly relates to religion, though a Protestant-Catholic dichotomy is hinted at with England and Holland showing superiority over France, Spain, and Portugal. The theme of the superiority of nondespotic representative government and risk-taking capitalism is clearly present. This idea is only hinted at and it would be wrong to make too much of it at this point in Mahan's writings, but it is intriguing in that Max Weber's *The Protestant Ethic and the Spirit of Capitalism* could not have been the source since that work was not written until 1904–5.

The bulk of Mahan's *The Influence of Sea Power* explained England's (then Britain's) rise to world dominance through effective use of sea power and, conversely, France's failure to defeat Britain largely because of its desire to be a land power rather than a sea power. Sumida has summarized Mahan's point most succinctly: "[W]hen circumstances favored both development by land or sea . . . the leaders of states were well-advised to prefer the latter to the former on the grounds that the return on investment—that is to say, success in war and increased national wealth as purchased by state-spending—was higher."[39]

Letters of congratulations poured in and favorable reviews appeared in the press. The book created a sensation in the U.S. Navy and the Royal Navy as well. Theodore Roosevelt, who would later review the book for *Atlantic Monthly*, wrote to Mahan:

> During the last two days I have spent half my time, busy as I am, in reading your book. That I found it interesting is shown by the fact that having taken it up, I have gone straight through and finished it. I can say with perfect sincerity that I think it very much the clearest and most instructive general work of the kind with which I am acquainted. It is a *very* good book—admirable; and I am greatly in error if it does not become a classic [emphasis in original].[40]

Numerous letters came from American and British officers, scholars, and politicians.[41] Reviews were uniformly favorable. Admiral Luce in the *New York Critic* hailed his protégé's work as "altogether exceptional." There was, he said, "nothing like it in the whole range of naval literature. . . . The work is entirely original in conception, masterful in construction, and scholarly in execution."[42] Mahan would undoubtedly have been thrilled by this encomium from his mentor. As he told Luce when sending him his complimentary copy,

Whatever usefulness the book may be found to have, the merit is ultimately due to yourself, but for whose invitation it would never have been undertaken. But for the impulse you gave, I should still have been contented to drift on, smitten with the indifference to the higher military considerations, which is too common in the service. It is, therefore, in every way fitting that you should receive this acknowledgment at my hands, and I wish at the same time to thank you for the start you gave me.[43]

In his review in the *Atlantic Monthly* Roosevelt wrote that *The Influence of Sea Power* was "the best and most important, and also by far the most interesting, book on naval history." He also praised Mahan for not manifesting "the shortcomings which make the average military man an exasperatingly incompetent military historian." Roosevelt was not interested solely in the book's historical merits, but also in its relevance to the present, in particular the fact, as he saw it, that "our greatest need is the need of a fighting fleet." Mahan's contribution was "a real service."[44]

The British edition, brought out by Sampson Low, Marston and Company, was a huge success, much to the delight of Roy Marston, company director.[45] Indeed, one could argue that the book caused a bigger stir in Britain than it did in the United States. British naval officers and naval historians, while astounded that an American had staked such a prominent place on their turf, were nonetheless full of praise for Mahan, who had explained in such a clear and elegant way why Britannia ruled the waves. As Puleston put it, "never have competitors been more generous in acknowledging the success of a rival."[46] The impact went beyond naval circles; former prime minister William Gladstone praised it, "regard[ing] it as one of the greatest of modern books." Field Marshal Lord Roberts, with whom Mahan later became friends, said the book "had given him more pleasure than any book he had read for many years."[47]

The scholarly reviews were generally positive as well. Captain Cyprian Bridge, RN (later Admiral Sir Cyprian) wrote a nineteen-page review for *Blackwood's Edinburgh Magazine* calling it "a very remarkable book" that "merit[ed] the closest attention of statesmen." Bridge recognized that the book was written "for the benefit of the author's fellow-citizens," but thought the lessons for British naval and political leaders were clear: "[they] may learn from it how their country achieved her present position amongst the nations, and how that position may be maintained."[48]

Professor John Knox Laughton of the Royal Naval College, Britain's foremost naval historian, wrote a thirty-four-page review for the *Edinburgh Review*. Laughton's review, titled "Captain Mahan on Maritime Power," was "perhaps the most knowledgeable and detailed analysis Mahan's book received in the

English-speaking world at the time of its publication."[49] Though critical in some respects (though less strongly than Seager suggests), Laughton said, "[W]e have nothing but compliments to pay to the author on the ability with which he has fulfilled his task." He praised Mahan's analysis, which demonstrated "a fulness [sic], a professional insight, and a literary skill altogether foreign to our naval histories."[50] Mahan wrote to Luce that "[I] considered myself fortunate to come off so easy at his hands, for he probably knows more naval history than any English speaking man living."[51]

A number of British reviewers recognized that Mahan's book was written mainly for an American audience, "to rekindle in the hearts of his fellow-citizens some desire to contest the supremacy of the seas," as Laughton put it. Contrary to Seager's interpretation, Laughton did not see this as any threat to Britain since he added the disclaimer (which Seager did not quote) "in so far, at any rate, as the necessities of home defence render it advisable and geographical conditions may render it feasible."[52] Sumida has suggested that Mahan never intended that the United States should attempt to rival British naval supremacy but rather that the two should cooperate.[53]

Another factor that rendered Mahan's writing so significant in Britain was the beginning of a German naval buildup and the subsequent anxiety this caused in both naval and political arenas. Those who wanted funds spent on the enlargement and modernization of the Royal Navy were quoting Mahan to bolster their case.[54]

It took a few more years for *The Influence of Sea Power* to circulate through Europe and then Asia, but Mahan's reputation was now set. Even the usually cynical Seager had to admit that "with the possible exception of Harriet Beecher Stowe's *Uncle Tom's Cabin*, published in 1852, no book written in nineteenth-century America by an American had greater immediate impact on the course and direction of the nation."[55] In the meantime Mahan was already at work on the sequel, which would take the British-French struggle up to the defeat of Napoleon. The War College was in a "period of suspended animation" while the Coasters Island facility was being refurbished, and no classes were held in 1890 and 1891. Mahan was named president again on the orders of the new Secretary of the Navy, Benjamin F. Tracy, but he was allowed to stay at home in New York City "on special duty" so he could continue working on his lectures and new book.[56] Mahan was happy with the arrangement.[57]

Mahan had another concern, apart from his writing and the college, and that was his daughter Helen. In July 1890, a month before her seventeenth birthday, Mahan wrote her two lengthy letters. He was then briefly in Newport and the children were in Bar Harbor vacationing with their grandmother Evans.

The first letter, dated July 9, 1890, was essentially a homily on the development of Christian character. The immediate issue that inspired it was that "Mamma has told me that you had asked her how you could make yourself care for persons whom you do not naturally love." Mahan praised her for recognizing this trait and reassured her that it was not "a *fault* or sin, for which you are originally responsible." The cause was original sin or humanity's fallen nature. It was nonetheless "a very serious *defect*, against which you are bound as a Christian to strive." Always a stickler for theological precision, Mahan pointed out that indifference to others—a defect he admitted that he, too, had struggled with for many years—was "not as bad as hatred or ill-will." Nonetheless, it was "as much opposed to that charity, or love, which our Lord and His apostles dwell upon as the great distinctive grace of the Christian character." The key to overcoming this indifference was, first, to "do works of kindness," though he cautioned her to remember that such works "cannot save us." Second, she should "pray continually to God to change your nature in this respect—give you a loving heart. It will take time, but never despair of it."

The cause of Helen's distress was that she did not have much time for her grandmother and felt guilty about it. Her father acknowledges this. "I know that she has shown such a very marked partiality for Lyle, that it is not to be wondered at [that] she has lost the affection of her other grandchildren." Mahan did not condemn Helen, but he gave sound advice on how to cope. Helen had a duty both to her grandmother and to God to be kind, and she could do that duty through prayer and effort, regardless of whether Grannie deserved it. "Go to see her frequently, and not grudgingly or of necessity, remembering that God loves a *cheerful* giver." Some might see this as laying a further guilt trip on Helen, but in fact it is the opposite. He is relieving her of the burden of liking her grandmother and suggesting that she can show kindness anyway.

Mahan concluded the letter with an admonition to be careful with whom she associated. "Your friends seem to be very kind and fond of you," but he and her mother were concerned "that they are in their aims and principles entirely worldly—living that is for this world, and not for the next." He did not tell her not to associate with them, only "to be careful" not to become too attached to "the comforts and pleasures of this world." He concluded with a reminder that life was short and the only things that would endure were the fruits of the spirit, "love, joy, peace."[58]

Seager's animus toward Mahan's religious beliefs causes him to put the worst possible construction on this letter, characterizing it as an old-fogeyish sermon by a religious fanatic who does not want his teenage daughter to have any fun. But in his effort to make Mahan appear a pious, tyrannical father, he overlooks or deliberately ignores several key points. He says that Mahan "bluntly told the 17-year-old girl to avoid the company of those around her" whom her father considered worldly.[59] But Mahan did no such thing. He did not tell her to drop her friends, only to be careful about their interests. Indeed, Seager uncharitably characterizes Helen as a "wallflower" who was "not very pretty and not very popular."[60] Her prettiness may be a matter of subjective judgment, but she hardly could be called unpopular given Mahan's concerns about her friends. Perhaps because he has no empathy with Mahan's outlook, Seager overlooks the virtues of this letter. Of course it is a sermon, but, surely, given her upbringing Helen could not have found anything strange about that. Nor did Mahan try to make Helen feel guilty; he went to pains not to. Indeed, Seager misses the whole point that Mahan was not trying to berate, discourage, or depress Helen, but rather to comfort and encourage her. After all, it was Helen herself who had first brought up the issue by asking her mother for advice.[61]

Neither of the Mahan daughters married, a fact Seager uses to try to prove that Mahan was a dictatorial, prudish, Victorian father. In fact, he specifically blames Mahan for this, saying that "Mahan successfully crushed the desire of both of his daughters for personal independence" and "seal[ed] them off from possible suitors."[62] Seager states that Helen "died in 1963, at age 89, unpursued, unimpaired, and unmarried. Her sister Ellen died in 1947 at age 70 in a similar state of grace."[63]

Mahan's wife, Elly, with daughters Ellen (left) and Helen (right), 1906 (*Naval Historical Collection, Naval War College*)

The question of why the Mahan daughters never married is a complex one. There might be many reasons, and many of these we might have no knowledge of. One answer that suggests itself may be that their mother pressured them to stay home to be her companions. This happened to Mahan's sister Jane and to Elly Mahan's sister Rosalie.[64] But there is no hard evidence that this was what happened to Helen and Ellen. Seager's blaming Mahan for this is not only uncharitable, but inaccurate. Mahan fully expected his daughters to marry, as indicated by his letter to Helen of July 20, 1890. In that letter he wrote to her that he was going to discuss "a subject which may seem somewhat strange, particularly at your present age; but it is one upon which you are sure to hear, probably already have heard, a good deal of light nonsense talked."[65] Seager also claims that Mahan was having a "conflict" with Helen over her interest in young men, but there is no evidence of such a conflict and the letter contains no suggestion of it either.[66] Seager is so intent upon portraying Mahan as a sexually repressed prude that he contradicts himself in his own explanation of this letter. In his 1977 biography of Mahan he characterizes Helen as a homely, socially backward wallflower, yet in his 1980 article he claims that she is too involved with worldly friends and activities. Seager also, in both these pieces, conflates this letter with the one just discussed, giving the reader the impression that it was one long letter.[67] In any case, Mahan was not discouraging Helen from marriage nor portraying marriage as a worldly desire to be shunned, as Seager implies. The letter makes it clear that Mahan expects that she will marry inasmuch as he refers to "the happiness of your future home, the well being of your husband and children." Nor did Mahan think it wrong that Helen was thinking about men or even eyeing up possible prospects; in fact, Mahan's only concerns were that she not dwell excessively on the subject and that she not evaluate men based on superficial qualities such as "money [or] good looks." The most important task was to commit the matter to God and seek his guidance. "Put yourself under His care. . . . Ask Him that if He wishes you to marry He may guide you to the man to whose care He will entrust you, and whose happiness and home it may be your privilege to make." He urged her "to begin and take a Christian view of marriage," referring to the words of the marriage service in the Book of Common Prayer. In short, the peace and happiness of her future home "may depend upon the prayer you are saying and the thoughts you are thinking now." There is nothing antimarriage in the letter.[68]

While in the midst of working on the *Sea Power* sequel Mahan was approached by D. Appleton & Co. to contribute a volume on David Farragut for their Great Commanders series. Mahan agreed because he wanted to "say something for the Navy."[69] He finished the book within six months and it was published in October 1892. Though the book was something of a rush job, Mahan based his manuscript on Farragut's own papers (as supplied by Farragut's son, Loyall) and correspondence with Farragut's surviving associates.[70]

Of particular interest in this serviceable biography is Mahan's stress upon Farragut's devotion to God and family. Mahan identified with Farragut. Farragut was a devout Christian and an Episcopalian who was constant in prayer and in seeking divine guidance. For instance, Mahan quotes Farragut as saying, "I hope for success, shall do all in my power to secure it, and trust to God for the rest" and "I am always hopeful; put my shoulder to the wheel with my best judgment, and trust to God for the rest."[71] Mahan noted that when in battle, at crucial points when his original plans seem thwarted and he was unsure whether to advance or retreat, he prayed. "In this extremity the devout spirit that ruled his life . . . impelled him to appeal to Heaven for guidance." Farragut prayed, "O God, who created man and gave him reason, direct me what to do. Shall I go on?" "'And it seemed,' said the admiral, 'as if in answer a voice commanded, "Go on!"'" Mahan applauded this "profound dependence on the will of the Almighty."[72] He also lauded Farragut's devotion to his wife. "It was an attachment also not merely professed in words, but evidenced by the whole course of his life and conduct. Infidelity or neglect of a wife was in truth, in the estimation of Admiral Farragut, one of the most serious blots upon a man's character, drawing out always his bitterest condemnation."[73] Farragut's "rare strength of character" was a key part of his success as an officer and commander in battle. Not surprisingly, Mahan also applauded him for being a regular churchgoer.[74]

The book received good reviews, and Seager says that its publication so close to *The Influence of Sea Power upon the French Revolution and Empire* allowed it to "bask in the reflected glow of the vastly more important work." This seems unfair inasmuch as the book was praised by numerous sources in America and Britain.[75] Mahan himself was not altogether satisfied with the work, citing his lack of "data," by which he presumably meant primary sources; he also found "discouraging" the book's lack of financial success. Still he must have been gratified by the good reviews because he saved all the clippings.[76] Though Seager calls *Farragut* "thoroughly mediocre," not all historians agree.[77] William N. Still Jr., who wrote the chapter on Farragut for James Bradford's 1997 anthology *Quarterdeck and Bridge*, says that the biography has held up well over the years and that Mahan's "characterization of Farragut is the most perceptive of any to date."[78]

In December 1891 Mahan was called to Washington to assist Secretary Tracy in formulating plans for a possible U.S. naval action against Chile because of the infamous bar fight in Valparaiso in which two American sailors were killed and dozens more injured. Mahan's work was minimal. "Mr. Tracy kept matters in his own hands. . . . Nor do I remember that I was ever directed to consult anyone else in the Dept." He wrote a couple of memos, which seem to have been totally ignored.[79] Mahan's time was not completely wasted, however, because he had a meeting with Tracy during which the secretary asked him what he wanted to do next. Mahan replied that he wanted to finish his second book in the Sea Power series. Tracy replied, "Why don't you finish it?" and added, "Do you want to go as Prest. of the War College?" Mahan answered in the affirmative.[80] Since Mahan did not have to go to Newport until July 1892, this gave him additional time at home in New York for writing. The college, housed in a new building, reopened in September 1892.[81]

In November 1892 *The Influence of Sea Power upon the French Revolution and Empire* was published in two volumes by Little, Brown in the United States and Sampson Low, Marston in Britain (a small portion of it had previously appeared as an article, "Pitt's War Policy," in the July 1892 issue of *Quarterly Review*).[82] The second Sea Power work was longer than the first because it was much more detailed and relied much more extensively on primary sources.[83] The new work had two heroes: William Pitt the Younger in the political realm and Horatio Nelson in the naval realm. Mahan's admiration for Britain and its political, commercial, and naval prowess had an added element in this work: his disdain for revolutionary and Napoleonic France. The French, he said, "knew no mean between anarchy and servile submission," while the British had "respect for law, for established authority, for existing rights" and a national character that was "conservative while progressive."[84] Sumida points out that Mahan "did not believe that Britain's victory over France was predetermined"—at least not from a worldly standpoint—citing Mahan's view that the two sides were "closely matched" and "so even a balance, the wisest prophet cannot foresee how the scale will turn."[85] Interestingly, five years later Mahan raised the question of whether the events that made Britain the world's pre-eminent sea power were not "accidents" but rather "the exhibition of a Personal Will, acting through all time, with the purpose deliberate and consecutive, to ends not yet discerned." Mahan, though, was merely posing the question. God's design always remained to some extent mysterious and Mahan acknowledged that. The outcome of a specific war did not directly translate to "the judgment of God," for Mahan believed that in "a case of possible war arising, God has given us a conscience, with revealed data, and necessary faculties for decision; I therefore should no more expect enlightenment as to His judgment upon the case, by recourse to War, than I should by tossing a penny."[86]

Mahan was nervous about how his work would be received in Britain. He wrote to Major George Sydenham Clarke (later Sir George, then later Lord Sydenham), a British military writer and lower-level cabinet officer, "I shall look with interest and some anxiety to the reception of my coming book on your side."[87] His worry was unnecessary as the reviews were good on both sides of the Atlantic. Theodore Roosevelt actually reviewed the book twice, and in *Atlantic Monthly* Roosevelt said that in "philosophic spirit and grasp of his subject in its larger aspects, he is not approached by any other naval writer whom we can at the moment recall." In *Political Science Quarterly*, in a review of both Sea Power volumes, Roosevelt said that Mahan had founded "a new school of naval historical writing" and that all Americans should be proud "that an officer of our own navy should have written such books." Roosevelt was particularly interested in the lessons Americans should learn from these books: "that we must have a great fighting navy, in order to hold our proper position among the nations of the earth and to do the work to which our destiny points."[88] John Knox Laughton in the *Edinburgh Review* thought the second Sea Power work "even more important" than the first because "important as it is to naval affairs, [it] is still more so to the statesman, the administrator, the ship-owner, the merchant and the tradesman."[89] A. H. Johnson in the *English Historical Review* (reviewing both Sea Power volumes), while chiding Mahan for relying too heavily on French sources, nonetheless said that "these volumes stand without a rival; and their lessons are equally valuable to the historian, the statesman, the naval strategist, and the tactician."[90]

Mahan was pleased with his output, and though he was not making much money from the books he could work at his own pace and took satisfaction in his work. Writing fifteen years later, he said, "I now often recall with envy the happiness of those days, when the work was its own reward, and quite sufficient, too, almost as good as a baby."[91]

Family matters also preoccupied Mahan at this time. As the eldest, not to mention the most successful, Alfred was protective of his brothers and tried to help them when he could. He even brought Fred, a captain in the Army Corps of Engineers, to the Naval War College in the fall 1892 term to lecture on coast defenses, possibly in an attempt to add a little luster to Fred's resume.[92]

On March 8, 1893, Mahan's mother died at the home she shared with her sister Jane Swift in Elizabeth, New Jersey. During the last years of her life she was an invalid, and Mahan commented to his wife that "those who loved her best could scarcely desire her continuance here." But according to Puleston, who interviewed Mahan's sister Jane, "her strong sense of humor asserted itself to the end and she amused those about her with her witty comments on life as viewed from her bedroom." She took pride in Alfred's success and "had all the reviews of his books read to her." Mahan accompanied her remains to West Point, where she was buried next to her husband.[93] Mrs. Mahan and her sister donated land they had inherited from their grandfather James Jay for the building of the Church of the Atonement in Tenafly, New Jersey. They also contributed toward the construction of the church and "presented a very valuable set of altar vessels. . . . Mr. Alfred Mahan furnished the Bible and Prayer Book."[94]

More bad news, or so it seemed at the time, came Mahan's way in March. He was being sent back to sea. In November 1892 Grover Cleveland defeated the incumbent Benjamin Harrison for the presidency, portending a big change at the Navy Department. The Cleveland administration was not disposed to a large navy or an imperialistic outlook. Francis M. Ramsey, head of the Bureau of Navigation and as such the head detailer, was no fan of Mahan or the Naval War College. Ramsey had long wanted Mahan back at sea, but Secretary Tracy had always intervened to get Mahan assignments that allowed him to write. That was about to change with the appointment of Hilary Herbert as the new Secretary of the Navy.[95]

Mahan unwittingly exacerbated the situation by opining on events in Hawaii. On January 30, 1893, he wrote a letter to the editor of the *New York Times* on "the recent revolution in Hawaii," in which American sugar planters assisted by American military forces seized control of the islands and were immediately recognized by the U.S. minister as a prelude to annexation. Mahan supported annexation, but in his letter asked rhetorically if the United States was "ready to undertake" the "great extension of our naval power" that would be necessary to defend the islands. He also expressed concern about "the great number of Chinese" who lived in Hawaii and whether the islands would become "an outpost of European civilization or of the comparative barbarism of China."[96]

As a result of the letter, Walter Hines Page, editor of *The Forum*, asked Mahan to write an article on this same topic for the March issue. This gave Mahan only a week to work on it, but he thought he should accept because the article might be "useful for the Navy."[97] The article was published as "Hawaii and Our Future Sea Power," and it expanded on the themes raised in the letter, making two points. First, control of Hawaii—or at least keeping it out of the hands of a hostile power—was necessary to protect the west coast of America. Second, the building of an isthmian canal would make the United States a Pacific power, like it or not, and would necessitate defending our Pacific interests. To deal adequately with these two issues the United States needed a navy equal to Great Britain's. This was not, he stressed, to compete with them, but to be a "cordial" partner to "the great nation from whose loins we sprung."[98]

The article did not sit well with the anti-annexationist Cleveland administration. That, in combination with the mutual animosity between him and Ramsey, ensured that he was going back to sea against his wishes. Seager makes much of this, but overlooks the obvious changes that had occurred in Mahan's life. Whether Mahan liked sea duty or not was irrelevant at this point; he was fifty-two years old and due to retire in 1896. Most important was that he had found his life's work—writing and teaching on naval matters—and felt that was the sphere where he could make the maximum contribution to the Navy. Many others thought so too, and powerful friends in Washington, including Roosevelt, Henry Cabot Lodge, and Admiral Luce, lobbied hard for him to stay at the Naval War College. A number of serving officers, including Capt. George Dewey, came to his defense and one, Frederick McNair, volunteered to go to sea in his place.[99] McNair told Dewey, who then told Mahan's brother Fred, that "he [McNair] considers that what you are doing is of so much more importance, that he would be willing to volunteer to go to sea to have you left on shore."[100] William McCarty Little, Mahan's colleague at the Naval War College, also was outraged, citing various encomiums to Mahan including "the Jomini of the Water." He expressed bafflement that the Prophet of Sea Power "is in danger of being taken from the War College and sent to sea!"[101] Theodore Roosevelt put it even more bluntly: "Oh, what idiots we have to deal with!"[102] Herbert and Ramsey had their way, nonetheless, and Mahan was assigned to take command of the cruiser USS *Chicago*, as Ramsey reportedly declared, "It is not the business of a naval officer to write books."[103] Nevertheless, Mahan had the last laugh, since the two-year European tour of the *Chicago*, though not without its difficulties, turned into a personal victory tour for the naval officer who wrote books.

Mahan took command of the *Chicago* on May 11, 1893. She was undergoing a refit at the Brooklyn Navy Yard in preparation for a voyage that would consist mainly of "friendly visits" to European nations. The destinations were places of interest to Mahan even though he really had no desire to leave the United States. On the minus side was that the *Chicago* was going to serve as the flagship of the commander of the European Station, Rear Adm. Henry Erben. In Puleston's words, Erben "shared Ramsey's views concerning naval officers with literary aspirations. Anyone acquainted with Erben and Mahan would have known they were hopelessly incompatible."[104]

Already at work on his next project, a biography of Lord Nelson, as well as committed to writing some articles on current issues for *Atlantic Monthly*, Mahan hoped to get some reading done, and possibly even some writing, while at sea. He was aware, however, that this might be an unrealistic hope. He wrote to Horace Scudder, editor of *Atlantic Monthly*, "I am preparing to exert myself in the literary way; but what I can accomplish under these difficulties remains to be seen."[105]

The *Chicago* put to sea on June 18, headed for Queenstown, Ireland. On the first day out he wrote to his wife (using her nickname Deldie) that while he did not yet mind the separation he knew he would soon. He contrasted himself with Nelson, who "never really cared for his wife after the first few years."[106] This situation certainly did not apply to Mahan, who was always happiest at home with his family, as evidenced by writing constantly to his wife while away. He also wrote letters to each child as well as to his sister Jane, although the letters to Lyle have not survived. At the time Helen was nineteen, Ellen was fifteen, and Lyle was twelve.[107] Rapidly deteriorating relations with Erben and an injury to his leg combined with Mahan's dislike of being at sea made the cruise a difficult one.[108] The compensation came with Mahan's discovery that he was a celebrity in naval and diplomatic circles throughout Europe, but especially in Britain.

When the *Chicago* arrived in Queenstown there were already invitations waiting inviting Mahan to a variety of dinners given by political and naval bigwigs. John Hay (Lincoln's former secretary) wrote Mahan from London, "All the people of intelligence are waiting to welcome you."[109] On July 30, when the *Chicago* arrived at the Isle of Wight for the Cowes Regatta (a major event on the royal calendar), he received an invitation from Queen Victoria to dine at her residence there, Osborne House. The admiral was invited, too, almost as an afterthought. Mahan wore full dress uniform and "ate dinner with my sword on for the first time in my life." In addition to the queen, Mahan met the Prince of Wales (the future Edward VII), his son the Duke of York (the future George V), and another of the queen's grandsons, Kaiser Wilhelm II. The queen told Mahan she had heard of his books, though Mahan suspected she had been "coached." But the Duke of York, a professional naval officer, had read the books and talked with Mahan about them. Mahan also met for the first time a man who would become a close friend, Field Marshal Lord Roberts (known as "Bobs"). Bobs, it turned out, was a huge fan. "He told me some one had sent him the first [Sea Power] book, but he himself had bought the second, and after some flattering words, I said, Yes, my Lord, but it is better to have done something as you did in Afghanistan than only to have written something." Interestingly, the kaiser, who would soon become a devotee of Mahan's theories, seems not to have spoken to him that night, although the captain of the kaiser's yacht did. The following day one of the queen's younger sons, the Duke of Connaught (Prince Arthur), a professional army officer, came on board the *Chicago*.[110]

Mahan in command of the USS *Chicago*; sketch by Gribayeitoff, 1894 *(U.S. Naval Institute Photo Archive)*

As the *Chicago* proceeded to Southampton, then to London, Mahan was wined and dined by the high and mighty. Erben was always invited as a courtesy, but it was clear who the guest of honor really was. The admiral did not appreciate playing second fiddle to a subordinate, and Erben probably felt like a useless appendage when he was invited to a dinner in Mahan's honor given by the First Lord of the Admiralty, Earl Spencer. So great had Mahan's reputation become that three previous first lords also attended.[111] He also had dinner with Professor Laughton, "who has given me some points about Nelson," but he soon told his wife that he found the London whirlwind a bit of a strain. "I am tiring a little of the racket—a quiet hour over a book suits me much better and I had rather see your dear faces around me than hear any more compliments."[112]

Just before leaving England he received good news from the United States in the form of a letter from Cdr. French E. Chadwick informing him, "The War

College is safe. The Secy [Herbert] read your last book (on Sea Power) and that convinced him. He told me some time since he was opposed to it. He now tells me he has informed Ramsey that he has changed his mind." Mahan reported this to Luce and quoted the Bible verse "In quietness and confidence shall be your strength [Isaiah 30:15]." He also told his wife, "I scarcely knew till I got this how keenly I had felt the report of the College abolition—the tears came to my eyes of mingled relief and exultation."[113]

The *Chicago* left Britain in early September 1893 and cruised the Mediterranean, visiting France, Portugal, Spain, Gibraltar, Italy, Turkey, Syria, Egypt, and Algeria before returning to England in May 1894. Mahan's difficult relations with Erben came to a head in December 1893 when the admiral gave him a less-than-sterling fitness report. He graded Mahan as follows:

Professional ability	Tolerable
Attention to duty	Tolerable
General conduct	Excellent
Sobriety	Excellent
Health	Good
Efficiency of men under his control	Tolerable, except in the matter of divisional exercises where her condition is good

Erben appended an explanation of his "Tolerable" rating in professional ability.

I state herewith that Capt. Mahan always appears to advantage to the service in all that does not appertain to ship life or matters, but in this particular he is lacking in interest, as he has frankly admitted to me. His interests are entirely outside the service, for which I am satisfied he cares but little, and is therefore not a good naval officer. He is not at all observant regarding officers tending to the ship's general welfare or appearance. Nor does he inspire or suggest anything in this connection. In fact, the first few weeks of the cruise she was positively discreditable. In fact, Capt. Mahan's interests lie wholly in the direction of literary work, and in no other way connected to the service.[114]

Erben did not do Mahan the courtesy of informing him of what the report said and Mahan did not find out about it till January 22, 1894. He was understandably upset over the "Tolerable" ratings and the addendum and felt they were unjust. He was particularly incensed over the implication that "there has been any willful neglect." He told his wife "we can well believe God will bear me clear—for I have kept my work before Him." He requested her prayers for this situation. He was worried not only about his reputation, but also that a negative report would give ammunition to those, especially Ramsey, who wanted to shut down the War College.[115]

Mahan prepared a detailed rejoinder to be sent to Herbert, completed with some assistance from two of his most trusted junior officers, Lt. Arthur Nazro and Lt. Thomas Rodgers. Mahan thought that most of Erben's remarks were baseless and that he could successfully counter every point. Two items in particular galled him. One was Erben's calling the *Chicago*'s condition "positively discreditable" in the first few weeks of the cruise. Mahan answered this by citing how little time he had to get her ready before sailing, how he had been incapacitated by a knee injury, and, most importantly, how Erben's previous inspection in October 1893 made no mention of any deficiencies. The other issue was Erben's charge that Mahan admitted he lacked interest in his duties as commanding officer. It was, of course, no secret that Mahan had not wanted this assignment and would have much preferred to work on his writing, but Mahan thought it "hardly fair to press a casual remark, whose precise words I can not now recall, to the implication that I take no interest in my duties. . . . The question is not what I feel, but what I do; and the test of what I do is the results obtained." Mahan also assured Secretary Herbert that he had a strict rule to not "touch my literary work until the ship's work for the day is over." Mahan concluded his fifteen-point response by asking for a "general inquiry into the condition and efficiency of the *Chicago*, and my conduct and action as her captain."[116]

Mahan also sought the help of Theodore Roosevelt, Henry Cabot Lodge, and his wife's cousin, David B. Ogden, a New York lawyer who was a friend of Roosevelt's. Once word of this controversy got out, other admirals, including Luce, sprang to his defense. Roosevelt, Lodge, and Ogden thought it was best to handle the matter in a low-key way. Lodge met with Herbert and learned that the secretary thought Erben's charges were "not serious enough to warrant any action or further consideration." He also told Lodge to tell Mahan "what he could not say in an official letter, that he had nothing but the kindest feeling toward you." More to the point, the secretary said "there was no reason for you to make yourself uneasy and that when the ship went out of commission, she would be rigidly inspected by a first-class board, and that you would have an opportunity if you desired to meet all the criticism of Erben, to receive vindication in the report of the inspectors." Lodge also said that the secretary agreed with Lodge's own opinion that Mahan's works were "an honor to the American Navy." Mahan told Elly that he "consider[ed] this settlement satisfactory" and felt vindicated.[117] Relations between Mahan and Erben remained awkward—an "armed truce" according to Puleston—but Mahan seemed to triumph in the end. Erben was frustrated that the Navy Department backed Mahan. Mahan basked in fulsome lionization when the *Chicago* returned to England.[118] Throughout the ordeal Mahan relied on the support of his ever-loyal wife and, of course, on God. "How a thing like this teaches me to know God and the power of the Holy Spirit. It is worth all the trouble." This was before he knew how the matter would turn out. In low moments he said he found his situation "desolating . . . but a great comfort to know God rules all." If it were not "for the support God gives me I believe I should go to pieces."[119] When vindication came he told Elly that they must not seek revenge lest they lose "God's protection on which we all rely."[120]

In the midst of all this, Mahan's concern for his children and their spiritual state was a frequent theme in letters to them and their mother. Helen, the oldest, was now twenty. He expressed to her, not for the first time, his worry that she was associating with unbelievers. Not, he said, that he "wish[ed] to control your choice of friends, nor to limit your range of thought." Rather he was concerned that unbelievers would instill doubt in her mind, "that miserable doubting feeling, based upon no reasonable convictions." Possibly he sensed that her doubts, if indeed she had any, were of an intellectual nature. He assured her that he, "certainly a man of brains," found "the truths of Christianity satisfying to my intellect and my only firm support in doubt and trouble." If doubts should assail her "God will not leave you in the dark."[121] This is just the sort of advice that Seager loves to ridicule and present as evidence that Mahan did not want her to marry. Again, this assertion ignores Mahan's references to his daughter marrying in the future. "Of course, if you marry, you will transfer both your work and your support elsewhere."[122] As for Ellen ("Nellie"), now almost seventeen, far from Mahan's desiring her to be an isolated homebody, he was concerned that she get out and make new friends. She had "too little variety of companionship." He prayed "that God will send her friends" and that she would be encouraged to find interesting activities. He worried that she was perhaps feeling guilty for some "vague sinfulness or wrong doings" without having done any "specific wrong act." If so, it was "a snare of the devil." She needed to be assured that her "suffering" was not her fault. "God in His time will reward faithfulness."[123]

In September 1894 Lyle, now thirteen, entered Groton School in Groton, Massachusetts, headed by the Reverend Endicott Peabody (invariably referred to as "the Rector"). Mahan's concern, as always with his children, was that Lyle, even though away from home, would "feel that he is always with God." He also wanted to make sure that Lyle was "following the prayers I gave him after his confirmation."[124] Such constant advice and worry may seem to some pedantic, self-righteous, and smugly pious, but Mahan's children, whether they appreciated it at the time, always recognized its sincerity. Lyle in later years stated that he recognized that his father's faith was "not of the lip-service kind."[125]

Mahan also worried about his brother Fred. It is not clear what Fred's difficulties were, though Alfred thought some of them were career-related. Fred served on the Light House Board and apparently incurred the wrath of the Corps of Engineers (in which he was a captain) because he was too "friendly" toward Navy interests.[126] Alfred's letter to Elly also hinted at marital problems.

> I am distressed about Fred. Poor fellow; now is the time wife and children come in—and one says heartily—it is not good for man to be alone. I fear too that Fred, without meaning to, has by his mistaken abstention from church, etc. lost touch with God, who stands by one so marvelously under such trials as the present. "His (not our) faithfulness and truth shall be my shield and buckler." I shall write him again.[127]

Whatever the situation was, Alfred continued to have a close relationship with Fred.

Not surprisingly, Mahan took a keen interest in divine service on board ship. The ship's chaplain was F. F. Sherman, and Mahan and Sherman apparently got along and Sherman mostly did an adequate job. One cannot imagine Mahan being silent with either his wife or the Navy Department if he thought Sherman theologically or pastorally deficient. There was one episode, however, when Sherman started to preach on presidential use of force against labor rioters. Mahan interrupted the sermon, but Erben said, "Sit down, Mahan. Let him go ahead." Mahan wanted Sherman to stick to biblical exposition and stay away from politics, but Erben sided with Sherman and rescinded Mahan's request (possibly even an order) to vet the chaplain's sermons ahead of time.[128]

From September 1893 to May 1894 the *Chicago* cruised the Mediterranean. Even though he was preoccupied with the Erben matter there were aspects of the cruise that Mahan enjoyed. One was visiting biblical sites in Turkey and Syria such as Patmos, Tarsus, and Smyrna.[129]

He also enjoyed socializing in Villefranche, France, with a wealthy British family, Mr. and Mrs. George Schiff, who vacationed there. He greatly admired their daughter Rosie, even wishing that Lyle was old enough to court her. As much as he liked the social life he enjoyed with the Schiffs in both France and England, he lamented that they had no "religious feeling."[130] Elly contemplated taking a trip to England to join her husband, an idea, despite its logistical difficulties, "I should dearly love." Alas, uncertainty as to the *Chicago*'s movements made her abandon the idea.[131]

The *Chicago* returned to England on May 9, 1894, and Mahan received another round of honors, tributes, and dinners. Erben was invited to most of these but frequently claimed indisposition and excused himself. It was galling to him to play second fiddle to a lower-ranking officer whom he disliked and to see that officer lauded by British political and naval figures. Erben's discomfort was obvious to all, and even the British prime minister, the Earl of Rosebery, remarked to Mahan that Erben's "position is difficult—for after all he is much in that of chaperon to debutante."[132] Mahan was invited to numerous dinners and banquets, celebrated the queen's birthday with the Royal United Service Institution, and dined at Trinity House with the Prince of Wales. What pleased him most was a dinner in his honor at the Royal Navy Club, where he became the first foreigner to be so honored since the club's founding. He also gave a lengthy interview with the *Pall Mall Gazette* in which he upheld the notion of British naval superiority.[133]

In June the *Chicago* went to Antwerp, Belgium, for a long overdue over-haul. Among the visitors to the ship when she was opened to the public were a twenty-year-old Sandhurst cadet named Winston Churchill and his younger brother Jack, who were traveling on the continent with their tutor. They "examined it as closely as the authorities would let us," Winston told his mother, but it is not clear whether the captain was on board at the time.[134]

Mahan returned to England for a brief visit in June and was awarded honorary degrees from both Cambridge and Oxford. He received an LLD from Cambridge on June 18 in "a private audience, before the accustomed officials and some few visitors from outside." This was followed by a "few hours of easy social intercourse with a few eminent persons."[135] Two days later he went to Oxford to receive a DCL. This was a public ceremony in the Sheldonian Theatre with full academic regalia, a procession through town, and numerous dignitaries including the prime minister, Lord Rosebery. Mahan wore his full dress uniform under a scarlet gown. The event, he said later, was "a curious combination of impressiveness and horse-play." Rosebery told him that he "had beaten the record" for receiving degrees from both universities in the same week.[136] Mahan admitted to his wife that he enjoyed the "adulation," going so far to say he "craves" it but at the same time "despise[s]" it. To succumb to his own publicity would be "debasing," but he trusted in God to not let that happen. He even prayed, "God keep me in vivid recollection of my own nothingness."[137]

At this same time Mahan received a letter from Poultney Bigelow, foreign correspondent for the *New York Herald* based in London. It contained news the significance of which has ever since been debated. On May 26, 1894, Bigelow had received a telegram from the emperor of Germany, Wilhelm II, in which the kaiser said "I am just now, not reading but devouring Captain Mahan's book [*The Influence of Sea Power upon History*]; and am trying to learn it by heart. It is a first-class work and classical in all points. It is on board all my ships and constantly quoted by my Captains and officers." Bigelow forwarded a copy of the telegram to Mahan. Mahan had no direct response to this, at least none that has survived, though he did meet the kaiser once again at Cowes. The queen gave a dinner on board the royal yacht to which Mahan was invited and at which the kaiser was also present. The kaiser's aide told Mahan that "the E[mperor] was much interested in my book." The kaiser, normally a stickler for protocol, was so eager to speak to Mahan that he buttonholed him without waiting for a formal presentation so that Mahan "was taken unawares." Mahan, however, was so preoccupied with his instructions on how to greet the queen that he could not even recall what Wilhelm said. The conversation was short, though. "[W]e had not exchanged two sentences" when they were interrupted by the queen's aide, who snagged Mahan for a presentation to Her Majesty.[138] Puleston later recorded that in 1919 a U.S. Navy lieutenant, Scott Unested, had been shown the kaiser's study in his now-abandoned palace. "On the shelves in easy reach of the Kaiser's armchair were Mahan's works on sea power, both in English and German. They were extensively underscored and contained many marginal notes." Puleston, though unfortunately not giving many details, was later in touch with the exiled kaiser, who was eager to help him with his biography of Mahan. "The former Emperor remembers perfectly having made these notes and later directed that the German properties he had owned be searched in order that the books might be made available to the writer; but they have disappeared, possibly having been sold by the caretaker."[139] Mahan himself does not seem to have paid very much attention to the kaiser's accolades.[140]

A bit of good news came Mahan's way when he learned that Erben was going to be replaced by Rear Adm. William A. Kirkland, whom Mahan had known since 1860. He was apprehensive at first, but he soon realized that he had nothing to fear from his new commanding officer. Apart from Kirkland's tendency to profanity, Mahan had nothing else to fault; "Kirkland is very nice to me" and did not interfere in the running of the ship.[141] In contrast to Erben, who had given Mahan another negative fitness report, Kirkland gave him high marks and even wrote an unsolicited letter to Secretary Herbert praising Mahan "as an act of justice," presumably to counteract Erben's reports. Mahan, he said,

> is a careful yet bold Navigator, never afraid of his ship. He is a just and careful administrator of the Regulations and Laws of the Navy, to his officers and crew. He is indefatigable in his efforts to obtain the best results in efficiency so far as he is permitted by the Regulations. He is subordinate and cheerful in carrying out the instructions of his superiors. Of his abilities and his gentlemanly and officer-like conduct, every one is aware.[142]

Mahan's relations with Kirkland remained cordial which undoubtedly made his life easier.

While on his various shore leaves in England, Mahan always attended church on Sunday unless circumstances prevented it, and even on those occasions he felt guilty. "I myself am ill at ease over the occasional neglects into which I have been betrayed. I do not think, however, I would willingly or wilfully omit church." He was not, however, impressed with the churchgoing habits of the aristocracy. "I fear church is being put sadly in the background of English society of the upper class."[143] In contrast, the royals attended church every Sunday; Mahan went once with Queen Victoria's cousin, the Duke of Cambridge (Prince George), who was commander-in-chief of the British army, with whom he would remain on friendly terms.[144]

A variety of rumors swirled around Mahan. One was that the *Chicago* would be sent to China to show the flag during the Sino-Japanese War. Another was that Mahan would be offered the superintendency of the Naval Academy. The latter prospect did not thrill him, but he told his wife he would take it if it meant the *Chicago* could some home sooner. Nothing, however, came of any of these rumors.[145]

In January 1895 Lyle, while at Groton, became ill with measles, then pneumonia. His mother left the girls alone in New York and went to Groton to nurse him. Lyle remembered that she was there six weeks, but his sister Ellen remembered it as only three weeks (Ellen's recollections are generally more reliable as to dates and details). Years later both siblings stated that their mother did not tell their father of the illness because she did not want to worry him. They were wrong in this; Elly did tell her husband about Lyle's illness, though not the extent of its seriousness. She also neglected to write him frequently, though she did not stop altogether as Ellen later claimed. Mahan pressed his wife for more letters, saying, "Don't lose your thought of others because the boy has the measles." And Ellen claimed he told her, "Your mother never neglected me like this before." When Mahan came home Elly told him how ill Lyle actually had been. According to Lyle, who was in bed in an adjoining room when this conversation took place, "He certainly was terribly shocked and asked over and over again if she was sure that I was all right now." This was a revealing moment for Lyle, who later claimed that his father did not show much affection. "It was the first inkling I had of the feeling which lay beneath the surface."[146]

After another turn around the Mediterranean, the *Chicago* finally headed home in February 1895, arriving in New York harbor on March 23. Contrary to Seager's negative view of Mahan's seamanship, the captain brought the ship in and docked her perfectly without the assistance of a pilot.[147]

During the *Chicago*'s voyage Mahan's aunt, Jane Okill Swift, and Elly's mother, Ellen Kuhn Evans, died leaving significant bequests to Mahan and his wife. These, along with earnings from his writings and a Navy pension, convinced him that he could retire. His plan was to get a year's leave and then retire in September 1896, by which time he would have completed forty years of service (including his time at the Naval Academy, which in those days counted toward retirement). "A year's leave and then retire, that is my present aim; and I hope that with Auntie's and your mother's leavings and my hoped for earnings we may get on."[148] Secretary Herbert wanted him to stay in the Navy but was sympathetic to Mahan's desire to continue writing. He wrote to Naval War College president Capt. Henry Taylor, "I shall endeavor to provide for him a place that will be agreeable to him and afford opportunities for pursuing his literary work."[149]

Seager characterizes the *Chicago* cruise as two years of "sheer misery."[150] Certainly Mahan was frequently unhappy; the separation from his family, the boredom of shipboard routine, his deteriorating relations with Erben, and lack of opportunity to work on his writing projects all took their toll. But Seager's description of the tour overlooks the positives, including the honorary degrees, the socializing in London and Villefranche, the hobnobbing with royalty and political figures, and the new friendships with Royal Navy leaders and British naval scholars. Mahan enjoyed all these things, as a careful reading of his letters clearly indicates.

Mahan remained captain of the *Chicago* until her decommissioning on May 1, 1895, after which Herbert called him to Washington for a meeting. The happy result was assignment "to temporary duty in connection with the Naval War College and Torpedo School." This essentially meant he could stay in New York and work on his life of Nelson.[151]

After returning home Mahan and his wife bought a home at 160 West Eighty-Sixth Street. During his absence in the *Chicago* Elly had built a "cottage" in Quogue, Long Island (the Mahans had been renting a summer cottage there since 1893). She was heavily involved in the planning and direction of the contractors, and this no doubt helped to keep her occupied while her husband was away. The new cottage was called Slumberside and was on one acre of land about two hundred yards from the ocean. The Mahans divided their time between New York City and Quogue for the next ten years.[152] In addition to working on the Nelson biography, Mahan began to write articles on contemporary naval and diplomatic issues, most of which were later collected and published as books. He gave lectures at the Naval War College in June and received an honorary LLD from Harvard on June 26.[153] He also at this time copied and dated a motto from the Bible: "It is better to trust in the Lord than to put any confidence in man" [Psalm 118:8].[154]

He continued to perform occasional naval duties, including a court-martial and more lectures in Newport. He was also distracted by problems with his youngest brother Dennis Jr. The three Mahan brothers were to divide the proceeds from the sale of their aunt Jane Swift's property (their sister Jane received a separate bequest). Dennis, who needed the money, wanted a quick sale, while Alfred thought that if they held on to it for a while it would increase in value. The siblings were not exactly fighting over the will, but Dennis was being difficult. Alfred tried to keep the peace among all of them. Dennis' problems were many: an invalid wife, a child, indebtedness, and a drinking problem. Alfred seems to have felt protective toward him, more so than Fred did. Alfred reminded Fred that "we can't ignore the duties of blood." Fearing that Dennis would make foolish financial decisions, "We must try, as quietly and unobtrusively as we can, to keep him safe in his business matters, for the sake of himself and his family." Alfred was particularly concerned about two possibilities, both of them bad. One was that Dennis might die, and the other was that he might get thrown out of the Navy for drunkenness, as "he has had one or two narrow shaves already."[155] Alfred told a family friend, "We must try and keep peace between Fred and Dennis. The latter is trying at times and Fred's patience is small."[156] The property was divided quickly and Alfred's worst fears, fortunately, did not come true. Dennis remained in the Navy, though not without further problems, retired as a commodore, and lived until 1925.[157]

Mahan had intended to put in for retirement in September 1896, but held off because of the shocking possibility that the United States might go to war with Britain. This might seem far-fetched, but for a brief period in 1895–96 it seemed possible. The cause, which seems so obscure today, was the United States' attempt to intervene in a dispute between Britain and Venezuela over the boundary of British Guiana. Secretary of state Richard Olney (speaking for President Cleveland) sent a strongly worded letter to the British government urging accession to the American offer to arbitrate and suggesting that a British refusal to comply was a violation of the Monroe Doctrine. The British foreign secretary, the Marquess of Salisbury, replied four months later, basically telling the United States to mind its own business. This was followed by a belligerent message from President Cleveland that some took to be threatening war. The situation put Mahan in a dilemma, as he was no fan of Cleveland and of course was a staunch anglophile and had numerous friends and admirers in Britain. He also felt that as a serving officer he should make no public statement. Nevertheless he was pressured to make one. It was a difficult time for him, and it came in the midst of the settlement of his aunt's will and his worries about Dennis.[158]

Firstly, he believed it would be wrong to retire while war threatened. He wrote to his old friend Ashe, "I shrank from the appearance of retiring while possible trouble from an overt source remained."[159] He told British naval scholar James Thursfield that "as an officer I of course express no opinion upon the justice of our cause or the cause of our government. In case of war it would remain to me only to do the duty for which I have been brought up."[160] The prospect of war with Britain upset him for both military and emotional reasons. He told Thursfield that "as a matter of personal feeling and even more of personal conviction I am absolutely with you in the belief that no greater evil can possibly happen to either nation or to the world than such a war."[161] He also wrote to Rear Admiral Bouverie Clark of the Royal Navy, whom he had known since his time on the *Wachusett* in the South Pacific, "I will not believe war possible—if it comes, and I am in it, I think I shall have to request the admiralty to hoist on your ships some other flag than the British—for, save our own, there is none other on which I should be so reluctant to fire."[162] To another English friend, Colonel J. B. Sterling, Coldstream Guards, Mahan reported that he had recently turned down a request from "two very wise and somewhat prominent men" to become involved in an effort to establish a "Permanent Tribunal of Arbitration between Great Britain and the United States." Mahan opposed the idea in principle; he believed no nation should entrust "its conscience with any other keeping than its own." He did nevertheless assure Sterling, quoting his own answer to the two aforementioned gentlemen, that "[i]n my honor, reverence, and affection, Great Britain stands only second to my own country. As the head of the English-speaking race outside our borders, I feel for her what Mr. [Arthur James] Balfour has not ineptly called race patriotism."[163]

Happily for Mahan, the situation resolved itself when the British government, preoccupied with the Boers in South Africa, agreed to arbitration. He felt safe in requesting retirement and he was officially retired on November 17, 1896.[164] This merited a mention in the *New York Times*, which reported that he "would have been promoted to the rank of Commodore in a few months." Mahan was well aware of this but told Ashe that he was willing to forgo the increased pay in the interests of working on his writing without fear of "interruption by the Department." He hoped he could "more than make good the loss by writing." He also told Ashe that once retired he hoped to write about "the State, Church, and social movement about me."[165]

Mahan's two-volume *The Life of Nelson: The Embodiment of the Sea Power of Great Britain* was published in March 1897. Even Seager agrees that it "was probably his best book, certainly his best-researched" because it was based so heavily on primary sources.[166] Mahan had desired to "produce the definitive life," and certainly most contemporary historians thought it "pre-eminently the best biography of Nelson so far published."[167] Mahan thought Nelson the quintessential naval commander. While not whitewashing Nelson's flaws, he presented a Nelson he clearly admired as "the one man who in himself summed up and embodied the greatness of the possibilities which Sea Power comprehends,—the man for whom genius and opportunity worked together, to make him the personification of the Navy of Great Britain."[168] Sumida, in his perceptive analysis of *Life of Nelson*, points out that Mahan admired Nelson for his "mastery" of "political, administrative and military skills," a combination "rare in any single man." Most important, though, in Mahan's view, was Nelson's decisiveness in seeking out and destroying the enemy.[169]

Leaving it to the naval historians to critique Mahan's analysis of Nelson's battles, it is more relevant to this work to look at two aspects of Mahan's biography: Nelson's religious faith and his extramarital affair with Emma, Lady Hamilton. Nelson was the son of an Anglican rector, a factor that would have counted for a lot with Mahan, though not as much as Nelson's personal faith in God. Still, Nelson had a good moral upbringing, which Mahan acknowledged was important and contributed to his "kindly sweetness," gratitude toward those who helped him, and his exemplification of "the charity which is kind and thinketh no evil."[170] Mahan praised Nelson's numerous references in his letters to God's guidance and his gratitude for God's blessings. Nelson was a regular churchgoer, regularly held divine service on the *Victory*, and enjoyed discussing sermons with the chaplain. Mahan lauded all these activities and said, "In the sense of profound recognition of the dependence of events upon God, and the obligation to manifest gratitude in outward acts, Nelson was from first to last a strongly religious man."[171] Such sentiments could have been simply standard-issue religious talk. Mahan knew this, of course, and commented, "Although always reverently thankful to the Almighty for a favorable issue of events, there does not seem to have been in him any keen consciousness of personal dependence [upon God]."[172]

Nelson's most egregious breach of morality was his liaison with Lady Hamilton. This was difficult for Mahan to deal with inasmuch as his admiration for Nelson was so great and Nelson's misconduct was so flagrant. Many naval historians then and now viewed it as irrelevant to Nelson's tactical skill and leadership abilities, but for Mahan, who was as interested in Nelson's character as he was in his skill, it clearly posed a problem. Mahan used adverbs such as "unfortunately" and "unhappily" in discussing this distasteful affair, "the otherwise almost inexplicable but enduring infatuation which enslaved his later years, and has left the most serious blot upon his memory."[173] Exacerbating

Nelson's misbehavior was the fact that Emma was the wife of a close friend, Sir William Hamilton. Betrayal of marriage vows was a worse sin in Mahan's eyes, but betrayal of a friend was still deplorable.[174]

Mahan concluded that Nelson treated his wife Frances well enough, but that he was never ardently in love with her and quickly grew bored with her, a boredom exacerbated by her childlessness (though she had a child by her first husband). Nelson, said Mahan, needed someone who "enkindled his ardent imagination, or filled for him the place of an ideal, which his mental constitution imperatively demanded as an object of worship." His wife never fulfilled this.[175] Mahan certainly did not approve of Emma Hamilton as a substitute wife. Indeed, Nelson's choice of lover shocked him. "The pitifulness of it is to see the incongruity between such faith, such devotion, and the distasteful inadequacy of their object." Mahan did not deny that Nelson really loved Emma or that he was faithful to her, but that did not excuse the breaking of his marriage vows or his "glory[ing] in the public exhibition" of his illicit relationship.[176] Mahan's comment on what the Nelsons lacked is as good a description as any of what he thought Christian marriage should be: "an enduring wedded love which strikes root downward and bears fruit upward, steadily growing in depth and devotion as the years roll by."[177]

Despite this great lapse in judgment and behavior, Mahan's view of Nelson was overwhelmingly positive. Not only was Nelson the greatest naval officer of all time, but he was the man whose victory at Trafalgar turned the tide against Napoleon. Nelson's mission in life—the reason he was put here by God—was to defeat "the pure military despotism of Napoleon."[178] Mahan summed up Nelson's career and life in the following words:

> Sharer of our mortal weakness, he has bequeathed to us a type of single-minded self-devotion that can never perish. . . . War may cease, but the need for heroism shall not depart from the earth, while man remains man and evil exists to be redressed. Whenever danger has to be faced or duty to be done, at cost to self, men will draw inspiration from the name and deeds of Nelson.[179]

Despite Seager's admission that *Life of Nelson* was "probably [Mahan's] best book," he is scathing in his ridicule of it.[180] In his 1980 article "A Biography of a Biographer," Seager characterizes *Life of Nelson* as a combination of hagiography and prudery. He even takes gratuitous swipes at Mahan's wife (whom he calls "unexciting" and "plain") and daughters. Seager also claims that Mahan, madly grasping for a plausible explanation of how his otherwise upright hero could "flee to the arms of a beautiful, clever, amoral, sexually aggressive tart like Emma," blames the liaison on a head wound Nelson received at the Battle of the

Nile.[181] Mahan made no such claim in the pages Seager cites as evidence for this, but gave more plausible reasons for Nelson's infatuation.[182]

Seager also claims that Mahan, while generally earning favorable reviews, was panned by British reviewers for his moralistic condemnation of the affair.[183] This is a highly selective, even exaggerated, misreading of those reviews. William O'Connor Morris in the *Fortnightly Review* praised Mahan's "admirable, just, and discerning . . . treatment of this most unhappy subject."[184] James R. Thursfield in the *Quarterly Review* was a little harder on Mahan, taking him to task for allowing Nelson's "pitiful tragedy" to "overhang his whole career." He nonetheless praised Mahan for not allowing "the maudlin sentiment which allows the glamour of a rather tawdry romance to silence the moral judgment altogether."[185] In the *Edinburgh Review* John Knox Laughton, who had recently published his own book, *The Nelson Memorial: Nelson and His Companions in Arms*, praised Mahan as one who "alone, among his biographers, has fully brought out the inner workings of Nelson's character" and said his criticism of Nelson was "just."[186] George Sydenham Clarke in *The Nineteenth Century* did think Mahan spent too much time on the affair, which he found "somewhat irritating," but he praised the book as being "a picture, drawn in fine lines by a master hand, in which the significance of the events chronicled stands out in true proportion." He rated it "the best life of Nelson that has yet appeared."[187] Seager's contention that "Mahan brought down on his head the polite laughter of British reviews" is simply a gross exaggeration.[188]

As with any work of history some reviewers had minor quibbles, and one amateur naval historian, Francis Badham, had a literary shootout with Mahan in the pages of the *English Historical Review,* but the book was generally lauded. Favorable reviews and personal letters poured in to Mahan. To correct some of the minor errors Mahan put out a second, revised edition in 1899. While Seager berates *Life of Nelson* not only for its alleged preaching but for attempting to fit Nelson into a rigid set of "universal principles and laws," not all modern historians take that cramped view.[189] Sumida, in an incisive analysis of *Life of Nelson* in his *Inventing Grand Strategy*, has a much clearer sense of what Mahan was striving for. "What really mattered to Mahan was Nelson's power of command." Mahan showed that Nelson embodied "the cardinal virtues of naval leadership," which were "intelligence, understanding of sound principles, and resolution." These lessons were timeless.[190]

CHAPTER 6

A PUBLIC CHRISTIAN

I n 1897 Mahan published *The Interest of America in Sea Power, Present and Future,* which consisted of a collection of previously published articles dating from December 1890 to October 1897.[1] Most of Mahan's later books were of this same type.[2] The book's most obvious relation to religion is Mahan's penchant for quoting Bible verses. These are too numerous to mention in their entirety, so one example will have to suffice. In "The Isthmus and Sea Power," which originally appeared in the October 1893 *Atlantic Monthly,* Mahan referred to U.S. foreign policy as "sounding brass and a tinkling cymbal" (1 Corinthians 13:1).[3] Most readers of that day would have recognized these quotes from the King James Version of the Bible right away. In "A Twentieth Century Outlook," which originally appeared in the September 1897 *Harper's Monthly,* Mahan revealed for the first time in print three significant ways his Christian faith impacted his view of history and contemporary events. One axiom that he seems never to have doubted, but was only now discussing, was that God controlled human history. This did not negate the importance of human will or action, but ultimately God was in control and in his "providence" decreed the working of events for his own purposes.[4] Mahan's second theme was that "Christian civilization" was the highest form of human society and that Christianity had to spread around the world. "The great task now before the world of civilized Christianity, its great mission, which it must fulfill or perish, is to receive into its own bosom and raise to its own ideals those ancient and different civilizations by which it is surrounded and outnumbered." He was speaking particularly of China, India, and Japan.[5] Despite the unfashionable nature of this view today—not to mention Mahan's unapologetic belief in the truth of Christianity and the superiority of Christian civilization—it should be pointed out that Mahan's view was not in any way based on a belief in *racial* superiority. He described himself as "[o]ne who believes that God has made of one blood all nations of men who dwell on the face of the whole earth" and decried any Christian who held "any movement of aversion to mankind outside his own race." That being such, he certainly believed that Christianity created the highest achieving and most moral type of society. He did, however, caution that Christian civilization (especially American and British) might become too materialistic and lose sight of the spiritual truths, in which case it is "limited in hope and love to this world, [and] I know not what we have to offer to save ourselves or others."[6]

Mahan's third theme was his belief in the inevitability of conflict and warfare as long as humans lived in this world. Based on his belief in original sin and the innate depravity of humankind, he believed that war was intrinsic to the human condition. This might be a deplorable fact of life, but because armed conflict was sometimes necessary to stop the spread of evil, the soldier's vocation, especially the Christian soldier's, was a noble one. "Conflict is the condition of all life, material and spiritual; and it is to the soldier's experience that the spiritual life goes for its most vivid metaphors and its loftiest inspirations."[7]

In the first chapter, "The Strategic Features of the Caribbean Sea and the Gulf of Mexico," which originally appeared in the October 1897 *Harper's Monthly*, Mahan concluded his discussion with another assertion that God, exercising "Personal Will," acted "throughout all time, with purpose deliberate and consecutive, to ends not yet discerned." In the context of this article, Mahan was claiming that Britain's naval supremacy since the time of Cromwell was not an accident but part of God's plan.[8] The reviews were generally favorable, though all discussed the historic, military, and diplomatic aspects of the articles rather than Mahan's few comments of a religious nature. Mahan's friend, Lieutenant Colonel Sir George Sydenham Clarke, wrote that Mahan was "brilliant," but he found the book a "disappointment."[9] Mahan did not take offense, and while he claimed that Clarke did not understand "my dominant ideas," he assured Clarke that "I do not find that you have transgressed towards me either as a reviewer or as a friend." Clarke saw numerous problems in the world and was not optimistic about their solutions. Interestingly, Mahan, even though a strong believer in the concept of original sin, took issue with this. "I don't know where you stand theologically, but it seems to me that the old reproach to the Israelites, that though they saw the *works* they did not know the *ways* after forty years, has its lesson for us today; and that too whether we accept a personal Providence, as I do, or whether not. Surely things get better rather than worse."[10] This may seem a surprising statement from one who believed human beings were by nature sinners, but his optimism was based entirely on God's works, not those of humankind. Mahan believed that God was working things out for his own ends, which by definition had to be good.

Even though *The Interest of America in Sea Power* was not nearly as significant a book as the Sea Power series or *Life of Nelson*, it was translated into Japanese (1899), French (1903), Italian (1904), and German (1909).[11] This was no doubt a sign of its author's increasing importance on the world naval scene.

On June 11, 1897, Alfred and Elly Mahan celebrated their silver wedding anniversary while they were summering at Slumberside in Quogue. The event filled Mahan with joy, as he wrote to his sister thanking her for her present.

Mahan in his fifties *(U.S. Naval Institute Photo Archive)*

> It is certainly something, not unparalleled but I fear rare, not only to have had twenty five years of happiness, but to find that the end is better than the beginning; that although youth is gone, at no time have things been so entirely well with us. For myself at least the indisposition to live my life over again is not from dissatisfaction with the past, but from firm enjoyment of the present. I should be inclined from my experience to say it is quite logical to put the golden wedding last—the golden age *is* last.[12]

Mahan also received an honorary LLD from Yale on June 30. As he had already received an LLD from Harvard, he remarked tongue-in-cheek to the family lawyer, "My law knowledge will soon be immense."[13]

As the Cuban crisis worsened and diplomatic relations with Spain deteriorated in the winter and spring of 1898, Mahan went ahead with plans to take his family to Europe for a vacation. He even withdrew Lyle early from his senior year at Groton so that he too could come. While doing so he assured "the

Rector," Endicott Peabody, how pleased he was "with the growth and development of Lyle's character and moral turn" which showed "the wholesome influence exerted by yourself and your associates."[14] Mahan must have been pleased with Lyle's academic work, too, as he had been accepted by Columbia University and would enter in the fall.[15]

Mahan had planned the vacation for a long time. It was to last six months, and as Lyle recalled, his father had "mapped out exactly" the itinerary.[16] The trip was scheduled to begin on March 26, but with war with Spain seemingly imminent after the sinking of the USS *Maine* on February 15, 1898, Mahan wondered if he ought to go. He might be recalled to active duty or his services might be needed in some other capacity. He was told by the Navy Department that there was no need to cancel the trip.[17]

Mahan, who has so often been maligned as an imperialist and a warmonger, took a calm attitude toward the sinking of the *Maine*. In a letter to his British friend, Colonel J. B. Sterling, he wrote, "The thought of treachery is not admissible until proved, and I myself do not see any indication of it as yet."[18] Only a week after the sinking Mahan gave a speech in Princeton to the New Jersey Chapter of the Society of the Cincinnati, advising them to "be very cautious in forming hasty conclusions in reference to such things as this disaster. People are liable to jump at conclusions at a great national crisis like this which might involve them seriously."[19]

Theodore Roosevelt, then occupying the key position of Assistant Secretary of the Navy, sought Mahan's views constantly and the two had a lengthy correspondence (some of which has been lost). Although Warren Zimmermann in *First Great Triumph* claims that "Mahan's views in reply were as hawkish as his own [Roosevelt's]," that does not actually seem to be the case. Mahan's replies to hypothetical tactical questions were not the same as expressing eagerness for a war to occur.[20]

The Mahans sailed for Europe as scheduled on March 26. While in Rome he learned that Congress had declared war on Spain on April 19. On April 25, while still in Rome, he received orders from Secretary Long recalling him to active duty and ordering him to report to Washington. An English reporter asked Mahan how long the war would last, and Mahan replied, "About three months," an accurate prediction.[21] Mahan set sail at once while his wife and children continued their trip as planned.

Mahan was appointed to the Naval War Board along with Adm. Montgomery Sicard and Capt. Arent Crowninshield. Three of its original members (including Theodore Roosevelt) had left it for combat commands. Mahan's duty, however, was considered active service, and a portrait of the Naval War Board shows him in uniform.[22] The board's duties were vaguely defined; Seager calls it "a peculiar cross between a college debating society and a War College faculty seminar."[23] Mahan himself thought it was a bad idea, and the day after reporting for duty he sent Long a memo recommending that the Naval War Board be abolished and replaced by "a single officer, to be known by such title as may seem convenient to designate his duties," something along the lines of a chief of staff or chief of naval operations. He thought that a board's accountability was too diffuse. He wanted to see one person in charge with "single, individual responsibility, which alone achieves results in war."[24] Long disagreed, but Mahan continued to push for a naval general staff for years.[25]

Mahan did yeoman work on the board, and while none of it could be considered earthshaking, he contributed much and learned much. In 1906 at the request of the Navy Department, he wrote a detailed report, "The Work of the Naval War Board of 1898," which also included his own judgment and critique of the board and the premises on which it functioned.[26]

It was the annexation of the Philippines as a result of the war that brought about a turning point in Mahan's thinking about American expansion. Though he was soon to acquire a reputation as an expansionist—even an imperialist— he was not one in 1898. Prior to the Spanish-American War his only interest in territorial expansion was the acquisition of Hawaii, which he strongly supported, but only because of its importance as a naval base that would be necessary if an isthmian canal was to be built. A canal would, like it or not, make America a Pacific power, and a base in Hawaii would be necessary to protect the West Coast. He had no interest in acquiring territory for its own sake or for its commercial value. His interest in Hawaii was strictly military.[27] He showed no interest in acquiring Cuba or in supporting the insurgents.[28]

Despite Julius Pratt's claim in *Expansionists of 1898* (1936) that Mahan was instrumental in setting the stage intellectually for the annexation of the Philippines, a claim many historians have repeated, Mahan was actually ambivalent about it.[29] His initial interest was in acquiring only a coaling or naval station, possibly Manila, Subic Bay, or Luzon.[30] While he later came to acceptance of annexation of the entire Philippine archipelago, he always remained ambivalent about it. Dewey's victory at Manila and what it portended took him by surprise. "It has opened a vista of possibilities which were not by me in the least foreseen." The unexpectedness of this development and the prospect of the duty it thrust upon the United States filled him with "awe" and provoked the thought that "the will of man seems to count for little."[31] He wrote to George Sydenham Clarke that he foresaw that "our nation will be forced to feel that we cannot abandon to any other the task of maintaining order in the land which we have been led to interpose. 'Chance' said Frederick the Great. 'Deus vult' [God wills it] say I."[32] The "any other" to which he referred was certainly Germany. The fear that Germany, which had ships observing in Manila Bay, had designs on the Philippines may also have pushed Mahan toward a total annexation position.[33] He remained lukewarm about annexation however. In 1900 he told the Alumni Club of the City College of New York that the United States had been "pitch-forked" into the Philippines, which did not necessarily preclude the possibility that God had done the pitchforking.[34] When writing his memoirs in 1907 he presented annexation as a duty "which must be accepted," saying that preserving "personal freedom to the private Philippine islander" was more important than political independence, though not incompatible with it.[35]

While Mahan was working on a new book, *Lessons of the War with Spain*, he was distracted yet again by problems with his brother Dennis. While serving on the USS *Badger*, Dennis was involved in an "unfortunate incident," the nature of which is not known, but whatever it was, it was bad enough that he was in danger of being court-martialed as well as being denied promotion to lieutenant commander. Alfred, usually not one to ask favors or indulge in special pleading, interceded on his brother's behalf and sought the help of Secretary Long. Alfred pointed out that Dennis had been ill "and had been given an opiate by the surgeon." He was also, according to Alfred, so disappointed that he had not been able to get into combat during the recent war that his health was affected. Alfred directly asked Long to quash the court-martial, not only on the grounds of showing mercy to Dennis but to prevent the Mahan name from being dragged through the mud. Alfred feared that the tabloids, especially William Randolph Hearst's *New York Journal* (for which Alfred refused to write even though offered a hefty fee), would enjoy getting some mileage out of a Mahanian embarrassment. Alfred's plea was based on two generations of the family's service to their country. "My father was long in the service of the country, and was the instructor of many of the bravest and best of its soldiers. Every one of his sons has belonged to one or the other of the strong arms of the Government, and all their days have stood ready to render faithful service." He also reminded Long that the name of Mahan "has become familiar to foreign navies, not to its own credit only, but also to that of the service with which it has been associated." He concluded by saying that the Mahan name "came to us untarnished from our father" and that he hoped the family's service "standing to our credit, may now serve to shield and protect the good name our father bore and gave to his children."[36] Long came through for the Mahans; there was no court-martial and Dennis even received his promotion. Alfred was grateful and wrote Long a letter of profuse thanks. He realized that Long was opening himself up to the charge of showing favoritism, and so he owed Long all the more gratitude. Presuming that Long had "an unwillingness to drag a name honorably connected to the Navy, through the mire of publicity" Mahan thanked him for his "mercifulness and kindness" and concluded, "I thank you with my whole heart for this relief from apprehension and anxiety."[37]

Even though he was busy with the war board and his writing, he began to take advantage of retirement and the opportunity it gave him to devote more time to church activities and writing on religious topics. Mahan got published in the religious press because of Silas McBee, who in 1896 became editor of the New York–based weekly Episcopal newspaper *Churchman* (not an official church publication). Though Mahan had been subscribing to *Churchman* for many years, he first made the acquaintance of McBee in May 1897. McBee wished to meet Mahan to discuss foreign missions. This was a subject that interested Mahan but on which he had no firsthand knowledge since he had met few missionaries, Anglican or otherwise, on his travels. It is not known whether the meeting actually took place though Mahan did invite McBee to his home.[38] While their relationship was not strong enough to be labeled a partnership, it was nonetheless a positive one despite their theological differences. McBee was a keen ecumenist and devotee of the social gospel movement, and Mahan most definitely was not, but they did have a common interest in world missions. Seager characterizes McBee as a "strong expansionist" though he neglects to mention that this was for missionary rather than political or military reasons, and he suggests that this was the main reason McBee was eager to publish Mahan in the pages of *Churchman*. This may or may not have been the case, but Mahan's writing for *Churchman* covered many topics besides missions and expansion. Certainly McBee did publish Mahan frequently starting in September 1899. At first the contributions were letters to the editor, but they expanded to include book reviews and articles.[39]

Mahan was reluctant at first to take on writing or speaking commitments "on religious subjects" for fear of not having enough time to work on his naval writing. "I should have no time to grow in my special line, which is sufficiently known." He stressed to McBee that his naval writing was his God-given vocation and that he tried to bring into it a Christian viewpoint, if appropriate. "As far as indications go, to treat a certain range of secular subjects, imparting to them, when it can be done without straining, a coloring consistent with religious thought, is the line marked out for me by Providence."[40] Mahan must have changed his mind quickly, though, since it was only a few days later that his first letter to the editor was published.[41]

Mahan was also now willing to involve himself in church controversies. One of these was the case of Charles A. Briggs, a Presbyterian minister and professor at Union Theological Seminary in New York. Briggs considered himself a staunch defender of higher criticism (a method of studying scripture from a literary and historical viewpoint as though it were like any other ancient document) and a militant opponent of "traditionalists," in Briggs' own phrase.[42] He was tried for heresy and acquitted, but was subsequently suspended by the General Assembly of his church in 1893. In 1898 he announced that he was seeking ordination as an Episcopal priest in the Diocese of New York.[43] Mahan was one of "several prominent churchpeople" who wrote letters of objection to Bishop Henry C. Potter, although the letters had no effect as the ordination took place on May 14, 1899.[44] While Mahan's role in this affair was minimal, it did show that he was not shy about making his views known to the bishop or protesting the bishop's action.

On the recommendation of Secretary of State John Hay, President William McKinley appointed Mahan as a member of the United States delegation to the First Hague Conference, held from May 16 to July 29, 1899. The other members of the delegation were Andrew Dickson White, diplomat and former president of Cornell University; Stanford Newell, U.S. minister to the Netherlands; Seth Low, president of Columbia University; Capt. William Crozier, U.S. Army; and George F. W. Holls, secretary and legal counsel to the delegation.[45] It was as a result of Mahan's participation in this conference that his views on war began to receive publicity as well as criticism in certain circles.

Called by Czar Nicholas II, the Hague Conference was a manifestation of a movement called universal arbitration (or "arbitration"), which was much in vogue at the time. The idea was that if international disputes could be arbitrated, war could be avoided. The advocates of this view wished to carry it one step further and make arbitration mandatory (which would, of course, entail setting up some sort of international tribunal to hear cases). Thus, if *all* international disputes could be subject to *mandatory* arbitration, war could be ended *forever*, or so it was thought. This idea appealed greatly to those who identified themselves as part of the burgeoning progressive movement, and particularly its religious wing, the social gospel movement. Many social gospelers and other progressives latched onto this notion with great enthusiasm because it suited their belief that humankind was progressing morally as well as materially and that war would become obsolete.

It is essential to understand Mahan's views on warfare as well as his critique of the social gospel movement. The social gospel movement, which was then in its heyday, attempted to make Christianity more relevant to social and economic problems. Mahan's objection, as stated in a 1903 article, was that the social gospel reversed the priority of the two great commandments; it elevated love of neighbor over love of God. Put another way, it focused the Christian's attention on "external benevolent activities" rather than on building a personal relationship with Jesus Christ. He considered this a "capital mistake." Not that Mahan was against benevolent activities—he was not although he strongly disapproved of the social gospelers' infatuation with socialism—but he thought they were the "fruit" of Christian life, not the essence of that life itself.[46]

Though he had not yet written about war from a Christian perspective, he seemed to have a fully formed view of it by this time. The starting point for understanding Mahan's view of war is not the nature of war itself, but rather the nature of humanity. Mahan believed in original sin, the doctrine that states that because of Adam and Eve's disobedience in the Garden of Eden, the entire human race (with the sole exception of Jesus) has an inborn predisposition to sin. All people sin and all are in need of a savior, and because humans are sinful they do bad things.[47] Violence, and eventually war, are the result. It is important to grasp that because of his theological views, Mahan did *not* view human nature as constantly improving, an idea that was a staple of progressive thought. Therefore, he thought war never could or would be eliminated, a view that was the basis of his argument with pacifists.

That all humans are sinful, so evident to Mahan from his study of scripture and history, did not in his view negate the existence of good in the world or the view that there might be relative levels of good and evil. Nor did it negate the necessity or utility of societal controls like government to keep to a minimum the damage that evil could do. This inevitably entailed government-sanctioned use of force.

Though Mahan does not cite Augustine of Hippo (354–430) in his writings, it is nonetheless clear that his views on war stem, at least indirectly, from Augustine's "just war" theory. This should not be surprising since Augustine's ideas could have come to Mahan from any number of sources. Most just-war theories, whether they spring directly from Augustine or not, are similar because they are all based on the same premise, namely the reality of original sin. The thrust of Augustine's argument is that while war is *an* evil, it is not *the worst* evil. In fact, war is sometimes necessary to prevent a worse evil. This does not mean that all wars are just. Augustine distinguishes among such factors as the reasons for the war, attempts made to avoid it, the means used to fight it, and the authority by which it is ordered. Basically Augustine says that war is permitted if it is authorized by a legitimate authority, is fought for a just reason (defense against direct aggression or to protect a weaker party), is used only as a last resort, and is fought by means proportional to attaining victory without spilling over into needless slaughter.[48] Mahan was in the same camp, and while he did not oppose arbitration on an ad hoc basis, he was opposed to mandatory arbitration.[49]

Undoubtedly, not all of the ninety-six delegates at the Hague Conference shared the lofty goals that it was ostensibly designed to reach. Many were experienced diplomats who were there simply to get the best deal they could for their nation in terms of arms limitations treaties. But a surprising number seemed to subscribe to the notion that even if war itself could not be outlawed, many of its nastier aspects could. Five of the six of the American delegates held to this view, the lone naysayer being Mahan. When President McKinley had appointed Mahan to the U.S. delegation, the other members were not altogether pleased because Mahan, alone among them, "had very little, if any, sympathy with the main purposes of the conference."[50] Those words were written by Andrew Dickson White, one of the American delegates. White kept a diary during the proceedings and it provides an illuminating view of both Mahan's role at the conference and White's constant frustration with his opposition to arbitration. White considered Mahan to be wedded to old-fashioned militaristic ideas and admitted to his diary that he was "embarrassed" by Mahan's retrograde views, although he considered Mahan "a man of the highest character and of great ability."[51]

Two issues in particular caused friction between Mahan and the more idealistic delegates. One was the attempt by the conference to ban the use of "asphyxiating bombs." Mahan's position was that such weapons had not been fully tested and developed, so any discussion of their use or the damage they could cause was purely hypothetical. He also argued that the United States should never prohibit itself from using a weapon out of misplaced idealism because a less scrupulous enemy was unlikely to be bound by such prohibitions. Finally he noted that other weapons currently used, including the torpedo, also brought their victims a horrible death, but no one was proposing to ban them.[52]

The second issue had to do with a proposal to allow neutral hospital ships to pick up survivors of naval engagements. Mahan thought this was an unfair use of neutrality and reasoned that a neutral ship voluntarily entering a war zone was not neutral at all. He believed it would avoid legal problems with neutral nations if hospital ships flew the flag of the nation to which they had offered their services.[53] This question became tied up with technical issues revolving around the legal definition of neutrality, which were not easily explained to the general public. Nonetheless Mahan came off looking hardhearted, as though he was opposed to rescuing drowning sailors.[54]

After he returned home in August 1899, even though he had a number of other projects in the works, he wrote "The Peace Conference and the Moral Aspect of War," which appeared in the October 1899 issue of *North American Review* (later reprinted in both *Lessons of the War with Spain* [1899] and *Some Neglected Aspects of War* [1907]). In this article Mahan maintained that the desire to end war by means of arbitration had a built-in fallacy that its advocates refused to recognize, namely that arbitration itself was a form of coercion. In Mahan's view, arbitration was even worse than war in that it coerces the conscience and binds it ahead of time to unforeseen situations.[55] Mahan also made the Augustinian point that it is moral for a state to go to war when "no other means of overcoming evil remains." War, which is not a good in itself, had achieved good things, for instance ending slavery in the United States, which measures short of war could not. One of the biggest fallacies of the advocates of arbitration was their assumption that war was the *worst* evil. To Mahan (as to Augustine) clearly it was not. Christianity did not require nations to relinquish the power of the sword in this world (a reference to Romans 13:4) and the use of that power was sometimes necessary to prevent a worse evil.[56]

Lessons of the War with Spain, and Other Articles was published in November 1899. The bulk of it was a series of articles titled "Lessons of the War with Spain," which had appeared in *McClure's* magazine from December 1898 to April 1899, along with a few other previously published articles including the aforementioned "The Peace Conference and the Moral Aspect of War." Apart from "Peace Conference," Mahan made a few points in other articles that are germane to the discussion. In "Lessons of the War with Spain" he mocked the panic that affected some on the East Coast who feared a Spanish invasion. Spain could barely defend its few remaining colonies let alone invade the United States, and Mahan ridiculed this fear as "unmeasured, irreflective, and therefore irrational." He blamed it, however, on "that false gospel of peace" that looks only to the preservation of physical comfort, and "in its argument against war strives to smother righteous indignation or noble ideals by appealing to the fear of loss and casting the pearls of peace before the swine of self-interest."[57] In another interesting article, "The Relations of the United States to their New Dependencies," which had originally appeared in, of all places, *Engineering magazine* in January 1899 under the title "American Duties to her New Dependencies," Mahan addressed directly for the first time America's new role as a colonial power. Mahan thought that the role had been "forced upon" the United States and not deliberately sought. The model the United States should follow was, not surprisingly, Great Britain, a "strong" and "beneficent" power, unlike Spain, which he characterized as "inhumanly oppressive" and "tyrannically exacting." The United States should look upon its new possessions "with their *yet* minor races" [emphasis added] as wards for whom we should do what is best.[58]

Not surprisingly, his views on warfare, indeed his very status as a military commentator, generated some unfavorable comments in social gospel circles, especially within its growing pacifist movement. Not all these critics were *absolute* pacifists, that is to say against all war at any time for any reason. Most, in fact, were not. Nevertheless, they were what could be termed *functional* pacifists. They did not oppose all wars that had been fought in the past; some they could identify as having been fought for a moral purpose. The most obvious example was the Civil War, which (at least from the Union perspective) they could see as good because it resulted in freeing the slaves. This should not be surprising when one considers that many of these social gospel pacifists considered themselves spiritual heirs of the abolitionists. What was turning them into functional pacifists at the beginning of the twentieth century was their belief that while war may once have had a moral purpose, that was no longer the case because humanity had morally evolved. War had become a relic of the barbarian past. It is immediately evident, then, why they found Mahan's views so objectionable.

In 1900, attorney Wallace Rice took on Mahan in the pages of a progressive magazine, *The Dial*. The attack seems to have been triggered by the publication of *Lessons of the War with Spain*, which contained a reprint of "The Peace Conference and the Moral Aspect of War." Rice considered Mahan a warmonger and a hypocrite for clothing his views in the garb of Christianity. Mahan, Rice said, "fails to show any higher notion of right than is held in the word might." This was not surprising, according to Rice, since Mahan's profession "is the art of killing his fellows." Just in case the reader did not get it the first time Rice repeated this charge at the end of the article. He was particularly incensed that Mahan saw war as having a moral justification and that Mahan even invoked the name of God. Rice did not agree with Mahan's view that a nation's acting in its own self-interest is compatible with the larger purposes of Providence. "Captain Mahan forgets the appeal to the national conscience and the God he has been invoking and says baldly: 'it [American expansion] is our interest.'" He concluded his review by reiterating that Mahan's "profession is the art of killing his fellows and that he is far too eager professionally to discern any of the possibilities of peace."[59] There is no indication that Mahan ever responded to this article.

One pacifist to whom he did respond was philanthropist Grace Hoadley Dodge, probably because she sent him a personal letter rather than attacking him in public. Unfortunately Dodge's letter to Mahan has been lost, but they had obviously corresponded previously, as Mahan makes reference in the first line of his response to "the time of my last writing." That must have been recently as the topic under discussion was his article in *North American Review*, "The Peace Conference and the Moral Aspect of War." Dodge was apparently going to publish some sort of book or pamphlet advocating arbitration and planned to include articles by delegates Seth Low and George Holls but nothing by Mahan. It is not clear why she actually wrote to him, but he told her that omitting his article did not rankle him because of "petty jealousy," but rather because the anti-arbitration viewpoint was "relegat[ed] to an inferior position of the moral side of the question" in her proposed publication. He told her that the pro-arbitration advocates were deluded in their belief that war was the worst of all evils. "The shocking evils of war have so impressed their imaginations, that they fail to recognize its moral character. Yet worse things can happen to a man—far worse—than to be mangled by a shell, or to a nation than to be scourged by war." He reminded her "that there are contingencies which do not admit arbitration" and unless the pro-arbitration lobby admitted this "I do not believe you will have scored a step in the nation's advance."[60]

Two current wars were also preoccupying Mahan at the moment, the first being the Philippine Insurrection led by Emilio Aguinaldo against U.S. occupation. While Mahan had no doubt that military force must be used to put down the rebellion, he was not the hard-charging imperialist that some critics make him out to be. Nor did he view the Filipinos as an inferior race whose lot in life was to be ruled by their betters. Mahan preferred to view America's new possessions as dependencies, not colonies, the distinction being that a colony could someday "become incorporated into the mother country." The formerly Spanish possessions clearly, in his view, did not fit that category. He viewed the Filipinos as a type of dependent who needed looking after and thought that Army and Navy officers were "the best possible guardians," better than politicians, because they were used to dealing with enlisted men.[61] This may sound paternalistic, and certainly Seager thinks so, but it warrants notice that nowhere does Mahan say that the Filipinos are racially inferior or inherently incapable of self-government.[62] What he actually says is that they are "in the childhood state of development."[63] Mahan had made a similar comment to Daniel Gilman, president of Johns Hopkins University, when he wrote, "Races, like men, have a childhood."[64] More will be said on Mahan's use of the word "race," but the obvious should be pointed out here, namely that childhood is not a permanent condition. Mahan viewed these dependencies as fully capable of maturing.

In a letter to Theodore Roosevelt, Mahan used the phrase "naturally treacherous," which Seager makes much of to show that Mahan was a paternalistic Anglo-Saxon supremacist who viewed the Filipinos as ungrateful wards who needed a pat on "their empty, noble, and soon-to-be baptized heads." That they would be naturally treacherous and noble at the same time is a puzzle, but in any case the letter to Roosevelt is a bit more nuanced than Seager acknowledges. First of all, it is not clear whether "naturally treacherous" refers to all Filipinos or just those in the insurrection. That it may be the latter is indicated by Mahan's later use of the phrase "petty chiefs, impatient of restraint" to describe those rebelling against U.S. rule. But whatever the shortcomings of the Filipinos, they were explained by Mahan as the result of "hav[ing] endured Spanish soldiery [for] three centuries."[65]

Mahan also played a minor role in facilitating the creation of an Episcopal diocese for the Philippines. He was elected a member of the Episcopal Church's Board of Missions in 1900, replacing the recently deceased Cornelius Vanderbilt II. He was also an active member of the Church Club of New York, an association of Episcopal laymen.[66] Mahan and another member, Francis Greene, were instrumental in getting the Church Club of New York (and other church clubs around the country) to petition the General Convention, due to meet in October 1901, to set up a missionary Diocese of the Philippines and appoint a bishop. New York's Bishop Potter was an enthusiastic proponent of the idea and raised $1,500 for the bishop's salary and $25,000 for a permanent endowment, while the Church Club of New York raised a further $13,000. Charles Henry Brent was chosen as the first bishop, and Mahan sent a glowing letter to Navy Secretary Long introducing Brent and urging Navy cooperation in Brent's efforts, "so far as it can be properly extended . . . for both Bishop Brent and his future work I personally have the utmost value."[67]

It would be useful here to discuss Mahan's use of the word "race," since that word is used so frequently in his books. It is also an issue that needs clarification, because some writers have accused Mahan of being a racist.[68] Mahan used the term "race" frequently, and he has been often misunderstood. Simply put, Mahan was not a racist as that term is used today, meaning someone who views certain groups as inferior based on inherent and inherited genetic traits and physical characteristics. Mahan did not use the term "race" in that way. Occasionally he used it to mean the human race, but most often he used "race"—as did many of his contemporaries—to mean what we would call today nationalities or ethnic groups. Most importantly, the distinctions among them were based not on biology, but on culture, and therefore were changeable, not permanent. So while Mahan, for example, did believe that Anglo-Saxon civilization was superior, this was a cultural judgment—mainly based on law, politics, and religion—rather than a biological one.[69] Mahan himself viewed as unchristian any notion of biologically based prejudice. In a reference to Acts 17:26 he said, "One who believes that God has made of one blood all nations of men who dwell on the face of the whole earth cannot but check and repress, if he ever feels, any movement of aversion to mankind outside his own race."[70] He also addressed this same issue in a letter to the *Times* of London in 1913. "Personally, I entirely reject any assumption or belief that my race is superior to the Chinese or to the Japanese. My own suits me better, probably because I am used to it, but I wholly disdain, as unworthy of myself or of them, any thought of superiority."[71]

Likewise, based on biblical reasons, Mahan did not share in the casual anti-Semitism so common in his day. Abraham, because of his faith, was "the father, begetter, of all them that believe whether Jew or Gentile."[72] Mahan said of himself, "I am without anti-Semitic feeling. That Jesus Christ was a Jew covers his race for me."[73]

Mahan's first publication in *Churchman* was in September 1899. This was the first of many contributions to that paper, which continued until his death. Though printed as a letter to the editor, it was written in response to a request from the editor, Silas McBee, to comment on George Parkin's review of David Starr Jordan's book *Imperial Democracy*.[74] Parkin was a Canadian scholar, well-known imperialist, and defender of the British Empire. Jordan, the president of Stanford University, was a peace activist and anti-imperialist. Mahan had not read Jordan's book, so did not feel qualified to comment on it, but he did make some general comments on the expansion issue from a Christian perspective. In the letter, he made a key point about himself and his view of the role of the state. First of all, he stressed that his views of all things "depend upon my convictions as a Christian and a Churchman—the strongest convictions that I entertain; for to me the Church is a greater fact than any State, and Christianity is more than any political creed." The thrust of his argument then turned to the duties and opportunities of the state when confronted with possession of new "dependencies." The state, an institution ordained by God, has certain duties just as the church and individual Christians do. Because the state as such is not Christian, the duties may not be as clear-cut, especially regarding the new dependencies. Mahan saw it as logical and scriptural, however, to see "the divine hand" at work in bringing the peoples of the dependencies under American control. Mahan is clear on the point that recent events do not "constitute a call to expansion," only that "the future of several peoples, heretofore unused to, and probably not yet fit for, self-government, is not to be solved, Christianly, by washing our hands and sending them about their business." The question, he readily admitted, was a complicated one and would not be solved by platitudes, "stock phrases," and "political proverbs." The Christian should not be discouraged, but should pray and seek the Holy Spirit's guidance.[75] This letter shows, if nothing else, that Mahan was not the jingoistic expansionist of stereotype, but a much more nuanced thinker from both a religious and political perspective.

Mahan also watched closely another war taking place at this time, the Boer War (1899–1902). This resulted in numerous letters to the editors of various New York newspapers, four articles, three of which were later reprinted in several of his books, and one book, *The Story of the War in South Africa, 1899–1900*.[76] It is no surprise that with his strong anglophilia and so many friends in the British armed forces, Mahan would side with Britain, but to assume that he did so unreflectively is not accurate. When the war first started he admitted that he was "painfully ignorant of the details of the matter" and that it was important to "keep an eye on the facts" before jumping to a conclusion. He was disturbed, though, that some newspapers, including the *New York Times* were siding with the Boers without knowing all the facts and were taking a "truculent" attitude toward Britain. "If Great Britain is wrong, by all means let us have the truth, but the disposition seems to be to prejudge, and to *assume* that the cause of essential justice is that of the Boers [emphasis in original]."[77]

In an article in the March 1900 issue of *North American Review*, "Merits of the Transvaal Dispute," Mahan concluded that the British were meeting the criteria of a just war and were acting out of the "highest moral duty."[78] Mahan was particularly incensed that Americans of Irish descent, invariably Democrats, were speaking out against the British and urging the United States to offer to mediate the dispute. Mahan was convinced that they were doing this solely out of anti-British spite, not because they cared about the Boer cause.[79] Mahan felt strongly that the United States should stay out of the fray and not do anything to antagonize the British, who had been true friends, particularly in supporting the United States in the war against Spain. "The importance of good-feeling between U.S. and G.B. is so great, and her service to us two years since so marked, that misdirected abuse by us will be most regrettable and ungrateful."[80] He was also annoyed that American anti-imperialists who were against the U.S. presence in the Philippines were claiming that the two situations were analogous and were using anti–Boer War feeling to stir up opposition to the U.S. war against the Philippine rebels.[81] Mahan thought the Boer government was "a corrupt and oppressive oligarchy" and was especially angered when Boer representatives came to America to drum up support for their cause. He wrote to the pro-Boer *New York Evening Sun* that the Boers were "like babies" in their complaining. The editor published the letter under the headline "Captain Mahan in Savage Mood."[82] Mahan's support was certainly appreciated in British government and military circles and by friends such as Vice-Admiral Bouverie Clark and Field Marshal Lord Roberts.[83]

While not directly related to his support of the Boer War—though that surely did not hurt—in May 1900 Mahan received the Chesney Gold Medal from the council of the Royal United Service Institution for his contribution to the British Empire through his Sea Power series and *Life of Nelson*. The medal was sent to him by the Duke of Cambridge, president of the RUSI. In his letter of thanks to the prince, Mahan said, "I value even more highly [than being awarded the medal], if that be possible, the assurance that in such competent judgment, my works have contributed in some degree to the welfare of the British Empire, the strength of which is so essential to the cause of our English-speaking race, and of mankind in general."[84]

In 1900 Mahan published *The Problem of Asia and Its Effect upon International Policies*, also a collection of previously published articles. Part I, "The Problem of Asia," was based on a series of articles that had been published in *Harper's*, while Part II, "Effect of Asiatic Conditions on World Policies," and Part III, "Merits of the Transvaal Dispute," appeared in *North American Review*. From a religious point of view there are a number of interesting points Mahan made in this book. It is easy to see some elements of this book as racist, as Seager clearly does, but one must remember that Mahan used the word "race" in a cultural, not a biological, sense. Mahan divided the world into three major racial groups, which he called the Slavic, the Asiatic, and the Teutonic.[85] The Teutonic included Britain, the United States, and Germany. But Mahan was willing to include the Japanese in that category as well, or at least suggested that if they were not there yet, they soon would be. While Seager ridicules the notion of turning the Japanese into Teutons, likening it to Hitler's making the Japanese "honorary Aryans," it would seem to indicate that not only were Mahan's categories not biological, but that they were fluid, not fixed. As the Japanese became Europeanized, they were "repeating the experience of our Teutonic ancestors."[86] Most important to Mahan in this process was the acceptance of Christianity. He was hopeful—overly so—at the prospect of Christianizing Japan and thought it key to that nation's development as a major sea power.[87]

As for the Chinese, they needed to be Christianized too, though the situation of missionaries was precarious during the Boxer Rebellion, which was taking place as Mahan wrote these articles. As a keen supporter of foreign missions, Mahan felt strongly that Christian preaching should be allowed in China. He defended this on free speech grounds. No Chinese should be compelled to listen, however. The Chinese government's animus against Christian missionaries was "absurd" and would only hinder China's advancement, which he equated with adopting "the mental and moral equipment of European civilization."[88]

The Slavs (meaning Russia), while Christian, were backward politically because of their form of government, an absolute monarchy, which Mahan referred to as "Czardom." Its size, its "immense population," and its expansionist impulse all gave Mahan a "deep-rooted distrust" of Russia.[89] While he viewed Russia as the natural enemy of both Britain and Germany, he also thought, in the long run, that "the hallowing traditions of a common Christianity" would provide the "common spirit" to assimilate the races to each other. Such sentiments may seem unrealistic, but he had faith in the reconciling power of Christianity.[90]

These views hardly square with the stereotype of Mahan as either a racist or a cultural imperialist. While he clearly wished the Asians would become Christians—and probably wished the Russians would become Anglicans—he did not believe that a common Christian culture required "the merging of national characteristics."[91] Those who label Mahan a social Darwinist ignore his faith, not only in the unifying aspect of Christianity, but also in his belief that the strength of the United States (and Britain as well) "rests in the common political and legal tradition" that can absorb and assimilate "all other social and racial types with which it has been brought into political association."[92] The "Asian peoples," Mahan believed, needed to be brought "within the compass of the family of Christian states; not by fetters and bounds imposed from without, but by regeneration promoted from within."[93]

The year 1901 also saw the publication of *Types of Naval Officers*, a study of six British admirals from the age of sail, each of whom embodied a certain characteristic. Four of the chapters had previously been published as articles. Of most interest for our purposes is the chapter on Sir Edward Pellew, later Lord Exmouth. Although Sir James Saumarez is briefly mentioned as a very religious man, Pellew is the only one whose religious beliefs Mahan discusses. Although Mahan mildly criticizes Pellew's "narrow Protestant feeling," which manifested itself in a shrill anti-Catholicism, Mahan was full of admiration for Pellew's deep faith. "Lord Exmouth was a deeply religious man. Strong as was his self-reliance in war and tempest, he rested upon the Almighty with the dependence of a child upon its father." Mahan also pointedly remarked, lest any reader think religious faith was not compatible with the demands of a military life, that these admirals of strong Christian faith such as Pellew, Saumarez, and "our own Farragut" were "lion-hearted, masculine men who had passed their lives amid the storms of the elements and of battle."[94]

Once retired from the Navy, Mahan began public speaking on religion at church and sometimes secular events. He also now had more time to devote to one of his favorite organizations, the Church Missionary Society for Seamen, later known as the Seamen's Church Institute (SCI). He had joined the organization in

1867 and was a member of the Board of Managers from 1867 to 1896, served as corresponding secretary in 1897 and 1898, and was lay vice president from 1898 to 1914. He became a patron in 1875, which meant he contributed at least $100 every year.[95] Retirement gave him more time to devote to the organization, and he often addressed their meetings and gave fund-raising pitches to other church audiences. His first recorded address for the SCI was given on April 10, 1897. It is not documented where the speech was given or to whom, though it was most likely an Episcopal church audience. Mahan opened his address with an affecting description of the merchant seaman, far from home, friendless in New York City, and prone to find enticing vices. "He arrives a wanderer, flits for a few days through the streets, and then, again a wanderer, he departs." If young he is particularly vulnerable to "the beginnings of evil." Mahan said, "Men who are not touched by this will be troubled by nothing." In requesting a generous response from donors, Mahan also noted that these seamen are not merely objects of charity, but through their profession they contribute to the wealth of the city.[96]

He also addressed the annual meeting of the society in December 1898 and urged the Episcopal Church to add a third field of missionary activity; along with foreign and domestic should be added the sea. "When the Church as a body recognizes that the sea as well as the land demands her motherly care, that she should seek to build up the character of seamen by spreading among them the light of the gospel, the need for the separate and highly specialized effort of our Society may cease." Unfortunately, the church at large "pay[s] little heed to seamen" and so the work of the SCI was essential, providing the men with material as well as spiritual sustenance and giving them an alternative to the usual temptations. "Help is asked to maintain and extend this beneficent work. Whose duty is it to aid?"[97]

He gave another address to the SCI in March 1902 titled "The Well Being of the Seaman in Port." Bishop Potter was in attendance. One of the purposes of this address was to raise money to purchase a launch to facilitate the SCI's work in protecting the mariners from crimps. Crimp was a general term denoting anyone in port who took advantage of a seaman, particularly cheating him out of his money. Crimps would often sail out to meet incoming ships and loan sailors money at exorbitant rates. They also used to steer seamen to boarding houses or saloons that charged high rates, and worked to get seamen drunk or drugged in order to then rob them. The SCI's president, the Reverend Archibald Mansfield, thought that if the SCI had a launch that could also go out to meet the ships he could put a dent in the crimps' activity. Mahan's speech was to help achieve this goal. While pointing out that mariners' working and living conditions had improved, the seamen still needed wholesome recreation and spiritual sustenance. But it was time to take a more aggressive role in counteracting the crimps; "we have a certain aggressive warfare to carry on against those whose livelihood depends largely on anticipating our benevolent work, getting hold of the seamen before they know where they are and manipulating their stay in port to their own pecuniary gain." The new launch would "extend our sphere of operations, aggressive and protective."[98] The funds were raised and the SCI purchased a launch, which was named *Sentinel*.[99] When in 1906 Mansfield thought the SCI needed a new and shorter name it was Mahan who suggested the new name, Seamen's Church Institute.[100]

Mahan also began speaking to Episcopal parishes. In March 1899 he spoke at Holy Trinity Church in Brooklyn. This was something of an emotional speech, especially for someone as introverted as Mahan, because he emphasized his personal experience of the Christian faith and the trustworthiness of God. This was a significant event for him as he considered it his first *public* testimony.[101] The main thrust of the address was that he knew from "*personal* experience of the battle of life" that Christianity was true [emphasis in original].[102] The personal (or experiential) did not negate the intellectual. He explained that he based his life "upon a full intellectual acceptance of the Christian faith, as explicitly set forth in the historic creeds—the Apostles' and the Nicene Creeds. In those, and in the Word of God, I have found, and find, not merely comfort and strength but intense intellectual satisfaction." But this was not enough for a complete Christian life. One needed a personal relationship with God and this could come only through the gift of the Holy Spirit. Intellect alone could not account for this. Any positive effect his address might have on his hearers would itself be the work of the Holy Spirit. Mahan also mentioned several times the phrase "thirty years" referring to the length of time he had been a believer, though he did not explicitly mention if this refers to his conversion experience at the age of twenty-nine.[103] He concluded with "the reiteration of my sure and joyful confidence, that I have tried God these many years and found Him ever faithful," and rejoiced "that once at least I am able publicly to lay at His feet in words—however poor my deeds—that all that I have, all that I am, all that I have accomplished, has been of Him and through Him."[104] This address is a powerful testimony; one could even call it evangelical, albeit of the dignified stiff-upper-lip variety.

Later that same month Mahan gave an address at the Church of the Holy Trinity in Middletown, Connecticut. This address, titled "The Practical in Christianity," was included in the 1910 edition of Mahan's own religious work, *The Harvest Within*. Though more theological than the previous address, it was still highly personal, with a reference to the "thirty years," a personal relationship with God, and the importance of the Holy Spirit. Mahan again emphasized "the intellectual satisfaction that I derive from God's word" but, of course, stressed that "only through Christ" does he know anything at all. This speech emphasized more the importance of the sacraments (baptism and holy communion) as a means of having union with Christ. There can be no real Christian life, he said, "disunited from Christ's person" and "[o]ur spiritual life depends absolutely on union with Him."[105] The main thrust of the address was to argue against the currently popular notion that there was a distinction between practical or moralistic (good) Christianity and dogmatic (bad) Christianity. Mahan argued that there was no such distinction within a proper understanding of Christianity. The "formulation of Christian Truth—which is dogma" is "the solid foundation on which alone the scheme of Christian morality securely rests." Right knowledge leads to right action, but the knowledge of which he speaks is not knowledge about God, but personal union with Jesus Christ. The truly "*practical* Christian" is the one who is united to Christ in faith and draws all strength from him "Whose power has never failed [emphasis in original]."[106]

Mahan was always an active church member regardless of where he lived. His daughter Ellen listed nine Episcopal parishes that she remembered attending.[107] Two have already been discussed, St. George's in New York City and

Mahan with grandson Alfred Thayer Mahan II (*Naval Historical Collection, Naval War College*)

St. John's in Newport, Rhode Island. We have already discussed St. George's in the context of Lyle's baptism and Helen's confirmation, both of which took place at Trinity, Wall Street, instead of St. George's, the parish to which the Mahans belonged. There seemed to be some sort of dissatisfaction with the rector, William Rainsford. This may have been because of the rector's involvement with the social gospel movement, of which Mahan disapproved, or it may have been because of a more personal reason, as was hinted at in the dispute over Helen's confirmation. At this point, then, it may be useful to lay to rest a canard about Mahan. In his *Naval Aristocracy* Karsten, clearly no fan of Mahan nor of the Episcopal Church, claims that Mahan resigned from the vestry (which Karsten calls a "parish board") of Trinity Church because the "pastor appointed a workingclass layman to the parish board as a democratic measure." He compares Mahan unfavorably to J. Pierpont Morgan, who "confined himself to a written protest" while Mahan "felt compelled to resign."[108] Karsten cited as his source a book by sociologist E. Digby Baltzell, *Philadelphia Gentlemen: The Making of a National Upper Class*, published in 1958.[109] Baltzell tells essentially the same story but identifies the parish as St. George's and the rector as Rainsford. He says Mahan resigned from the vestry when Rainsford put a "member of the working class" on the vestry, but cited no source for this claim.[110] Baltzell had the correct parish and rector where there was, indeed, a dispute over having working-class representation on the vestry. There was even a resignation, but it was not Mahan's. In fact the story is completely untrue for the simple reason that Mahan was never on the vestry at St. George's.[111] The resignation was from none other than the senior warden, J. Pierpont Morgan (although the rector talked him out of it), and Rainsford himself related this story in his memoirs.[112]

What is the source of this canard against Mahan? For it surely is a canard, suggesting both snobbery and hypocrisy. Since Baltzell gave no source, the trail ends there. We will never know why Baltzell confused Mahan with J. P. Morgan. A more interesting question is why Karsten accepted Baltzell's story at face value without checking for a source or even noting that there was none. One can only surmise that Karsten was perhaps a little too eager to accept an anecdote that portrayed Mahan in a bad light without checking its veracity. The only vestries Mahan served on were St. John's, Newport, and Church of the Atonement, Quogue, where he became senior warden, the highest lay position in an Episcopal parish.[113]

In 1902 Mahan was elected president of the American Historical Association (AHA), of which he had been a member probably since 1894 or 1895. He was one of the original subscribers to the association's journal, the *American*

Historical Review (*AHR*), but rarely wrote for it, even though invited, mainly because the journal paid so poorly compared to the high rates he could earn from commercial publications. He also had his own set of rules about which books he would or would not review. He would not review books by people he disliked, nor would he review bad books by people he did like![114] Nonetheless in 1901 he was offered the vice presidency of the AHA, accepting on the condition that when he succeeded to the presidency (as was the practice in the AHA) he would not have any administrative duties. He had always found these "distasteful" and wanted to devote himself to his writing "without distraction."[115] But the offer of the vice presidency with its assumption of succession to the presidency was "more than acceptable, more than welcome to me and I thank you for it very sincerely."[116]

Mahan did succeed to the presidency and on December 26, 1902, at the annual meeting held in Philadelphia, delivered his presidential address, titled "Subordination in Historical Treatment." It was published in the AHA *Annual Report*, but never in the *AHR* because it had already been promised to *Atlantic Monthly*, where it appeared under the title "The Writing of History" in the March 1903 issue. It was later reprinted in Mahan's *Naval Administration and Warfare* (1908) and is considered Mahan's most explicit explanation of his philosophy of history.[117]

After some disclaimers about his lack of academic credentials and his coming to the study of history "late in life" and as part of his "past profession," he got to the gist of his argument, which was that the accumulation of facts for their own sake was a useless endeavor. The facts had to be "subordinated" by "selective grouping" to the "one dominant thought or purpose of the designer."[118] In Mahan's own work this was, of course, the Sea Power books. "Facts, however explanative and laboriously acquired, are but the bricks and mortar of the historian." The purpose of history was not to accumulate facts or even to arrange them in a narrative, but to enlighten the "man in the street" so that he could learn something significant, particularly what errors to avoid. To not do so was to fail in the historian's duty.[119]

More pertinent to our purposes was Mahan's open declaration that God ruled human history and worked it out for his own purposes. History itself was the "plan of Providence" and each event "becomes as it were a fully wrought and fashioned piece, prepared for adjustment in its place in the great mosaic, which the history of the [human] race is gradually fashioning under the Divine overruling." The study of history, properly done, "will present a majestic ideal unity corresponding to the thought of the Divine Architect, realized to His creature."[120]

Seager mocks this address, seeming to forget—or choosing to ignore—that Mahan was a man of his times. The providential theme was not that unusual, nor considered unprofessional, in that day. In 1937 Julius Pratt analyzed that aspect of the speech as seriously as the other aspects. While Pratt raised philosophical and analytical questions about Mahan's approach, he accepted Mahan's "religious prepossessions" as a legitimate approach to history. Pratt acknowledged that Mahan's faith was key to understanding his writings, but he did not see that as detracting from their value. His main criticism of the presidential address was that Mahan did not recognize "that each human generation might find a new significance in the same historical episode."[121] Theology aside, Seager also does not seem to recognize that Mahan's subordinationist ideas were common at the time as part of the "speculative" approach to history, the search for the One Big Idea that explains much if not everything.[122] Even though Mahan was not impressed with most academic historians, claiming they made simple concepts too complicated, his contemporaries in the academic world generally viewed him respectfully.[123]

In his discussion of "Subordination," Seager discusses probable influences on Mahan's philosophy of history. One was Edward Meyrick Goulburn's *Thoughts on Personal Religion* (1865), which Mahan first read as a young man on the *Iroquois*. Years later he told his daughter Helen that this book "more than any other has affected my spiritual life." This work "lies unseen among the foundations of my best thought."[124] The influence here is quite plausible, as Goulburn had said, "The first thing to be done by a person bent upon studying any large subject such as History . . . is to limit the field of his researches, and draw a circle around it." One can see the relation to Mahan's idea of subordination.[125] While Seager ridicules Goulburn for his Christian orthodoxy, he reserves his strongest invective for the alleged influence of Milo Mahan's numerology theories on Alfred's thought. Seager devotes six pages of his biography of Mahan to explicating Milo's theory of divine numerology, insisting it was the source of Alfred's theory of subordination. The implication is that Milo's theory was nonsense and, therefore, so was Alfred's.[126]

In 1863 Milo published a book titled *Palmoni; or, The Numerals of Scripture*. This was followed by a sequel, *Mystic Numbers*, published in 1875. Both these books were examples of biblical numerology, the searching of scripture for patterns of numbers and mathematical relationships that were thought to prove the divine authorship of the universe and explain the course of human history. Palmoni was the Hebrew noun used in Daniel 8:13 that in the marginal note of the King James Version was rendered as "the numberer of secrets."[127]

Seager both exaggerates the eccentricity of numerology in the nineteenth century and asserts without evidence that it had a major influence on Alfred. There have always been factions within Christianity that have seized on numerology as the key to understanding scripture and world events, even continuing to the present day, as a search of the Internet confirms. Certainly today this study is confined to fringe groups that are considered beyond the pale of legitimate theological scholarship, but it was not always so. In the nineteenth century numerology had respectable adherents and, while not exactly mainstream, was nonetheless considered a legitimate field of inquiry. Milo himself was influenced by Henry Browne's *Ordo Saeclorum: A Treatise on the Chronology of the Holy Scriptures* (1844). A British theologian, Francis Hooper, also published a book titled *Palmoni* in 1851, with the subtitle *An Essay of the Chronological and Numerical Systems in Use Among the Ancient Jews.* That the book was published by Oxford University Press is an indication that the topic was considered legitimate scholarship. It is not known if Milo was aware of or had read Hooper's book.[128]

More to the point is Seager's assertion that Alfred was strongly influenced by *Palmoni* and *Mystic Numbers*, which through guilt by association would make Alfred as much of a kook as Seager thinks Milo was. The problem with this claim is that there is no evidence for it. We do not even know if Alfred read *Palmoni* or *Mystic Numbers*, and even if we grant for the sake of argument that Alfred read *all* his uncle's works there is still no evidence that he ever voiced an opinion of these two books. He never mentions either in his correspondence or his memoirs. Seager surely knew this or he would have cited a source if it existed.[129] The only time Alfred ever expressed any interest in numerology was when he was a young officer aboard the *Iroquois* and made a diary entry expressing his confusion about "the received chronology of the Bible" and a "discrepancy" he had found. This entry was dated January 10, 1869. *Palmoni* was published in 1863. If he consulted his uncle's book, or was even aware of it, he did not mention it.[130] That both Milo and Alfred believed that God was the creator of the universe and that the universe ran in an orderly manner was hardly shocking. It did not mean that numerology had any influence on Alfred.

It may well be that Alfred was more influenced by Milo's *The Spiritual Point-of-View* (1863), a response to the allegedly heretical writings of John William Colenso, the Anglican bishop of Natal. Colenso held a number of unorthodox views (including that Christians should tolerate African polygamy), but his notoriety rested on a series of treatises he wrote on the Pentateuch (the first five books of the Old Testament), the book of Joshua, and Paul's epistle to the Romans, in which he denied the historical accuracy of the Bible. Many theologians, including Milo, wrote refutations. Milo's was titled *The Spiritual Point-of-View; or, The Glass Reversed: An Answer to Bishop Colenso*. Milo defended the scriptures as infallible but maintained that not everything in them had the same importance. Not all parts had the same function or were equally edifying. The key was to understand that the Bible was "infallibly true from the spiritual point of view."[131]

For our purposes what is most interesting are Milo's comments on history, which show a much more sophisticated understanding than Seager gives him credit for. Milo criticized Colenso for imposing nineteenth-century standards of history, "modern, rationalistic, matter-of-fact," on ancient peoples who had a different understanding of what history was, and then finding them wanting. Milo likewise saw no conflict between science and faith, concluding that God did not need to reveal everything about the physical universe all at once.[132] While there is no fully developed philosophy of history in the book, Alfred may have gotten more out of it than he would have from the complex formulae of *Palmoni*.

In June 1903 Mahan delivered the commencement address at Dartmouth College. He was also awarded a Doctor of Laws degree at the ceremony.[133] The address was titled "Personality and Influence." It was a long speech taking up eleven and a half pages in *Letters and Papers*.[134] The gist of it was that the "spirit of the age" was an "impulse towards concentration and organization of power." One saw this in the political, economic, and social realms. Mahan thought this trend was dangerous since it quashed individual freedom, initiative, and independence and concentrated power in the hands of a few. It also fostered a sense of helplessness in the face of unstoppable forces. Mahan believed the way to counteract this was to recognize and act upon the force of personality. Personality was "the supreme moral influence, itself of mixed good and evil" that each person possessed but needed to cultivate and use. He told the graduates they were "not impotent playthings of fortune, but actors in a series of events, great and small." Everyone needed a moral purpose in life, and in order to use one's life for good one had also to preserve individuality and independence.[135]

In the second half of the speech he transitioned to a religious theme, stating that it was "not the assertion of personality, but its consecration" that was the "theme" of the address. Personality (or individualism) without a high moral character was not only useless but dangerous. A good personality manifests itself in good action; "what a man is, that he does." The highest way to consecrate the personality was to be in "the service of God," and the best way to do that was to follow the way of Jesus Christ, "the August Personality whose influence upon our civilization transcends that of all others." This was not an overtly evangelistic address since Mahan was not, at least directly, urging the audience to seek a

personal relationship with Christ. Instead he focused more on the positive influence of Christianity on civilization and the influence of individual Christians on
their societies. In a more subtle way, though, he was encouraging that kind of
relationship since he stressed the primacy of faith as the source of good works
and the necessity of "Faith, Hope, Love" (1 Corinthians 13:13) in forming a
good character. None of this, he suggests, is possible without knowing Jesus.
"We shall be like Him, when we shall see Him as He *is*" (1 John 3:2) (emphasis
in original).[136] We also get a clue to his view of reforming society when he said
in his closing paragraph, "We shall never regenerate mankind unless we see success in the regeneration of its units [i.e., individuals]" and that can only come
through growth in the Christian life.[137]

On February 4, 1904, the Russo-Japanese War began. Much of it was fought
at sea, and even though Mahan had not followed it closely he was commissioned to write articles on it for *Collier's* and *National Review*. These gave him
an opportunity to earn some ready cash, which proved useful as he and his
family took two trips to Europe from 1904 to 1906.[138] Mahan was hampered in
his analysis by lack of firsthand information and had to rely entirely on press
accounts. While this was not ideal from a historian's perspective, it was something Mahan could relate to as a naval officer, since a military commander often
had to make decisions based on incomplete knowledge. "It is indispensable to
get the fullest data that can be had . . . but it is no less indispensable than to
go forward, working from the basis of what has been learned, however imperfectly, and advancing tentatively, but finally towards the solution of the difficulty
immediately in hand."[139]

Mahan's view of the war (and Japan's defeat of Russia at the Battle of
Tsushima) was ambivalent. He was not sorry to see Russia receive a comeup-
pance in Asia, and he thought some of Japan's grievances were legitimate. But
he was also concerned about the emergence of Japan as a rival to U.S. interests,
particularly given anti-American rioting that had taken place in Japan following the Treaty of Portsmouth (negotiated by Theodore Roosevelt), which ended
the war.[140]

Mahan was also concerned about Japanese immigration to America, a
hotly contested issue at the time. Seager tries to make Mahan appear racist, but
Mahan's views were much more nuanced. It bears repeating that Mahan's prejudices were actually cultural, not racial. His concern was over assimilation, not
racial superiority as such.

The issue of Japanese emergence as a great power was a controversial one
at the time. Connected to it was the question of whether and how Japanese
immigrants would assimilate to Western cultures, especially American or

Canadian. Mahan wrote in the *Times* of London that while he doubted that Japanese would be easily assimilable, he did not see that condition as "permanent" because of their "virile qualities." Although Seager tries to portray this as anti-Japanese, he has a hard time making the charge stick. Mahan himself disavowed any notion of racial superiority over the Japanese (and Chinese as well) and reminded readers that he had been stationed in Japan for more than a year and had enjoyed "the charming geniality and courtesy of her people" and over the following forty years had "repeatedly met their military officers, diplomats, or private gentlemen."[141]

Mahan, it will be recalled, had befriended the Japanese midshipmen attending the Naval Academy in the late 1870s and "often had the pleasure of entertaining them in my home." One in particular, Tasuka Serata, became close to Mahan because they were both Christians. Far from being a racist, Mahan had a high view of the Japanese, particularly their naval officers. Although most, unlike Serata, were not Christians, Mahan did not hold this against them—though of course he hoped they would convert—but admired them for their devotion to their emperor and their openness to "the progress of Christendom."[142]

In 1905 Mahan published *Sea Power in Its Relations to the War of 1812*, which completed the Sea Power series.[143] On June 29, 1906, Mahan was promoted to rear admiral on the retired list as a result of legislation passed by Congress advancing to the next highest rank all retired naval officers who had served in the Civil War. This law was passed to rectify an oversight in a law passed eight years previously. That law had encouraged retirements in a top-heavy officer corps by allowing those retiring to do so at a higher rank, but it had excluded those already retired. "The consequence" as Mahan pointed out, "was that men who had served the four years Civil War were outranked and outpaid by men without war service." Mahan himself "felt no grievance" as he had retired voluntarily, "but it was unfair to those retired compulsorily for age or health." The 1906 legislation corrected this. Mahan was more than happy to get a pay raise, but "'Captain Mahan' has become almost a nom de plume for me, and I am a little perplexed about changing it."[144] He continued to use "Captain A. T. Mahan" or "A. T. Mahan, Captain" on the title pages of his books even though his friends and naval contemporaries began to address him as admiral.

The year 1907 saw the publication of two more books. One was his autobiography, *From Sail to Steam*, which has already been cited extensively. Most of it had already appeared as articles in *Harper's Weekly* and *Harper's Monthly* from February to December 1907.[145] Except for the occasional aside about the providential course of history, Mahan does not discuss his religious views in this book.[146] The second book was *Some Neglected Aspects of War*, which contained some previously published articles as well as some new material. The book contained "The Peace Conference and the Moral Aspect of War" that had been previously published in *Lessons of the War with Spain* and discussed above. For our purposes the most significant new material appeared in the preface and the article "War from the Christian Standpoint."

In the preface, Mahan discussed an anonymous letter he had received from someone in England signed "A Lover of my Fellow Creatures." The writer said that upon reading one of Mahan's articles on the Hague Conference,

> I . . . deeply regret to find that you have used the great talent God gave you for the welfare of mankind to uphold and encourage instead War which is literally Hell upon earth, and the curse of mankind, at this exceedingly critical period when your opinion might have proved a feather weight in the scale in favour of International Arbitration. May God forgive you, and lead you to an altered and better mind.[147]

Mahan took umbrage at this charge. He was willing to accept disagreement and he was a good enough historian to know that there were many and conflicting interpretations of a given issue. But he did not care for the implication that his views were unchristian or that he was in need of God's forgiveness for holding them.

> To ask thus solemnly that God may forgive a man is to pronounce his guilt before God. Why? Because of the antecedent assumption, that all War is so certainly and entirely wicked, that a man cannot without sin present before the audience of his kind such considerations as those contained in the article, herein republished, "The Practical Aspect of War." That the author thereof may be conscientiously assured of the rightness of his contention counts for nothing, no opposite side of the case is admitted, as to War.[148]

Mahan went on to say that the writer "takes the seat of the Almighty, and unhesitatingly declares the wickedness of his fellow. Judgment is passed by one neither commissioned nor competent to it; a procedure as unchristian in spirit, and in manifestation, as War can be."[149]

The other article, though technically not new, was being published for the first time. It was "War from the Christian Standpoint," which had been a speech given to the Church Congress in Providence, Rhode Island, on November 15, 1900. The speech had not been published at the time, but Admiral Luce had seen a copy or possibly been in the audience. Mahan wrote him, "Thank you for your kind words about 'War from a Christian Standpoint.' They convinced myself."[150]

Mahan's argument in "War from the Christian Standpoint" was essentially Augustinian, as explained above. Mahan never actually cited Augustine, but claimed he had arrived at his position solely from studying the Bible. His argument was based on three points. First, Jesus used force to expel the moneychangers from the Temple; moreover, he did so "not on his own behalf," but for the benefit of those who were being exploited. Second, no Christian soldier mentioned in the New Testament was ever told that his faith required him to abandon the profession of arms. Third, God has given authority (the "power of the sword") to the state "to defend the right."[151] Wars were sometimes necessary because "in the present imperfect and frequently wicked state of mankind, evil easily may, and often does, reach a point where it must be controlled, perhaps even destroyed, by physical force." Contrary to what some of his detractors over the years have claimed, Mahan in no way glorified war; he admitted it was evil but believed it was "justified" as "a remedy for greater evils."[152] He also drew a distinction between the individual and the state as it related to the appropriateness of a pacifist stance. It was permissible, he thought, for an individual Christian to practice pacifism or nonviolence, if so led by the Holy Spirit, as that would require surrender only of one's own rights. But he viewed it as immoral for a Christian to surrender the rights of others. Nations, he pointed out, are not the same as individuals, but are trustees of their citizens' rights; hence those who hold positions in government would be behaving in an immoral way if they turned their personal pacifism into public policy. Mahan concluded on a tolerant note, stating that he was not troubled by Christian pacifists because they were following their own consciences.[153]

A more extensive attack on Mahan was launched by Lucia Ames Mead, an anti-imperialist and peace activist, in *The Arena,* a progressive social gospel magazine, in 1908. It is not clear that her article is a book review, but it seems to have been written as a response to the publication of *Some Neglected Aspects of War.* Mead, who considered herself an "abolitionist of war" and a member of "the new peace party," denied that she was an absolute pacifist, but she stated her belief that "human nature doubtless is improving." She expressed confidence that war would end "within a century," but worried that influential people such as Mahan could derail the process with their retrograde views. That Mahan was a professed Christian was even more dismaying to her. "When, therefore, a distinguished naval expert and exemplary Christian gentleman discourses on this theme and tells us that war is inevitable, the layman is overawed and dumb." Her belief in human progress was unbounded, and she assailed Mahan for doubting it. Mead claimed that Mahan "ignores the fact that, in this age of endless forms of organization, rapid communication and widespread education, the progress of past centuries is now being equaled in decades, not merely in material achievements, but in mental and spiritual advance." She also, not surprisingly, supported the arbitration movement and condemned Mahan for rejecting it. She claimed that Mahan was unconcerned with justice and had an ulterior motive for his view of warfare, namely the continued existence and expansion of the Navy. She admitted no protective or defensive function of a navy. "A navy exists simply that it may fight another navy." War is evil "because it never aims at justice" and, in any case, is uncivilized and outmoded. Her belief in peace rested on her belief in progress and "constructive, courageous statesmanship that forestalls enmity and turns it into bonded friendship."[154] There is no evidence that Mahan responded to Mead's attack.

In addition to writing on war and peace issues, Mahan continued to speak and write about internal issues in the Episcopal Church. His first published article (as distinct from a letter to the editor) in *Churchman* appeared in the April 25, 1903, issue. It was actually the printed version of a speech he had given to the Church Club of New York on March 25 titled "The Apparent Decadence of the Church's Influence." This is the speech in which Mahan gave important information about his own conversion experience, but that was really an aside to the bulk of the speech, which was about the decline of the Episcopal Church's influence in American society. Mahan's concern was that church membership was declining, not in absolute numbers but in percentage of the population. The number of clergy was not increasing, but barely holding steady. This latter development particularly disturbed him. It showed that the church was "deficient in the spiritual vigor" necessary for a church to grow and to inspire a man to consider the priesthood. It was not difficult for Mahan to diagnose the cause of the symptoms. It was that the church had reversed the priority of the two Great Commandments and had made loving one's neighbor more important than loving God. Put another way, the problem was the influence of the social gospel movement. Benevolence to others had superseded loving God; not that that requirement was abandoned. "It is simply quietly relegated to a secondary place." Apart from being unscriptural, it made no sense theologically since, as Mahan pointed out, "The love of God is the one sure motive and source for the love of man." The solution was a return to what he called "personal religion," which unfortunately was no longer being preached or taught. He claimed that the social gospelers in the Episcopal Church were criticizing concern over one's own salvation as selfish. He strongly objected to this view and asserted that by "walk[ing] hand in hand" with Jesus a person became more, not less, unselfish and sacrificial. Humanitarian concerns and activities can never be a substitute for a personal relationship with Jesus Christ. The solution to the church's "decadence" was to return to personal religion "preached once more openly from the pulpit." This alone would reach and inspire the people in the pews.[155]

This article was prefaced by a long editorial (presumably written by McBee, an avid proponent of the social gospel) taking to task both Mahan for his retrograde views and the Church Club for setting the topic. While flattering Mahan as "the greatest living naval statesman" and a devoted Christian, the editor claimed that the notion of personal religion was wrong because it was too individualistic and therefore "self-centered." He even went so far as to say that the idea of saving one's own soul was "a distinctly pagan doctrine" that "denies the Gospel at its core." The only measure of Christian love is "working for others."[156]

McBee's critique, however, misrepresented Mahan's argument. Mahan nowhere said that saving one's own soul was the only or most important purpose of Christianity. In fact, he did not use "soul" terminology at all. The essence of his article was the importance for the individual believer of having a personal relationship with the savior Jesus Christ. This made a person more, not less, concerned with the good of others. McBee, who was nothing if not fair, published two letters supporting Mahan's position in the May 9 issue. One was from Frederick Dan Huntington, bishop of Central New York, who compared the current liberalism in the Episcopal Church to early nineteenth-century Unitarianism, a movement he claimed was already outmoded. The other letter was from a layman, William H. Nielson of Plainfield, New Jersey, who said the editorial unjustly distorted the plain meaning of Mahan's article.[157]

Mahan tried to view everything in life from a Christian perspective and thought deeply about the theological meaning of all that happened, whether to world powers or to his own family. This included even the deaths of his beloved dogs. Jomini died on December 15, 1900. Mahan wrote, "He was over twelve, but seemed well and jolly till he broke down all of a sudden." After a week of futile treatments he was euthanized to "put an end to his suffering."[158]

By 1905 the Mahans had another dog, Rovie, breed and age unknown, who was killed by an automobile. Mahan, terribly upset, comforted himself with the thought that Rovie's death was quick. "The injuries must have been all internal; and they were mercifully so complete that death followed almost immediately." Better for Rovie that he had not experienced "Jomini's week of suffering." Rovie was buried in his blanket. "I laid by him the old bone, and a stick on the lawn which he had latterly laid great store by, larking with me and crunching it." Meditating on God's purposes for this sad occasion, Mahan concluded that God had spared Rovie a greater sorrow and that Christ had died for Rovie, too. "But if, as we know, not a sparrow falls to the ground without our Father [Matthew 10:29], we may be sure that our Father and his [Rovie's] Father had taken this little dog from some sorrow. Sure I am that Christ did not die for man alone."[159]

Health problems of one sort or another, affecting most of the family, were the cause of a trip to Europe in the spring of 1907. Sometime prior to April, Mahan's doctor "suddenly discovered, or at least for the first time told me, that my arteries and heart were showing signs of age and this place [baths at Bad Nauheim, Germany] might help." His wife Elly had already planned a trip for herself because of her respiratory condition, a result of influenza in 1904. Mahan had not wanted to go, but the trip to Bad Nauheim "I fear is destined to be a regular annual function during the life of my wife and myself."[160] Younger daughter Ellen was there in the hopes of getting rid of "scarlatina" and "inflammatory rheumatism" she had contracted on a previous trip to Europe. Helen, the elder daughter, was there to find help for what Seager calls "her continuing nervous condition."[161]

At some point, probably in 1893, Helen, who possessed musical talent, began assisting her teacher, Mrs. Morgan, with pupils. Then she began taking on her own pupils and began to "feel somewhat overwhelmed," according to her mother. Seager contends that Mahan wanted her to remain dependent and discouraged her teaching and by implication her ability to earn an independent income.[162] But Mahan's letters do not support this thesis. He sympathized with Helen's feelings and encouraged her, saying that "you have an adequate knowledge of music, and probably a faculty for teaching—all which is in your favor."[163] Far from discouraging her from earning money, he applauded it and, fearing his retirement pay would be reduced, thought that the family would need her income in the future. "Of course, if you marry, you will transfer both your work and your support elsewhere." His main concern seemed to be her health and that her work habits be regular rather than "by fits and starts."[164] It is true that in November 1894 Helen was treated by a doctor and was not particularly happy about it. "I am sorry to hear from mamma that you are uneasy under Dr. Warren's administrations. I do not find fault with you for it."[165] The only thing we know about her ailment is that "the doctor finds you run down from the effect of the winter's drive." What this actually means, we do not know. Part of her exhaustion, if that is what it was, was due not only to overwork but to a busy social life, including taking up fencing. Mahan warned her not to "be out late on Saturday night." It is not true, as Seager claims, that she was ordered by the doctor to spend fourteen hours in bed. That prescription was for her mother, not her. We simply do not know what Helen's problem was, but it was probably exacerbated by her concern over her mother's health.[166] According to Seager, Helen had "another, more severe, nervous breakdown" in 1905. This may possibly have been true, but again the evidence is ambiguous. The only mention of it is in a letter from Mahan to his publisher John Brown in which he refers to "my daughter who is suffering from an approach to nervous prostration, and forbidden by the doctor to see more than one visitor a day." Which daughter, however, is not identified. In a footnote Seager identifies her as Helen, but no source is given. Another letter cited by Seager as a source for Helen's illness makes no mention of Helen, or her sister, or any illness. Even if we assume the daughter in question was Helen, Mahan called her difficulty "no serious trouble."[167] Whatever Helen's problem was, we hear no more about it, as neither her sister Ellen nor her brother Lyle made any mention of it in their recollections.

Another source of stress affecting Mahan's own health may have been touchy relations with Lyle and his new wife. Lyle had graduated from Columbia in 1902 before marrying Madeline Johnson in 1904 in a "large fashionable" wedding that was reported in detail in the *New York Times*. She gave birth to the Mahans' only grandchild, Alfred Thayer Mahan II, in July 1905.[168] Even though Mahan delighted in his grandson, there was, as Lyle said, "friction that unfortunately existed between my wife and my parents," for which he blamed himself.[169]

Prior to traveling to Germany, Mahan gave an address to the Episcopal Church Club of Philadelphia on February 25, 1907, titled "Some Practical Considerations Concerning the Spiritual Life." This was a long address that took up more than twelve pages in *Letters and Papers*, and the audience may have found it tedious. It was vintage Mahan, stressing the themes of a Trinitarian God, the reliability of the scriptures, and the necessity of working hard at spiritual growth, the goal of which was to "increase in the knowledge of God and in likeness to Him." He did not emphasize so much the necessity of a personal relationship with Christ, possibly because the audience was composed of fellow Episcopalians already serious about their faith. He stressed practical steps one could take, guided by the Holy Spirit, that would help a believer become closer to Christ. Without these practical steps, a believer would fall into "spiritual decay." He was referring to such things as daily prayer, family prayer, Bible reading, attending Sunday services, receiving communion, tithing, and "daily watchfulness over acts, to conform them to Christ's words." These may seem like small steps, but they added up to a closer walk with God.[170]

Back in Bad Nauheim in 1907, Mahan was bored, called the place "dull," and chafed at his doctor's orders to cut down on physical exercise (he was an avid walker.) "My girls say I am getting fussy and irritable." He did, however, acknowledge that the baths had done wonders for Elly. "Not only did it restore her after a dangerous illness, but now at 55 she is more like what she was at 30 than at 40."[171]

While there Mahan answered a letter from Hugh R. Monro, a Presbyterian layman who was president of the American Tract Society, seeking Mahan's support for an ecumenical organization. Mahan was willing to support the organization, but only on the condition that all its members believe in "the eternal Godhead of our Lord Jesus Christ." He would not be a part of any organization or movement that welcomed Unitarians or other non-Trinitarians. "In a most proper and most Christian eagerness to subordinate other points on which we differ, I fear lest the impulse may lead us to ignore this one foundation, apart from which the whole building will rest upon sand."[172] A few weeks later Mahan contributed to statements of support for the American Movement, an organization for lay and foreign missions. (It is not clear if this is the same organization of which Monro wrote, but the timing and purpose would seem to indicate so.) They were holding a meeting in London on May 28, 1907. Mahan wanted to attend but his doctor would not allow it, so he sent a statement, and while the original has been lost, an excerpt of it was published in the *Times* of London. Mahan believed the organization was manifesting the "Power of the Gospel of the Lord." As Christians of different denominations worked together in the mission field, they "will ultimately find the solution of the worst of our home problems—namely, our corporate separateness from one another."[173]

After returning home to Quogue in June 1907, Mahan entered the hospital on September 25 for a prostatectomy, "a pretty severe course of treatment, involving an operation which will keep me quiet and off all duty for the better part of a month."[174] He was in the hospital for four weeks but thought that "the general gain is obvious." He did not heal properly, however, and had to have a second operation in December. As Elly told Admiral Luce, "The first wound had healed in such a peculiar way (very unusual they say) that it formed an impassable barrier." This caused him "intense agony," but the second operation was successful and he "is so happy to be free from the dreadful pains." By January he was much better and resuming correspondence himself.[175]

According to Seager, the aftermath of Mahan's illness brought on "nothing less than a serious breakdown of his religious faith occasioned by the intense pain through which he had passed and his inability to bear it with the Christian fortitude he thought God demanded." He cites two sources for this, one a quote from daughter Ellen's recollections. "He bore pain very badly and seemed to be completely unnerved by it." Ellen did say this, though not in connection with his operation or a crisis of faith. Seager also cites a letter to Luce in November 1907 in which Mahan said, "[A]t present I am greatly discouraged, my own practical piety having broken down miserably under some recent troubles." Clearly he was having some difficulty, but whether it was a crisis of faith or spiritual "breakdown" is impossible to say because we know so little about it. What Seager calls a crisis may simply have been part of the normal ups and downs that every Christian goes through, exacerbated by illness and pain.[176]

Interestingly, Ellen does make reference to a crisis at about this same time, 1906–7, but it did not seem directly related to Mahan's illness. She is mysterious about it and never explains what actually happened, but it affected both parents and might have been related to finances, since she mentions it in the context of her grandmother leaving a bequest to her mother. "Then [ca. 1906] my parents received a blow which altered everything for us. From my father and mother something had gone which they were never to get back." This is dramatic language, all the more intriguing because she never tells what the blow was. But it did not seem to have caused a crisis of faith for her father, for according to Ellen it was her father's faith that saved the day. "Papa took command of the situation at once, his faith never faltered, he pointed out the way which we, as a family, should take. He showed us the true balance between head and heart which a Christian should keep and, above all, he kept it himself."[177]

Seager makes no reference to this episode at all, though he claims that Mahan's next book, *The Harvest Within*, was written "in propitiation for his weakness and as an act of contrition." This is doubtful because in the same letter to Luce that Seager cites as a source for this claim, Mahan stated that he was already working on the book before his illness.[178]

Despite his illness, Mahan remained involved with church activities and speaking engagements. One church organization with which he had recently become involved was the American Church Institute for Negroes, an offshoot of the Board of Missions. The conditions of blacks, especially in the South and especially in the Episcopal Church, was an issue that concerned him. Mahan did not write often—in fact barely at all—on the specific question of race relations in the United States, but we can piece together some of his comments to discern his views. He did say that he saw a "great superiority" of white over black, but, as was usually the case when he discussed "race," the issue was cultural and not biological. "That is, the question was not one of colour, but of assimilation as involved in race character."[179]

In 1898 Mahan privately commented on, but publicly stayed out of, an argument playing out in the press over the blame that should attach to American society and the U.S. government over the treatment of African Americans. In a letter to McBee, Mahan acknowledged "the undeniable wrongs and shortcomings in the case of the negro and the Indian," but praised McBee for his editorial, which had emphasized the gains made by blacks since the Civil War, rather than indicting the nation as evil. Mahan singled out for criticism in this regard Bishop Potter of New York and Dr. William Reed Huntington, rector of Grace Church in New York City, whose negative comments he thought to be unhelpful and unchristian. Mahan's position was that the situation of black Americans was improving and that white Episcopalians ought to aid in that improvement. He admired "the more hopeful augury of Mr. Booker Washington" and told McBee of his own encounter with a black clergyman. "I lately had a visit from a colored presbyter [priest] from Richmond, Rev. J. W. Johnson, who spoke similarly hopefully of the upward progress of his race, while not concealing his keen sense of the inequality of treatment he and his brethren still receive in our Church South." Mahan was confident "that under our civilization the negro *is* advancing; the movement is upward" (emphasis in original).[180]

In 1906 Mahan was invited to be a trustee of the new American Church Institute for Negroes. This organization was actually a renamed and revamped version of an older organization, the Protestant Episcopal Freedman's Commission to Colored People, which had been established in 1865 to provide education for the newly freed slaves. It was dissolved in 1878 but was re-established under its new name to provide oversight and funding for Episcopal-affiliated black schools and colleges.[181] Mahan was enthused about this cause and on at least one occasion took a trip with the other trustees to St. Augustine's School in Raleigh, North Carolina. (This trip was also the occasion for a reunion with Sam Ashe, whom he had not seen in thirty-five years.) According to David Greer, who succeeded Potter as bishop of New York in 1908 and was also the president of the American Church Institute, Mahan "was one of the most regular attendants at its meetings."[182]

On November 21, 1908, Mahan was in Annapolis, where he delivered the main address at the dedication of the memorial window at the Naval Academy chapel to Rear Adm. William T. Sampson. Sampson had been a midshipman at the academy when Mahan was there and had been the victor in the battle of Santiago in the Spanish-American War. The speech was long and, according to the *Army and Navy Journal*, "was heard only imperfectly." It was later published in the Naval Institute *Proceedings*. Most of the address was a rehashing and praising of Sampson's naval career, and there was no mention of Sampson's religious beliefs. The lesson of Sampson's life, Mahan told the assembled midshipmen and officers, was "to value character above every professional gain." To emulate Sampson they should put duty above glory.[183]

In 1908 the Mahans decided to sell Slumberside, their house in Quogue, and build a new one. The impetus came from his wife and daughters, who found the house too small and, since it was unheated, available for only a few months of the year. This necessitated finding a rental in the city for the remainder of the year. The new house, Marshmere, had a furnace and a soundproof study for Mahan. According to Ellen, "It took my father some time to get used to this house, Marshmere; he rather hankered after the older house, but gradually the beauty of the view and peacefulness of the surroundings appealed and I think he became quite reconciled."[184]

The Harvest Within: Thoughts on the Life of the Christian, published in 1909, was Mahan's only book-length treatment of religion. Part personal testimony, part biblical analysis, part expository sermon, it represents Mahan's attempt to sum up and present in an organized fashion the full scope of his Christian beliefs. He originally wanted to title it *Fragments That Remain*. He considered himself old by this time and wanted to gather and organize his thoughts (the fragments) while there was still time to encourage "fellow-combatants in the battle of life." That title was already taken, however, so, in corroboration with his publisher James McIntyre at Little, Brown, he decided on *The Harvest Within*.[185] The book was "governed by a leading idea" in the same way that the Sea Power series was. In this case the idea was love for Jesus Christ, inspired not so much by his deeds as by "the excellence of His Person, and by realization of personal relation to Him." Mahan asserted, as he had on a number of occasions, that many well-meaning Christians got the order of love and good works reversed. Love for Jesus had to come first; the good works would follow from that. "The riches of Christ are unsearchable, but chief among them is the gift of love for Himself. It is a gift, not an acquisition."[186]

The book was divided into five chapters: Power, Likeness, Intercourse, Fulfilment, and Hope. Though the book was 262 pages, its theme revolved around the necessity of a personal relationship with Jesus Christ. Mahan also used phrases such as "vital union with Christ" and "dwelling in Christ and Christ in him."[187] Attempting to summarize the book would be tedious, but it has some interesting features that give us more insight into Mahan.

Most obvious is Mahan's thorough knowledge of the Bible. He had been studying it seriously since he was a young man and at the age of nearly seventy he was thoroughly at home in it. Practically every page had scriptural references. That is not to say, of course, that others would always agree with his interpretations, but his facility with scripture was impressive, especially for a layman, and he did not hesitate to get into debates with clergy with whom he disagreed. Mahan, who under his uncle's direction had read widely in theology, including the liberals of the day, refused to get sucked in to the argument of literal versus figurative interpretations, seeing it as a distraction from his larger point. While he leaned more to the conservative side and certainly viewed scripture as inerrant, he was not a literalist. Twice in the book he asserts that the meaning of the verse is clear whether one interprets it literally or figuratively.[188]

Though Mahan did not deal with the issue at great length, he did reflect on God's purposes in human history. While this may seem like a philosophical issue, Mahan made it a practical one in tying it to the importance of giving thanks to God, thankfulness implying some acknowledgment of past events. "Forgetfulness and unbelief are twins." Some Christians fail to associate cause and effect and do not acknowledge God's providence in everything, and according to Mahan Christians need to cultivate "the habit of seeing God's hand in all things." He acknowledged that discerning God's purposes in history (including one's own life) was not easy, but it was the *habit* of seeking God's purposes that was important. "This is not the pretense that one sees clearly at once the significance of each event; but that the habit exists of recognizing distinctly that each is from God; that it is so accepted; and that the meaning and outcome are pondered from that point of view." As in history, so in a person's life. "Each [event] has its appointed work." What befalls the Christian is not chance nor without purpose. "Love underlies each experience."[189]

While Mahan did not discuss political or historical controversies as such, he did include a brief discussion of slavery in the Bible. Though Seager (as discussed in chapter 2) implies that Mahan did not care about the slavery issue, it was in fact an issue about which he cared deeply.[190] He had thought about the theological implications of slavery and felt strongly that the Bible should not be blamed for it. Rather than acceding to the charge that the Bible justified slavery, Mahan believed that defenders of slavery had misused the Bible. He listed in a footnote eleven verses pertaining to slavery and argued that, taken individually or together, their thrust was against slavery rather than for it. "Only within a half-century has slavery disappeared from Christendom; but its disappearance was insured from the moment the power of Christ became incarnate." Christ himself took on the flesh of humanity "common to master and to slave." Paul did not advocate social revolution, but abolition was implied "in his exposition of love as by Jesus Christ commanded, with a direct application to slavehood." Christianity had made the slave a brother or sister in Christ; "the slave ceased to be only a chattel, and became a member of Christ. To this there could be but one logical result."[191]

Mahan also believed that there was plenty of historical evidence for the truth of Christianity. God did not demand blind faith. "Belief without reason is not faith but credulity." While we cannot see the physical Jesus, we have "His Life, His Words, His Resurrection." He particularly stressed the evidence for the Resurrection since it was "the foundation truth of Christianity" and was not a question "of merely speculative curiosity, but of immediate vital importance to the individual and to the [human] race." The reasons he offered were (1) eyewitness accounts and (2) the changes in the lives of believers even to the point of willingness to be martyred. The Resurrection, Mahan said, was established by evidence "sufficient, intellectually, to establish any ordinary historical incident" and was the only plausible explanation for the apostles' behavior. He posed the question, if the Resurrection did not occur, then what explains the apostles' belief that it did?[192]

Mahan also believed, though he did not dwell on it, that science and Christian faith were not incompatible. Science dealt with the physical universe, "an array of secondary causes, which are manifestations of God's creative power." The Bible, however, was not a science textbook but dealt with "the primary Personal cause, God." While God worked "*with* man's natural efforts" in the study of science, God as Holy Spirit worked "*in* man" in developing faith and sanctifying to good deeds (emphases in original). The Bible taught the latter, not the former.[193]

He was not troubled by inconsistencies in the gospel accounts and did not see it as threatening when they were the subject of historical analysis. They were not written by Jesus himself but by his followers, which the gospel writers freely admit. The inconsistencies and seemingly conflicting statements were in his view witness to their authenticity, since "the inference is fair that the evidence has not been tampered with, but given to the best of the writer's ability." He was not at all threatened by the so-called higher criticism and believed that the Bible could more than hold its own against professional theologians.[194]

Seager mercilessly derides *The Harvest Within*, calling it "a dull exercise in Mahan's post-surgery enthusiasm for Christ." He also calls it "unoriginal," "tiresome," and "arrogant."[195] But the book was far more than an effort to cope with postsurgery depression. It was the result of a lifetime of reflection, prayer, and study. What's more, according to one naval historian the book is actually original and sophisticated. Sumida, in his *Inventing Grand Strategy*, gives an analysis of *The Harvest Within* in the context of Mahan's naval writings. Sumida believes that it "merits special consideration in a study of Mahan's writing on navies and naval power."[196] In addition to using the "leading idea" as in the Sea Power series, Sumida sees Mahan as "view[ing] the true acceptance of Christianity as comparable in nature to an act of critical command decision-making in war because both initiatives had to be undertaken in the face of uncertainty."[197] Just as a naval commander had to make life-or-death decisions based on the information available to him at the moment, which he knows is incomplete, so the Christian does as well. This is where faith comes in, which then needs to be followed by an act of will. "This is Faith, even when exercised in other than religious matters. . . . It is a high military virtue, to which in its perfection few attain; one chief factor in military success or unsuccess."[198] While the rational analysis of available information was important, the great commander (for example, Nelson) had to use emotion as well because "emotion is power." Sumida's great insight is his seeing how Mahan makes the connection between command in war and the Christian life. In both spheres success "was not simply a matter of following rules . . . [but] was propelled by a combination of an individual's intellectual and emotional activity."[199] A key part of both intellect and emotion was experience, which "Mahan believed was the best preceptor of true Christian consciousness, [and] of naval command."[200]

The only other historical work that analyzes *The Harvest Within*—though not nearly as cogently as Sumida's—is Joe L. Dubbert's *A Man's Place: Masculinity in Transition* (1979), a study of Victorian ideas of masculinity and how men of that era tried to combat what they saw as the feminization of society. With minimal evidence, Dubbert categorizes Mahan as one who "asserted that modern man needed an image of a virile, energetic Jesus Christ." He states that *The Harvest Within* was a book written for men and claims that "Mahan perceived God as a strong masculine figure capable of vengeful anger when necessary. The New Testament, with its preachment of love had been misinterpreted, having been read as an argument against forceful action." The problem with this argument is that there is no evidence for it, and Dubbert's comments on *The Harvest Within* indicate only a superficial reading of it. While it is probably true that Mahan would not have cared for a feminized Jesus, there is no indication that this was an issue that concerned him. The clear thrust of *The Harvest Within* is the necessity of a personal relationship with Jesus Christ, not the need for a more manly Jesus. Dubbert's quotations from the book are taken out of context and distorted to suit his argument. The notion that Mahan presents a vengeful Old Testament God at the expense of a loving New Testament one is ludicrous. Mahan goes on at great length about the love of Jesus, sometimes on the very page Dubbert cites to show the opposite. In any case, Dubbert's reliability is suspect since, in discussing Mahan's life, he gets a number of facts wrong and seems to have confused Alfred with his father.[201]

There was one glitch in the publication of *The Harvest Within*. Mahan was keen that the cover of the book be decorated with the Greek letters Alpha and Omega, signifying the beginning and the end, a symbol of God. He even gave Little, Brown specific instructions as to how they should look. Unfortunately, the design resembled his initials ATM superimposed over each other. He was "sensitive" to the fact that it might look egotistical and wished the design to be modified in future editions.[202]

The book was published in England by Longmans, Green rather than his usual publisher, Sampson Low, Marston, as Mahan thought the former more suitable to publish religious works. He was disappointed, however, that Longmans did not do enough to publicize the book.[203] He sent several copies to prominent American Episcopalians including David Greer, bishop of New York and president of the American Church Institute for Negroes; William C. Doane, bishop of Albany and son of his uncle's friend Bishop George Washington Doane; William Reed Huntington, rector of Grace Church, New York City; and various laypeople. He also sent one to the Archbishop of Canterbury, Randall Davidson. Responses have not survived, but Huntington kept the book, put his own personal bookplate in it, and saved Mahan's letter.[204]

Seager states that the book did not enjoy good sales, but it did go through two additional editions.[205] Only *Churchman* and *The Guardian* (a High Church Anglican paper in London) reviewed it—which disappointed Mahan—but the reviews were favorable. *Churchman* lauded him for showing "a keen sense of the responsibility of laymen" and for not allowing his secular occupation "to obscure the sphere of obligation imposed upon him as a Churchman." *Churchman* also printed an excerpt from the book, and while no copy of *The Guardian*'s review survives, Mahan seemed pleased with it.[206]

The years after the publication of *The Harvest Within* saw no letup in Mahan's activities in the church or his writings on religious topics. He was not, however, as reported by Seager, a delegate to the Episcopal Church's General Convention.[207] His interest in missions continued unabated. In June 1909 he sent a long letter to the editor to *Churchman* encouraging lay support for missions and explaining the theological premises behind his plea. He stressed that he was speaking for himself and not as a member of the Board of Missions. The church's missionary activity was expanding but the funding was no longer sufficient, and some projects might have to be cut back or shut down altogether. Mahan did not want to see that happen. "The fact is, that the work of missions is the work of Jesus Christ and the duty is to Him." He told his readers that the excuse that one has already given and others have not is not a good one. The "willingness to give is a grace, and giving itself a privilege." The Christian should "use this grace in proportion to his ability to give, entirely unaffected by what others do." He also took to task some other Board of Missions members who were reluctant to make an appeal for funds to the church at large because such an appeal "will infallibly come upon those who already have given and largely sustained the work." He disagreed because those who held this attitude "estimate the demand chiefly as a tax levelled by men, and not as a privilege extended by God." Mahan was not interested in arguments about who was or was not doing his fair share—the cost of funding missionary work was estimated at eighty cents per communicant—but in whether each church member was fulfilling his duty to God as God guided him.[208]

Though he did not attend, Mahan played a behind-the-scenes role at the World Missionary Conference in Edinburgh in 1910 as an advisor to Seth Low (fellow delegate to the First Hague Conference), who headed the American delegation. The conference's Report VII relied heavily on a paper prepared by Mahan and quoted large portions of it verbatim.[209]

Mahan took an interest in everything affecting the Episcopal Church, especially in parishes to which he had once or currently belonged. Even though he had not attended Trinity Church in Newport, Rhode Island, for many years, in 1911 he supported the campaign of its rector, Stanley C. Hughes, to foster observance of Sunday as the Lord's Day, a practice that was becoming increasingly lax. The rector of Trinity, Wall Street, William T. Manning, also supported him. Mahan's letter to Hughes was published in the parish newsletter as well as in the *New York Times* (presumably with Hughes's permission). After commending Hughes for his stand, Mahan wrote, "You will expect criticism, the type of which is familiar to us. I beg to express to you my own strong personal admiration of the stand openly taken and my deep conviction of the imminent necessity for it." The *Times'* coverage of this issue is indicative of the importance of Trinity, Wall Street in the larger church; because of the parish's great wealth its rector was often considered more important than the bishop of New York! The headline read "Manning Approves Lord's Day Protest," but the article also shows the importance of Mahan as a prominent layman, with the subheading reading "Admiral Mahan Also Indorses Newport Clergy's Condemnation of Sunday Non-Observance."[210]

Mahan also involved himself in an issue in which he had a great interest as well as firsthand experience. The concept of universal arbitration was making a comeback. On November 8, 1911, the Episcopal Diocese of New York at its annual convention passed a resolution recording "its hearty approval" of proposed arbitration treaties between the United States, Great Britain, and France and expressing "the hope that they may speedily be ratified by the Senate."[211] The Episcopalians were not the only ones supporting the treaties. A group called the American Peace and Arbitration League was asking clergymen of all denominations to observe November 26, 1911, as "Unity Sunday" and preach sermons urging ratification of the treaties. Much to Mahan's dismay, "a long list of clergy of this city [New York]" had signed up to do just that. In response Mahan fired off identical letters to the *New York Times* and the *New York Evening Post*.

Mahan's opposition to the Episcopal resolution, however, rested not on his personal objection to the arbitration treaties themselves but rather on his view of the proper relationship of church and state. Mahan's letter to the editor posed two questions: (1) What is the role of the church as institution in the political process and (2) what is the role of the individual Christian as citizen?

Mahan analyzed the first question strictly from a scriptural point of view without any reference to the Constitution or the First Amendment. He opened his argument with an implicit question: What is the purpose of the Episcopal diocese's resolution and such events as "Unity Sunday"? The purpose, he answered, "avowedly is for the Church to bring pressure to bear upon the State, in the matter of an action which is committed to the State, and is not committed to the Church. In other words, the Church is to be used as an instrument of political agitation." Why was this wrong? Mahan offered one major reason and three minor ones. First, "neither the Church nor clergy, as such, have any expert knowledge" in the fields of diplomacy or constitutional law. Additionally, experts in those fields—and here he cited John Bassett Moore, an authority on international law, and former secretaries of state Richard Olney and Elihu Root—differed among themselves as to both the wisdom and constitutionality of the proposed treaties and made persuasive arguments on both sides. Hence the issue did not lend itself to determining a distinctively Christian position. Finally, the only ones who had "any duty to take action" on the treaties were the senators themselves. But the major reason for Mahan's objection to the church's involvement in politics was that church and state occupied separate spheres, each with its separate responsibilities, and one should not intrude on the other. The church "exceeds her legitimate functions, and so do the individual clergy, when, as Church or as clergy, they endeavor to bring pressure to bear upon the State in its own divinely appointed sphere." Without quoting it directly, Mahan alluded to the scriptural warrant (Luke 20:25) for his viewpoint. "To use the master's expression, the Church is intruding into the things of Caesar, the temporal power of his day." To drive home the point, Mahan called on historical precedent to back him up. "The attempt of the clergy [to involve the church in politics] is simply an intrusion into the sphere of the state, recalling the Calvinist theocracy of Geneva and early New England, and the monstrous claims of the mediaeval Church to decide whether citizens owed allegiance to this ruler or that."

Mahan then turned his guns on his fellow Episcopalians in the Diocese of New York. The delegates to the annual convention (including laymen as well as clergy) had exceeded their authority. To pass a resolution on a secular matter was to "usurp power [and] do that for which they have no commission from God or man." Their action in fact "was really null; for not only had they no commission from their constituency, but that constituency, the Church at large in the diocese, was incompetent to authorize their course."

Did this mean that Mahan believed that Christians or an individual's Christian beliefs should play no role in politics? Absolutely not. The crucial distinction was one between the Christian as individual citizen and the church as institution. In their capacity as citizens Christians could participate in the political arena as much as they liked. "As citizens it is not only their privilege, but their right, and may be their duty, to do their utmost to forward any measure of public policy that commends itself to their judgment." If the delegates of the diocesan convention wished to take a stand on the arbitration treaties, "they could have got together during or after convention, and taken the same action while distinctly disavowing representative capacity," in other words, making it clear that they were speaking as private individuals and not as representatives of the Episcopal Church.[212]

In any event the arbitration treaties did not pass the Senate, so Mahan, the anti-arbitrationist, was vindicated.[213] But the arbitration movement continued in fits and starts; the mainline Protestant churches generally continued to support it, and Mahan continued to speak out against church involvement in politics. In our own time, when most Christian churches have lobbying agencies in Washington and religious organizations speaking out on political issues is taken for granted, Mahan's letter provides an instructive perspective on church-state relations.

In 1912 Mahan got into a dispute with Norman Angell, a British Labour politician, writer, and antiwar activist. Angell had written a book, *The Great Illusion*, published in 1911. Angell's belief, though framed in secular terms, was similar to the social gospel view of war with which Mahan had previously done battle. Angell believed that war was now obsolete, not so much because human behavior was getting better, but because the European economies were so intertwined that war no longer made any sense. The *illusion* referred to in the title was that European nations believed that their economic prosperity depended on their being able to deter aggression, thus necessitating a strong military. "At the root of the whole armament difficulty lies the theory that economic advantage goes with the exercise of military force."[214]

The book also contained numerous attacks on Mahan, some of which he construed as personal, such as Angell's remark that Mahan's theories were "all moonshine and very mischievous moonshine."[215] An irate Mahan prepared extensive notes that showed how angry he was. He accused Angell of "bias," "argument ad hominem," and "gross travesty."[216] He got his chance to fire back when the *North American Review* published in March 1912 his detailed critique of Angell's book, which took a calm scholarly tone but was harsh nonetheless.[217] Mahan maintained that "the fundamental proposition of the book is a mistake." Both human nature and the facts of history refuted it. Nations have gone and will continue to go to war against their economic self-interest on numerous occasions. Angell's view "is not only to misread history but to ignore it." Nations did not maintain armaments with an eye to "speedy return of dollars and cents" but to defend themselves against aggressors. Not only did he disagree with Angell's view of war and economics, he expressed amazement at Angell's total disregard of history. "Much of the argument of *The Great Illusion* turns upon the allegation that the past is in many respects so wholly past that arguments based upon its experience are no longer valid."[218] Such a casual dismissal of history and such a naive view of human nature shocked Mahan.

Angell replied in the June 1912 issue of *North American Review*.[219] He did not claim that Mahan had misunderstood him nor did he attempt to refute any of Mahan's arguments. He simply asserted that Mahan was wrong and that his views were outmoded. He conceded Mahan's point that he ignored history since he openly claimed that history was irrelevant. He said that he was a believer in progress and that war was an outmoded way of settling disputes between nations; "we have passed out of that state of development." He believed that the character of humanity was changing for the better and that the only purpose of religion was "the improvement of society." He condemned Mahan for being a "militarist" and said that Mahan's writings showed the "limitation" of the military mindset. Mahan's advocacy of a strong military and his belief in the inevitability of war as part of the human condition "is the doctrine of savagery."[220]

It is one of the ironies of the Angell-Mahan dispute that it was Angell who was the racist and social Darwinist, not Mahan. Angell maintained that one of the reasons war had been bad for Europe was that the "racially better people" got killed, "leaving the stock to be perpetuated by its worst elements."[221] Mahan drafted a reply but never published it. It would probably have been a pointless exercise anyway since he and Angell were operating on two different planes. Seager claims that Angell had gotten the better of Mahan in this controversy, but one could argue that subsequent events proved that Mahan's view of human nature was more accurate.[222]

In 1913 Mahan got into yet another controversy with an author. This time it was an American novelist with the improbable name of Winston Churchill (no relation to the British statesman). Ironically, the American Churchill was also a graduate of the Naval Academy (class of 1894) but never served on active duty, resigning his commission shortly after graduation.[223] Churchill wrote a social gospel novel titled *The Inside of the Cup*. It was serialized in *Hearst's* magazine in 1912 and then published in book form in 1913. The social gospel novel was a genre popular in the late 1800s and early 1900s. These novels invariably featured a male protagonist, usually a Protestant clergyman, who is initially a traditional orthodox Christian. He then has a crisis of faith that is resolved by rejecting a literal interpretation of scripture and embracing a form of ministry that is essentially social work.[224]

The Inside of the Cup, though virtually unknown today, was the number one bestseller in America in 1913 and number three in 1914. It is the story of a young Episcopal priest named John Hodder, who, through his reading of modern philosophy and higher criticism theology, has a crisis of faith. He begins to see his wealthy parishioners as hypocritical, corrupt, and tied to an outmoded theology. He also has a romance with a liberated young woman who defies her father to become a landscape architect. Hodder resolves his crisis by devoting himself to serving the poor, but his congregation balks at his radicalism and he is tried for heresy. Even though he wins the girl in the end, he also becomes an advocate for divorce, viewing it as wrong to stay in a loveless marriage. Though a bestseller, the novel was extremely controversial and in the book version Churchill included an afterword defending himself against accusations of heresy.[225]

Mahan reviewed the novel in the August 30, 1913, issue of *Churchman*. Not surprisingly, he disliked it. In notes prepared for himself he stated that he found it inconceivable that anyone could not grasp that Jesus alone had "the words of eternal life" [John 6:68].[226] In his review Mahan said that the book was both "bad art" and bad theology. He criticized Churchill for presenting a "parody and caricature" of Christianity. The characters were stereotypes, with orthodox Christians presented as "dishonest and worldly" while those who embraced liberalism and the social gospel were "the lovable and the noble." Apart from the characterizations, Mahan took Churchill to task for three things. One was Churchill's advocating that church members and clergy who no longer believed in traditional Christian teachings remain in their churches and seek to subvert them from within. Mahan considered this dishonest. Second, he rejected Churchill's advocacy of divorce if the parties fell out of love. Not only was this a misunderstanding of love, confusing it with emotions and "inclinations," but divorce for such a reason was contrary to the word of God. Third was Churchill's setting up of law (bad) and liberty (good) in opposition to each other, a theological heresy known as antinomianism. Mahan closed by urging "serious readers of this book [to] beware of half truths."[227]

Churchill's rebuttal was printed in the October 11, 1913, edition. He maintained that Christianity in general, and the Episcopal Church in particular, should include within its ranks those who disagree with traditional Christian teachings. He claimed that Christianity was constantly evolving and that belief in Jesus as Lord and Savior did not require belief in orthodox doctrine, which in his view was based on ancient, outmoded, and unscientific sources. He called

Mahan's view—which held to the Nicene Creed as the summary of Christian belief—as "mitigated catholic orthodoxy." Churchill said this view was wrong, or at best outmoded, because it was "inconsistent with democracy," "supernatural," and "monarchical," attributes unsuited to the modern age. Churchill asserted that the modern Christian's development took place in three stages: obedience to the authority of the church based on fear (the level at which he claimed Mahan was stuck); individualism (an improvement but still bad); and "service, the highest state."[228] Despite the social gospel sympathies of the editor, an editorial in the same issue essentially sided with Mahan, accusing Churchill of attributing to the Episcopal Church beliefs and practices that were Roman Catholic.[229]

In the summer of 1913 Mahan wrote an introduction to the biography of Tasuka Serata, a vice admiral in the Imperial Japanese Navy, who was a Christian. Mahan had known Serata when he had been at the Naval Academy (class of 1881). The biography was going to be written by Lieutenant Commander K. Asami, also a Christian, who had written Mahan in March asking him to write the introduction. "Knowing your interest in the cause of religion and humanity, I venture to write." The book would be in Japanese, of course, but Asami hoped that some or all of it would be published in English as well. Asami thought the book would, in addition to promoting Christianity in Japan, promote international peace and "good feeling between your country and ours." A contribution from Mahan "would have great influence upon our officers, who are all familiar with your works."[230] Mahan replied in May, saying yes, and Asami thanked him profusely, hoping that Mahan would give a message that "will cause many to think of the power of Christ to make all men one."[231]

Mahan's introduction was essentially a sermon on the theme of unity in Christ, which ties all Christians together regardless of race or national origin. Though he had not seen Serata since 1880, "there was, and is, between Serata and myself a bond stronger than ordinary friendship. He was then, and until death continued to be, an avowed Christian, as I, too, then was and still am. In Christ there is for His followers a unity exceeding other ties." Since one of the purposes of the book was to encourage other Japanese to convert to Christianity, Mahan also explained that Christianity and devotion to the emperor as "temporal Sovereign" were not incompatible. Christ, however, was the "Sovereign of a nation which shall have no end." In Christ's kingdom there will be only one citizenship and all citizens will share a common trait, "likeness to Christ." Probably meant for an audience of Japanese naval officers, Mahan's introduction also stressed that Jesus Christ was a "Hero" and "a good patriot." Even though Japan had not yet fully embraced Christianity, it had "adopted its fruits" and thus gained the admiration of Europe.[232] Asami was happy with Mahan's contribution. He did finish the biography, but unfortunately no copy of it in either Japanese or English has ever been found.[233]

The summer of 1913 was indeed busy for Mahan. He wrote a great deal, which included published work, notes for himself, and drafts of speeches. One was an essay written for the Board of Missions called "The Purpose of a Life Work." Most definitions of happiness involved "that satisfaction with one's self and one's surroundings." There was nothing wrong with happiness, but the way most people chose to seek it—through "pleasure, wealth, power, knowledge, reputation, amusement, ease, and whatever others there be"—was not the way to find it. The only true happiness was the joy and peace that come through union with Christ. Even a life of service to God and humanity, if followed for its rewards, would not make someone truly happy. Only seeking the Kingdom of God, regardless of vocation, for its own sake would bring true joy because one would be in the "Presence" of Christ.[234]

At about this same time he wrote an essay called "The Christian Doctrine of the Trinity." It does not appear to have been published or given as a speech, so he might have written it for himself. It is not one of Mahan's best pieces, jumping as it does from topic to topic without a clear point, so it may have been nothing more than draft notes for a future speech or article. It strikes a somber note, talking about a Christian having to undergo "purging, pruning, suffering" in order to bear more fruit so that God may be glorified.[235]

During the last year and a half of Mahan's life (mid-1913 to late 1914) he became involved in controversies regarding the Episcopal Book of Common Prayer. Mahan had held strong opinions on the topic of Episcopal liturgy ever since he was a teenager, but this was the first time he had ever written on the topic. The impetus was the 1913 General Convention at which prayer book revision was a hot topic. Debate spilled over into the pages of *Churchman*, and Mahan took on the challenge of defending the traditionalist view.

During Mahan's lifetime two prayer books were used in the Episcopal Church, the 1789 and the 1892. There is no indication that Mahan was particularly bothered by any changes introduced in the 1892 book, undoubtedly because the changes were minimal.[236] Though in later years Mahan objected to the "tinkering" done in "previous revisions," it is not clear whether he meant the 1892 book itself or the more extensive revisions proposed in the *Book Annexed* of 1883 that were rejected by General Convention.[237] Historians of the liturgy agree that the 1892 book was extremely conservative in terms of revision because of the fear of party strife within the church. There was, however, a significant minority that was disappointed in the lack of change in the 1892 book and quickly organized to lobby for further revision. This lobby, pushing for a new Book of Common Prayer, was much in evidence at the 1913 General Convention, which had authorized a commission to propose revisions.[238]

In the November 8, 1913, issue of *Churchman*, Mahan wrote an article called "Freedom in the Use of the Prayer Book," in which he took to task the Reverend Dr. Charles L. Slattery, rector of Grace Church, New York City, and a supporter of prayer book revision. The main change Slattery advocated was the introduction of options as to choice of psalms, lessons, and canticles in morning prayer. Mahan said he understood the need for latitude in certain special occasions, especially when there were large numbers of non-Episcopalians present. But for regular worship in the congregation he was against these changes, for two reasons. One, introduction of options negated the concept of *common* prayer, Anglicans all over the world saying the same prayers and listening to the same scripture readings on any given Sunday. Second, extending too much liberty to clergy to make changes put the congregation at the mercy of the priest's personal likes and dislikes. He also found it disturbing that the advocates of change suggested that the present form of worship was "monotonous and wearisome." If that were so, Mahan charged, then it was the fault of the clergy themselves for not providing adequate instruction as to what the various parts of the service meant and how they fit together in common worship.[239]

Mahan's articles on the prayer book in *Churchman* attest to his vast knowledge of Anglican/Episcopal liturgy. Some of his arguments are extremely detailed and may be of interest only to liturgical scholars, but they reveal his love of the liturgy and how important it was to him personally. These articles also show a passion that even his other religious articles lack. In the April 11, 1914, issue of *Churchman*, he wrote an article on the Te Deum, a canticle (sung prayer) regularly used in the Sunday morning prayer service. He saw this canticle as "one of the most complete, as well as most majestic, of hymns truly Catholic [i.e., universally Christian]." He was outraged that some prayer book revisionists were proposing to give the clergy the option to drop it. He analyzed it line by line, explaining its power and beauty, and concluded with a "strong appeal—protest, if I may say so" against giving clergy this option. He reiterated his objection to abandoning catholic worship "under the guise of extending liberty."[240]

A few months later Mahan got involved in another debate that became known as the "starch controversy." The episode began with an article titled "The Sources of the Church's Strength and Weakness," by the Reverend Dr. Walker Gwynne, rector of Calvary Church, in Summit, New Jersey, which appeared in the July 25, 1914, issue of *Churchman*. The very first weakness Gwynne mentioned was a liturgical rigidity, which he referred to as "starch," implying lack of flexibility. After unfavorably comparing the present practice of Anglicanism to "the methods of the Primitive Church," Gwynne continued,

> [R]espectability and conformity were too long the rule, and still remain too much the rule among us. Our Prayer Book services and our habits are still hard and stiff with the starch which we have inherited from many generations, and which most of us, even with the best intentions, find it hard to get rid of. Let us hope that the new Joint Commission of the General Convention on the revision and enrichment of the Prayer Book, while retaining with all tenacity the rich treasure of our sacramental offices, will take some of the starch out of our choir [i.e., daily] offices, and give us more freedom in the use especially of the psalter, the lectionary and the canticles.[241]

Mahan wasted no time in returning fire, and his letter to the editor appeared in the August 8, 1914, issue. For starters, Mahan took exception to the word "starch," which he said was "ill chosen, as lacking in the seriousness and reverence with which the subject should be treated." Gwynne's agenda—prayer book revision—was no secret, but Mahan detected that Gwynne's ultimate goal went beyond simply revision of certain sections of the daily office.

> "Starch" it appears, consists in that "respectability and uniformity" characteristic of the set services; and the remedy proposed is expressed in the hope that the present Joint Commission on the Revision of the Prayer Book "will take out some of the starch," by giving "more freedom in the use *especially* [emphasis Mahan's], of the Psalter, the Lectionary and the Canticles." "Especially" indicates that the hope extends beyond these.

As before, Mahan objected to the introduction of *options* into the service, which to his mind destroyed the concept of *common* prayer.

> [T]he proposition of Dr. Gwynne is that in the Morning and Evening Prayer—Sundays not excepted—the entire service from the Lord's Prayer to the Creed is to be at the discretion of the officiating clergyman; not as regulated by the Church for a *common* [emphasis in original] worship, and be made merely that of the particular congregation; disconnected in fact, as in form, from all other congregations. It thus dismisses the catholicity of St. Paul, that "with one accord ye may with one mouth glorify God" (Rom. xv. 6); a oneness of utterance which he connects explicitly with oneness of mind and purpose—"likemindedness."

Not loath to use sarcasm, Mahan commented,

> For completeness, Dr. Gwynne's suggestion needs only the addition—entirely congruous—that, when the officiating clergyman prefers, he shall substitute

extemporary prayer for the prayers following the Creed. Under such a system no congregation can know what form the worship of another is taking, and there will be no common praise or prayer beyond the four walls of the building. We shall have abandoned the catholic practice of the Church and adopted that of the purely Protestant separatist bodies that surround us.

To Mahan common prayer was the cornerstone of Anglican worship. That he took it seriously is evident from this letter as well as his response to Slattery. He even pointed out in his response to Gwynne that "common praise" as expressed through the canticles was "a nobler function than even that of common prayer." Thus it galled him that Gwynne had called for more leeway in choice of canticles. Though Gwynne had not directly said so, Mahan assumed that one of the reasons Gwynne wanted more options was that worshipers found the Venite and Te Deum "monotonous or wearisome." Mahan could not believe "[t]hat any one with a moderately intelligent understanding of the structure and association of the Canticles" could find them so, but if that was the case he put the blame squarely on the clergy. The remedy for such a deplorable situation was not more options in the services but better teaching of the services as presently structured.

> The trouble is that the clergy do not put their own minds to the comprehension of these great hymns much less instruct their people. Whatever "starch" there is, is in the uninstructed intelligence and apathetic imagination of the worshippers; and this fault will not be remedied by the Church abandoning her own function of governance of worship to a body of dissociated clergymen acting independently from Sunday to Sunday.

There was a certain amount of experimentation already being practiced, and Mahan concluded his letter with a jab at the liturgical indignities to which he had been subjected. "As for the laity, under the system—if adopted—I trust they have imagination enough to fancy what they will get. We already have a certain amount of experience."[242]

Gwynne responded in the August 22, 1914, issue. Apparently he had no stomach for a war of words with Mahan, as he backed off his own argument with some haste. In a letter titled by the editor "'Starch' Again," Gwynne blamed the editor for omitting sentences in his original article that changed his meaning and caused Mahan to misunderstand him. "Two whole sentences at this point were omitted, in which I referred to the 'many and diverse tongues, and races, and civilizations,' the result of our tremendous tide of immigration, which form one of our greatest problems. It was in regard to these conditions that I expressed the hope that the General Convention would 'give us more freedom.'" This was an irrelevant point since the fact that immigrants were coming to

America had no bearing on Mahan's view of common prayer. The implication of Gwynne's argument was that having more options in the services would make the Episcopal Church more appealing to immigrants. Given Mahan's argument for the importance of *common* prayer, Gwynne's new tactic would certainly not sway him. Indeed, with a more ethnically diverse congregation, Mahan's point would be borne out. It was common prayer that united an otherwise diverse group of people into a worshiping congregation and into the larger Anglican communion.

Gwynne tried another ploy, claiming that Mahan misunderstood his use of the word "starch." He now claimed that what he meant by that term was "our too frequently assumed social superiority, our coldness of manner, our eminent respectability, and our too frequent lack of adaptation for work among the uncultured or unchurched multitudes." This, too, was a flimsy argument since the "starch" segment of his original article clearly referred to liturgical practice, not to missions or evangelism or ecumenical relations.

He also tried to assure Mahan that they were really on the same side after all. He was, he said, "a rubrical rigorist" and sympathized with Mahan "in his laymen's dislike of the too frequent liberties that some of the clergy take in this connection." He claimed that allowing more options in the offices would take away the excuse that some priests used to justify those "liberties." He also pointed out that some of the same suggestions he made were being made in England by "competent liturgical scholars."[243] If this letter made any impression on Mahan, we do not know, as he chose not to respond. Perhaps he thought he had gotten the better of Gwynne or that he had nothing to add to his original argument.

In any case the contention did not end there. A layman named Charles Fiske came to Gwynne's defense in the August 29, 1914, issue. Making the argument even more strongly than Gwynne, Fiske maintained that "the Church's worship is a formal, ceremonial, inflexible function, out of touch with the thought of men and insensitive to the world's need." Part of the problem was the liturgy itself and the traditional Anglican attitude toward it, which Fiske felt turned "Sunday worship [into] a thing apart, a sacred performance of an unchanging rite, not the living expression of an intense desire." But a good part of the problem lay with the laity, whom Fiske thought "do not possess the devotional instinct to such a degree as to find in this use of the ordinary methods of worship a sufficient expression of a great and pressing desire."

Of particular concern to Fiske was the outbreak of war in Europe. He expressed his dismay that the prayer book made no provision for special prayers nor allowed the clergyman to compose his own.

> The awful tragedy of the European war emphasizes for Churchmen the need either of greater adaptability in the use of the Book of Common Prayer or of a wider and more frequent exercise of their liturgical functions by the Bishops. With all Europe plunged into a war at whose possibilities of multiplied horror the civilized world stands aghast, it does seem the height of absurdity that in the thousands of our churches not one word of prayer should be uttered for a speedy peace or the triumph of justice and righteousness.

Fiske complained that at the church he had attended the previous Sunday there was no mention of the war in the sermon. His complaint may have had validity, but it hardly seemed fair to blame the prayer book for it. In any case, he took the opportunity presented by the war to push his case for prayer book revision that would include "the right to introduce extemporaneous prayer" and "the addition of more prayers for particular occasions."[244]

Mahan responded that same day (though his letter did not appear till the September 12 issue) and took Fiske to task for his ignorance of the prayer book, which Mahan maintained already had plenty of suitable prayers. He said that he "deeply share[d]" Fiske's "broad sympathy shown for the peoples of Europe distressed by the war," but he disagreed with Fiske's proposed solution. "It is doubtless difficult for a Liturgy to provide beforehand petitions calculated for an unforeseen catastrophe of exceptionable magnitude; but extempore prayers are a remedy worse than the disease, if so be that the Prayer Book provide resources adequate to the occasion. I think it does in this case, if ministers and people will use their brains."

He then illustrated this with examples such as "the petition of the Litany for all Christian Rulers,—governments,—and of the other, that 'unity, peace and concord' be granted to all nations." He also pointed out that there were places in the liturgy, including immediately after the creed in morning prayer, where it was perfectly appropriate for the officiant "to call the attention of the people to the desolating strife." While he conceded that exceptional calamities such as war might call for "additional supplications," acceptable if used in the appropriate place, he deplored Fiske's using the war as an excuse to elasticize the starch. "It is said that exceptional cases make for bad legislation, and, while the present may point the need for enrichment by additional prayers, to use it to promote so-called elasticity is to be deprecated."[245]

Thus ended the "starch controversy," but Mahan was not done with the subject of liturgical revision. He wrote a two-part article, "Prayer Book Revision," which appeared in the October 10 and October 17, 1914, issues of *Churchman*. Part I reiterated points already made in previous articles and letters to the editor, namely that allowing options ruined the catholicity of worship, that the laity needed instruction in how the liturgy was put together, and that options put the congregation at the mercy of the priest's own agenda. Part II contained Mahan's own recommendations for change, but with the caveat that any changes made by the General Convention be made mandatory, not optional. His proposals involved extremely minute details of the liturgical services. Once again, these articles attest to Mahan's vast knowledge of the Anglican liturgy and its historical precedents.[246]

Though the prayer book issue consumed a good deal of his thought and time, Mahan continued to write on other aspects of religion as well. In October 1913 Charles W. Eliot, president of Harvard, spoke before a Unitarian conference in Buffalo, New York. His speech, titled "Twentieth-Century Christianity," was subsequently printed in the *New York Times* and then published as a pamphlet. Eliot considered Unitarianism a form of Christianity, though Mahan and many other Christians did not since Unitarians did not recognize the divinity of Jesus Christ but rather saw him as a great humanitarian teacher. Eliot's thesis was that science and higher criticism had made traditional Christianity outmoded, and, in addition, a religion that talked of God as king was outmoded as well. The only future of Christianity was in Unitarianism, and Unitarians themselves needed to propagate this view more vigorously.[247]

Mahan took to the pages of *North American Review* (April 1914 issue) to respond. While Eliot's article took up only one page in the *Times* magazine supplement, Mahan's article was ten pages long. He eviscerated Eliot's argument. Whatever else Unitarianism was, it was certainly not Christian and never would be. Whereas Eliot speculated on the future, Mahan "appeal[ed] to history in which Jesus Christ once lived on earth and as resurrected Lord still acted."[248]

To Mahan there was no common ground between orthodox Christianity and Unitarianism on this point. Jesus was either God or he was not. Mahan also expounded at length on the motivation of Christians throughout the centuries. Following a good teacher would not explain why so many had died or risked their lives and were still doing so in the name of Jesus. He also claimed that Christianity and its spread by missionaries were responsible for much of the material progress of the world. Some of his cultural chauvinism kicked in here since he clearly believed that Protestant societies were freer and more advanced than those dominated by Roman Catholicism or Eastern Orthodoxy, but even those were more advanced and improving than non-Christian societies. And even in those non-Christian societies, if their governments allowed Christianity to exist and allowed freedom for Christians to practice their religion, they would advance more quickly than those that did not. He cited Japan and China as examples. He did not claim that material and political progress was solely due to Christianity. "I simply state the unchallengeable fact that, wherever Christianity is, there coincidentally is progress; and that where Christianity is not, there is coincident decadence until Christianity enters." Unitarianism could not hope to match this record because only Jesus could inspire the devotion and the power his followers needed. "[A]dmiration for a long-dead teacher, such as Socrates," has not had anything near the impact on the world that Christianity has had. He concluded by charging that it was Unitarianism, a nineteenth-century construct stemming from eighteenth-century Deism, that was outmoded. It was Christianity that changed the world and would continue to do so.[249]

The rejoinder to Eliot was well-received in numerous quarters. Thomas Gailor, bishop of Tennessee, wrote, "I thank God for a layman who can state the faith as you have declared it."[250] Secretary of the Navy Josephus Daniels, a Methodist, wrote, "I have read with the greatest pleasure and profit your article in *The North American Review*, replying to Dr. Eliot. It is most helpful to the younger men to read your clear call to hold fast to the ancient landmarks our fathers set."[251]

In August 1914 Mahan returned to the arbitration issue, or rather the church did and Mahan responded. "The Mediatorial Office of the Church toward the State" appeared in the August 29, 1914, issue of *Churchman*. The United States had signed arbitration treaties with thirty nations, and the Episcopal Church was supporting the treaties. This article made essentially the same points as his previous letters on this topic, but it went into more detail on the church involving itself in politics, something he was adamantly against. The church and the state were created by God for different purposes and should not encroach upon each other. While individual Christians can and should be involved if called to do so—and every Christian at a minimum was called to be a good citizen—the church as an institution should not endorse specific policies. To do so is to usurp the legislature's function. Mahan was concerned that the church had lost sight of this and was becoming infected by a "spurious substitute" of political action instead of preaching the gospel. The only thing the church ought to be doing regarding political issues was praying for the nation, its leaders, and officeholders. This was what Mahan meant by "mediatorial." The church's one political function was prayer, that is, interceding with God for the state. Anything other than that was usurping the state's God-given function. Individual Christians should be the light and salt in society as they sought the Holy Spirit's guidance as to how best to serve their neighbors.[252]

CHAPTER 7

FINAL DAYS

Mahan continued to write about naval history and current geopolitical issues. Some books included reprints of previously published articles, while some contained new material. These books were *Naval Administration and Warfare* (1908), which included a reprint of his American Historical Association presidential address, *The Interest of America in International Conditions* (1910), *Naval Strategy Compared and Contrasted* (1911), *Armaments and Arbitration* (1912), which included his rejoinder to Angell, and *The Major Operations of the Navies in the War of American Independence* (1913), a revised version of a previous contribution to volume 3 of William Laird Clowes' *The Royal Navy: A History from the Earliest Times to the Present* (1898).[1] These books will not be discussed in detail since they do not reflect on religion in any way except for the occasional discussion of "just war" theory that reiterated what Mahan had said in earlier volumes.[2] *Naval Strategy*, a reworking of lectures delivered at the Naval War College between 1887 and 1911, is interesting in that it established another direct intellectual link to Mahan's father in the person of William Tecumseh Sherman. Alfred had stayed in touch with Sherman, and before Sherman died in 1891, he had read and commented on some of the drafts of Alfred's original lectures at the NWC. In this volume Alfred thanked him.[3]

In November 1912 Mahan and family went to Europe on what turned out to be his last trip abroad. Their first stop was London, where he visited his Royal Navy friends. One of the people he met with was the other Winston Churchill, now First Lord of the Admiralty. Churchill "told me he was about to read the book [*Naval Strategy*] upon the recommendation to him of one of the 'Sea Lords.'"[4] He also visited his brother Fred, who had retired from the Army and was now living in Paris. They visited Elly's sister in Pau, then went on into Italy.[5] While the Mahans were in Europe, the Balkan War had begun in which the Bulgarians, Serbs, Montenegrins, and Greeks were rebelling against the Ottoman Empire. Mahan was concerned that a regional conflict might lead to a general European war. He was eager to get home, though he claimed he was not "worried." Daughter Ellen used the word "uneasy" instead, remembering he wanted to "get my women folk out,—not to say my gray hairs, what I have of them."[6]

Mahan expounded on the war in a few places. Though Seager claims that he hated the Turks, this idea is not accurate. "I believe the individual Turk is not a bad sort, but any people more hopelessly unfit for governing, it is hard to imagine." Turkish misrule, he believed, was largely due to the practice of the Muslim religion and its refusal to let Christianity be practiced in its lands. "Turkish misrule is not because they are Turks, but because Mahomet has blinded their eyes to the Person of Christ." In fairness to Mahan, he also blamed the Balkan states (supposedly Christian) for turning on each other once they got rid of Ottoman rule, and in his view they had much less of an excuse.[7] He also blamed the European powers, "who had acquiesced in the miseries of the Turkish provinces, [then] intervened with a peaceful arbitrament on their own account, in their own interest," which Mahan said led to "a most cruel war." The Mahans arrived safely home in April 1913.[8]

Mahan also opined on another controversial topic of the day, women's suffrage, though how interested he really was in this issue is hard to say. It could not have been of consuming interest since only one instance can be documented in which he offered an opinion. Still, that opinion is interesting since he brought a Christian perspective to it. His papers contain an undated draft of what is labeled "A Speech," though if he actually gave the speech and to what audience we do not know. Mahan was against women having the right to vote, although his reason was most emphatically not because he thought women were too stupid to understand politics or even because he thought women were inferior to men in any way. His reasons—while hardly palatable today—were based on his scriptural understanding of the role of the sexes. His starting point was to claim that the issue was "not *equality* in any sense, but *identity* of social function" (emphases in the original). He stressed that Christianity did *not* teach inequality of the sexes. "The equality of the sexes has been the teaching of Christianity from the beginning; and nowhere else than where Christianity enters has that equality been found, because women have neither the physical nor the moral energy to compel it by brute force." Christianity, however, "emphasizes differentiation and desires identity of function." Women were made by God to "concentrate their ambitions and affections upon the home, the children, and all the sacred relationships attaching to these words." Entering "the outside hurly-burly

of masculine life" would "disperse their energies and modify their characters."
That was his view as a Christian, but the key question for any social or political issue was, was it good for the community? His answer was no. And it was
not so much because women's voting by itself would threaten the family, but
because—as pretty much everyone knew would happen—voting would "necessarily [open] the full range of all the political activities," which included running
for and holding public office. This would "reverse what has heretofore been fundamental in our society."[9]

In only one other place, also a draft document, did he discuss the role of
women, but it was not in the context of the suffrage issue. In his draft essay on
"The Christian Doctrine of the Trinity," he waxed eloquent on the role of the
Christian wife as "the priestess in the home," meaning that she functioned as
"the intercessor between God and the other members." These other members
included "the husband, the children, and most especially toward the servants."
By fulfilling the role with "constant intercession [and] prayer" the wife conse-
crated the home, "filling it with the beauty of holiness."[10] One can understand
why Mahan would have serious doubts about women's suffrage, but there is
no doubt that his views were sincerely held and indeed were common at the
time. It does not, though, seem to have been an issue to which he devoted
much attention.

In July 1913 J. Franklin Jameson, whom Mahan knew from his American
Historical Association days, was head of the Department of Historical Research
at the Carnegie Institution in Washington, D.C. He invited Mahan to become
a research associate for "one winter of five or six months." Mahan was not keen
on moving to Washington, even temporarily, and he was unclear on what his
duties would be. He was told it was to have a weekly chat with Jameson and "talk
informally to [the staff] about historical matters." The former was fine, but the
latter puzzled him. He feared it would require preparation, which would take
time away from his proposed research project, "a history of the United States
from the point of view of expansion."[11] Nonetheless the duties were light and the
money was good ($2,400), "an offer not to be disregarded in these hard times."
So he accepted the offer and was due to begin in November 1914.[12]

In the meantime a world war had broken out in Europe. Seager claims that
Mahan "had long assured his readers" that this war among the major powers
"would likely never happen" and that Mahan "was surprised by the sudden
onset" of the war. If Seager is trying to downgrade Mahan's status as a military pundit, he does not succeed. A look at Mahan's comments on the First and
Second Balkan Wars indicates that he foresaw trouble ahead.[13] Even before an
actual world war was under way, reporters sought out Mahan for his opinion,

which he was eager to give. As the initial Serbian crisis escalated, he advised Britain "to declare war at once," deeming it essential to that nation's reputation as a trustworthy ally. He expressed his confidence in the superiority of the Royal Navy. "Speaking from my standpoint, as an American, I tell you that there is only one navy in the world, and that the others are mere striplings by comparison."[14] Mahan blamed Europe as a whole for the war. "Europe now is reaping the harvest of past blunders which even at the time of their occurrence it was difficult to reconcile with sound statesmanship."[15] But at the same time, while not blaming Germany solely, he thought Germany bore a large share of the blame and must be defeated.[16] In handwritten notes he explained why he now wished to see Germany defeated even though in previous writings he had expressed a preference for the Teutonic culture over that of the Slav. "[T]he Teuton had come so under the domination not merely of an arrogant military caste, but of the ideas of that caste, that the immediate necessity of civilization is a defeat which shall humble them to the dust, but not crush them."[17]

Mahan made only two published statements on the war. One was an interview with the *New York Evening Post* published on August 3, 1914, while the other was an article in *Leslie's Illustrated Weekly Newspaper* that ran on August 20, 1914.[18] Afterwards the curtain of censorship fell. President Woodrow Wilson, trying to enforce American neutrality not only of action but of opinion, ordered "all officers of the Service, whether active or retired, to refrain from public comment of any kind upon the military or political situation on the other side of the water."[19] Mahan appealed to Secretary Daniels, claiming that a retired officer was no different than a private citizen and should not be "silenced," but to no avail. Daniels replied that pro-British bias would "trench upon the lines of American neutrality."[20] Mahan already had several articles lined up, but had to cancel them and in one case return the money already paid.[21] Mahan's family, notably his brother Fred and his sister Jane, believed this decision so upset him that it hastened his death.[22] Mahan suffered "a rather sharp heart attack" in mid-September, which he blamed on "pressure of work," possibly a reference to other small writing projects unconnected with the war, or letters to the editor.[23]

Elly and the daughters moved to Washington in late October 1914 after finding a suitable rental house. Mahan joined them there on November 1. His health worsened, though, and he wrote to one of Elly's in-laws that "I have dragged on from day to day without energy to take up my pen." He reluctantly performed two social duties: leaving his calling card at the White House and the Secretary of the Navy's office.[24] He also attempted a few visits to the Carnegie Institution. Jameson later commented, "He charmed us all by his kindness and by the courtesy he showed even to the youngest of the young women in the office."[25] He was

Portrait of Mahan by Alexander James *(Naval War College Museum)*

mostly homebound after November 9, when he began to be treated by Navy doctor, F. M. Pleadwell. He did make it to church (St. Thomas's) on November 15, where Rear Adm. Bradley A. Fiske, who had studied under Luce and Mahan at the Naval War College, spotted him in the congregation. "Admiral A. T. Mahan in church this morning. Looked well, but a little older. He joined in all the singing."[26] Later that same day he wrote to the doctor about how poorly he felt with stomach trouble and lack of sleep.[27] In mid-November, when he heard of the death of his old friend Field Marshal Lord Roberts, "he stood looking out of the window and drumming on the pane, saying, 'Lucky Bobs, lucky Bobs.'"[28]

On November 28 his doctor had him moved to the Naval Hospital in Washington. He did not seem to object. His daughter Ellen said that "he cheered up for a while when two nice young orderlies came to take him to the Naval Hospital. His whole expression was that of one who felt that everything was going to be all right and, as he was taken down stairs in a stretcher, he looked at me and winked."[29] In the hospital, shortly before his death, he looked at a tree outside his window and said to a nurse, "If a few more quiet years were granted me, I might see and enjoy these things, but God is just and I am content."[30] He declined rapidly and died at 7:15 in the morning on December 1.[31]

Mahan's funeral was held at St. Thomas's Church; the Reverend C. Ernest Smith presided. At Mahan's request there was no naval ceremony and he was buried in civilian clothes, reflecting his belief that there was no rank in heaven.[32] The service was a simple burial office. Mahan's cousin, Eugenia Cheston, attended and later wrote to Elly, "I was so glad we could be with you at this beautiful service at St. Thomas' Church. It seemed to me that the simplicity of it all was just what Cousin Alfred would have liked."[33] His remains were taken to Quogue and buried in the churchyard at Church of the Atonement. His tombstone also makes no reference to his rank. It reads simply, "Alfred Thayer Mahan United States Navy" with his dates.[34]

Mahan's death received extensive coverage, nationally and internationally, especially in Britain. It was the front-page story in the *New York Times*, and the *Times* reported stories in the British press as well. Tributes were published in many venues and Elly was swamped with personal letters.[35] Many discussed his Christian faith.

Secretary Daniels responded the very day of Mahan's death in a letter to Elly.

> Admiral Mahan was not only a fine type of Naval Officer, but possessed a lovable character that endeared him to all with whom he came in contact. . . . In your distress you must feel a solemn pride that throughout the world to-day his passing will be learned of with deep regret. . . . Your grief is shared not only by the Service he loved and long and nobly worked for, but by the Nation.[36]

The Navy Department issued its own public tribute as well, noting "no writer of modern times evinced a keener insight in the affairs of the world. . . . [H]is death leaves a void among naval and political authorities of the world that no author and writer can fill."[37]

The British, of course, were at war and counted Mahan as one of their naval saviors, not only for his cogent analyses of their past naval glories but, more to the point, for his tireless efforts to warn the British government of the German threat and the need to keep up British naval supremacy. Cecil Spring-Rice, the

British ambassador to the United States, wrote to Elly, "It is my duty on behalf of the British Admiralty to express the sorrow British sailors feel at the death of your husband. . . . The achievements of our sailors were his theme and their consequences his doctrine. . . . We remember also that he was a sincere friend of our country in times when friends are dear."[38] The *Morning Post* of London wrote, "In Admiral Mahan dies the greatest among naval historians. . . . This country owes to the great American a debt which can never be repaid, for he was the first elaborately and comprehensively to formulate the philosophy of British sea power, and from time to time, as occasions of difficulty arose, he published an essay or an article which indicated the right course for Britain to follow."[39] The *Daily Chronicle* of London said, "Admiral Mahan's death will come to the British people with a sense of acute personal loss."[40] The British Navy Records Society passed a resolution "to record their sense of the loss the British Empire has sustained" by the death "of one who so generously appreciated the real work of the Royal Navy."[41]

Many Americans weighed in as well. Historian James Ford Rhodes said, "I learned very much from him and always felt that, after an interview, I had made an intellectual advance . . . history and literature have suffered a great loss."[42] Even though Mahan had attended Columbia University for only two years, it was proud to claim him as an alumnus and published a lengthy tribute in the *Columbia University Quarterly*. Written by a longtime acquaintance, William Milligan Sloane, it praised Mahan's work for its perspicacity and lucid argument. "Were we to reckon the greatness of historical work by its contemporary influence, his would be a reputation which in the long list of modern historians in all lands cannot be exactly paralleled." Sloane referred to Mahan's religious faith. "Behind the historian was the man, a devout and orthodox Christian, with a strain of mysticism, inquiring into the divine purposes as revealed in the course of human events." He also defended Mahan against charges of being a warmonger; "the writer must enter a protest against the charge that he was at any time, in conversation or in his writings, an apostle of war. So far from that, he was preeminently an apostle of peace." His advocacy of a strong navy was "solely for the safety and dignity of the land which was dear to him."[43] Bradley Fiske paid tribute to Mahan's character as well as his intellect in a tribute in the U.S. Naval Institute *Proceedings*. "Duty, in whatever form it came, was sacred. Invariably he gave to its performance the best that was in him."[44]

The Outlook published two pieces on Mahan. An anonymous article published immediately after his death praised his astute judgment as well as his "deeply moral and religious nature." Praising him as "both a true warrior and a student of history," the writer, obviously concerned about how the European war would affect America, said, "America loses one whom just now she can ill afford to lose. For never was there a time when the problem of our country's defense more needed the influence of a man with Mahan's vision and sanity."[45] A few months later Theodore Roosevelt published his tribute titled "A Great Public Servant." He praised Mahan for his great works of naval history and for doing his best to convince the American public and their leaders of the necessity of a strong navy, a cause also dear to Roosevelt's heart. "But in the vitally important task of convincing the masters of us all—the people as a whole—of the importance of a true understanding of naval needs, Mahan stood alone. There was no one else in his class or anywhere near it." Roosevelt minced no words; Mahan was "the greatest naval writer in history." Highly critical of Wilson's handling of the European war, Roosevelt managed to get in a dig against "the present administration in Washington" and claimed that their understanding of the importance of the Navy was thirty years behind the times. Mahan's works, he concluded, should be read "by all Americans who desire to know what the real interest of their country demands in the way of thought and actions."[46]

Mahan would have no doubt felt vindicated by all the tributes, but he probably would have been the most moved by the ones that came from church friends, groups, and publications. Bishop Greer of New York wrote to Elly, "I shared with all the world the admiration for his eminent services to his chosen profession, and yet, beyond and above all that, I admired him for the beauty and charm of his Christian character." Greer, in his capacity as president of the American Church Institute for Negroes, also issued a statement saying that the organization had sustained "a very great loss." Mahan's "counsel and advice were always prized, and it will be difficult if not impossible to find anyone to fill his place."[47]

The Seamen's Church Institute, on whose board Mahan sat for forty-seven years, passed a resolution stating that he "was an absolutely conscientious member of the many Committees on which he willingly, faithfully, and graciously served." He was an "unfailing and unselfish" champion of the merchant seaman's welfare and "a man of God of superior intellect, and with profound religious convictions; a great Churchman and an ardent patriot."[48]

Even Trinity, Wall Street, a parish to which Mahan never belonged, issued a statement. "In the death of Admiral Mahan, the Church has lost one who may truly be described as a great layman, accepting with his whole heart the Church's teaching, interested and active in her work, illustrating her truth in his own Christian character and life." The resolution praised *The Harvest Within*, "which reveals both his unusual theological knowledge and the reality of his own spiritual experience. . . . It would be well if every Churchman would make himself familiar with this volume."[49]

Churchman, the publication to which Mahan had contributed so much, had two significant obituaries, one from a clergyman and one from a layman. The clergyman was George William Douglas, who had baptized Lyle many years before. He recalled his first meeting with Mahan at Lyle's baptism and called him "a Churchman to the core." Mahan combined "religious conviction with fine intellectuality." Douglas also believed that "in relation to history in general, Mahan had the keenest sense of the implication of the life and doctrine of Christ." Douglas then wandered off into a discussion of the war, which seemed slightly out of place in an obituary. He suggested that Mahan had been struggling with some guilt over having inadvertently contributed to the outbreak of the war through the influence of his Sea Power books on the German navy. There is actually no evidence of Mahan's feeling guilty in any way, at least not on that score. Douglas was, in his own words, one of those people who thought war, while justifiable in some cases in the past, was now outmoded. "Has not a new epoch now opened on the world? . . . [I]s it not evident that henceforth all war will be stupid? . . . [I]t is the duty of all Christians to devote themselves to expediting the means and methods for maintaining peace and averting war altogether." He tried to project those thoughts onto Mahan, but anyone who knew Mahan or his writings would hardly be convinced. Douglas also discussed Mahan's most recent passion, resisting revision of the prayer book. While praising Mahan "as a man of God—an unusually intelligent Christian," he himself was in favor of revision and could not resist a criticism of Mahan's position. He said that "some of us wished that he was less islanded in Anglicanism; that he were more flexible and genial. He did not sense sufficiently the popular mind and our average condition." Mahan would surely not have agreed with that claim, inasmuch as he viewed himself as speaking for the average layperson, the one who, like Mahan, did not want his liturgy messed about by meddling clerics! Nonetheless Douglas conceded that Mahan's concern with common prayer was genuine and based on the comfort the prayer book brought him on lonely sea voyages. While succumbing to the temptation to use the obituary to push his own agenda, Douglas' admiration was sincere, and he said in closing, "we leave our friend in God's safe keeping, where he wished to be—'Safe home: safe in port.'"[50]

Churchman's lay tribute was written by a fellow Episcopalian naval officer, Rear Adm. Charles H. Stockton. Stockton had known Mahan since his own midshipman days at the Naval Academy and had served under him at the Naval War College. He avoided controversial issues and gave a simple tribute to Mahan as a thinker and Churchman. "He had become an author, a thinker, an historian, and a naval statesman, but in it all and interwoven throughout was the earnest, sincere and devout Christian." This was as succinct a summary of Mahan's life as any.[51]

Mahan's fellow parishioners at Church of the Atonement, Quogue, also felt the loss. The rector, Frederick B. Carter, was by his own admission intimidated by having Mahan in his congregation. "He had a strong effect upon me whenever I preached, silently challenging me, as it were, to do my best, and I count it one of the greatest privileges of my life to have had him as a hearer for so many years during the summer."[52] Well might a priest feel intimidated by Mahan, knowing that Mahan was not in the slightest intimidated by him.

For all the honors heaped upon him in his lifetime and tributes given after his death, Mahan would probably have been most touched by that of his fellow parishioners in Quogue. A plaque was put up in the church in his honor by his "Friends and Fellow-Worshippers." It read "To the Glory of God. In Memoriam. Alfred Thayer Mahan 1840–1914 Rear-Admiral United States Navy. Great among the nations as an expounder of Sea-Power: Greater in the Kingdom of GOD as an example of a Christian man."[53] There could be no better summing up of Mahan's life than that.

Any discussion of Mahan's life, career, and writings is incomplete without taking into account his deep Christian faith and how he applied it to everything he did as an officer, historian, strategist, Churchman, son, husband, and father. To fail to understand this is to fail to understand Mahan.

NOTES

Abbreviations Used in the Notes

ATM	Alfred Thayer Mahan
DHM	Dennis Hart Mahan
GTS	General Theological Seminary
JMH	*Journal of Military History*
LC	Library of Congress
LPATM	*Letters and Papers of Alfred Thayer Mahan*, (Seager and Maguire, eds.)
MM	Milo Mahan
NWC	United States Naval War College
USMA	United States Military Academy
USNIP	United States Naval Institute *Proceedings*

INTRODUCTION

1. Henry L. Stimson and McGeorge Bundy, *On Active Service in Peace and War* (New York: Harper Brothers, 1948), 506. Stimson was secretary of war from 1940 to 1945.

2. See, for example, the essays in John B. Hattendorf, ed., *The Influence of History on Mahan* (Newport, R.I.: Naval War College Press, 1991), which discuss Mahan's impact on navies and naval history around the world.

3. Charles Carlisle Taylor, *The Life of Admiral Mahan* (New York: George H. Doran Co., 1920).

4. Ibid., 307.

5. Ibid., viii.

6. Ibid., vii–viii, x.

7. William D. Puleston, *Mahan: The Life and Work of Captain Alfred Thayer Mahan, U.S.N.* (New Haven, Conn.: Yale University Press, 1939), v.

8. Ibid., v–viii.

9. Robert Seager II, *Alfred Thayer Mahan: The Man and His Letters* (Annapolis, Md.: Naval Institute Press, 1977); Robert Seager II and Doris D. Maguire, eds., *Letters and Papers of Alfred Thayer Mahan*, 3 vols. (Annapolis, Md.: Naval Institute Press, 1975).

10. Seager, *ATM*, xi, 458.

11. Charles E. Neu, "*Review of Alfred Thayer Mahan: The Man and His Letters*," *Journal of American History* 65 (1979): 1167.

12. Richard Turk, "*Review of Robert Seager II, Alfred Thayer Mahan: The Man and His Letters*," *Military Affairs* 42 (1978): 160.

13. Peter Karsten, *The Naval Aristocracy: The Golden Age of Annapolis and the Emergence of Modern American Navalism* (New York: Free Press, 1972).

14. Reo N. Leslie Jr., "Christianity and the Evangelist for Sea Power: The Religion of Alfred Thayer Mahan," in Hattendorf, ed., *Influence of History on Mahan*, chap. 11; Jon Tetsuro Sumida, *Inventing Grand Strategy and Teaching Command: The Classic Works of Alfred Thayer Mahan Reconsidered* (Baltimore: Johns Hopkins University Press, 1997).

CHAPTER 1. FAMILY

1. Puleston, *Mahan*, vi, 1–3. Puleston did the most extensive research on the Mahan family background and Dennis' early life. He was aided in his research by a Norfolk lawyer, John B. Jenkins. See also Puleston-Jenkins correspondence in ATM Papers, LC.

2. Ibid., 3.

3. Ibid.

4. John Henry Hopkins Jr., ed., *The Collected Works of the Late Milo Mahan, D.D.* (New York, 1875) 3: iii; Taylor, Mahan, 3.

5. Puleston, *Mahan*, 4; Taylor, *Mahan*, 3; ATM, *From Sail to Steam: Recollections of Naval Life* (New York: Harper & Brothers, 1907), x.

6. Puleston, *Mahan*, 4–5.

7. Ibid., 4; ATM, *Sail to Steam*, xi; Thomas E. Griess, "Dennis Hart Mahan: West Point Professor and Advocate of Military Professionalism, 1830–1871" (PhD diss., Duke University, 1969), 4–5.

8. Jane Leigh Mahan, "Random Memories," *The Pointer*, March 15, 1929, 6.

9. Griess, "DHM," 93.

10. On Thayer's reforms and innovations, see Griess, "DHM," 68–114; Stephen E. Ambrose, *Duty, Honor, Country: A History of West Point* (Baltimore: Johns Hopkins University Press, 1966), 62–105; James L. Morrison Jr., "*The Best School*": *West Point, 1833–1866* (Kent, Ohio: Kent State University Press, 1986), 3–4, 23–26.

11. Griess, "DHM," 105–6, 111; for a detailed description of Dennis' cadet years see 90–114.

12. DHM to Esther M. Mahan, June 29, 1824, ATM Papers, LC.

13. Herman A. Norton, *Struggling for Recognition: The United States Army Chaplaincy, 1791–1865* (Washington, D.C.: Department of the Army, 1977), 24; Morrison, *"The Best School,"* 57; Joseph G. Swift, *The Memoirs of General Joseph Gardner Swift* (Worcester, Mass., 1890), 219.

14. Norton, *Struggling for Recognition*, 27–29.

15. Seager, *ATM*, 2.

16. DHM to Esther M. Mahan, June 29, 1824, ATM Papers, LC.

17. Griess, "DHM," 115–18.

18. Ibid., 119–21.

19. DHM to Mary Ann Charlton, June 25, 1827, ATM Papers, LC.

20. Griess, "DHM," 129; for a full description of Dennis' time at Metz, see 128–32.

21. Puleston, *Mahan*, 7; Anne Ayres, *The Life and Work of William Augustus Muhlenberg* (New York, 1880), 129–30; Alvin W. Skardon, *Church Leader in the Cities: William Augustus Muhlenberg* (Philadelphia: University of Pennsylvania Press, 1971), 5, 59, 77.

22. Griess, "DHM," 133–35; George W. Cullum, *Biographical Register of the Officers and Graduates of the U.S. Military Academy at West Point*, N.Y., 2nd ed. (New York, 1868), 1:256–57.

23. Puleston, *Mahan*, 11.

24. "Mahan Genealogy" (comp. Robert Seager, II), typescript; Lyle Evans Mahan, "My Recollections of My Grandmother," typescript, DHM Papers, USMA Library. Lyle's recollections were also reprinted; see Lyle Evans Mahan, "My Parents, Rear Admiral and Mrs. Alfred Thayer Mahan," in *Influence of History on Mahan*, John B. Hattendorf, ed. (Newport, R.I., Naval War College Press, 1991), 109–25.

25. Griess, "DHM," 147; for a complete listing of DHM's books, see 376–77; Morrison, *"The Best School,"* 49.

26. DHM, *An Elementary Treatise on Advanced-Guard, Out-Post, and Detachment Service of Troops, and the Manner of Posting and Handling Them in Presence of an Enemy*, rev. ed. (New York, 1864), title page.

27. William B. Skelton, *An American Profession of Arms: The Army Officer Corps, 1784–1861* (Lawrence: University Press of Kansas, 1992), 247.

28. Ibid., 172, 306, 319; Griess, "DHM," 306–7; Stephen E. Ambrose, "Dennis Hart Mahan," *Civil War Times Illustrated* 2 (Nov. 1963): 35.

29. Morrison, *"The Best School,"* 47.

30. Ibid., 49, 95; Ambrose, "DHM," 30; Griess, "DHM," 173.

31. Morrison, *"The Best School,"* 49.

32. Morris Schaff, *The Spirit of Old West Point, 1858–1862* (Boston: Houghton Mifflin, 1907), 68.

33. Quoted in Ambrose, *Duty, Honor, Country*, 102.

34. John F. Marszalek, *Sherman: A Soldier's Passion for Order* (New York: Free Press, 1993), 24; Ambrose, "DHM," 33.

35. John C. Tidball, "Getting Through West Point," in John C. Tidball Papers, USMA Library.

36. George W. Cullum, "Professor D. H. Mahan," *Army and Navy Journal* 9 (1871): 119–20, quoted in Griess, "DHM," 193.

37. DHM to Samuel Seabury III, May 4, 1831 (photocopy), ATM Papers, NWC Library.

38. DHM to Charles M. Conrad, Nov. 26, 1850, DHM Papers, USMA Library.

39. Norton, *Struggling for Recognition*, 37–38; Morrison, "*The Best School*," 57.

40. DHM to Conrad, Nov. 26, 1850, DHM Papers, USMA Library.

41. Ibid.; Morrison, "*The Best School*," 57; for a further discussion of this episode see Suzanne Geissler, "Professor Dennis Mahan Speaks Out on West Point Chapel Issues," *JMH* 69 (2005): 505–19.

42. Information supplied by Wayne Kempton, archivist of the Diocese of New York.

43. DHM to James B. McPherson, July 28, 1852 (photocopy), DHM Papers, USMA Library; original in James B. McPherson Papers, LC.

44. Hopkins, ed., *Collected Works*, 3: iii. Hopkins's biography of MM (introduction to Volume 3 of *Collected Works*) is also available at http://justus.anglican.org/resources/pc/usa/mahan/memoirs.html.

45. Ayres, *The Life and Work of William Augustus Muhlenberg*; William Wilberforce Newton, *Dr. Muhlenberg* (New York, 1890); Skardon, *Church Leader*; Byron D. Stuhlman, *Eucharistic Worship*, 1789–1979 (New York: Church Hymnal Corporation, 1988), 95; Thaddeus A. Schnitker, *The Church's Worship: The 1979 American Book of Common Prayer in a Historical Perspective* (New York: Peter Lang Pub., 1989), 81.

46. Edward R. Hardy Jr., "Evangelical Catholicism: W. A. Muhlenberg and the Memorial Movement," *Historical Magazine of the Protestant Episcopal Church* 13 (1944): 155–92.

47. John Frederick Woolverton, "William Augustus Muhlenberg and the Founding of St. Paul's College," *Historical Magazine of the Protestant Episcopal Church* 29 (1960): 192–218; Ayers, *Muhlenberg*, 100.

48. Newton, *Dr. Muhlenberg*, 46.

49. W. A. Muhlenberg, *The Ceremony and Address of the Laying of the Cornerstone of St. Paul's College* (New York, 1837), 10, quoted in Woolverton, "Muhlenberg," 200.

50. Woolverton, "Muhlenberg," 210–14.

51. Hopkins, ed., *Collected Works*, 3:iii; Skardon, *Church Leader*, 80–83; John B. Kerfoot, *Academical Degrees and Titles: An Address* (New York, 1854), 22–24.

52. Hopkins, ed., *Collected Works*, 3:iii.

53. William A. Muhlenberg to John B. Kerfoot, March 18, 1847, in Hall Harrison, *Life of the Right Reverend John Barrett Kerfoot* (New York, 1886), 1:127.

54. Puleston, *Mahan*, 9.

55. Hopkins, ed., Collected Works, 3:v–vi.

56. Ibid., 3:vi–viii.

57. Ibid., 3:x–xi; Powel Mills Dawley, *The Story of the General Theological Seminary: A Sesquicentennial History*, 1817–1967 (New York: Oxford University Press, 1969), 185–86.

58. Hopkins, ed., *Collected Works*, 3 xi; MM, *Church Missions: A Sermon Preached before the Society for the Advancement of Christianity in Pennsylvania* (Philadelphia, 1851).

59. Quoted in Dawley, *Story of GTS*, 186.

60. Hopkins, ed., *Collected Works*, 3:xii–xiii.

61. Quoted in Dawley, *Story of GTS*, 192.

62. Ibid., 192.

63. Ibid., 192.

64. Hopkins, ed., *Collected Works*, 3:ix.

65. MM, *An Exercise of Faith, In Its Relation to Authority and Private Judgment* (Philadelphia, 1855); *The Exercise of Faith: A Book for Doubters* (London, 1877); *The Comedy of Canonization* (New York, 1868).

66. MM, *A Church History of the First Seven Centuries to the Close of the Sixth General Council*, ed. John Henry Hopkins Jr., (New York, 1873), vii–viii.

67. Ibid., viii.

68. "Review of *A Church History of the First Three Centuries*," *North American Review* 91 (1860): 568–69; Seager, *ATM*, 607 n. 12.

69. Ibid., *ATM*, 8, 606 n. 11.

CHAPTER 2. YOUTH AND EARLY MANHOOD

1. Baptismal Record, Cadet Chapel, n.d., Archives, USMA Library; Norton, *Struggling for Recognition*, 37.

2. Puleston, *Mahan*, 12.

3. ATM, *Sail to Steam*, xiii.

4. Ibid., xiii; Puleston, *Mahan*, 14–15.

5. William Whitman Bailey, "Recollections of West Point" (n.d. ca. 1897, Brown University Library), quoted in Seager, *ATM*, 7.

6. Jane Mahan, "Random Memories," *The Pointer*, March 15, 1929, 6.

7. Ibid., 6–7; ATM, *Sail to Steam*, xiii.

8. Henry L. Abbot, Memoir of *Dennis Hart Mahan*, 1802–1871 (Washington, D.C., 1878), 36.

9. Puleston, *Mahan*, 15; "Recollections of Ellen Kuhn Mahan," ca. 1937–38, in *LPATM*, 3:724.

10. Puleston, *Mahan*, 15.

11. Ibid., 15; ATM to Samuel A. Ashe, Oct. 30, 1858, *LPATM*, 1:10–11; Samuel A. Ashe, "Memories of Annapolis," *South Atlantic Quarterly* 18 (1919): 204.

12. ATM to Mary Jay Okill, Nov. 10, 1847, *LPATM*, 1:1. The book Alfred refers to is *Agathos and Other Sunday School Stories* (New York, n.d.).

13. ATM to Ashe, Nov. 21, 1858, *LPATM*, 1:21.

14. ATM to J. Franklin Jameson, April 27, 1914, *LPATM*, 3:523–24.

15. Bailey, "Recollections," in Seager, ATM, 7.

16. ATM to Mary Okill Mahan, June 24, 1848, *LPATM*, 1:1; Francis Duncan, "Mahan: Historian with a Purpose," USNIP 83 (May 1957): 498.

17. Puleston, Mahan, 15; Seager, ATM, 7–8; ATM, *Sail to Steam*, v.

18. ATM, *Sail to Steam*, v.

19. Ibid., vi, 70–71.

20. Ibid., xiii.

21. Ibid., xiv.

22. Woolverton, "Muhlenberg," 193; Skardon, *Church Leader*, 84.

23. Skardon, *Church Leader*, 48–49, 61, 88–90; Harrison, *Kerfoot*, 1:33, 58–61, 127–29, 2:507.

24. Puleston, Mahan, 16; Harrison, *Kerfoot*, 1:180–81; I am indebted to St. James School historian Theodore Camp for this information. Camp to author, Feb. 27, 1998.

25. I am indebted to St. James School historian Theodore Camp for this information. Camp to author, Feb. 27, 1998.

26. ATM, *Sail to Steam*, xiv.

27. Ibid., xiv; Griess, "DHM," 202.

28. Course certificates, Columbia College, 1855–56, ATM Papers, NWC Library.

29. ATM to Ashe, Sep. 20, 1870, *LPATM*, 1:358.

30. ATM, "The Apparent Decadence of the Church's Influence," Churchman, April 25, 1903, 546.

31. ATM to Ashe, Jan. 1, 1859, *LPATM*, 1:45.

32. ATM, *Sail to Steam*, xiv.

33. ATM to Ambrose S. Murray, Jan. 14, 1856, *LPATM*, 1:2.

34. ATM, *Sail to Steam*, xiv–xv.

35. Ibid., xv–xvii.

36. ATM to Murray, April 14, 1856, *LPATM*, 1:2.

37. ATM, *Sail to Steam*, xvii.

38. ATM to Helen E. Mahan, Dec. 31, 1884, *LPATM*, 1:585–87; ATM to Jane L. Mahan, April 28, 1867, *LPATM*, 1:104–5.

39. Norton, *Struggling for Recognition*, 37–38.

40. Charles Todorich, *The Spirited Years: A History of the Antebellum Naval Academy* (Annapolis, Md.: Naval Institute Press, 1984), 17, 27, 80–81.

41. Ibid., 18, 57–60, 80; ATM, *Sail to Steam*, 71; Puleston, *Mahan*, 19, 21.

42. ATM, *Sail to Steam*, 71–73; Charles Welsh, Acting Secretary of the Navy, to ATM, Oct. 2, 1856, quoted in Taylor, *Mahan*, 6.

43. Seager, *ATM*, 12.

44. Todorich, *Spirited Years*, 152–53. Some events cited as examples of hazing were actually not, since they did not involve the abuse of plebes by upperclassmen. See also Mark C. Hunter, *A Society of Gentlemen: Midshipmen at the U.S. Naval Academy, 1845–1861* (Annapolis, Md.: Naval Institute Press, 2010), 69.

45. ATM, *Sail to Steam*, 54.

46. Seager, *ATM*, 21, 27.

47. Ibid., 12, 25.

48. ATM to Elizabeth Lewis, Oct. 16, 1857, *LPATM*, 1:3.

49. *LPATM*, 1:3 n. 3; Ashe's recollections of ATM are included in his article "Memories of Annapolis," cited below.

50. Ashe, "Memories of Annapolis," 204.

51. ATM to Ashe, Jan. 1, 1859, *LPATM*, 1:42. Seager takes this quote out of context and omits the crucial words "in this one respect"; see his *ATM*, 22.

52. ATM to George Blake, Dec. 7, 1857 (two separate letters on same date), *LPATM*, 1:4–5; George Blake Memorandum, Dec. 8, 1857, National Archives, Naval Records Division, quoted in Seager, *ATM*, 13.

53. Seager, *ATM*, 23.

54. ATM to Ashe, Nov. 18, 1858, *LPATM*, 1:26.

55. Seager, *ATM*, 21.

56. ATM to Ashe, Oct. 23, 30, 1858, *LPATM*, 1:6–7, 13.

57. Puleston, *Mahan*, 22.

58. Mahan to Ashe, Oct. 30, 1858, *LPATM*, 1:11–12. There were only twenty-one members in the class at this time. Seager puts the count at thirteen anti-Mahan, three pro-Mahan, and four neutral, though how he determined this is not at all clear. Seager, *ATM*, 609 n. 42.

59. DHM to ATM, n.d. (photocopy), DHM Papers, USMA Library; original in ATM Papers, LC.

60. DHM to ATM, Oct. 14, 1858, ibid.

61. ATM to Ashe, Dec. 5, 1858, *LPATM*, 1:30. See also Hunter, *Society of Gentlemen*, 125.

62. ATM to Ashe, Nov. 21, 1858, *LPATM*, 1:24.

63. DHM to ATM, May 19, 1859 (photocopy), DHM Papers, USMA Library; original in ATM Papers, LC.

64. ATM to Ashe, May 25, 1859, *LPATM*, 1:82.

65. DHM to ATM, May 19, 1859, DHM Papers, USMA Library.

66. Ashe, "Memories of Annapolis," 198; Puleston, Mahan, 19; Todorich, *Spirited Years*, 142–48; Karsten, *Naval Aristocracy*, 72–74.

67. Karsten, *Naval Aristocracy*, 75. We do not know for certain about the midshipmen of Mahan's time. Karsten's figures are for the period 1885–95; the academy did not begin keeping track of midshipmen's religious affiliation

until 1885. For suggested reasons for the predominance of Episcopalians in the officer corps (Army as well as Navy), see Morris Janowitz, *The Professional Soldier: A Social and Political Portrait* (New York: Free Press, 1960), 97–101; Peter Karsten, "Ritual and Rank: Religious Affiliation, Father's 'Calling,' and Successful Advancement in the U.S. Officer Corps of the Twentieth Century," *Armed Forces and Society* 9 (1983): 427–40.

68. Karsten, *Naval Aristocracy*, xiii, 74. Karsten, by his own admission, got this idea from Janowitz's famous work *The Professional Soldier*, which stated that "the Episcopal doctrine with its strong emphasis on authority, ceremony, and mission, supplies a positive religion for the military profession." Karsten puts a more negative interpretation on it. See Janowitz, Professional Soldier, 99; for Karsten's comments on same, see also his "Ritual and Rank," 427.

69. Todorich, *Spirited Years*, 147–48.

70. Karsten, *Naval Aristocracy*, 74; Karsten, "Ritual and Rank," 428.

71. Karsten also expands the term "High Church" to include Presbyterians and Congregationalists, thereby bending the term out of all recognition; see *Naval Aristocracy*, 73; Todorich, *Spirited Years*, 142–48.

72. The chaplain during Mahan's first year was Theodore B. Barrows, but we know nothing of Mahan's opinion of him. Todorich, *Spirited Years*, 144–46.

73. ATM to Ashe, Nov. 28, 1858, *LPATM*, 1:25.

74. ATM to Ashe, Oct. 24, 1858, *LPATM*, 1:8–9.

75. ATM to Ashe, Dec. 12, 1858, *LPATM*, 1:33–34.

76. ATM to Ashe, Feb. 7, 1859, *LPATM*, 1:58.

77. ATM to Ashe, Feb. 14, 1859, *LPATM*, 1:60.

78. ATM to Ashe, Dec. 5, 1858, *LPATM*, 1:30.

79. ATM to Ashe, March 20, 1859, *LPATM*, 1:69.

80. On Jones, see *Bureau of Naval Personnel, United States Navy Chaplains, 1778-1945* (Washington, D.C.: Government Printing Office, 1948), 141; Todorich, *Spirited Years*, 141, 143–46; William P. Leeman, *The Long Road to Annapolis: The Founding of the Naval Academy and the Emerging American Republic* (Chapel Hill: University of North Carolina Press, 2010), 138–39, 213–14. Jones' books were *Sketches of Naval Life* (New Haven, Conn., 1829); *Excursions to Cairo, Jerusalem, Damascus and Balbec from the United States Ship Delaware During Her Recent Cruise* (New York, 1836); *and Life-scenes from the Old Testament* (Philadelphia, 1868).

81. ATM to Ashe, Feb. 7, 1859, *LPATM*, 1:57.

82. ATM to Ashe, Nov. 12, 1858, *LPATM*, 1:18.

83. ATM to Ashe, March 19, 1859, *LPATM*, 1:69.

84. ATM to Ashe, Oct. 30, 1858, March 20, 1859, *LPATM*, 1:10, 69.

85. ATM to Ashe, Nov. 20, 1858, March 20, 1859, *LPATM*, 1:26, 69.

86. ATM to Ashe, Feb. 1, 20, May 1, 1859, *LPATM*, 1:54, 61, 79.

87. Puleston, Mahan, 23–24.

88. ATM to Ashe, Feb. 1, 1859, *LPATM*, 1:56.

89. Ibid., 1:56.

90. ATM to Ashe, Feb. 7, 1859, *LPATM*, 1:58.

91. ATM to Ashe, Dec. 12, 1858, *LPATM*, 1:34.

92. Ibid., 1:34.

93. ATM, *Sail to Steam*, 85.

94. Ibid.

95. Ibid., 87.

96. Ibid., 85–86.

97. Seager, *ATM*, 29; Puleston, *Mahan*, 25–26; ATM to Ashe, May 1, 1859, *LPATM*, 1:78.

98. Seager, ATM, 21, 14.

99. Puleston, Mahan, 26; ATM to Ashe, June 1, July 31, 1859, *LPATM*, 1:82–85.

100. ATM, *Sail to Steam*, 103; Puleston, *Mahan*, 27.

101. ATM to Ashe, July 31, 1859, *LPATM*, 1:85.

102. ATM to Ashe, Oct. 5, 1860, ATM to C. S. Newcome, Oct. 10, 1861, ATM to Ashe, July 26, 1884, *LPATM*, 1:88, 90, 573. Mahan described the *Congress* cruise in detail in *Sail to Steam*, 103–55.

103. ATM, *Sail to Steam*, 149.

104. Ibid., 153–54; ATM to Newcome, Oct. 10, 1861, *LPATM*, 1:89–90.

105. ATM to Gustavus Vasa Fox, Sep. 9, 1861, *LPATM*, 1:88–89; Puleston, *Mahan*, 31–33; Seager, *ATM*, 35.

106. ATM, *Sail to Steam*, 156–57.

107. Ibid., 158.

108. Ibid., 163–64.

109. Ibid., 91.

110. Ibid., 91–92.

111. Seager, *ATM*, 29.

112. Ibid., 29; see index entry for "Negroes" in *LPATM*, 3:856.

113. Puleston, *Mahan*, 35; ATM, *Sail to Steam*, 179–80.

114. ATM, *Sail to Steam*, 180–81.

115. Seager, *ATM*, 38, 612 n. 11; Karsten, *Naval Aristocracy*, 330.

116. Puleston, *Mahan*, 35.

117. Ibid.; see also ATM to Ashe, March 6, 1870, ATM, Diary, Feb. 8, 1869, *LPATM*, 1:353, 278.

118. ATM, *Sail to Steam*, 180–87.

119. Ibid., 187–88.

120. Ibid., 174–75.

121. Albert Gleaves, Life and Letters of Rear Admiral Stephen B. Luce, U.S. Navy (New York: G. P. Putnam's Sons, 1925), 6–7; on Luce's writings, see for example

Stephen B. Luce, "Christian Ethics as an Element of Military Education," The United Service 8 (Jan. 1883): 1–16 [repr. in USNIP 32 (1906): 1367–86]; "The Benefits of War," North American Review 153 (Dec. 1891): 672–83 [repr. as "War and Its Prevention," USNIP 30 (1904): 611–22].

122. MM to ATM, Oct. 3, 1864, quoted in Puleston, *Mahan*, 37–38 and Seager, *ATM*, 39–40. Seager claims in a footnote that the original is in the NWC Library but I was unable to locate it; Seager, *ATM*, 612 nn. 15–16.

123. ATM, *Sail to Steam*, 187; Puleston, *Mahan*, 38.

124. J. F. Green to ATM, July 12, 1864, John Dahlgren to ATM, Oct. 24, 1864, National Archives, Naval Records Division, cited in Seager, *ATM*, 612 n. 18.

125. Puleston, *Mahan*, 38–39; DHM, *Summary of the Course of Permanent Fortification (West Point*, N.Y., 1850); for a brief outline of DHM's course on permanent fortifications, see Griess, "DHM," 364–65.

126. ATM, *Sail to Steam*, 191–92.

127. Ibid., 192.

128. Ibid., 189–90.

129. Ibid., 188–89; Griess, "DHM," 339–40. Alfred's account of the event makes no mention of his father being there; neither does the *New York Times* account that appeared in the April 18, 1865, issue.

130. ATM, *Sail to Steam*, 193; ATM to Percival Drayton, June 26, July 1, 1865, *LPATM*, 1:91–92.

131. Seager, ATM, 41; ATM to Drayton, July 1, 1865, LPATM, 1:92; Puleston, Mahan, 40.

132. ATM, *Sail to Steam*, 91–92.

133. Puleston, *Mahan*, 29–30.

134. Griess, "DHM," 334–37.

135. DHM to Gouverneur Kemble, Sep. 26, 1864, DHM Papers, USMA Library (photocopy in ATM papers, NWC Library); Russell F. Weigley, "Dennis Hart Mahan," in *Dictionary of American Military Biography* (Westport, Conn.: Greenwood, 1984), 716.

136. On Kemble's dinner parties, see John S. D. Eisenhower, *Agent of Destiny: The Life and Times of General Winfield Scott* (New York: Free Press, 1997), 144–45.

137. DHM to Kemble, Sep. 26, 1864, DHM Papers, USMA Library. Dennis had actually conflated two separate Bible verses.

138. Ibid. Dennis had supported McClellan's efforts earlier in the war, but for reasons unclear broke with him; see Griess, "DHM," 332–33.

139. DHM to Kemble, Sep. 29, 1864, DHM Papers, USMA Library (photocopy in ATM Papers, NWC Library).

140. Griess, "DHM," 338. Dennis' negative view of Lee may have been influenced by the general feeling at West Point that West Pointers who had joined the Confederate Army were traitors. See James Tyrus Seidule, "'Treason Is Treason': Civil War Memory at West Point, 1861–1902," *JMH* 76 (2012): 427–52.

141. "Grant and Lee Compared," Cincinnati Daily Commercial, Aug. 19, 1864. A photocopy of this newspaper clipping is in DHM Papers, USMA Library.

142. Ibid. Another version of this article appeared as "Grant and Lee" in the *Army and Navy Journal* 1 (July 7, 1864): 758–59.

143. Griess, "DHM," 336–37.

144. Ibid., 337.

145. William T. Sherman to John A. Rawlins, Sep. 17, 1863, in William T. Sherman, *Memoirs of General W. T. Sherman* (New York: Library of American, 1990), 368.

146. Ambrose, *Duty, Honor, Country*, 101; Ambrose, "DHM," 30, 32–33.

147. Griess, "DHM," chap. 10; Weigley, "DHM," 717.

148. Hopkins, ed., *Collected Works*, 3:xvii–xx.

149. Ibid., xviii. Alfred's younger brother Dennis Jr. attended Burlington College.

150. MM, *The Healing of the Nations* (Albany, N.Y., 1855), 17.

151. Hopkins, ed., *Collected Works*, 3:xxviii–xxxi, 478–509. Milo's argument is strikingly similar to one Alfred would make forty-nine years later in two identical letters to the *New York Times* and *New York Evening Post, LPATM*, 3:433–35.

152. MM to Samuel Roosevelt Johnson, 1861, Deans' Papers, GTS Library; Dawley, *Story of GTS*, 196.

153. Samuel Roosevelt Johnson to Jackson Kemper, July 12, 1862, Samuel Roosevelt Johnson Papers, GTS Library, quoted in Dawley, *Story of GTS*, 196.

154. George Templeton Strong, *Diary*, ed. Allan Nevins and Milton Halsey Thomas (New York: Macmillan Co., 1952), 3:384.

155. Ibid., 3:398–99.

156. Samuel Seabury III, *American Slavery Distinguished from the Slavery of English Theorists, and Justified by the Law of Nature* (New York, 1861 [repr. Miami: Mnemosyne Pub. Co., 1969]).

157. MM, *Healing of Nations*, 12.

158. Hopkins, ed., *Collected Works*, 3:xxxi–xxxii.

CHAPTER 3. CRISIS AND CONVERSION

1. Puleston, *Mahan*, 41; see for example, ATM to Mary Okill Mahan, Feb. 16, April 28, 1867, *LPATM*, 1:97, 99–101.

2. ATM to Thornton A. Jenkins, Nov. 15, 17, 1865, *LPATM*, 1:93–94; ATM, *Sail to Steam*, 194.

3. ATM, *Sail to Steam*, 194; ATM to Mary Okill Mahan, Feb. 16, 1867, *LPATM*, 1:97.

4. Seager, *ATM*, 42; USS Muscoota log, National Archives, Naval Records Division.

5. ATM to Mary Okill Mahan, Feb. 16, 1867, *LPATM*, 1:97.

6. USS Muscoota log, National Archives, Naval Records Division; Seager, *ATM*, 42.

7. Seager, *ATM*, 42.

8. ATM to Mary Okill Mahan, April 18, 1867, *LPATM*, 1:99–100.

9. Ibid., 1:99–100.

10. ATM to Thornton A. Jenkins, Sep. 24, Oct. 27, 30, 1866, *LPATM*, 1:94–95.

11. Diary, May 16, 1868, *LPATM*, 1:160.

12. Seager, *ATM*, 43–44.

13. ATM to Mary Okill Mahan, Feb. 16, 1867, *LPATM*, 1:97. Mahan sometimes capitalized pronouns referring to God and sometimes not.

14. ATM to Mary Okill Mahan, May 3, 1867, *LPATM*, 1:101.

15. ATM to Thornton A. Jenkins, Jan. 2, 1867, *LPATM*, 1:95.

16. Seager, *ATM*, 44.

17. See note 13 above.

18. Puleston, *Mahan*, 40; for the actual letters see *LPATM*, 1:96–143, 333–54.

19. See, for example, Perry Miller, "'Preparation for Salvation' in Seventeenth-Century New England," in *Nature's Nation* (Cambridge, Mass.: Belknap Press, 1967), 50–77, or in *Journal of the History of Ideas* 4 (1943): 253–86.

20. Seager, *ATM*, 45–46.

21. See Patricia Caldwell, *The Puritan Conversion Narrative: The Beginnings of American Expression* (New York: Cambridge University Press, 1983). Even Karsten, who is not sympathetic to Mahan's religious outlook, recognizes this in his characterization of the diary as one that "could have been written by a seventeenth-century Calvinist." See Peter Karsten, "Review of *LPATM*, by Robert Seager II and Doris D. Maguire, eds.," *American Historical Review* 82 (1977): 454.

22. Seager, *ATM*, 613 n. 2. The diary is found in *LPATM*, 1:145–332; the original is in the ATM Papers, NWC Library.

23. Diary, Nov. 7, 1868, *LPATM*, 1:231.

24. See, for example, diary entries of Jan. 2, 13, 16, 1869, *LPATM*, 1:257, 261, 263.

25. Seager, *ATM*, 51, 614 n. 2. Gaul's diary is at the National Museum of the Marine Corps, Quantico, Virginia.

26. Elinor and James A. Barnes, eds., *Naval Surgeon: The Diary of Dr. Samuel Pellman Boyer* (Bloomington: Indiana University Press, 1963), 2:73.

27. See, for example, diary entries of July 31, 1868, March 7, 9 1869, *LPATM*, 1:198, 286, 287.

28. The best example of this is ATM, *The Harvest Within: Thoughts on the Life of a Christian* (Boston: Little, Brown, and Co., 1909).

29. Dairy, May 10, Nov. 30, Dec. 26, 1868, *LPATM*, 1:156, 240, 253.

30. Diary, May 17, 1868, *LPATM*, 1:160–61.

31. Diary, May 21, 1868, *LPATM*, 1:164.

32. Karsten, *Naval Aristocracy*, 73.

33. Diary, July 19, 1868, *LPATM*, 1:193.

34. Barnes and Barnes, eds., *Naval Surgeon*, 2:73.

35. Diary, Jan. 24, 1869, *LPATM*, 1:267.

36. Diary, July 5, 1868, *LPATM*, 1:184.

37. Diary, Dec. 20, 21, 1868, Jan. 24, 25, 1869, *LPATM*, 1:250–51, 267–68.

38. Diary, Jan. 3, 1869, *LPATM*, 1:257.

39. Diary, June 20, 1868, *LPATM*, 1:179.

40. ATM to Mary Okill Mahan, Feb. 22, 1868, *LPATM*, 1:130.

41. ATM to Mary Okill Mahan, March 1, 1868; diary, Jan. 24, 1869, *LPATM*, 1:133, 268.

42. These books are mentioned throughout the diary. Most (not all) are listed in Seager, *ATM*, 620–21 n. 48.

43. MM, *The Spiritual Point-of-View; or, The Glass Reversed: An Answer to Bishop Colenso* (New York, 1863).

44. Robert Bruce Mullin to author, March 16, 1998.

45. See, for example, diary, Jan. 22, May 11, 1869, *LPATM*, 1:266, 301.

46. Diary, Jan. 31, 1869, *LPATM*, 1:273–74.

47. Seager, *ATM*, 70–71.

48. Diary, Jan. 1, 1869, *LPATM*, 1:256.

49. Seager, *ATM*, 70; diary, Jan. 10, 1869, *LPATM*, 1:259–60. Milo's fascination with biblical chronology and numbers is seen in his *Palmoni; or, The Numerals of Scripture: A Proof of Inspiration; a Free Inquiry* (New York, 1863).

50. Seager, *ATM*, 70–71.

51. Diary, Sep. 13, 1868, *LPATM*, 1:218.

52. Seager, *ATM*, 71; diary, July 16, 1838, *LPATM*, 1:191–92.

53. Seager, *ATM*, 72.

54. Ibid., 72; *LPATM*, 1:149 n. 4.

55. ATM to Ashe, Oct. 9, 1868, *LPATM*, 1:339; diary, April 29, 30, May 4, 8, 1868, *LPATM*, 1:149. 152, 155.

56. ATM to Ashe, Oct. 9, 1868, *LPATM*, 1:339–40.

57. Diary, May 8, 1868, *LPATM*, 1:155–56.

58. Diary, May 10, 1868, *LPATM*, 1:156.

59. Seager, ATM, 74.

60. Diary, May 11, 1868, *LPATM*, 1:156–57.

61. Diary, May 13, 1868, *LPATM*, 1:158.

62. Diary, May 14, 1868, *LPATM*, 1:158–59.

63. Ibid., 1:159.

64. Diary, May 16, 1868, *LPATM*, 1:160.

65. Ibid., 1:160.

66. Diary, May 17, 1868, *LPATM*, 1:161.

67. Diary, May 19, 1868, *LPATM*, 1:162.

68. Diary, May 21, 22, 25, 1868, *LPATM*, 1:164–66.

69. Diary, May 27, 29, 30, 31, *LPATM*, 1:167–70.

70. Diary, May 30, 1868, *LPATM*, 1:169.

71. Diary, June 2, 5, 6, 7, *LPATM*, 1:171–74.

72. Diary, June 15, 1868, *LPATM*, 1:175.

73. Diary, June 20, 1868, *LPATM*, 1:178–79.

74. Diary, Aug. 20, 1868, *LPATM*, 1:209.

75. Diary, Sep. 6, 8, 10, 12, 1868, *LPATM*, 1:215–17.

76. ATM to Ashe, Oct. 10, 1868, *LPATM*, 1:340.

77. Diary, Sep. 24, 1868, *LPATM*, 1:223.

78. Diary, Feb. 8, 1869, *LPATM*, 1:278.

79. They saw each other again in March, May, and July 1869.

80. Diary, Aug. 30, 1869, *LPATM*, 1:329.

81. Diary, July 29, Aug. 4, 6, 1869, *LPATM*, 1:317–18, 322–23.

82. Diary, Aug. 16, 30, Sep. 5, 1869, *LPATM*, 1:327, 329, 330.

83. Theron Woolverton to ATM, July 8, 1883, ATM Papers, NWC Library; ATM to Helen Evans Mahan, April 19, 1894, *LPATM*, 2:260; Seager, *ATM*, 622 n. 62.

84. Diary, March 5, 1869, *LPATM*, 1:285.

85. ATM to Ashe, Oct. 10, 1868, *LPATM*, 1:340.

86. Diary, March 5, 1869, *LPATM*, 1:285.

87. Diary, May 17, 1869, *LPATM*, 1:307.

88. Seager, *ATM*, 60.

89. Diary, April 26, 1868, Sep. 10, 1869, *LPATM*, 1:146, 332.

90. Diary, Jan. 1, 29, 30, 1869, *LPATM*, 1:256, 272.

91. Diary, July 27, 28, 1869, *LPATM*, 1:317. Woolverton's sin is never actually identified in the diary, but based on Mahan's comments about Woolverton's way with women and his dramatic reaction to hearing about it, it seems likely to have been sexual.

92. Diary, May 29, June 5, 1868, *LPATM*, 1:169, 173.

93. Diary, July 12, 1868, *LPATM*, 1:188.

94. Diary, May 24, 1869, *LPATM*, 1:312.

95. Seager, *ATM*, 52, 615 n. 16; diary, Feb. 3, 6, March 5, Sep. 10, 1869, *LPATM*, 1:276, 277, 285, 332.

96. Diary, Feb. 8, 1869, *LPATM*, 1:278.

97. Diary, May 7, 1868, *LPATM*, 1:154.

98. Diary, June 15, 1868, *LPATM*, 1:175.

99. Diary, Aug. 6, 1868, *LPATM*, 1:201.

100. Diary, May 31, 1868, *LPATM*, 1:170.

101. Diary, July 15, 1868, *LPATM*, 1:191.

102. Diary, May 27, Dec. 23, 1868, Jan. 24, 1869, *LPATM*, 1:167, 252, 267.

103. Diary, Dec. 2, July 17, 1868, *LPATM*, 1:241, 192.

104. Seager, *ATM*, 46.

105. ATM to Mary Okill Mahan, Feb. 16, 1867, *LPATM*, 1:96; see also ATM to Mary Okill Mahan, March 1, 1868, 1:131, ATM to Ashe, Nov. 19, 1868, 1:348.

106. ATM to Mary Okill Mahan, March 1, 1868, *LPATM*, 1:131.

107. Diary, Dec. 17, 18, 1868, *LPATM*, 1:248–49.

108. Seager, *ATM*, 46–47.

109. Diary, Nov. 16, 1868, *LPATM*, 1:234.

110. Harry S. Stout, *The Divine Dramatist: George Whitefield and the Rise of Modern Evangelicalism* (Grand Rapids, Mich.: Eerdmans, 1991), 26–27.

111. *Mahan* Prayer, *LPATM*, 1:145.

112. *LPATM*, 1:314 n. 1; ATM, *Sail to Steam*, 263; Puleston, *Mahan*, 45; Seager, *ATM*, 62, 80.

113. ATM to Ashe, Jan. 17, 1879, *LPATM*, 1:352; ATM, *Sail to Steam*, 264; Puleston, *Mahan*, 46; Seager, *ATM*, 81.

114. ATM to Ashe, Jan. 17, 1870, *LPATM*, 1:352; enclosure in brackets is Seager's. See also Seager's comment on missing portion of letter, Seager, *ATM*, 622 n. 1.

115. Puleston, *Mahan*, 46–47. Neither of Mahan's children, Ellen or Lyle, mention this relationship in their recollections.

116. ATM to Ashe, March 6, 1870, *LPATM*, 1:353.

117. Ibid., 1:353–54.

118. ATM, *Sail to Steam*, 266–67; Puleston, *Mahan*, 47; ATM to Ellen Evans Mahan, Feb. 24, 1894, *LPATM*, 2:235.

119. ATM to Ashe, July 11, 1870, *LPATM*, 1:355.

120. Ibid., 1:355.

121. Information on the Evans family is found in Puleston, Mahan, 48; and Seager, *ATM*, 85.

122. Seager, *ATM*, 85–86, also 87–90.

123. ATM to Cdr. James Alden, Aug. 26, 1879, ATM to Ashe, Sep. 20, 1870, *LPATM*, 1:355, 357.

124. ATM to Alden, Sep. 1, 3, 8, 1870, *LPATM*, 1:356.

125. Hopkins, ed., *Collected Works*, 3: xlii.

126. Ibid., 3:xlii–xliii.

127. Ibid., 3:xlviii–xlix; MM, "Brief for the Defense," Special Collections, GTS Library. A copy can also be found online at http://justus.anglican.org/resources/pc/usa/mahan/brief.pdf.

128. Hopkins, ed., *Collected Works*, 3:xlviii–xlix.

129. Ibid., 3:xlix–xlx.

130. ATM to Ashe, Sep. 20, 1870, *LPATM*, 1:358.

131. ATM to Alden, Sep. 8, 1870, *LPATM*, 1:356.

132. ATM to Ashe, Sep. 20, 1870, ATM to Alden, Nov. 4, 1870, *LPATM*, 1:357–58.

133. ATM to Ashe, Sep. 20, 1870, *LPATM*, 1:357–58.

134. Seager, ATM, 85; ATM to Ashe, Sep. 20, 1870, ATM to Mary Okill Mahan, Aug. 15, 1871, *LPATM*, 1:357–58, 368–69.

135. ATM to Ellen Evans, Jan. 6, 1871, *LPATM*, 1:359.

136. Leah Robinson Rousmaniere, *Anchored within the Vail: A Pictorial History of the Seamen's Church Institute* (New York: Seamen's Church Institute of New York and New Jersey, 1995), 31.

137. ATM to Mary Okill Mahan, Aug. 15, 1871, *LPATM*, 1:368.

138. ATM to Ashe, Feb. 27, 1871, *LPATM*, 1:359–60.

139. ATM, "Address Delivered at Holy Trinity Episcopal Church, Brooklyn, New York," March 1899, *LPATM*, 3:598–602; ATM, "The Practical in Christianity," in ATM, *Harvest Within*, 263–80.

140. ATM to Ellen Evans, March 10, 22, April 3, 5, June 12, 1871, ATM to Ashe, April 25, 1871, *LPATM*, 1:360–66.

141. ATM to Ellen Evans, April 5, June 12, 1871, *LPATM*, 1:363, 366.

142. Puleston, *Mahan*, 50. Presumably, Puleston got this from the Mahan family.

143. ATM to Mary Okill Mahan, Aug. 15, 1871, *LPATM*, 1:368–69.

144. Abbot, *Memoir of DHM*, 34–35; Griess, "DHM," 341–42.

145. Griess, "DHM," 342.

146. Ibid., 341; Abbot, *Memoirs of DHM*, 35.

147. Seager, *ATM*, 89.

148. Griess, "DHM," 342.

149. ATM to Ashe, April 13, 1876, *LPATM*, 1:450.

150. Cadet Hugh L. Scott to mother, Sep. 24, 1871, Hugh L. Scott Collection, USMA Library.

151. Griess, "DHM," 343–46.

152. ATM to James Alden, Sep. 30, 1871, ATM to Daniel Ammen, Nov. 15, 1871, Jan. 22, 24, 1872, *LPATM*, 1:369–70.

153. Quoted in Puleston, Mahan, 50. No original source is given but presumably Puleston received this quote from a family letter. Lyle Mahan alludes to it in his "Recollections," 121.

154. The earliest source for the engagement and wedding is Puleston, *Mahan*, 50–51.

CHAPTER 4. FAMILY MAN AND BURGEONING AUTHOR

1. Puleston, *Mahan*, 51; Seager, *ATM*, 89–90; ATM to Daniel Ammen, Sep. 17, 21, Dec. 4, 12, 1872, ATM to Navy Dept., Sep. 19, 20, 1872, ATM to George Robeson, Dec. 2, 1872, *LPATM*, 1:371–73; see also 1:373 n. 2.

2. ATM to Ammen, Feb. 15, 1873, ATM to William R. Taylor, Feb. 17, 1873, *LPATM*, 1:373–74; Puleston, *Mahan*, 52; Seager, *ATM*, 90.

3. Puleston, *Mahan*, 52–53; Seager, *ATM*, 92–96.

4. Ellen Mahan to Mary Okill Mahan, Oct. 12, 1874, ATM Papers, LC. Mahan's wife will be referred to in footnotes as Ellen Mahan. Their daughter Ellen Kuhn Mahan will be referred to as Ellen K. Mahan.

5. Ellen K. Mahan, "Recollections," *LPATM*, 3:723.

6. Ellen Mahan to Mary Okill Mahan, Oct. 8, 9, 1873, ATM Papers, LC.

7. Charles O'Neil Diary, Dec. 20, 1873, May 14, Sep. 16, 1874, LC.

8. Ellen Mahan to Mary Okill Mahan, Sep. 13, 1874, ATM Papers, LC.

9. ATM to Robeson, Jan. 1, 1875, ATM to William A. Kirkland, Jan. 1, 1875, *LPATM*, 1:426–27.

10. ATM to Mary Okill Mahan, Feb. 1, 1875, *LPATM*, 1:427–29.

11. *Journal of the Proceedings of General Convention, 1874* (Hartford, Conn.: 1875), 185; Robert Prichard, *A History of the Episcopal Church* (Harrisburg, Pa.: Morehouse, 1991), 155–56, 184–86; George Hodges, A Short History of the Episcopal Church, rev. ed. (Cincinnati, 1974), 84–85.

12. ATM to Mary Okill Mahan, Feb. 1, 1875, *LPATM*, 1:427–29.

13. ATM to Mary Okill Mahan, March 3, 1875, *LPATM*, 1:431.

14. ATM to Ashe, June 17, 1876, *LPATM*, 1:454.

15. ATM to Ashe, May 15, 1875, *LPATM*, 1:432–33.

16. ATM to Ashe, May 21, 1875, *LPATM*, 1:433.

17. ATM to Ashe, May 21, July 1, 1875, *LPATM*, 1:434–35.

18. ATM to Ammen, Aug. 27, 30, Sep. 1, 1875, *LPATM*, 1:435–36.

19. ATM to L. E. Chandler, Oct. 2, 1875, *LPATM*, 1:436.

20. ATM to Ashe, Dec. 27, 1875, Jan. 27, 1876, *LPATM*, 1:436–42.

21. ATM to Washington C. Whitthorne, March 21, 1876, *LPATM*, 1:443–50. See also ATM to Ashe, Feb. 1, March 28, April 13, May 19, June 17, July 13, 1876, *LPATM*, 1:442–56.

22. ATM to Ashe, Dec. 27, 1875, *LPATM*, 1:439.

23. ATM to Ashe, June 17, 1876, *LPATM*, 1:455–56.

24. ATM to Ashe, June 17, July 23, Aug. 19, 21, 1876, *LPATM*, 1:454–59. For a complete discussion of the Robeson controversy and Mahan's role in it, see Seager, A*TM*, 103–15. Seager agrees with the Whitthorne Committee judgment.

25. ATM to Ashe, July 23, Aug. 19, 1876, *LPATM*, 1:456–58.

26. Puleston, *Mahan*, 56.

27. ATM to Ashe, Dec. 27, 1875, *LPATM*, 1:439.

28. ATM to Ashe, June 17, 1876, *LPATM*, 1:454.

29. ATM to Ammen, Oct. 11, 16, Dec. 5, 11, 1876, *LPATM*, 1:460–61.

30. ATM to Ammen, Dec. 11, 1876, *LPATM*, 1:461–62.

31. Ammen to ATM, Dec. 13, 1876, *LPATM*, 1:462 n. 1.

32. ATM to William Church, Nov. 25, 29, 1876, *LPATM*, 1:460–61.

33. ATM to Ammen, Dec. 29, 1876, *LPATM*, 1:462; Puleston, *Mahan*, 56; Seager, *ATM*, 118; ATM to Mary Okill Mahan, May 3, 1875, *LPATM*, 1:431.

34. ATM to Ashe, Oct. 21, 1877, *LPATM*, 1:463–64.

35. Puleston, *Mahan*, 56. This statement is probably based on remarks made in Lyle Mahan's "Recollections," 114, 124.

36. ATM to Ammen, July 11, Sep. 3, 6, 1877, ATM to Ashe, Oct. 21, 1877, *LPATM*, 1:462–64.

37. ATM to Ashe, Dec. 2, 1877, *LPATM*, 1:465.

38. ATM to Ashe, May 9, 1879, *LPATM*, 1:474; ATM, "Naval Education," *USNIP* 5 (Dec. 1879), 345–76.

39. Seager, *ATM*, 120.

40. ATM, "Naval Education," 347–48.

41. Ibid., 345.

42. Seager, *ATM*, 120.

43. ATM, "Naval Education," 348.

44. Ibid., 369–71.

45. Ibid., 375–76.

46. ATM, "Introduction to K. Asami's Biography of Tasuka Serata," *LPATM*, 3:688; Seager, *ATM*, 119, 628 n. 25; Taylor, *Mahan*, 266–68. Names of the other students are listed in Seager, *ATM*, 628 n. 25.

47. Puleston, *Mahan*, 59; ATM, *Sail to Steam*, 279–80.

48. ATM to Ashe, Nov. 13, 1880, *LPATM*, 1:487; ATM to Ellen K. Mahan, Oct. 18, 1884, *LPATM*, 1:580–81.

49. ATM to Ashe, Nov. 13, 1880, ATM to William D. Whiting, July 9, 15, 1880, *LPATM*, 486–87.483–84.

50. ATM to Ashe, Nov. 13, 1880, *LPATM*, 1:487.

51. ATM to Ashe, Dec. 21, 1882, *LPATM*, 1:543; Puleston, *Mahan*, 62.

52. Lyle Mahan, "Recollections," 122.

53. Ellen K. Mahan, "Recollections," *LPATM*, 3:721; Helen Mahan to ATM, Nov. 7, 1883, ATM Papers, NWC Library; Seager, ATM, 96–97, 625 n. 27; George William Douglas, "Rear Admiral Mahan," *Churchman*, Dec. 12, 1914, 766.

54. William F. P. Napier, *History of the War in the Peninsula and in the South of France, ed. Charles Stuart* (Chicago: University of Chicago Press, 1979).

55. ATM, *Sail to Steam*, 273.

56. Ellen K. Mahan, "Recollections," *LPATM*, 3:724; Lyle Mahan, "Recollections," 113.

57. ATM to Ashe, Dec. 21, 1882, *LPATM*, 1:543; Helen Mahan to ATM, Nov. 19, 1883, Nov. 9, 1884, ATM Papers, NWC Library; Puleston, *Mahan*, 63.

58. Ellen K. Mahan, "Recollections," *LPATM*, 3:723–24.

59. ATM, *The Gulf and Inland Waters* (New York, 1883).

60. ATM to Ashe, July 6, 1883, *LPATM*, 1:554; Charles Scribner's Sons to ATM, Dec. 15, 26, 30, 1882, Scribner Collection, Princeton University Library.

61. Puleston, *Mahan*, 64. Karsten states that Mahan was the third choice after Commo. James Walker and Cdr. George Dewey both turned down the offer. Karsten, *Naval Aristocracy*, 331, 349 n. 14.

62. Karsten, *Naval Aristocracy*, 331, 333.

63. ATM, *Gulf and Inland Waters*, v.

64. For a list of eyewitnesses see *LPATM*, 1:548 n. 2. Mahan's correspondence regarding the writing of the book can be found in *LPATM*, 1:546–56. See also Mahan's "Memorandum of a Conversation with James E. Jouett on the Battle of Mobile Bay, August 5, 1864," March 1883, *LPATM*, 3:555–56.

65. See, for example, ATM to Thomas H. Stevens, May 20, 1883, *LPATM*, 1:551.

66. ATM to Ashe, July 6, 1883, *LPATM*, 1:555.

67. ATM, *Gulf and Inland Waters*, 6.

68. See, for example, ATM to Ashe, July 6, 1883, *LPATM*, 1:554–55.

69. ATM, *Gulf and Inland Waters*, 3–4.

70. ATM to Ashe, July 6, 1883, *LPATM*, 1:554.

71. Samuel Dana Greene to ATM, June 23, 1883, quoted in Taylor, *Mahan*, 24.

72. Loyall Farragut to ATM, July 6, 1883, quoted in Taylor, *Mahan*, 24.

73. *Chicago Tribune*, July [?], 1883, clipping in ATM Papers, NWC Library.

74. *Army and Navy Journal*, July 1883, quoted in Taylor, *Mahan*, 24.

75. Theron Woolverton to ATM, July 8, 1883, James R. Soley to ATM, July 19, 1883, ATM Papers, NWC Library. For a list of other correspondents, see Seager, *ATM*, 633 n. 23.

76. ATM to John G. Walker, Aug. 6, Sep. 9, 1883; ATM to Ashe, Aug. 14, 1883; ATM to William E. Chandler, Sep. 9, 1883, *LPATM*, 1:556–59.

77. Lyle Mahan, "Recollections," 110; Ellen K. Mahan, "Recollection," *LPATM*, 3:721.

78. Helen Mahan to ATM, Nov. 19, Dec. 19, 1883, Jan. 6, 19, 1884, ATM Papers, NWC Library.

79. Helen Mahan to ATM, Jan. 25, 27, Feb. 8, 1884, ATM Papers, NWC Library.

80. Helen Mahan to ATM, Feb. 22, March 16, April 27, 1884, ATM Papers, NWC Library.

81. Helen Mahan to ATM, July 7, 1884, ATM Papers, NWC Library.

82. Helen Mahan to ATM, Sep. 7, 28, 1884, ATM Papers, NWC Library.

83. Helen Mahan to ATM, Sep. 28, Nov. 9, 1884, ATM Papers, NWC Library; ATM to Helen Mahan, Aug. 22, 1884, *LPATM*, 1:576.

84. ATM to Helen Mahan, Dec. 31, 1884, *LPATM*, 1:585–87.

85. Helen Mahan to ATM, March 8, 29, 1885, ATM Papers, NWC Library.

86. Puleston, *Mahan*, 71.

87. ATM to Lyle Mahan, Dec. 29, 1884, *LPATM*, 1:584.

88. ATM to Aaron Hughes, Dec. 18,1883, *LPATM*, 1:561; ATM to William C. Whitney, May 15, 1885, *LPATM*, 1:605.

89. ATM, *Sail to Steam*, 274, 267.

90. ATM to Luce, Sep. 4, 1884, *LPATM*, 1:577.

91. Luce to Boutelle Noyes, July 19, 1883, in Gleaves, *Life and Letters of Stephen B. Luce*, 162–64.

92. Puleston, *Mahan*, 69.

93. John B. Hattendorf, B. Mitchell Simpson III, and John R. Wadleigh, *Sailors and Scholars: The Centennial History of the U.S. Naval War College* (Newport, R.I.: Naval War College Press, 1984), 15.

94. Luce, "Naval Administration, III," *USNIP* 29 (Nov. 14, 1903): 1–13. See also Hattendorf, Simpson, and Wadleigh, *Sailors and Scholars*, 15–16.

95. Puleston, *Mahan*, 69.

96. Hattendorf, Simpson, and Wadleigh, *Sailors and Scholars*, 16–17; see also John D. Hayes and John B. Hattendorf, eds., *The Writings of Stephen B. Luce* (Newport, R.I.: Naval War College Press, 1975), 11, 28, 31. Luce also discusses the Artillery School at length in "War Schools," *USNIP* 9 (1883): 633–57.

97. Seager, ATM, 143; *LPATM*, 1:577 n. 2.

98. Hattendorf, Simpson, and Wadleigh, *Sailors and Scholars*, 17–18.

99. ATM to Luce, Sep. 4, 1884, *LPATM*, 1:577.

100. ATM, *Sail to Steam*, 273.

101. ATM to Luce, Sep. 4, 1884, *LPATM*, 1:577–78.

102. ATM to Luce, Nov. 5, 1884, March 23, Sep. 2, 1885, *LPATM*, 1:581, 597, 613.

103. Larrie D. Ferreiro, "Mahan and the 'English Club' of Lima, Peru: The Genesis of *The Influence of Sea Power upon History*," JMH 72 (2008): 901–6; Theodor Mommsen, *The History of Rome*, trans. William P. Dickson (London, 1869); ATM, *Sail to Steam*, 276.

104. ATM, *Sail to Steam*, 277. See also Puleston, *Mahan*, 69–70.

105. ATM, *Sail to Steam*, 277.

106. ATM to Luce, May 16, 1885, *LPATM*, 1:606–7.

107. ATM to Luce, May 16, 1885, *LPATM*, 1:606.

108. ATM to Whitney, Aug. 5, Sep. 19, 1885, *LPATM*, 1:612–14; ATM to Luce, Oct. 16, 1885, *LPATM*, 1:614. Some of Mahan's answers to exam questions can be found in *LPATM*, 3:557–58.

109. ATM to John G. Walker, Oct. 20, 1886, *LPATM*, 1:615; ATM to Luce, Oct. 21, 1885, *LPATM*, 1:615; Puleston, *Mahan*, 74; Seager, *ATM*, 166.

110. ATM to Luce, Oct. 21, 1885, *LPATM*, 1:615.

111. Puleston, *Mahan*, 74; ATM, *Sail to Steam*, 277.

112. ATM to Ashe, Jan. 13, 1886, *LPATM*, 1:621; ATM, *Sail to Steam*, 278.

113. ATM, *Sail to Steam*, 275–85; Puleston, *Mahan*, 74–80; Seager, *ATM*, 165–76, 636–67 n. 5.

114. ATM, *Sail to Steam*, 278–80; Léonard Lapeyrousse-Bonfils, *History of the French Navy (Paris, 1845)*; John Campbell, *Lives of the British Admirals* (London, 1742); Henri Martin, *A Popular History of France from the First Revolution to the Present Time* (Boston, 1877–82).

115. On DHM's use of Jomini, see Griess, "DHM," 221, 290, 314–20. Sherman, General Order No. 62, July 24, 1862, quoted in Griess, "DHM," 329.

116. Antoine Henri Jomini, *Histoire Critique et Militaire des Guerres de la Revolution* (Brussels, 1840–42); *Summary of the Art of War*, trans. by O. F. Winship and E. E. McLean (New York, 1854).

117. ATM, *Sail to Steam*, 282.

118. Ibid., 283. For a detailed discussion of Jomini's influence on Mahan, see Puleston, *Mahan*, 77–80. Sumida, *in Inventing Grand Strategy*, takes a slightly different view; see 23–24, 109–10 for his discussion of both Mahans and their uses of Jomini.

119. See *LPATM*, 1:615–34.

120. ATM to Ashe, Jan. 13, 1886, *LPATM*, 1:620–21.

121. Various letters, *LPATM*, 1:634–35.

CHAPTER 5. PROVIDENCE AND SEA POWER

1. Hayes and Hattendorf, eds., *Writings of Stephen B. Luce*, 13; ATM, *Sail to Steam*, 292.

2. ATM, *Sail to Steam*, 293; Hattendorf, Simpson, and Wadleigh, Sailors and Scholars, 23.

3. ATM, *Sail to Steam*, 293.

4. Ibid., 294; Hattendorf, Simpson, and Wadleigh, Sailors and Scholars, 24.

5. Hattendorf, Simpson, and Wadleigh, Sailors and Scholars, 24; ATM to Walker, Oct. 19, 1886, *LPATM*, 1:636–67.

6. Luce, "On the Study of Naval Warfare as a Science," in Hayes and Hattendorf, *Writings of Stephen B. Luce*, 45–68; also USNIP 12 (1886): 527–46.

7. ATM, "Reminiscences of Service at the Naval War College," *LPATM*, 3:663; Ellen K. Mahan, "Recollections," *LPATM*, 3:725.

8. Ellen K. Mahan, "Recollections," *LPATM*, 3:725; Lyle Mahan, "Recollections," 124.

9. Ellen K. Mahan, "Recollections," *LPATM*, 3:726.

10. Ibid., 3:721; Bruce J. Shaw, parish clerk, to author, Oct. 8, 1998; Zabriskie Memorial Church of St. John the Evangelist, "Parish History," http://www .saintjohns-newport.org/about.htm, accessed July 13, 2007.

11. ATM to Walker, Oct. 19, 1886, *LPATM*, 1:636–38. See also Puleston, *Mahan*, 83–84.

12. Luce to ATM, July 15, 1907, in Gleaves, *Life and Letters of Rear Admiral Stephen B. Luce*, 295–96; Hayes and Hattendorf, *Writings of Stephen B. Luce*, 68 n. 71; Puleston, *Mahan*, 83. Puleston may have heard this firsthand from Bliss.

13. ATM, *Sail to Steam*, 296.

14. Ibid., 296–99; Hattendorf, Simpson, and Wadleigh, *Sailors and Scholars*, 25–31; Puleston, *Mahan*, 84–88; Seager, *ATM*, 178–90.

15. ATM to Charles R. Miles, Nov. 22, 1888, *LPATM*, 1:666–69. This letter was subsequently published in USNIP 15 (1889): 57–60.

16. Luce to Theodore Roosevelt, Feb. 13, 1888, Theodore Roosevelt Papers, LC; Hayes and Hattendorf, *Writings of Stephen B. Luce*, 33; Hattendorf, Simpson, and Wadleigh, *Sailors and Scholars*, 28. On the Mahan-Roosevelt relationship see Richard W. Turk, *The Ambiguous Relationship: Theodore Roosevelt and Alfred Thayer Mahan* (New York: Praeger, 1987); and Warren Zimmermann, *First Great Triumph: How Five Americans Made Their Country a World Power* (New York: Straus & Giroux, 2002).

17. ATM to Scribner's, Sep. 4, 1888, *LPATM*, 1:657–58.

18. Scribner's to ATM, Sep. 18, 1888, Scribner Collection, Princeton University Library.

19. Caspar F. Goodrich to Charles S. Sperry, March 5, 1906, Archives, Record Group 1, NWC Library; Hattendorf, Simpson, and Wadleigh, *Sailors and Scholars*, 29–30.

20. See ATM correspondence to various parties, Dec. 1888–March 1889, *LPATM*, 1:672–79.

21. ATM, *Sail to Steam*, 302–3; Hattendorf, Simpson, and Wadleigh, *Sailors and Scholars*, 30–31.

22. ATM to Luce, Sep. 21, Oct. 7, 1889, *LPATM* 1:707, 711–13; Lyle Mahan, "Recollections," 124. See also Puleston, *Mahan*, 89–92; Seager, *ATM*, 193–98.

23. ATM to Luce, Oct. 7, 1889, *LPATM*, 1:711–12.

24. ATM to Luce, Oct. 7, 16, 1889, *LPATM*, 1: 712, 714.

25. For a list of all editions and translations, see John B. Hattendorf and Lynn C. Hattendorf, comps., *A Bibliography of the Works of Alfred Thayer Mahan* (Newport, R.I.: Naval War College Press, 1986), Sec. A2.

26. Sumida, *Inventing Grand Strategy*, 2.

27. ATM, *Influence of Sea Power upon History*, 1660–1783, 5th ed. (Boston, 1894; repr. New York, 1987), 25. All references are from the 1987 "Dover" edition, which is a reprint of the 5th edition, 1894.

28. John B. Hattendorf, "Alfred Thayer Mahan and his Strategic Thought," in *Maritime Strategy and the Balance of Power: Britain and America in the Twentieth Century*, ed. John B. Hattendorf and Robert S. Jordan (New York: Macmillan, 1989), 83.

29. ATM, *Influence of Sea Power*, 28–29.

30. ATM, "Subordination in Historical Treatment," in ATM, *Naval Administration and Warfare* (Boston: Little, Brown, and Co., 1908), 267–68.

31. See, for example, ATM to Hugh R. Monro, March 20, 1910, *LPATM*, 3:335–36.

32. ATM, *Influence of Sea Power*, 53.

33. Ibid., 50–52, 57.

34. Ibid., 53–55, 57.

35. Ibid., 57.

36. Ibid., 55–57.

37. Ibid., 57–58.

38. Ibid., 58–59.

39. Sumida, *Inventing Grand Strategy*, 32.

40. Roosevelt to ATM, 1890, quoted in Taylor, *Mahan*, 45.

41. See Taylor, *Mahan*, 45–46; Puleston, Mahan, 104–5; Seager, ATM, 208–12.

42. Luce, "*The Influence of Sea Power upon History*," The Critic 17 (July 26, 1890): 41–42, in Hayes and Hattendorf, *Writings of Stephen B. Luce*, 101–3.

43. ATM to Luce, May 7, 1890, *LPATM*, 2:10.

44. Theodore Roosevelt, "*Review of The Influence of Sea Power upon History*," Atlantic Monthly 66 (1890): 563–67.

45. Seager, ATM, 642 n. 21.

46. Puleston, *Mahan*, 110. On British response, see Puleston, *Mahan*, 104–10; Seager, ATM, 212–14.

47. Quoted in Taylor, *Mahan*, 46.

48. Cyprian B. S. Bridge, "*Review of The Influence of Sea Power upon History*," Blackwood's Edinburgh Magazine 148 (1890): 576–84.

49. John K. Laughton, "Captain Mahan on Maritime Power," *Edinburgh Review* 172 (1890): 420–53; Seager, *ATM*, 213.

50. Laughton, "Captain Mahan," 420, 453; for Seager's comments on Laughton's review see Seager, *ATM*, 213.

51. ATM to Luce, Dec. 20, 1890, *LPATM*, 2:34.

52. Laughton, "Captain Mahan," 453; Seager, *ATM*, 213.

53. Sumida, *Inventing Grand Strategy*, 82–92.

54. Puleston, *Mahan*, 107–8; Seager, ATM, 214.

55. Seager, *ATM*, 218.

56. ATM, *Sail to Steam*, 303; Hattendorf, Simpson, and Wadleigh, *Sailors and Scholars*, 30–31.

57. ATM, *Sail to Steam*, 303.

58. ATM to Helen Mahan, July 9, 1890, *LPATM*, 2:13–15, all emphases in original.

59. Robert Seager II, "Biography of a Biographer," in *Changing Interpretations and New Sources in Naval History: Papers From the Third United States Naval Academy Symposium*, ed. Robert W. Love Jr. (New York: Garland Publishing, 1980), 280; see also Seager, *ATM*, 220–21.

60. Seager, *ATM*, 220.

61. ATM to Helen Mahan, July 9, 1890, *LPATM*, 2:13.

62. Seager, "Biography of a Biographer," 280; see also Seager, *ATM*, 305, 313–14.

63. Seager, "Biography of a Biographer," 280.

64. Seager, *ATM*, 322–23.

65. ATM to Helen Mahan, July 20, 1890, *LPATM*, 2:15–17.

66. Seager, "Biography of a Biographer," 280.

67. Ibid., 280; Seager, *ATM*, 220–21.

68. ATM to Helen Mahan, July 20, 1890, *LPATM*, 2:16–17.

69. ATM to Benjamin F. Tracy, May 12, 1891, *LPATM*, 2:46.

70. Seager, *ATM*, 233–34, 648 n. 14; William N. Still Jr., "David Glasgow Farragut: The Union's Nelson," in *Quarterdeck and Bridge: Two Centuries of American Naval Leaders, ed. James C. Bradford* (Annapolis, Md.: Naval Institute Press, 1977), 145.

71. ATM, *Admiral Farragut* (New York, 1892), 252.

72. Ibid., 277–78.

73. Ibid., 267.

74. Ibid., 70, 307. In his retirement Farragut attended the Church of the Incarnation in New York City. There is a tablet there in his memory. This author also recalls seeing Farragut's copy of the Book of Common Prayer, showing his underlinings and notes, on display at the Naval Academy Chapel.

75. Seager, *ATM*, 235, 648 n. 15.

76. ATM to John M. Brown, July 2, 1897, *LPATM*, 2:517; Seager, *ATM*, 648 n. 15. The clippings are in the ATM Papers, NWC Library.

77. Seager, *ATM*, 233, 235; Seager, "Biography of a Biographer," 281.

78. Still, "Farragut," 145.

79. Seager, *ATM*, 235–36; ATM to Luce, Sep. 3, 1901, *LPATM*, 2:734.

80. ATM to Luce, Jan. 28, 1892, *LPATM*, 2:64.

81. Hattendorf, Simpson, and Wadleigh, *Sailors and Scholars*, 32–33.

82. ATM, *The Influence of Sea Power Upon the French Revolution and Empire, 1793–1812* (London, 1892); Seager, ATM, 231–37; ATM, "Pitt's War Policy," *Quarterly Review* 175 (1892): 70–101.

83. Seager, *ATM*, 216; Sumida, *Inventing Grand Strategy*, 33.

84. ATM, *French Revolution and Empire*, 2:371–72.

85. Sumida, *Inventing Grand Strategy*, 35–36; ATM, *French Revolution and Empire*, 2:201.

86. ATM, *The Interest of America in Sea Power, Present and Future (Boston, 1897)*, 307–8. The chapter in which this quote is found originally appeared as an article, "Strategic Features of the Caribbean Sea and the Gulf of Mexico," *Harper's New Monthly Magazine* 95 (1897): 680–91; ATM, "War from the Christian Standpoint," in *Some Neglected Aspects of* War (Boston: Little Brown & Co., 1907), 103–4. I am indebted to Jon Sumida for bringing this passage to my attention. See also Sumida, *Inventing Grand Strategy*, 98.

87. ATM to George Sydenham Clarke, Nov. 5, 1892, *LPATM*, 2:85.

88. Theodore Roosevelt, "Review of *The Influence of Sea Power Upon the French Revolution*," *Atlantic Monthly* 71 (1893): 556; Theodore Roosevelt, "Review of *The Influence of Sea Power upon History, 1660–1783* and *The Influence of Sea Power Upon the French Revolution and Empire, 1793–1812*," *Political Science Quarterly* 9 (1894): 171–72.

89. John K. Laughton, "Review of *The Influence of Sea Power upon the French Revolution and Empire*," *Edinburgh Review* 177 (1893): 484–85.

90. A. H. Johnson, "Review of *The Influence of Sea Power upon History and The Influence of Sea Power upon the French Revolution and Empire*," *English Historical Review* 8 (1893): 788. For further discussion of reviews see Seager, *ATM*, 232–33, 647–48 n. 13; Taylor, *Mahan*, 49–51.

91. ATM, *Sail to Steam*, 311.

92. ATM to Soley, Oct. 29, 1892, *LPATM*, 2:83.

93. ATM to Ellen Mahan, April 29, 1894, *LPATM*, 2:262; Puleston, *Mahan*, 132.

94. Samuel S. Vaughan, *The Little Church: One Hundred Years at the Church of the Atonement, 1868–1968* (Tenafly, N.J.: Church of the Atonement, 1969), 30.

95. Puleston, *Mahan*, 133–36; Seager, ATM, 245–46.

96. ATM to *New York Times*, Jan. 30, 1893, *LPATM*, 2:92–93; the letter was published on Feb. 1.

97. ATM to Horace Scudder, Feb. 3, 1893, *LPATM*, 2:94.

98. ATM, "Hawaii and Our Future Sea Power," in *Interest of America in Sea Power*, 39–55, originally in The Forum 15 (1893): 1–11.

99. Taylor, *Mahan*, 57–60; Puleston, *Mahan*, 133–36; Seager, *ATM*, 245–53; ATM to Roosevelt, March 1, 1893, *LPATM*, 2:96–97; ATM to Ramsey, March 17, 1893, *LPATM*, 2:98; ATM, *Sail to Steam*, 311–12.

100. Frederick Mahan to ATM, May 3, 1893, quoted in Taylor, *Mahan*, 60.

101. Quoted in Taylor, *Mahan*, 57.

102. Roosevelt to ATM, May 1, 1893, quoted in Taylor, *Mahan*, 58.

103. ATM, *Sail to Steam*, 311. It is not known precisely when and to whom Ramsey said this; see Seager, *ATM*, 649 n. 22.

104. Puleston, *Mahan*, 134–35.

105. ATM to Scudder, June 9, 1893, *LPATM*, 2:112.

106. ATM to Ellen Mahan, June 29, 1893, *LPATM*, 2:114.

107. Letters to his family can be found in *LPATM*, 2:113–409.

108. Puleston, *Mahan*, 135–36.

109. Quoted in ibid., 140.

110. ATM to Ellen K. Mahan, Aug. 1, 1893, ATM to Luce, Aug. 24, 1893, *LPATM*, 2:128–30, 144.

111. ATM to Ellen Mahan, Aug. 11, 1893, *LPATM*, 2:134–36.

112. ATM to Ellen Mahan, Aug. 11, 12, 1893, *LPATM*, 2:135–36.

113. French E. Chadwick to ATM, Aug. 10, 1893, quoted in both ATM to Ellen Mahan, Aug. 24, 1893, and ATM to Luce, Aug. 24, 1893, in *LPATM*, 2:142, 144.

114. Henry Erben, Fitness Report, A. T. Mahan, Capt., U.S.N., Dec. 31, 1893, *LPATM*, 2:221 n. 1.

115. ATM to Ellen Mahan, Jan. 22–23, 1894, *LPATM*, 2:210–12.

116. ATM to Herbert, Jan. 25, 1894, *LPATM*, 2:212–15.

117. Henry Cabot Lodge to ATM, Feb. 10, 1894, ATM Papers, LC; ATM to Ellen Mahan, March 4, 1894, *LPATM*, 2:139–40. Extensive correspondence on this matter among ATM, Roosevelt, Lodge, Ogden, and Mrs. Mahan is in ATM Papers, LC. See also Puleston, *Mahan*, 148–51; Seager, *ATM*, 281–88.

118. Puleston, *Mahan*, 150; Seager, *ATM*, 288–89.

119. ATM to Ellen Mahan, Jan. 15, 28, Feb. 10, 1894, *LPATM*, 2:216, 218, 224.

120. ATM to Ellen Mahan, March 13, 1894, *LPATM*, 2:230.

121. ATM to Helen Mahan, Jan. 31, 1894, *LPATM*, 2:220.

122. Seager, *ATM*, 312–15; ATM to Helen Mahan, Sep. 18, 1894, *LPATM*, 2:333.

123. ATM to Ellen Mahan, June 15, 1894, *LPATM*, 2:288–89.

124. ATM to Ellen Mahan, Oct. 11, 1893, June 29, 1894, *LPATM*, 2:163, 293.

125. Lyle Mahan, "Reminiscences," 113.

126. ATM to Ellen Mahan, Feb. 23, 1894, *LPATM*, 2:235.

127. ATM to Ellen Mahan, March 10, 1894, *LPATM*, 2:244.

128. J. M. Ellicott, "Three Navy Cranks and What They Turned," *USNIP* 50 (Oct. 1924): 1623–25; J. M. Ellicott, "With Erben and Mahan on the Chicago," *USNIP* 67 (Sep. 1941): 1237, 1240.

129. ATM to Ellen Mahan, March 4, 1894, ATM to Helen Mahan, March 16, 1894, *LPATM*, 2:241, 246–48.

130. ATM to Helen Mahan, Jan. 31, 1894, *LPATM*, 2:220.

131. ATM to Ellen Mahan, Feb. 10, Aug. 29, 1894, *LPATM*, 2:224, 322. For Seager's discussion of the Schiffs see *ATM*, 310–12. See also Puleston, *Mahan*, 150–51. Puleston refers to Mr. Schiff as Albert whereas Seager refers to him as George.

132. ATM to Ellen Mahan, June 1, 1894, *LPATM*, 2:278.

133. On Mahan's reception in England see Puleston, *Mahan*, 154–62, and Seager, *ATM*, 289–99; "Our Naval Supremacy: Captain Mahan's Opinion," *Pall Mall Gazette*, May 10, 1894, clipping in ATM Papers, NWC Library.

134. Martin Gilbert, *Churchill: A Life* (New York: Henry Holt, 1991), 45. No other Churchill biography mentions this episode.

135. ATM, *Sail to Steam*, 314; ATM to Ellen Mahan, June 20, 1894, *LPATM*, 2:290.

136. ATM, *Sail to Steam*, 314–16; ATM to Ellen Mahan, June 20, 23, 1894, *LPATM*, 2:290–91. For the text of the Oxford Orator (translated from Latin) see Taylor, *Mahan*, 71–72.

137. ATM to Ellen Mahan, June 11, 23, 1894, *LPATM*, 2:277, 291.

138. Wilhelm II to Poultney Bigelow, May 26, 1894; Bigelow to ATM, May 26, 1894, quoted in Taylor, *Mahan*, 131. ATM to Ellen Mahan, Aug. 10, 1894, *LPATM*, 2: 311–12. The kaiser's telegram is reproduced in Taylor, *Mahan*, 129.

139. Puleston, *Mahan*, 159 n. 1.

140. Ibid., 159; Taylor, *Mahan*, 131.

141. ATM to Ellen Mahan, Aug. 29, 1894, *LPATM*, 2:322. On the Erben-Kirkland change of command see Puleston, *Mahan*, 159–60; Seager, ATM, 300–302.

142. William A. Kirkland to Herbert, Feb. 28, 1895, ATM Papers, LC; also reported in *New York Herald*, March 24, 1895, clipping in ATM Papers, NWC Library.

143. ATM to Helen Mahan, June 5, 1894, *LPATM*, 2:280.

144. ATM to Ellen K. Mahan, Sep. 10, 11, 1894, *LPATM*, 2:325–26.

145. ATM to Ellen Mahan, Aug. 17, Oct. 19, 1894, *LPATM*, 2:315, 349.

146. On Lyle's illness see Lyle Mahan, "Recollections," 116, 124; Ellen K. Mahan, "Recollections," *LPATM*, 3:727; ATM to Ellen Mahan, Feb. 6, 11, 24, 1895, *LPATM*, 2:400, 402, 405.

147. Letters from this last part of the voyage and the decommissioning period are in *LPATM*, 2:393–414. See also Puleston, *Mahan*, 163–65; Seager, *ATM*, 303–7.

148. ATM to Ellen Mahan, Oct. 19, 1894, *LPATM*, 2:349.

149. Herbert to Henry Taylor, Feb. 23, 1895, Henry C. Taylor Papers, LC.

150. Seager, *ATM*, 308.

151. ATM to Ramsey, May 1, 7, 1895, *LPATM*, 2:414.

152. Puleston, *Mahan*, 166–67; Seager, *ATM*, 324–25.

153. Puleston, *Mahan*, 168–69; Seager, ATM, 327–31; ATM to Ramsey, June 27, 29, 1895, ATM to John M. Brown, June 30, 1895, *LPATM*, 2:420–21.

154. ATM, Motto, June 20, 1895, *LPATM*, 2:420.

155. ATM to Frederick A. Mahan, Dec. 15, 1895, *LPATM*, 2:438–39.

156. ATM to Augustus T. Gillender, Dec. 26, 1895, *LPATM*, 2:440.

157. "Dennis Hart Mahan [Jr.]," http://ourworld.compuserve.com/homepages/michael_patteson_4/dmahan.htm, accessed June 9, 1999. Dennis retired from the Navy in 1909 but was recalled to active duty during World War I.

158. For discussion of how this issue affected Mahan, see Puleston, *Mahan*, 169–71, and Seager, *ATM*, 333–37.

159. ATM to Ashe, Jan. 3, 1897, *LPATM*, 2:482.

160. ATM to James R. Thursfield, Jan. 10, 1896, *LPATM*, 2:441.

161. Ibid., 2:441.

162. ATM to Bouverie F. Clark, Jan. 17, 1896, *LPATM*, 2:444.

163. ATM to J. B. Sterling, Feb. 13, 1896, *LPATM*, 2:445.

164. On Mahan's retirement see Puleston, *Mahan*, 171, and Seager, *ATM*, 336.

165. *New York Times*, Nov. 18, 1896, quoted in Seager, *ATM*, 664 n. 12; ATM to Ashe, Jan. 3, 1897, Nov. 7, 1896, *LPATM*, 2:482, 471.

166. Seager, *ATM*, 340; Sumida, *Inventing Grand Strategy*, 36–37.

167. Puleston, *Mahan*, 173; Taylor, *Mahan*, 79.

168. ATM, *The Life of Nelson: The Embodiment of the Sea Power of Great Britain*, 2d ed. (Boston, 1899), 1:v.

169. Sumida, *Inventing Grand Strategy*, 37.

170. ATM, *Nelson*, 1:4–5, 20–21, 32.

171. Ibid., 1:96, 173, 263, 2:110, 159–60.

172. Ibid., 2:110.

173. Ibid., 1:ix, 32–33.

174. Ibid., 2:57–59.

175. Ibid., 1:42–43, 65, 67–68, 71–72, 90–91.

176. Ibid., 1:68.

177. Ibid., 1:71.

178. Ibid., 1:96–97.

179. Ibid., 2:397.

180. Seager, "Biography of a Biographer." This article includes a brief discussion of Mahan's *Farragut*, but most of it is a mocking critique of *Nelson*.

181. Ibid., 280, 284–85.

182. Ibid., 292 n. 17; ATM, *Nelson*, 1:350–51, 370–72, 385–88.

183. Seager, "Biography of a Biographer," 285–86; Seager, *ATM*, 342–43.

184. William O'Connor Morris, "Captain Mahan's 'Nelson,'" *Fortnightly Review* 61 (1897): 898.

185. James R. Thursfield, "The Life of Nelson," *Quarterly Review* 187 (1898): 132–33, 144.

186. John K. Laughton, "Captain Mahan's 'Life of Nelson,'" *Edinburgh Review* 186 (1897): 94, 101.

187. George S. Clarke, "Nelson," *The Nineteenth Century* 41 (1897): 899, 894–95, 905.

188. Seager, "Biography of a Biographer," 284.

189. For discussion of reviews, reactions, and the Badham controversy, see Taylor, *Mahan*, 78–87; Puleston, *Mahan*, 172–80; Seager, *ATM*, 340–48. See also Francis P. Badham, "Nelson and the Neapolitan Republicans," *English Historical Review* 13 (1898): 261–82; ATM, "The Neapolitan Republicans and Nelson's Accusers," *English Historical Review* 14 (1899): 471–501.

190. Sumida, *Inventing Grand Strategy*, 37, 39.

CHAPTER 6. A PUBLIC CHRISTIAN

1. ATM, *Interest of America in Sea Power*.

2. Randall Craig Schluter, in his dissertation "Looking Outward for America: An Ideological Criticism of the Rhetoric of Captain Alfred Thayer Mahan, USN, in American Magazines of the 1890s" (PhD diss., University of Iowa,

1995), analyzes Mahan's "rhetoric" in his articles from the period from 1890 to 1898 that appeared in *North American Review, Atlantic Monthly,* and *Harper's Monthly.* These magazines appealed to upper- and upper-middle-class elites with an interest in foreign policy and made up Mahan's "public sphere." His analysis of these magazines and Mahan's contributions to them is interesting but is marred by a strong anti-Mahan bias that sees him as an Anglo-Saxon cultural supremacist, navalist, and expansionist. He even suggests that Mahan's ideas contributed to the Cold War. He is not sympathetic to Mahan's religious viewpoints and sees them basically as an ideological smokescreen for Anglo-Saxon supremacy. See especially 231–34, 237–39.

3. ATM, *Interest of America in Sea Power,* 95.

4. Ibid., 243, 251, 264.

5. Ibid., 243.

6. Ibid., 245.

7. Ibid., 264, 268.

8. Ibid., 307–8. In the table of contents this article is listed as "Strategic Features of the Caribbean Sea and the Gulf of Mexico," but on page 271 where the article begins the title is given as "Strategic Features of the Gulf of Mexico and the Caribbean Sea."

9. George S. Clarke, "Captain Mahan's Counsels to the United States," *The Nineteenth Century* 43 (1898): 292–93. For discussion of reviews see Seager, *ATM,* 351–53.

10. ATM to Clarke, Feb. 22, 1898, *LPATM,* 2:543, emphases in original.

11. Hattendorf and Hattendorf, *Bibliography,* section A5.

12. ATM to Jane L. Mahan, June 10, 1897, *LPATM,* 2:515, emphasis in original.

13. ATM to Gillender, June 28, 1897, *LPATM,* 2:516; see also ibid.

14. ATM to Endicott Peabody, Feb. 18, 1898, *LPATM,* 2:542.

15. Seager, *ATM,* 667 n. 4.

16. Lyle Mahan, "Recollections," 117.

17. Puleston, *Mahan,* 186; Seager, *ATM,* 360.

18. ATM to Sterling, March 4, 1898, *LPATM,* 2:545.

19. ATM, "The Sinking of the U.S.S. *Maine*: Remarks to the New Jersey Chapter of the Society of the Cincinnati," Feb. 22, 1898, *LPATM,* 3:592; speech was reported in *New York Times,* Feb. 23, 1898.

20. Zimmermann, *First Great Triumph,* 237. On the Roosevelt-ATM correspondence, see Puleston, *Mahan,* 182–85; Seager, *ATM,* 360–63, 668 n. 7; William F. Livezey, *Mahan on Sea Power,* rev. ed. (Norman: University of Oklahoma Press, 1980), 133–34; Turk, *Ambiguous Relationship,* 37–55.

21. Long to ATM, cable, April 25, 1898, quoted in Taylor, *Mahan,* 88; Puleston, *Mahan,* 187.

22. Portrait reproduced in Taylor, *Mahan,* between pages 86 and 89.

23. Seager, *ATM,* 369.

24. ATM to Long, May 10, 1898, *LPATM*, 2:551–52.

25. Seager, *ATM*, 370. Mahan later developed some of these ideas in his article "The Principles of Naval Administration, Historically Considered," which originally appeared in the June 4, 1903, issue of *National Review* and was reprinted in ATM, *Naval Administration and Warfare*.

26. ATM, "The Work of the Naval War Board of 1898," Oct. 29, 1906, *LPATM*, 3:627–43.

27. ATM, "Hawaii and Our Future Sea Power," in *Interest of America in Sea Power*, 39–45.

28. Seager, *ATM*, 358. In his article "Strategic Features of the Caribbean Sea and the Gulf of Mexico," Mahan's only interest in Cuba was its military and naval importance. See ATM, *Interest of America in Sea Power*, 271–314.

29. Julius W. Pratt, *Expansionists of 1898: The Acquisition of Hawaii and the Spanish Islands* (Baltimore: Johns Hopkins University Press, 1936), 12–17. See also Walter LaFeber, *The New Empire: An Interpretation of American Expansion 1860–1898* (Ithaca, N.Y.: Cornell University Press, 1963), 62, 85–87.

30. ATM, Report of Naval War Board, Aug. 15–20, 1898, *LPATM*, 2:582–83.

31. ATM to John S. Barnes, July 21, 1898, *LPATM*, 2:566.

32. ATM to Clarke, Aug. 17, 1898, *LPATM*, 2:579–80.

33. ATM to Long, July 23, 1898, *LPATM*, 2:567.

34. ATM, "Remarks to the Associate Alumni of the College of the City of New York," Feb. 24, 1900, *LPATM*, 3:603.

35. ATM, *Sail to Steam*, 324–25.

36. ATM to Long. Oct. 6, 1898, *LPATM*, 2:597–98.

37. ATM to Long, Oct. 10, 1898, *LPATM*, 2:599.

38. ATM to Silas McBee, May 12, 1897, *LPATM*, 2:508.

39. Abstract of Silas McBee Papers, University of North Carolina Library, http://www.lib.unc.edu/mss/inv/m/McBee.Silas.html, accessed July 10, 2010; *LPATM*, 2:654 n. 2.

40. ATM to McBee, Sep. 8, 1899, *LPATM*, 2:654–55.

41. ATM, letter to editor, *Churchman*, Sep. 9, 1899, reprinted in *LPATM*, 2:661–63.

42. Carl E. Hatch, *The Charles A. Briggs Heresy Trial, Prologue to Twentieth-Century Liberal Protestantism* (New York: Exposition Press, 1969), 17.

43. Ibid., 131; James Elliott Lindsley, *This Planted Vine: A Narrative History of the Episcopal Diocese of New York* (New York: Harper & Row, 1984), 241.

44. Lindsley, *This Planted Vine*, 241; George Hodges, *Henry Codman Potter* (New York, Macmillan Co., 1915), 306. Mahan's letter is referred to by both Lindsley and Hodges, but never actually cited by either. A more recent biography of Potter by Michael Bourgeois, *All Things Human: Henry Codman Potter and the Social Gospel in the Episcopal Church* (Champaign: University of Illinois Press, 2003), does not mention Mahan. There is no extant copy of Mahan's letter.

Both Wayne Kempton, archivist of the Diocese of New York, and I searched for it without success. I am also grateful to the Rev. James Elliott Lindsley for sharing his recollections of his research with me; Lindsley to author, Aug. 20, 26, Oct. 15, 1997.

45. Puleston, *Mahan*, 204–5; Seager, *ATM*, 406–8.

46. ATM, "Apparent Decadence," 545, 547.

47. See, for example, ATM to Hugh R. Munro, May 20, 1910, *LPATM*, 3:335–36.

48. Augustine, *Political Writings*, ed. Henry Paolucci (Chicago: Gateway, 1962), 162–83. For a good analysis of Augustine's "just war" theory see George Weigel, *Tranquilitas Ordinis: The Present Failure and Future Promise of American Catholic Thought on War and Peace* (New York: Oxford University Press, 1987), 28–32.

49. Suzanne Geissler, "Mahan versus the Pacifists," in *New Interpretations in Naval History*, ed. Randy Carol Balano and Craig L. Symonds (Annapolis, Md.: Naval Institute Press, 2001), 183–99.

50. Andrew D. White, *Autobiography of Andrew Dickson White* (New York: Century Co., 1905), 2:347.

51. Ibid., 2:347.

52. Ibid., 2:319–20; ATM report to U.S. delegation, *LPATM*, 2:650–52.

53. White, *Autobiography*, 2:343; ATM report to U.S. delegation, *LPATM*, 2:646–49.

54. For a fuller discussion of Mahan at the Hague Conference see Taylor, *Mahan*, 94–101; Puleston, *Mahan*, 204–17; Seager, *ATM*, 409–16.

55. ATM, "The Peace Conference and the Moral Aspect of War," in *Some Neglected Aspects of War*, 24–26. This article can also be found in *Lessons of the War with Spain and Other Articles* (Boston, 1899), 207–38. Mahan's argument about the coercive nature of arbitration anticipates Reinhold Niebuhr's similar argument in *Moral Man and Immoral Society* (New York: Scribners, 1932).

56. ATM, "The Peace Conference," 30, 49–50. Mahan also makes clear in this article his disdain for the Fugitive Slave Act of 1850, which made it a federal crime to assist a runaway slave and forbade free states from offering refuge to runaways, and his belief that this was one of the (admittedly rare) occasions when it was permissible for a Christian to refuse to obey the law. He felt so strongly about this that he likened refusing to return an escaped slave to an early Christian refusing to sacrifice to the Roman emperor; see 27, 39.

57. ATM, *Lessons of the War with Spain*, 45.

58. Ibid., 242–46. I emphasized the word "yet" to indicate that Mahan viewed the colonized peoples as simply undeveloped, not inherently inferior.

59. Wallace Rice, "Some Current Fallacies of Captain Mahan," *The Dial*, March 16, 1900, 198–200.

60. ATM to Grace Hoadley Dodge, Jan. 4, 1900, *LPATM*, 2:675–76. In *LPATM* the recipient of this letter is identified as "Mr. Dodge" with the notation "No further identification has been found," *LPATM*, 2:675 n. 1. But in Seager, *ATM*,

the recipient is identified as Grace Hoadley Dodge; see 413, 671 n. 14. Dodge's proposed publication does not seem to have come to fruition.

61. ATM, "A Distinction Between Colonies and Dependencies," Nov. 30, 1898, *LPATM*, 3:596. This was a speech to the New York State Chapter of the Colonial Order, as reported in the *New York Times*, Dec. 1, 1898.

62. Seager, *ATM*, 420.

63. ATM to Lodge, Feb. 7, 1899, *LPATM*, 2:627.

64. ATM to Daniel C. Gilman, Oct. 23, 1898, *LPATM*, 2:605.

65. ATM to Roosevelt, Jan. 25, 1902, *LPATM*, 3:6–7; Seager, *ATM*, 420–21.

66. Taylor, *Mahan*, 264; James Elliott Lindsley, *The Church Club of New York* (New York: Church Club of New York, 1994), 192.

67. Lindsley, *Church Club*, 39–40; ATM to Long, Feb. 9, 1902, *LPATM*, 3:10–11. See also Ian Tyrrell, *Reforming the World: The Creation of America's Moral Empire* (Princeton, N.J.: Princeton University Press, 2010), 193. For further discussion of the Episcopal mission to the Philippines see Kenton J. Clymer, *Protestant Missionaries in the Philippines, 1898–1916: An Inquiry into the American Colonial Mentality* (Urbana: University of Illinois Press, 1986), 6, 16–17.

68. Karsten, *Naval Aristocracy*, 213–18; Seager, *ATM*, 478–80 and passim. Even the editors' introduction to my own article refers to him as holding "a racist vision not uncommon to his day"; see editors' introduction, Geissler, "Mahan versus the Pacifists," 189.

69. These are my own conclusions based on a close reading of Mahan's works, but they are in agreement with those expressed by Bates M. Gilliam in "The World of Captain Mahan" (PhD diss., Princeton University, 1961), 112–14.

70. ATM, *Interest of America in Sea Power*, 246.

71. ATM to *Times* (London), June 23, 1913, *LPATM*, 3:495.

72. Diary, Jan. 3, 1869, *LPATM*, 1:258.

73. ATM, *Sail to Steam*, 220.

74. ATM to McBee, Aug. 27, 1899, *LPATM*, 2:654.

75. ATM, letter to editor, *Churchman*, Sep. 9, 1899; also in *LPATM*, 2:661–63. The term "Churchman" with an uppercase C, though rarely used nowadays, was a synonym for Episcopalian, usually referring to a layman. See also Tyrrell, *Reforming the World*, 192–96.

76. See ATM's correspondence in the period Sep. 1899 to Jan. 1903, *LPATM*, 2:656–3:51. For a discussion, albeit a cynical one, of ATM's views on the Boer War, see Seager, *ATM*, 421–28. ATM, *The Story of the War in South Africa, 1899–1900* (London: Sampson Low, Marston & Co., 1900 [repr. New York: Greenwood, 1968]).

77. ATM to McBee, Sep. 23, 1899, *LPATM*, 2:656–57.

78. ATM, *The Problem of Asia and Its Effects upon International Policies* (Boston: Little, Brown, and Co., 1900), 205–6, 230. This article was reprinted in both *Problem of Asia* and *War in South Africa*.

79. See, e.g., ATM to McBee, Oct. 13, 1899, ATM to Thursfield, Oct. 28, 1899, ATM to James Ford Rhodes, Jan. 30, 1900, *LPATM*, 2:664–65, 679–80.

80. ATM to McBee, Oct. 13, 1899, *LPATM*, 2:664.

81. ATM to Rhodes, Jan. 30, 1900, *LPATM*, 2:680; ATM, "The Transvaal and the Philippine Islands," *The Independent*, Feb. 1, 1900.

82. ATM to *New York Evening Sun*, n.d. [1900], ATM Papers, NWC Library.

83. ATM to Clark, Dec. 19, 1900, May 3, 1901, *LPATM*, 2:699–700, 721–22; Roberts to ATM, Jan. 23, 1900, Clark to Charles Taylor, n.d. [1919 or 1920], in Taylor, *Mahan*, 187–88, 179–80.

84. ATM to Duke of Cambridge, July 10, 1900, *LPATM*, 2:691.

85. Seager, *ATM*, 460–67; ATM, *Problem of Asia*, 111.

86. Seager, *ATM*, 464; ATM, *Problem of Asia*, 149.

87. ATM, *Problem of Asia*, 108–11, 147–51, 154.

88. Ibid., 168–69.

89. Ibid., 24; see also ATM to Leopold J. Maxse, Feb. 21, March 7, May 27, 1902, *LPATM*, 3:12–13, 27.

90. ATM to Maxse, Feb. 21, March 7, 1902, *LPATM*, 3:12–13; ATM, *Problem of Asia*, 90–93. I have been unable to find any reference by Mahan to the Russian Orthodox Church.

91. ATM, *Problem of Asia*, 91.

92. Ibid., 194.

93. Ibid., 154.

94. ATM, *Types of Naval Officers Drawn from the History of the British Navy* (Boston: Little, Brown, and Co., 1901), 454–55, 476. Seager never discusses this book at all, though Puleston includes a chapter on it; Puleston, *Mahan*, 28.

95. *LPATM*, 3:590 n. 1; Rousmaniere, *Anchored within the Vail*, 31.

96. ATM, "A Statement on Behalf of the Church Missionary Society to Seamen in the Port of New York," April 10, 1897, *LPATM*, 3:590–91.

97. ATM, "Presentation to the Annual Meeting of the Church Missionary Society to Seamen in the Port of New York," Dec. 13, 1898, *LPATM*, 3:597.

98. ATM, "The Well Being of the Seaman in Port," March 21, 1902, *LPATM*, 3:606–7. On crimps, see Rousmaniere, *Anchored within the Vail*, 12–14, 29–33.

99. Rousmaniere, *Anchored within the Vail*, 30.

100. Ibid., 33.

101. Ibid., 3:598–602.

102. Ibid., 3:598.

103. Ibid., 3:599–600.

104. Ibid., 3:602.

105. ATM, "The Practical in Christianity," March 22, 1899, in *The Harvest Within*, 266–70, 274.

106. Ibid., 265–66, 278, 280.

107. These are listed in Ellen K. Mahan, "Recollections," *LPATM*, 3:721.

108. Karsten, *Naval Aristocracy*, 74.

109. Ibid., 97 n. 55.

110. E. Digby Baltzell, *Philadelphia Gentlemen: The Making of a National Upper Class* (Glencoe, Ill.: Free Press, 1958), 233.

111. Henry Anstice, *History of St. George's Church in the City of New York, 1752–1811-1911* (New York: Harper & Bros., 1911). Anstice lists all the vestry members up to the date of publication and Mahan's name is nowhere among them. I am indebted to Wayne Kempton, archivist of the Diocese of New York, for tracking down this source.

112. William S. Rainsford, *The Story of a Varied Life* (Garden City, N.Y.: Doubleday, Page & Co., 1922), 277–84.

113. On Mahan's activities at Church of the Atonement, Quogue, see Richard F. Welch, "Alfred Thayer Mahan," *Long Island Forum* (Winter 1999): 29; additional information was supplied to the author by George Maxwell, archivist of Church of the Atonement, Quogue, N.Y.; George Maxwell to author, Sep. 22, 2000.

114. Seager, *ATM*, 440–41; ATM to J. Franklin Jameson, Dec. 27, 1897, Dec. 24, 1899, *LPATM*, 2:533, 674–75.

115. ATM to James Ford Rhodes, Jan. 3, 1901, *LPATM*, 2:701.

116. ATM to Rhodes, Jan. 3, 1901, *LPATM*, 2:701.

117. Hattendorf and Hattendorf, *Bibliography*, D78; ATM, "Subordination in Historical Treatment," in *Naval Administration and Warfare*, 245–72.

118. ATM, "Subordination," 247–49, 251, 253–55.

119. Ibid., 253, 251–52.

120. Ibid., 267–68, 271.

121. Seager, *ATM*, 442–43; Julius W. Pratt, "Alfred Thayer Mahan," in *The Marcus W. Jernegan Essays in American Historiography*, ed. William T. Hutchinson (Chicago: University of Chicago Press, 1937), 215–16.

122. See , for example, Mark T. Gilderhus, *History and Historians: A Historiographical Introduction*, 7th ed. (Upper Saddle River, N.J.: Prentice Hall, 2010), chap. 4.

123. ATM, *Sail to Steam*, 86; G. P. Gooch, *History and Historians in the Nineteenth Century*, rev. ed. (Boston: Beacon Press, 1959), 394–96.

124. Seager, *ATM*, 443–44; ATM to Helen Mahan, June 14, 1896, *LPATM*, 2:458. On Goulburn see Albert Frederick Pollard, "Goulburn, Edward Meyrick," *Dictionary of National Biography*, 1901 supplement, http://eu.wikisource.org/wiki/Goulburn_Edward_Meyrick_(DNB01), accessed July 27, 2011.

125. Edward M. Goulburn, *Thoughts on Personal Religion* (New York, 1865), quoted in Seager, *ATM*, 444.

126. Seager, *ATM*, 445–50.

127. MM, *Palmoni*, title page; MM, *Mystic Numbers: A Key to Chronology* (New York, 1875).

128. MM, *Palmoni*, 6; Henry Browne, *Ordo Saeclorum: A Treatise on the Chronology of the Holy Scripture* (London, 1844); Francis Hooper, *Palmoni: An Essay of the Chronological and Numerical Systems in Use Among the Ancient Jews* (Oxford, 1851).

129. See Seager's footnotes for this section of *ATM*, 674–75.

130. Diary, Jan. 10, 1869, *LPATM*, 1:259–60.

131. MM, *Spiritual Point-of-View*, 3, 7–8, 14–15.

132. Ibid., 20, 23–25.

133. ATM to William J. Tucker, June 8, 1903, *LPATM*, 3:62–63.

134. ATM, "Personality and Influence," June 24, 1903, *LPATM*, 3:608–19.

135. Ibid., 3:608–12.

136. Ibid., 3:613–19.

137. Ibid., 3:619.

138. Puleston, *Mahan*, 249–53; Seager, *ATM*, 469–76; ATM, "Appreciation of Conditions in the Russo-Japanese Conflict," Parts I and II, *Collier's Weekly* 32 (Feb. 20, 1904): 7–8, and *Collier's Weekly* 33 (April 30, 1904): 10–13; ATM, "Some Considerations of the Principles Involved in the Present War," *National Review* 44 (Sep. 1904): 27–46 (reprinted in *Naval Administration and Warfare*, 131–73); ATM, "Some Reflections upon the Far-Eastern War," *National Review* 47 (May 1906): 383–405 (reprinted as "Retrospect upon the War between Japan and Russia," in *Naval Administration and Warfare*, 133–73).

139. ATM, "Principles Involved in the War between Japan and Russia," in *Naval Administration and Warfare*, 90; Puleston, *Mahan*, 250.

140. ATM, "Principles Involved in the War between Japan and Russia," 172; ATM to William H. Henderson, May 17, 1910, ATM to Clark, Sep. 11, 1908, *LPATM*, 3:342, 263.

141. ATM, "Japan Among the Nations: Admiral Mahan's Views," *Times* (London), June 23, 1913, *LPATM*, 3:495–99; see also ATM, *Naval Strategy Compared and Contrasted with the Principles and Practice of Military Operations on Land* (Boston: Little, Brown, and Co., 1911), 197.

142. ATM, "Introduction to Asami's Biography of Serata," *LPATM*, 3:688–90.

143. ATM, *Sea Power in Its Relations to the War of 1812* (Boston: Little, Brown, and Co., 1905).

144. Puleston, *Mahan*, 275; ATM to Luce, July 11, 1906, ATM to Clark, Jan. 15, 1907, *LPATM*, 3:163, 203.

145. Hattendorf and Hattendorf, *Bibliography*, A13.

146. ATM, *Sail to Steam*, 324.

147. ATM, *Some Neglected Aspects of War*, xiii.

148. Ibid., xiii.

149. Ibid., xiv.

150. ATM to Luce, Sep. 3, 1901, *LPATM*, 2:735.

151. ATM, "War from the Christian Standpoint," in *Some Neglected Aspects of War*, 104–8.

152. Ibid., 99–100.

153. Ibid., 106, 113.

154. Lucia Ames Mead, "Some Fallacies of Captain Mahan," *The Arena* 40 (1908): 163–70. Mead was an officer of the Anti-Imperialist League, the Women's Peace Party, and the International League for Peace and Freedom. See John M. Craig, *Lucia Ames Mead and the American Peace Movement* (Lewiston, N.Y.: Edwin Mellen Press, 1990).

155. ATM, "Apparent Decadence," 545–47.

156. "Erroneous Assumptions About the Decadence of the Church," *Churchman*, April 25, 1903, 537–38.

157. Frederick Dan Huntington and William H. Nielson, letters to the editor, *Churchman*, May 9, 1903, 614–15.

158. ATM to Mary E. Powel, Dec. 16, 1900, *LPATM*, 2:699.

159. ATM to Ellen K. Mahan, Aug. 20, 1905, *LPATM*, 3:137–38.

160. ATM to Clark, May 20, 1907, *LPATM*, 3:212.

161. ATM to Maxse, Jan. 15, 1906, ATM to Ashe, Sep. 9, 1907, *LPATM*, 3:152, 228; Seager, *ATM*, 573.

162. Seager, *ATM*, 314–15, 573.

163. ATM to Helen Mahan, Oct. 28, 1893, *LPATM*, 2:170. Seager's version of this episode is in *ATM*, 314–16.

164. ATM to Helen Mahan, Sep. 18, 1894, *LPATM*, 2:333.

165. ATM to Helen Mahan, Nov. 18, 1894, *LPATM*, 2:364.

166. ATM to Helen Mahan, Dec. 26, 1894, *LPATM*, 2:378–79; ATM to Ellen K. Mahan, Jan. 4, 1895, *LPATM*, 2:381; ATM to Ellen Mahan, Jan. 25, 1895, *LPATM*, 2:393; Seager, *ATM*, 315.

167. Seager, *ATM*, 315, 573; ATM to Brown, April 7, 1905, *LPATM*, 3:128. Seager also cites a letter to Leopold Maxse, Sep. 14, 1905, *LPATM*, 3:141, as a source but the letter makes no mention of Helen; see Seager, *ATM*, 661 n. 10.

168. Seager, *ATM*, 318; Puleston, *Mahan*, 254, 258; Ellen K. Mahan, "Recollections," *LPATM*, 3:719; *New York Times*, Oct. 23, 1904.

169. Lyle Mahan, "Recollections," 119. Lyle was married twice more, to Millicent Moore and Marion McCallum; see *LPATM*, 3:720 n. 10.

170. ATM, "Some Practical Considerations Concerning the Spiritual Life," Feb. 25, 1907, *LPATM*, 3:644–56.

171. ATM to Clark, May 20, 1907, *LPATM*, 3:212–13.

172. ATM to Hugh R. Monro, May 7, 1907, *LPATM*, 3:210–11.

173. *Times* (London), May 30, 1907, in *LPATM*, 3:657.

174. ATM to Ashe, Sep. 23, 1907, *LPATM*, 3:230–31.

175. ATM to Clark, Oct. 31, 1907, Ellen Mahan to Luce, Dec. 3, 1907, ATM to Luce, Jan. 27, 1908, *LPATM*, 3:232–33, 235, 236. For a list of other correspondence discussing the operation and its aftermath see Seager, *ATM*, 686 n. 11.

176. Seager, *ATM*, 574–75; Ellen K. Mahan, "Recollections," *LPATM*, 3:724; ATM to Luce, Nov. 18, 1907, *LPATM*, 3:234.

177. Ellen K. Mahan, "Recollections," *LPATM*, 3:728.

178. Seager, *ATM*, 575; ATM to Luce, Nov. 18, 1907, *LPATM*, 3:234.

179. ATM to *Times* (London), June 23, 1913, *LPATM*, 3:498.

180. ATM to McBee, Nov. 27, 1898, *LPATM*, 2:616–17.

181. "Records of the American Church Institute Processed and Opened for Research," http://www.episcopalarchives.org/acin.html, accessed July 16, 2012; "American Church Institute," http://www.episcopalarchives.org/Afro-Anglican_history/exhibit/divergence/acin2.php, accessed July 16, 2012.

182. ATM to Ashe, Oct. 25, 1906, *LPATM*, 3:190; David H. Greer, statement on death of ATM, Dec. 8, 1914, in Taylor, *Mahan*, 266.

183. ATM to Charles W. Stewart, June 5, 1908, ATM to Ashe, Nov. 30, 1908, *LPATM*, 3:248–49, 270–71; ATM, "Address at Unveiling of the Sampson Memorial Window," *USNIP* 35 (March 1909): 271–82.

184. Seager, *ATM*, 563; Ellen K. Mahan, "Recollections," *LPATM*, 3:729.

185. ATM, *Harvest Within*, v–vi; ATM to James W. McIntyre, Jan. 7, April 16, 1909, ATM to Little, Brown, April 12, 1909, *LPATM*, 3:274, 297.

186. ATM, *Harvest Within*, vii–viii.

187. Ibid., 2–3.

188. Ibid., 153, 226.

189. Ibid., 162–64, 167, 224–26.

190. ATM, letters to editor, *New York Times*, June 23, 1913, Sep. 10, 1914, *LPATM*, 3:498, 542.

191. ATM, *Harvest Within*, 141.

192. Ibid., 27, 29, 31–32, 34–37, 40–46.

193. Ibid., 141.

194. Ibid., 48–50.

195. Seager, *ATM*, 576.

196. Sumida, *Inventing Grand Strategy*, 76–77.

197. Ibid., 77.

198. ATM, *Harvest Within*, 24.

199. Ibid., 253; Sumida, *Inventing Grand Strategy*, 78.

200. Sumida, *Inventing Grand Strategy*, 79.

201. Joe L. Dubbert, *A Man's Place: Masculinity in Transition* (Englewood Cliffs, N.J.: Prentice-Hall, 1979), 137, 139, 72.

202. ATM to Little, Brown, April 1, 5, June 3, 1909, *LPATM*, 3:294–95, 304.

203. ATM to McIntyre, Jan. 7, 1909, ATM to Little, Brown, June 28, July 2, 1909, *LPATM*, 3:274, 305–6.

204. ATM to Little, Brown, May 22, June 28, 1909, *LPATM*, 3: 302, 305; ATM to William Reed Huntington, May 26, 1909, Diocese of New York Archives.

205. Seager, *ATM*, 576, 686 n. 12; Hattendorf and Hattendorf, *Bibliography*, A16.

206. "Captain Mahan's Interpretation of the Faith" ATM, "Christian Convictions," and *Churchman*, Aug. 21, 1909, 272, 282–83; "Faith in Action," *Guardian* (London), Aug. 18, 1909, 1286; ATM to Little, Brown, Aug. 31, 1909, *LPATM*, 3:310.

207. Seager, *ATM*, 577. Seager misread his source, ATM to Ashe, Sep. 23, 1907, *LPATM*, 3:231. Mahan was never a delegate to General Convention; this was confirmed by Wayne Kempton, archivist of the Diocese of New York, in an e-mail to author, July 27, 2012.

208. ATM, letter to editor, *Churchman*, June 5, 1909, 815–16.

209. Tyrrell, *Reforming the World*, 193; Brian Stanley, "Church, State, and the Hierarchy of 'Civilization': The History of the 'Mission and Government' Conference, Edinburgh, 1910," in *The Imperial Horizons of British Protestant Missions, 1880–1914*, ed. Andrew Porter (Grand Rapids, Mich.: Eerdmans, 2003), 61–62.

210. ATM to Stanley C. Hughes, quoted in "Manning Approves Lord's Day Protest," *New York Times*, Oct. 3, 1911, reprinted in *LPATM*, 3:423.

211. *Diocese of New York Convention Journal*, 1911, 59; "New York Convention," *Churchman*, Nov. 18, 1911, 720.

212. ATM, letter to editors of *New York Times* and *New York Evening Post*, Nov. 21, 1911, *LPATM*, 3:433–35. The letter was published in the *Evening Post* on Nov. 23 and in the *Times* on Nov. 24.

213. William J. Jackman, *History of the American Nation* (Chicago: Hamming, 1915), 6:1701.

214. Norman Angell, *The Great Illusion* (New York: G. P. Putnam's Sons, 1911), 29, 336.

215. Ibid., 308–9.

216. ATM, notes on *Great Illusion*, ATM Papers, LC.

217. ATM, "The Great Illusion," *North American Review* 195 (1912): 319–32; revised version reprinted in ATM, *Armaments and Arbitration, or the Place of Force in the International Relations of States* (New York: Harper & Brothers, 1912), 121–54.

218. Ibid., 322–24, 327, 331.

219. Norman Angell, "'The Great Illusion': A Reply to Rear-Admiral A. T. Mahan," *North American Review* 195 (1912): 754–72.

220. Ibid., 754, 758, 767, 772.

221. Ibid., 768.

222. ATM, draft reply to Angell, ATM Papers, LC; Seager, *ATM*, 590–91.

223. Robert W. Schneider, *Novelist to a Generation: The Life and Thought of Winston Churchill* (Bowling Green, Ohio: Bowling Green University Popular Press, 1976), 11–20.

224. Winston Churchill, *The Inside of the Cup* (New York: Macmillan, 1913); Erin A. Smith, "'What Would Jesus Do?': The Social Gospel and the Literary Marketplace," *Book History* 10 (2007): 193–221.

225. Smith, "What Would Jesus Do?" 199, 211–13; Schneider, *Novelist to a Generation*, 172–75.

226. ATM, "Thoughts on the Words of St. Peter," July 7, 1913, *LPATM*, 3:682.

227. ATM, "The Inside of the Cup," *Churchman*, Aug. 30, 1913, 277, 289–90.

228. Winston Churchill, "The Inside of the Cup: A Reply to Admiral Mahan," *Churchman*, Oct. 11, 1913, 479–80.

229. "Mr. Winston Churchill and Admiral Mahan," *Churchman*, Oct. 11, 1913, 478.

230. K. Asami to ATM, March 1913, quoted in Taylor, *Mahan*, 267.

231. Asami to ATM, 1913, quoted in Taylor, *Mahan*, 267–68.

232. ATM, "Introduction to K. Asami's Biography of Tasuka Serata," *LPATM*, 3:688–92.

233. Taylor, *Mahan*, 268; Hattendorf and Hattendorf, *Bibliography*, B19.

234. ATM, "The Purpose of a Life Work," ca. 1913, *LPATM*, 3:693–97.

235. ATM, "The Christian Doctrine of the Trinity," ca. 1913–14, *LPATM*, 3:714–16.

236. On the differences between the 1789 and 1892 books see Schnitker, *Church's Worship*, 86–88; Stuhlman, *Eucharistic Worship*, 95–101.

237. ATM to Frederick Burgess, April 6, 1914, *LPATM*, 3:521–22; Stuhlman, *Eucharistic Worship*, 98–99.

238. Stuhlman, *Eucharistic Worship*, 95–101; Schnitker, *Church's Worship*, 86–88, 98.

239. ATM, "Freedom in the Use of the Prayer Book," *Churchman*, Nov. 8, 1913, 623–24. In 1912 Slattery had invited Mahan to speak at Grace Church, although we do not know on what topic. Mahan turned him down, citing health reasons. ATM to Charles Slattery, June 1, 1912, *LPATM*, 3:461.

240. ATM, "The Structure of the Te Deum Considered Devotionally," *Churchman*, April 11, 1914, 467–68.

241. Walter Gwynne, "The Sources of the Church's Strength and Weakness," *Churchman*, July 25, 1914, 114–15.

242. ATM, letter to the editor, *Churchman*, Aug. 8, 1914, 189. In his article on the Te Deum he had also made reference to a church he had visited recently (which he would not name) where a number of innovations had already been made; see ATM, "Structure of the Te Deum," 468.

243. Gwynne, letter to editor, *Churchman*, Aug. 22, 1914, 257.

244. Charles Fiske, letter to editor, *Churchman*, Aug. 29, 1914, 289.

245. ATM, letter to editor, *Churchman*, Sep. 12, 1914, 356.

246. ATM, "Prayer Book Revision, I," *Churchman,* Oct. 10, 1914, 465–66; ATM, "Prayer Book Revision, II," *Churchman,* Oct. 17, 1914, 497–98.

247. Charles W. Eliot, "Twentieth-Century Christianity," *New York Times,* Jan. 11, 1914, SM2.

248. ATM, "Twentieth-Century Christianity," *North American Review* 199 (April 1914): 589–98. Mahan originally sent his rejoinder to the *New York Times,* "but they refused without reading it. I gave them a piece of my mind." ATM to Francis Greene, April 15, 1914, *LPATM,* 3:523.

249. ATM, "Twentieth-Century Christianity," esp. 591–94, 595, 597–98.

250. Thomas Gailor to ATM, ca. April 1914, quoted in Taylor, *Mahan,* 263.

251. Josephus Daniels to ATM, ca. April 1914, quoted in Taylor, *Mahan,* 263.

252. ATM, "The Mediatorial Office of the Church toward the State," *Churchman,* Aug. 29, 1914, 278–79, 291.

CHAPTER 7. FINAL DAYS

1. Of these books those not previously cited are ATM, *The Interest of America in International Conditions* (Boston: Little, Brown, and Co., 1910); *Naval Strategy Compared and Contrasted with the Principles and Practice of Military Operations on Land* (Boston: Little, Brown, and Co., 1911); *The Major Operations of the Navies in the War of American Independence* (Boston: Little, Brown, and Co., 1913).

2. See, for example, ATM, *Naval Administration and Warfare,* 105, 138; *Interest of America in International Conditions,* 41–42; *Armaments and Arbitration,* 116–20.

3. ATM, *Naval Strategy,* 124.

4. ATM to Little, Brown, March 8, 1913, *LPATM,* 3:491.

5. ATM to Clark, March 24, 1913, *LPATM,* 3:491.

6. Ibid., 3:492; Ellen K. Mahan, "Recollections," *LPATM,* 3:720.

7. Seager, *ATM,* 595; ATM to Clark, March 24, 1913, *LPATM,* 3:492; ATM, "Introduction to K. Asami," *LPATM,* 3:690; ATM, "Thoughts on the Righteousness of War," ca. July 1913, *LPATM,* 3:683–84; ATM to Little, Brown, April 23, 1913, *LPATM,* 3:493; For more on Mahan's view of Turks see ATM, "Twentieth-Century Christianity," 594, 596–97; ATM to Clark, Oct. 6, 1913, *LPATM,* 3:510–11.

8. ATM, "Why Not Disarm," ca. Sep. 1913, *LPATM,* 3:686–87; published as "The Folly of the Hague," *National Sunday Magazine,* Sep. 28, 1913.

9. ATM, "Women's Suffrage," n.d., *LPATM,* 3:712–13.

10. ATM, "The Christian Doctrine of the Trinity," n.d., *LPATM,* 3:715.

11. Jameson to ATM, July 16, 1913, ATM Papers, LC; ATM to Jameson, July 22, 1913, Feb. 6, 1914, *LPATM,* 3:504–5, 518–19.

12. ATM to Robert Woodward, Jan. 29, 1914, *LPATM,* 3:517; ATM to Clark, Oct. 1, 1914, *LPATM,* 3:549.

13. Seager, *ATM*, 597–98; ATM to Clark, March 24, 1913, *LPATM*, 3:492; ATM, "Why Not Disarm?" ca. Sep. 1913, *LPATM*, 3:685–87.

14. ATM, "The Origin of the European War," *New York Evening Post*, Aug. 3, 1914, 1, reprinted in *LPATM*, 3:698–700; ATM, fragment of unidentified newspaper interview, ca. Aug. 1914, quoted in Taylor, *Mahan*, 281, reprinted in *LPATM*, 3:701.

15. ATM, "About What Is the War?" ca. Aug. 1914, *LPATM*, 3:705.

16. ATM to Daniels, Aug. 15, 1914, *LPATM*, 3:541-42; ATM, "Origins of the European War," "Sea Power in the Present European War," *Leslie's Illustrated Weekly Newspaper*, Aug. 20, 1914, reprinted in *LPATM*, 3:698, 707, 710.

17. Quoted in Puleston, *Mahan*, 351.

18. ATM, "The Origin of the European War" and "Sea Power in the Present European War."

19. Woodrow Wilson to Daniels, Aug. 6, 1914, reprinted in Taylor, *Mahan*, 275. The Secretary of the Army received a similar letter.

20. ATM to Daniels (two letters), Aug. 15, 1914, *LPATM*, 3: 540–42; Daniels to ATM, Aug. 18, 1914, ATM Papers, LC and *LPATM*, 3:542 n. 1.

21. Seager, *ATM*, 599–600; Puleston, *Mahan*, 341–42; Taylor, *Mahan*, 277–80.

22. Frederick A. Mahan to Roosevelt, Feb. 11, 1915, quoted in Seager, *ATM*, 689 n. 31 and *LPATM*, 3:539 n. 3; Frederick A. Mahan to unidentified, May 1915, quoted in Taylor, *Mahan*, 277; Lyle Mahan, "Recollections," 120.

23. ATM to Wilmot A. Brownell, Sep. 21, 1914, ATM to Clark, Oct. 1, 1914, *LPATM*, 3:547, 548–49.

24 ATM to Rebecca L. Evans, Nov. 10, 1914, *LPATM*, 3:552.

25. Quoted in Puleston, *Mahan*, 353; see also Seager, *ATM*, 689 n. 32.

26. Bradley A. Fiske, *From Midshipman to Rear-Admiral* (New York: Century Co., 1919), 561.

27. ATM to F. M. Pleadwell, Nov. 15, 1914, quoted in Seager, *ATM*, 601–2. Original in LC but Seager does not indicate what collection; see Seager, *ATM*, 689 n. 32.

28. Ellen K. Mahan, "Recollections," *LPATM*, 3:730.

29. Ibid., 3:730.

30. Taylor, *Mahan*, 295.

31. Puleston, *Mahan*, 354. Lyle claimed that "the death was unexpected and I was not informed of the seriousness of his condition in time to see him before he died." But Ellen's recollections indicate that the death was soon expected once he entered the hospital. It is possible that Lyle said this to assuage his guilt over not making it to Washington in time. See Lyle Mahan, "Recollections," 119; Ellen Mahan, "Recollections," *LPATM*, 3:730.

32. Taylor, *Mahan*, 285; "Admiral Mahan, Naval Critic, Dies," *New York Times*, Dec. 2, 1914.

33. Eugenia Cheston to Ellen Mahan, Dec. 12, 1914, quoted in Taylor, *Mahan*, 285.

34. Photo of his tombstone, Hattendorf, *Influence of History on Mahan*, 126.

35. "Admiral Mahan, Naval Critic, Dies," "British Tributes to Mahan," *New York Times*, Dec. 2, 1914. For sample of tributes see Taylor, *Mahan*, 283–304; Puleston, *Mahan*, 355–58.

36. Daniels to Ellen Mahan, Dec. 1. 1914, quoted in Taylor, *Mahan*, 289.

37. Quoted in "Admiral Mahan, Naval Critic, Dies," *New York Times*, Dec. 2, 1914.

38. Cecil Spring-Rice to Ellen Mahan, Dec. 2, 1914, quoted in Taylor, *Mahan*, 283.

39. *Morning Post* (London), Dec. 2, 1914, excerpt quoted in "British Tributes to Mahan," *New York Times*, Dec. 2, 1914; full text quoted in Taylor, *Mahan*, 287.

40. *Daily Chronicle* (London), Dec. 2, 1914, excerpt quoted in "British Tributes to Mahan," *New York Times*, Dec. 2, 1914.

41. Navy Records Society Minutes, Dec. 1, 1914, quoted in Taylor, *Mahan*, 291.

42. Rhodes to Ellen Mahan, Dec. 3, 1914, quoted in Taylor, *Mahan*, 291.

43. William Milligan Sloane, "Two American Historians: Alfred Thayer Mahan," *Columbia University Quarterly* 18 (1916): 109–12.

44. Bradley A. Fiske, "Tribute to Mahan," *USNIP* 42 (Jan.–Feb. 1915): 2.

45. "Admiral Mahan," *Outlook* 108 (1914): 798–800.

46. Theodore Roosevelt, "A Great Public Servant," *Outlook* 109 (1915): 85–86.

47. Greer to Ellen Mahan, n.d.; Greer, resolution of American Church Institute for Negroes, Dec. 5, 1914, quoted in Taylor, *Mahan*, 271, 266.

48. Resolution, Board of Managers, Seamen's Church Institute of New York, Dec. 16, 1914, quoted in Taylor, *Mahan*, 265.

49. Trinity Church, New York City, tribute, quoted in Taylor, *Mahan*, 288.

50. George William Douglas, "Rear Admiral Mahan," *Churchman*, Dec. 12, 1914, 766, 779.

51. Charles H. Stockton, "Alfred Thayer Mahan: An Appreciation," *Churchman*, Dec. 19, 1914, 796–97.

52. Quoted in Taylor, *Mahan*, 262. It is not known if this quote is from a eulogy, a written tribute, or a private letter.

53. Photo of plaque in Taylor, *Mahan*, opposite 260.

SELECTED BIBLIOGRAPHY

MANUSCRIPT SOURCES

Diocese of New York
    Archives
General Theological Seminary Library
    Deans' Papers
    Samuel Roosevelt Johnson Papers
    Special Collections
Library of Congress
    Alfred Thayer Mahan Papers
    James B. McPherson Papers
    Charles O'Neil Diary
    Theodore Roosevelt Papers
    William T. Sherman Papers
    Henry C. Taylor Papers
National Archives
    Naval Records Division
Princeton University Library
    Scribner Collection
United States Military Academy Library
    Archives
    Dennis Hart Mahan Papers
    Hugh L. Scott Collection
    John C. Tidball Papers
United States Naval War College Library
    Archives
    Alfred Thayer Mahan Papers

PRIMARY BOOKS

Abbot, Henry L. *Memoir of Dennis Hart Mahan, 1802–1871.* Washington, D.C., 1878.

Angell, Norman. *The Great Illusion.* New York: G. P. Putnam's Sons, 1911.

Armstrong, Benjamin, ed. *21st Century Mahan: Sound Military Conclusions for the Modern Era.* Annapolis, Md.: Naval Institute Press, 2013.

Barnes, Elinor and James A., eds. *Naval Surgeon: The Diary of Dr. Samuel Pellman Boyer.* 2 vols. Bloomington: Indiana University Press, 1963.

Browne, Henry. *Ordo Saeclorum: A Treatise on the Chronology of the Holy Scriptures.* London, 1844.

Campbell, John. *Lives of the British Admirals.* London, 1742.

Case, Carl. *The Masculine in Religion.* Philadelphia: American Baptist Publication Society, 1906.

Churchill, Winston. *The Inside of the Cup.* New York: Macmillan Co., 1913.

Clowes, William Laird. *The Royal Navy: A History from the Earliest Times to 1900.* Vol. 3. London: Sampson Low, Marston and Co., 1898. Reprint, London, 1996.

Conant, Robert. *The Virility of Christ.* Chicago: privately printed, 1915.

Fiske, Bradley A. *From Midshipman to Rear-Admiral.* New York: Century Co., 1919.

Forbes, John Murray. *A Brief Reply to Certain Strictures of a Protestant Journal on a Late Discourse by Dr. Forbes on the Immaculate Conception.* New York, 1855.

Fosdick, Harry Emerson. *The Manhood of the Master.* New York: Association Press, 1911.

Halleck, Henry Wager. *Elements of Military Art and Science.* New York: 1846. Reprint, Westport, Conn.: Greenwood Press, 1971.

Hayes, John D., ed. *Samuel Francis DuPont: A Selection from His Civil War Letters.* Ithaca, N.Y.: Cornell University Press, 1969.

Hayes, John D., and John B. Hattendorf, eds. *The Writings of Stephen B. Luce.* Newport, R.I.: Naval War College Press, 1975.

Holls, Frederick W. *The Peace Conference at The Hague and Its Bearings on International Law and Policy.* New York: Macmillan Co., 1900.

Hooper, Francis J. B. *Palmoni: An Essay of the Chronological and Numerical Systems in Use Among the Ancient Jews.* Oxford, 1851.

Hopkins, John Henry, Jr., ed. *The Collected Works of the Late Milo Mahan, D.D.* New York, 1875.

Hutchins, Charles Lewis. *Carols Old and Carols New.* Boston: Parish Choir, 1916.

Jomini, Henri. *Histoire Critique et Militaire des Guerres de la Revolution.* Brussels, 1840–42.

———. *Summary of the Art of War.* Translated by O. F. Winship and E. E. McLean. New York, 1854.

Jones, George. *Excursions to Cairo, Jerusalem, Damascus and Balbec from the United States Ship Delaware During Her Recent Cruise.* New York, 1836.

———. *Life-scenes from the Old Testament*. Philadelphia, 1868.

———. *Sketches of Naval Life*. New Haven, Conn., 1829.

Kerfoot, John B. *Academical Degrees and Titles: An Address*. New York, 1854.

Lapeyrousse-Bonfils, Léonard. *History of the French Navy*. Paris, 1845.

Long, John D. *The New American Navy*. New York: Outlook Co., 1903.

Mahan, Alfred Thayer. *Admiral Farragut*. New York, 1892.

———. *Armaments and Arbitration or the Place of Force in the International Relations of States*. New York: Harper & Brothers, 1912. Reprint, Port Washington, N.Y.: Kennikat Press, 1973.

———. *From Sail to Steam: Recollections of Naval Life*. New York: Harper & Brothers, 1907. Reprint, New York: Da Capo Press, 1968.

———. *The Gulf and Inland Waters*. New York, 1883.

———. *The Harvest Within: Thoughts on the Life of a Christian*. Boston: Little, Brown, and Co., 1909.

———. *The Influence of Sea Power upon the French Revolution and Empire, 1793–1812*. London: 1892. Reprint, St. Clair Shores, Mich.: Scholarly Press, 1970.

———. *The Influence of Sea Power upon History, 1660–1783*. 5th ed. Boston, 1894. Reprint, New York, 1987.

———. *The Interest of America in International Conditions*. Boston: Little, Brown, and Co., 1910.

———. *The Interest of America in Sea Power, Present and Future*. Boston, 1897. Reprint, New York: Books for Libraries Press, 1970.

———. *Lessons of the War with Spain, and Other Articles*. Boston, 1899.

———. *The Life of Nelson: The Embodiment of the Sea Power of Great Britain*. 2d ed. rev. Boston, 1899. Reprint, Grosse Pointe, Mich.: Scholarly Press, 1968.

———. *The Major Operations of the Navies in the War of American Independence*. Boston: Little, Brown, and Co., 1913.

———. *Naval Administration and Warfare, Some General Principles, with Other Essays*. Boston: Little, Brown, and Co., 1908.

———. *Naval Strategy Compared and Contrasted with the Principles and Practice of Military Operations on Land*. Boston: Little, Brown, and Co., 1911.

———. *The Problem of Asia and its Effect upon International Policies*. Boston: Little, Brown, and Co., 1900.

———. *Retrospect and Prospect: Studies in International Relations, Naval and Political*. Boston: Little, Brown, and Co., 1903.

———. *Sea Power in its Relations to the War of 1812*. Boston: Little, Brown, and Co., 1905.

———. *Some Neglected Aspects of War*. Boston: Little, Brown, and Co., 1907.

———. *The Story of the War in South Africa, 1899–1900*. London: Sampson Low, Marston & Co., 1900. Reprint, New York: Greenwood Press, Pub., 1968.

———. *Types of Naval Officers Drawn from the History of the British Navy*. Boston: Little, Brown, and Co., 1901.

Mahan, Dennis Hart. *Elementary Treatise on Advanced-Guard, Out-Post, and Detachment Service of Troops, and the Manner of Posting and Handling Them in Presence of an Enemy*. Rev. ed. New York, 1864.

———. *Summary of the Course of Permanent Fortification*. West Point, N.Y., 1850.

Mahan, Milo. *A Church History of the First Seven Centuries to the Close of the Sixth General Council*. Edited by John Henry Hopkins Jr. New York, 1873.

———. *Church Missions: A Sermon Preached before the Society for the Advancement of Christianity in Pennsylvania*. Philadelphia, 1851.

———. *The Comedy of Canonization*. New York, 1868.

———. *The Exercise of Faith: A Book for Doubters*. London, 1877.

———. *An Exercise of Faith, In Its Relation to Authority and Private Judgment*. Philadelphia, 1855.

———. *The Great-hearted Shepherd*. New York, 1859.

———. *The Healing of the Nations*. Albany, N.Y., 1855.

———. *Mystic Numbers: A Key to Chronology*. New York, 1875.

———. *Palmoni; or, The Numerals of Scripture: A Proof of Inspiration; a Free Inquiry*. New York, 1863.

———. *The Spiritual Point-of-View; or, The Glass Reversed: An Answer to Bishop Colenso*. New York, 1863.

———. *The Way of Life*. New York, 1877.

Martin, Henri. *A Popular History of France from the First Revolution to the Present Time*. 3 vols. Boston, 1877–82.

Mead, Lucia Ames. *Swords and Ploughshares: or the Supplanting of the System of War by the System of Law*. New York: G. P. Putnam's Sons, 1912.

Mommsen, Theodor. *The History of Rome*. Translated by William P. Dickson. London, 1869.

Mullin, Robert Bruce, ed. *Moneygripe's Apprentice: The Personal Narrative of Samuel Seabury III*. New Haven, Conn.: Yale University Press, 1989.

Napier, William Francis Patrick. *History of the War in the Peninsula and in the South of France*. Edited by Charles Stuart. Chicago: University of Chicago Press, 1979.

Pierce, Jason. *The Masculine Power of Christ*. Boston: Pilgrim Press, 1912.

Procter, Francis. *A New History of the Book of Common Prayer*. Revised by Walter Howard Frere. London: Macmillan Co., 1941.

Rainsford, William S. *The Story of a Varied Life*. Garden City, N.Y.: Doubleday, Page & Co., 1922.

Schaff, Morris. *The Spirit of Old West Point, 1858–1862*. Boston: Houghton Mifflin, 1907.

Seabury, Samuel III. *American Slavery Distinguished from the Slavery of English Theorists, and Justified by the Law of Nature*. New York, 1861. Reprint, Miami, Fla.: Mnemosyne Pub. Co., 1969.

Seager, Robert II, and Doris D. Maguire, eds. *Letters and Papers of Alfred Thayer Mahan*. 3 vols. Annapolis, Md.: Naval Institute Press, 1975.

Sherman, William T. *Memoirs of General W. T. Sherman*. New York: Library of America, 1990.

Strong, George Templeton. *Diary*. Edited by Allan Nevins and Milton Halsey Thomas. New York: Macmillan Co., 1952.

Strong, Josiah. *Expansion under New World-Conditions*. New York: Baker & Taylor Co., 1900.

Suter, John W. *Life and Letters of William Reed Huntington, A Champion of Unity*. New York: Century Press, 1925.

Swift, Joseph G. *The Memoirs of General Joseph Gardner Swift*. Worcester, Mass., 1890.

Westcott, Allan, ed. *Mahan on Naval Warfare: Selections from the Writings of Rear Admiral Alfred Thayer Mahan*. Boston: Little, Brown, and Co., 1918. Reprint, Mineola, N.Y.: Dover Publications, 1999.

White, Andrew D. *Autobiography of Andrew Dickson White*. New York: Century Co., 1905.

PRIMARY ARTICLES AND CHAPTERS

"Admiral Mahan." *The Outlook* 108 (1914): 798–800.

"Admiral Mahan's Warning." *Fortnightly Review* 94 (1910): 224–34.

Angell, Norman. "'The Great Illusion': A Reply to Rear-Admiral Mahan." *North American Review* 195 (1912): 754–72.

Ashe, Samuel A. "Memories of Annapolis." *South Atlantic Quarterly* 18 (1919): 197–210.

Badham, Francis P. "Nelson and the Neapolitan Republicans." *English Historical Review* 13 (1898): 261–82.

Bridge, Cyprian. Review of *The Influence of Sea Power upon History*. *Blackwood's Edinburgh Magazine* 148 (1890): 576–84.

"Captain Mahan's Interpretation of the Faith." *Churchman*, Aug. 21, 1909, 272.

Churchill, Winston. "The Inside of the Cup: A Reply to Admiral Mahan." *Churchman*, Oct. 11, 1913, 479–80.

Clarke, George Sydenham. "Captain Mahan's Counsels to the United States." *Nineteenth Century* 43 (1898): 292–300.

———. "Nelson." *Nineteenth Century* 41 (1897): 893–906.

Douglas, George William. "Rear Admiral Mahan." *Churchman*, Dec. 12, 1914, 766, 769.

Eliot, Charles W. "Twentieth Century Christianity." *New York Times*, Jan. 11, 1914, SM2.

Greenwood, Frederick. "The Incendiary Mahan." *Blackwood's Edinburgh Magazine* 163 (1898): 563–65.

Gwynne, Walter. "The Sources of the Church's Strength and Weakness." *Churchman*, July 25, 1914, 114–15.

"Influence of America's Great Naval Strategist on the War in Europe." *Current Opinion* 58 (1915): 103–4.

Johnson, A. H. Review of *The Influence of Sea Power upon History* and *The Influence of Sea Power upon the French Revolution and Empire*. *English Historical Review* 8 (1893): 784–88.

Laughton, John K. "Captain Mahan on Maritime Power." *Edinburgh Review* 172 (1890): 420–53.

———. "Captain Mahan on Maritime Power: Review of *The Influence of Sea Power upon the French Revolution and Empire.*" *Edinburgh Review* 177 (1893): 484–518.

———. "Captain Mahan's 'Life of Nelson.'" *Edinburgh Review* 186 (1897): 84–113.

Luce, Stephen B. "Christian Ethics an Element of Military Education." United States Naval Institute *Proceedings* 32 (1906): 1367–86.

———. "Naval Administration, III." United States Naval Institute *Proceedings* 29 (Nov. 14, 1903): 1–13.

———. "On the Study of Naval Warfare as a Science." United States Naval Institute *Proceedings* 12 (1886): 527–46.

———. "War and Its Prevention." United States Naval Institute *Proceedings* 30 (1904): 611–22.

Mahan, Alfred Thayer. "Address at the Unveiling of the Sampson Memorial Window." United States Naval Institute *Proceedings* 35 (1909): 271–82.

———. "The Apparent Decadence of the Church's Influence." *Churchman*, April 25, 1903, 545–47.

———. "Christian Convictions." *Churchman*, Aug. 21, 1909, 282–83.

———. "Freedom in the Use of the Prayer Book." *Churchman*, Nov. 8, 1913, 623–24.

———. "The Great Illusion." *North American Review* 195 (1912): 319–32.

———. "The Inside of the Cup." *Churchman*, Aug. 30, 1913, 277, 289–90.

———. "The Mediatorial Office of the Church Toward the State." *Churchman*, Aug. 29, 1914, 278–79, 291.

———. "Naval Education." United States Naval Institute *Proceedings* 5 (Dec. 1879): 345–76.

———. "The Neapolitan Republicans and Nelson's Accusers." *English Historical Review* 14 (1899): 471–501.

———. "Prayer Book Revision, Part I." *Churchman*, Oct. 10, 1914, 465–66.

———. "Prayer Book Revision, Part II." *Churchman*, Oct. 17, 1914, 497–98.

———. "The Seaman." *Youth's Companion* 87 (1913): 603–4.

———. "The Structure of the Te Deum Considered Devotionally." *Churchman*, April 11, 1914, 467–68.

———. "Twentieth-Century Christianity." *North American Review* 199 (April 1914): 589–98.

———. "The Youth of Admiral Farragut." *Youth's Companion* 74 (1900): 328–29.

Mahan, Jane Leigh. "Random Memories." *The Pointer*, March 15, 1929, 6–7, 23.

Mahan, Lyle Evans. "My Parents, Rear Admiral and Mrs. Alfred Thayer Mahan." In *The Influence of History on Mahan*, edited by John B. Hattendorf. Newport, R.I.: Naval War College Press, 1991.

Mahan, Milo. "On Confession." In Charles Norris Gray, *Statement on Confession*. New York, 1872.

———. "Who Was James, The Lord's Brother." In Samuel Seabury III, *Mary the Virgin: As Commemorated in the Church of Christ*. New York, 1868.

Mead, Lucia Ames. "Some Fallacies of Captain Mahan." *Arena* 40 (1908): 163–70.

Morris, William O'Connor. "Captain Mahan's 'Nelson.'" *Fortnightly Review* 61 (1897): 895–910.

"New York Convention." *Churchman*, Nov. 18, 1911, 720.

Review of *A Church History of the First Three Centuries*. *North American Review* 91 (1860): 568–69.

Rice, Wallace. "Some Current Fallacies of Captain Mahan." *The Dial* 28 (March 16, 1900): 198–200.

Roosevelt, Theodore. "A Great Public Servant." *The Outlook* 109 (1915): 85–86.

———. Review of *The Influence of Sea Power upon the French Revolution and Empire*. *Atlantic Monthly* 71 (1893): 556–59.

———. Review of *The Influence of Sea Power upon History*. *Atlantic Monthly* 66 (1890): 563–67.

———. Review of *The Influence of Sea Power upon History* and *The Influence of History upon the French Revolution and Empire*. *Political Science Quarterly* 9 (1894): 171–73.

Sloane, William Milligan. "Two American Historians." *Columbia University Quarterly* 18 (1916): 109–12.

Stephens, H. Morse. "Some Living American Historians." *World's Work* 4 (1902): 2322–23.

Stockton, Charles H. "Alfred Thayer Mahan: An Appreciation." *Churchman*, Dec. 19, 1914, 796–97.

Thursfield, James R. "The Life of Nelson." *Quarterly Review* 187 (1898): 126–52.

SECONDARY BOOKS

Allen, Ethan. *Clergy in Maryland of the Protestantism Episcopal Church Since the Independence of 1783*. Baltimore, 1860.

Ambrose, Stephen E. *Duty, Honor, Country: A History of West Point*. Baltimore: Johns Hopkins University Press, 1966.

Anstice, Henry. *History of St. George's Church in the City of New York, 1752–1811–1911*. New York: Harper & Brothers, 1911.

Appleby, Joyce, Lynn Hunt, and Margaret Jacob. *Telling the Truth About History*. New York: W. W. Norton & Co., 1994.

Ayres, Anne. *The Life and Work of William Augustus Muhlenberg.* New York, 1880.

Baltzell, E. Digby. *Philadelphia Gentlemen: The Making of a National Upper Class.* Glencoe, Ill.: Free Press, 1958.

Brewer, Clifton H. *A History of Religious Education in the Episcopal Church to 1835.* New Haven, Conn.: Yale University Press, 1924.

Bureau of Naval Personnel. *United States Navy Chaplains, 1778–1945.* Washington, D.C.: Government Printing Office, 1948.

Caldwell, Patricia. *The Puritan Conversion Narrative: The Beginnings of American Expression.* New York: Cambridge University Press, 1983.

Clymer, Kenton J. *Protestant Missionaries in the Philippines, 1898–1916: An Inquiry into the American Colonial Mentality.* Urbana: University of Illinois Press, 1986.

Cooling, Benjamin F. *Benjamin Franklin Tracy: Father of the Modern American Fighting Navy.* Hamden, Conn.: Archon, 1973.

Craig, John M. *Lucia Ames Mead (1856–1936) and the American Peace Movement.* Lewiston, N.Y.: Edwin Mellen Press, 1990.

Cullum, George W. *Biographical Register of the Officers and Graduates of the U.S. Military Academy at West Point, N.Y.* 2d ed. New York, 1868.

Davis, George T. *A Navy Second to None: The Development of Modern American Naval Policy.* New York: Harcourt, Brace & Co., 1940.

Dawley, Powel Mills. *The Story of the General Theological Seminary: A Sesquicentennial History, 1817–1967.* New York: Oxford University Press, 1969.

Dubbert, Joe L. *A Man's Place: Masculinity in Transition.* Englewood Cliffs, N.J.: Prentice-Hall, 1979.

Dupuy, R. Ernest. *Sylvanus Thayer: Father of Technology in the United States.* West Point, N.Y.: Association of Graduates, United States Military Academy, 1958.

Eisenhower, John S. D. *Agent of Destiny: The Life and Times of General Winfield Scott.* New York: Free Press, 1997.

Fishburn, Janet Forsythe. *The Fatherhood of God and the Victorian Family: The Social Gospel in America.* Philadelphia: Fortress Press, 1981.

Gleaves, Albert. *Life and Letters of Rear Admiral Stephen B. Luce, U.S. Navy.* New York: G. P. Putnam's Sons, 1925.

Gooch, G. P. *History and Historians in the Nineteenth Century.* Rev. ed. Boston: Beacon Press, 1959.

Grenville, John A. S., and George B. Young. *Politics, Strategy, and American Diplomacy: Studies in Foreign Policy, 1873–1917.* New Haven, Conn.: Yale University Press, 1966.

Hacker, Louis M. *The Shaping of the American Tradition.* New York: Columbia University Press, 1947.

Hagan, Kenneth J. *American Gunboat Diplomacy and the Old Navy, 1877–1889.* Westport, Conn.: Greenwood Press, 1973.

Harrison, Hall. *Life of the Right Reverend John Barrett Kerfoot.* New York, 1886.

Hatch, Carl E. *The Charles A. Briggs Heresy Trial: Prologue to Twentieth-Century Liberal Protestantism.* New York: Exposition Press, 1969.

Hatchett, Marion J. *Commentary of the American Prayer Book.* San Francisco: Harper Collins, 1995.

Hattendorf, John B., ed. *The Influence of History on Mahan.* Newport, R.I.: Naval War College Press, 1991.

Hattendorf, John B., and Lynn C. Hattendorf, comps. *A Bibliography of the Works of Alfred Thayer Mahan.* Newport, R.I.: Naval War College Press, 1986.

Hattendorf, John B., B. Mitchell Simpson III, and John R. Wadleigh. *Sailors and Scholars: The Centennial History of the U.S. Naval War College.* Newport, R.I.: Naval War College Press, 1984.

Hendrix, Henry J. *Theodore Roosevelt's Naval Diplomacy: The U.S. Navy and the Birth of the American Century.* Annapolis, Md.: Naval Institute Press, 2009.

Herrick, Walter R., Jr. *The American Naval Revolution.* Baton Rouge: Louisiana State University Press, 1966.

Hodges, George. *Henry Codman Potter: Seventh Bishop of New York.* New York: Macmillan Co., 1915.

Holmes, David L. *A Brief History of the Episcopal Church.* Valley Forge, Pa.: Trinity Press International, 1993.

Hunter, Mark C. *A Society of Gentlemen: Midshipmen at the U.S. Naval Academy, 1845–1861.* Annapolis, Md.: Naval Institute Press, 2010.

Janowitz, Morris. *The Professional Soldier: A Social and Political Portrait.* New York: Free Press, 1960.

Karsten, Peter. *The Naval Aristocracy: The Golden Age of Annapolis and the Emergence of Modern American Navalism.* New York: Free Press, 1972.

Kennedy, Paul M. *The Rise and Fall of British Naval Mastery.* London: Macmillan Press, 1983.

LaFeber, Walter. *The New Empire: An Interpretation of American Expansion 1860–1898.* Ithaca, N.Y.: Cornell University Press, 1963.

Leeman, William P. *The Long Road to Annapolis: The Founding of the Naval Academy and the Emerging American Republic.* Chapel Hill: University of North Carolina Press, 2010.

Lindsley, James Elliott. *The Church Club of New York: The First Hundred Years.* New York: Church Club of New York, 1994.

———. *This Planted Vine: A Narrative History of the Episcopal Diocese of New York.* New York: Harper & Row, 1984.

Livezey, William E. *Mahan on Sea Power.* Rev. ed. Norman: University of Oklahoma Press, 1980.

Lovell, John P. *Neither Athens nor Sparta?: The American Service Academies in Transition.* Bloomington: Indiana University Press, 1979.

Marszalek, John F. *Sherman: A Soldier's Passion for Order.* New York: Free Press, 1993.

Millis, Walter. *Arms and Men: A Study of American Military History.* New York: G. P. Putnam's Sons, 1956.

Morrison, James L., Jr. *"The Best School": West Point, 1833–1866.* Kent, Ohio: Kent State University Press, 1986.

Newton, William Wilberforce. *Dr. Muhlenberg.* New York, 1890.

Northup, Lesley A. *The 1892 Book of Common Prayer.* Lewiston, N.Y.: Edwin Mellen Press, 1993.

Norton, Herman A. *Struggling for Recognition: The United States Army Chaplaincy, 1791–1865.* Washington, D.C.: Department of the Army, 1977.

Novick, Peter. *That Noble Dream: The "Objectivity Question" and the American Historical Profession.* New York: Cambridge University Press, 1988.

Parsons, Edward Lambe, and Bayard Hale Jones. *The American Prayer Book: Its Origins and Principles.* New York: Charles Scribner's Sons, 1946.

Pratt, Julius W. *Expansionists of 1898: The Acquisition of Hawaii and the Spanish Islands.* Baltimore: Johns Hopkins University Press, 1936.

Prichard, Robert W. *The Nature of Salvation: Theological Consensus in the Episcopal Church, 1801–73.* Urbana: University of Illinois Press, 1997.

Puleston, William D. *Mahan: The Life and Work of Captain Alfred Thayer Mahan, U.S.N.* New Haven, Conn.: Yale University Press, 1939.

Rappaport, Armin. *The Navy League of the United States.* Detroit: Wayne State University Press, 1962.

Rousmaniere, Leah Robinson. *Anchored within the Vail: A Pictorial History of the Seamen's Church Institute.* New York: Seamen's Church Institute of New York and New Jersey, 1995.

Schneider, Robert W. *Novelist To a Generation: The Life and Thought of Winston Churchill.* Bowling Green, Ohio: Bowling Green University Popular Press, 1976.

Schnitker, Thaddeus A. *The Church's Worship: The 1979 American Book of Common Prayer in a Historical Perspective.* New York: Peter Lang Pub., 1989.

Schurman, Donald M. *The Education of a Navy: The Development of British Naval Strategic Thought, 1867–1914.* Chicago: University of Chicago Press, 1965.

Seager, Robert II. *Alfred Thayer Mahan: The Man and His Letters.* Annapolis, Md.: Naval Institute Press, 1977.

Shepherd, Massey Hamilton, Jr. *The Oxford American Prayer Book Commentary.* New York: Oxford University Press, 1950.

Shulman, Mark Russell. *Navalism and the Emergence of American Sea Power, 1882–1893.* Annapolis, Md.: Naval Institute Press, 1995.

Skardon, Alvin W. *Church Leader in the Cities: William Augustus Muhlenberg.* Philadelphia: University of Pennsylvania Press, 1971.

Skelton, William B. *An American Profession of Arms: The Army Officer Corps, 1784–1861.* Lawrence: University Press of Kansas, 1992.

Spector, Ronald. *Professors of War: The Naval War College and the Development of the Naval Profession.* Newport, R.I.: Naval War College Press, 1977.

Sprout, Harold and Margaret. *The Rise of American Naval Power, 1776–1918.* Princeton, N.J.: Princeton University Press, 1939.

———. *Toward a New Order of Sea Power: American Naval Policy and the World Scene, 1918–1922.* Rev. ed. Princeton, N.J.: Princeton University Press, 1943.

Steer, Roger. *Guarding the Holy Fire: The Evangelicalism of John R. W. Stott, J. I. Packer, and Alistair McGrath.* Grand Rapids, Mich.: Baker Pub. Group, 1999.

Strausz-Hupe, Robert. *Geopolitics: The Struggle for Space and Power.* New York: G. P. Putnam's Sons, 1942.

Stuhlman, Byron D. *Eucharistic Worship, 1789–1979.* New York: Church Hymnal Corporation, 1988.

Sumida, Jon Tetsuro. *Inventing Grand Strategy and Teaching Command: The Classic Works of Alfred Thayer Mahan Reconsidered.* Baltimore: Johns Hopkins University Press, 1997.

Sweetman, Jack. *The U.S. Naval Academy: An Illustrated History.* Annapolis, Md.: Naval Institute Press, 1979.

Sydnor, William. *The Real Prayer Book: 1549 to the Present.* Wilton, Conn.: Morehouse, 1978.

Taylor, Charles Carlisle. *The Life of Admiral Mahan.* New York: George H. Doran Co., 1920.

Todorich, Charles. *The Spirited Years: A History of the Antebellum Naval Academy.* Annapolis, Md.: Naval Institute Press, 1984.

Trask, David F. *The War with Spain in 1898.* New York: Macmillan Co., 1981.

Turk, Richard W. *The Ambiguous Relationship: Theodore Roosevelt and Alfred Thayer Mahan.* New York: Praeger, 1987.

Tyrrell, Ian. *Reforming the World: The Creation of America's Moral Empire.* Princeton, N.J.: Princeton University Press, 2010.

Van Amringe, John H., et al. *A History of Columbia University, 1754–1904.* New York: Columbia University Press, 1904.

Vance, Norman. *The Sinews of the Spirit: The Ideal of Christian Manliness in Victorian Literature and Religious Thought.* Cambridge: Cambridge University Press, 1985.

Vaughan, Samuel S. *The Little Church: One Hundred Years at the Church of the Atonement, 1868–1968.* Tenafly, N.J.: Church of the Atonement, 1969.

Vlahos, Michael. *The Blue Sword: The Naval War College and the American Mission, 1919–1941.* Newport, R.I.: Naval War College Press, 1980.

Weigley, Russell F. *The American Way of War: A History of United States Military Strategy and Policy.* New York: Macmillan Co., 1973.

West, Richard S., Jr. *Admirals of American Empire.* New York: Greenwood Press, 1948.

Williams, William Appleman. *The Tragedy of American Diplomacy.* 2nd rev. ed. New York: W. W. Norton & Co., 1972.

Zimmermann, Warren. *First Great Triumph: How Five Americans Made Their Country a World Power.* New York: Farrar, Straus & Giroux, 2002.

SECONDARY ARTICLES AND CHAPTERS

Allin, Lawrence C. "The Naval Institute, Mahan, and the Naval Profession." *Naval War College Review* 31 (Summer 1978): 29–48.

Ambrose, Stephen E. "Dennis Hart Mahan." *Civil War Times Illustrated* 2 (Nov. 1963): 30–35.

Bederman, Gail. "'The Women Have Had Charge of the Church Work Long Enough': The Men and Religion Forward Movement of 1911–1912 and the Masculinization of Middle-Class Protestantism." *American Quarterly* 41 (1989): 432–65.

Berge, William H. "Voices for Imperialism: Josiah Strong and the Protestant Clergy." *Border States* 1 (1973). http://spider.georgetowncollege.edu/htallent/border/bs1/berge.htm. Accessed July 25, 2010.

Bower, Stephen E. "The Theology of the Battlefield: William Tecumseh Sherman and the U.S. Civil War." *Journal of Military History* 64 (2000): 1005–34.

Carpenter, Ronald H. "Admiral Mahan, 'Narrative Fidelity', and the Japanese Attack on Pearl Harbor." *Quarterly Journal of Speech* 72 (1986): 290–305.

Corgan, Michael T. "Mahan and Theodore Roosevelt: The Assessment of Influence." *Naval War College Review* 33 (Nov.–Dec. 1980): 89–97.

Crowl, Philip A. "Alfred Thayer Mahan: The Naval Historian." In *Makers of Modern Strategy From Machiavelli to the Nuclear Age*, edited by Peter Paret. Princeton, N.J.: Princeton University Press, 1986.

Downs, Robert B. "Ruling the Waves: Alfred T. Mahan's *The Influence of Sea Power upon History, 1660–1783.*" In *Books That Changed America.* New York: Macmillan Co., 1970.

Duncan, Francis. "Mahan: Historian with a Purpose." United States Naval Institute *Proceedings* 83 (1957): 498–503.

Ellicott, J. M. "Three Navy Cranks and What They Turned." United States Naval Institute *Proceedings* 50 (1924): 1623–25.

———. "With Erben and Mahan on the *Chicago*." United States Naval Institute *Proceedings* 67 (1941): 1237–40.

Ferreiro, Larrie D. "Mahan and the 'English Club' of Lima, Peru: The Genesis of *The Influence of Sea Power upon History.*" *Journal of Military History* 72 (2008): 901–6.

Field, James A., Jr. "Alfred Thayer Mahan Speaks for Himself." *Naval War College Review* 29 (Fall 1976): 47–60.

———. "American Imperialism: The 'Worst Chapter' in Almost Any Book." *American Historical Review* 83 (1978): 644–83.

Foner, Philip S. "Why the United States Went to War with Spain in 1898." *Science and Society* 32 (1968): 39–65.

Geissler, Suzanne. "The Admiral Versus the Rector: A Naval Historian Speaks Out on Prayer Book Revision." *Anglican and Episcopal History* 82 (2013): 166–79.

———. "Mahan versus the Pacifists." In *New Interpretations in Naval History*, edited by Randy Carol Balano and Craig L. Symonds. Annapolis, Md.: Naval Institute Press, 2001.

———. "Professor Dennis Mahan Speaks Out on West Point Chapel Issues, 1850." *Journal of Military History* 69 (2005): 505–19.

Godfrey, Jack E. "Mahan: The Man, His Writings and Philosophy." *Naval War College Review* 21 (March 1969): 59–68.

Gordinier, Glenn S. "Evangelists, Landsharks, and the Character of Seamen's Benevolence in Nineteenth-Century America." *The Log of Mystic Seaport* 43 (Summer 1991): 31–37.

Gough, Barry M. "The Influence of History on Mahan." In *The Influence of History on Mahan*, edited by John B. Hattendorf. Newport, R.I.: Naval War College Press, 1991.

Hacker, Louis M. "The Holy War of 1898." *American Mercury* 21 (1930): 316–26.

———. "The Incendiary Mahan: A Biography." *Scribner's Magazine* 95 (1934): 263–68, 311–20.

———. "Introduction." In *The Influence of Sea Power upon History, 1660–1783*. New York, 1957.

Hagan, Kenneth J. "Alfred Thayer Mahan: Turning America Back to the Sea." In *Makers of American Diplomacy: From Benjamin Franklin to Henry Kissinger*, edited by Frank J. Merli and Theodore A. Wilson. New York: Charles Scribner's Sons, 1974.

Hardy, Edward R., Jr. "Evangelical Catholicism: W. A. Muhlenberg and the Memorial Movement." *Historical Magazine of the Protestant Episcopal Church* 13 (1944): 155–92.

Hattendorf, John B. "Alfred Thayer Mahan and His Strategic Thought." In *Maritime Strategy and the Balance of Power: Britain and America in the Twentieth Century*, edited by John B. Hattendorf and Robert S. Jordan. New York: Macmillan Co., 1989.

———. "The Caird Lecture, 2000: The Anglo-French Naval Wars (1689–1815) in Twentieth Century Naval Thought." *Journal for Maritime Research*, June 2001. Journal on-line. Available from http://www.jmr.nmm.ac.uk. Accessed July 17, 2003.

Herrick, Walter R., Jr. Review of *The Naval Aristocracy*, by Peter Karsten. *Journal of American History* 60 (1973): 147–48.

Holmes, James R. "What's the Matter with Mahan?" United States Naval Institute *Proceedings* 137 (May 2011): 34–39.

Israel, Jerry. Review of *Alfred Thayer Mahan: The Man and His Letters*, by Robert Seager II. *Reviews in American History* 6 (1978): 370–72.

Karsten, Peter. "Armed Progressives: The Military Reorganizes for the American Century." In *The Military in America: From the Colonial Era to the Present*. Rev. ed., edited by Peter Karsten. New York: Free Press, 1986.

―――. "The Nature of 'Influence': Roosevelt, Mahan and the Concept of Sea Power." *American Quarterly* 23 (1971): 585–600.

―――. Review of *Letters and Papers of Alfred Thayer Mahan*, by Robert Seager II and Doris D. Maguire, eds. *American Historical Review* 82 (1977): 454.

―――. "Ritual and Rank: Religious Affiliation, Father's 'Calling,' and Successful Advancement in the U.S. Officer Corps of the Twentieth Century." *Armed Forces and Society* 9 (1983): 427–40.

Kennedy, Paul. "Mahan Versus Mackinder: Two Interpretations of British Sea Power." In *Strategy and Diplomacy*. London: Allen & Unwin in association with Fontana Paperbacks, 1983.

Kramer, Paul A. "Empires, Exceptions, and Anglo-Saxons: Race and Rule Between the British and United States Empires, 1880–1910." *Journal of American History* 88 (2002): 1315–53.

LaFeber, Walter. "A Note on the 'Mercantilistic Imperialism' of Alfred Thayer Mahan." *Mississippi Valley Historical Review* 48 (1962): 674–85.

―――. Review of *Letters and Papers of Alfred Thayer Mahan*, by Robert Seager II and Doris D. Maguire, eds. *Journal of American History* 64 (1977): 744–48.

Leslie, Reo N., Jr. "Christianity and the Evangelist for Sea Power: The Religion of Alfred Thayer Mahan." In *The Influence of History on Mahan*, edited by John B. Hattendorf. Newport, R.I.: Naval War College Press, 1991.

Miller, Perry. "'Preparation for Salvation' in Seventeenth-Century New England." In *Nature's Nation*. Cambridge. Mass.: Belknap Press, 1967.

Moley, Raymond. "Mahan's Long Shadow." *Newsweek*, July 18, 1966, 100.

Neu, Charles E. Review of *Alfred Thayer Mahan: The Man and His Letters*, by Robert Seager II. *Journal of American History* 65 (1979): 1166–69.

Northup, Lesley A. "Public Response and the Nineteenth-Century Prayer Book Revision Process." *Anglican and Episcopal History* 64 (1995): 173–94.

―――. "William Reed Huntington: First Presbyter of the Late Nineteenth Century." *Anglican and Episcopal History* 62 (1993): 193–213.

O'Connor, Raymond G. "The Imperialism of Sea Power [Review of *Letters and Papers of Alfred Thayer Mahan*, by Robert Seager II and Doris D. Maguire, eds.]." *Reviews in American History* 4 (1976): 409–14.

Palmer, Michael A. "'The Soul's Right Hand': Command and Control in the Age of Fighting Sail, 1652–1827." *Journal of Military History* 61 (1997): 679–705.

Pollard, Albert Frederick. "Goulburn, Edward Meyrick." *Dictionary of National Biography*, 1901 Supplement. http://en.wikisource.org/wiki/Goulburn,_Edward_Meyrick_(DNB01). Accessed July 27, 2011.

Pollock, Thomas R. "The Historical Elements of Mahan's Doctrine." *Naval War College Review* 35 (July–Aug. 1982): 44–49.

Pratt, Julius W. "Alfred Thayer Mahan." In *The Marcus W. Jernegan Essays in American Historiography*, edited by William T. Hutchinson. Chicago: University of Chicago Press, 1937.

Puleston, William D. "Mahan: Naval Philosopher." *Scribner's Magazine* 96 (1934): 294–98.

Rosenberg, Charles E. "Sexuality, Class and Role in 19th-Century America." *American Quarterly* 25 (1973): 131–53.

Schurman, Donald M. "Mahan Revisited." In *Maritime Strategy and the Balance of Power: Britain and America in the Twentieth Century*, edited by John B. Hattendorf and Robert S. Jordan. New York: Macmillan, 1989.

Seager, Robert II. "Alfred Thayer Mahan." *Dictionary of American Military Biography*, 711–14. Westport, Conn.: Greenwood Press, 1984.

———. "Alfred Thayer Mahan: Christian Expansionist, Navalist, and Historian." In *Admirals of the New Steel Navy*, edited by James C. Bradford. Annapolis, Md.: Naval Institute Press, 1990.

———. "Alfred Thayer Mahan: Navalist and Historian." In *Quarterdeck and Bridge: Two Centuries of American Naval Leaders*, edited by James C. Bradford. Annapolis, Md.: Naval Institute Press, 1997.

———. "A Biography of a Biographer: Alfred Thayer Mahan." In *Changing Interpretations and New Sources in Naval History: Papers From the Third United States Naval Academy Symposium*, edited by Robert W. Love Jr. New York: Garland Publishing, 1980.

———. "Ten Years Before Mahan: The Unofficial Case for the New Navy, 1880–1890." *Mississippi Valley Historical Review* 40 (1953): 491–512.

Seidule, James Tyrus. "'Treason Is Treason': Civil War Memory at West Point, 1861–1902." *Journal of Military History* 76 (2012): 427–52.

Smith, Erin A. "'What Would Jesus Do?': The Social Gospel and the Literary Marketplace." *Book History* 10 (2007): 193–221.

Smith, Richard W. "Mahan's Historical Method." United States Naval Institute *Proceedings* 90 (1964): 49–51.

Sprout, Margaret Tuttle. "Mahan: Evangelist of Sea Power." In *Makers of Modern Strategy: Military Thought From Machiavelli to Hitler*, edited by Edward Mead Earle. Princeton, N.J.: Princeton University Press, 1943.

Stanley, Brian. "Church, State, and the Hierarchy of 'Civilization': The Making of the 'Mission and Government' Conference, Edinburgh, 1910." In *The Imperial Horizons of British Protestant Missions, 1880–1914*, edited by Andrew Porter. Grand Rapids, Mich.: Eerdmans, 2003.

Starr, Harris Elwood. "Milo Mahan." *Dictionary of American Biography*. 12:210–11.

Still, William N., Jr. "David Glasgow Farragut: The Union's Nelson." In *Quarterdeck and Bridge: Two Centuries of American Naval Leaders*, edited by James C. Bradford. Annapolis, Md.: Naval Institute Press, 1997.

Turk, Richard W. Review of *Alfred Thayer Mahan: The Man and His Letters*, by Robert Seager II. *Military Affairs* 42 (1978): 160.

Watts, R. B. "The End of Sea Power." United States Naval Institute *Proceedings* 135 (Sep. 2009): 40–44.

Weigley, Russell F. "Dennis Hart Mahan." In *Dictionary of American Military Biography*, 714–18. Westport, Conn.: Greenwood, 1984.

Welch, Richard F. "Alfred Thayer Mahan." *Long Island Forum* (Winter 1999): 23–30.

Williams, T. Harry. "The Military Leadership of North and South." In *Why the North Won the Civil War*, edited by David Donald. New York: Collier Books, 1962.

Woolverton, John F. "W. R. Huntington: Liturgical Renewal and Church Unity in the 1880's." *Anglican Theological Review* 48 (1966): 175–99.

———. "William Augustus Muhlenberg and the Founding of St. Paul's College." *Historical Magazine of the Protestant Episcopal Church* 29 (1960): 192–218.

DISSERTATIONS

Berge, William H. "The Impulse for Expansion: John W. Burgess, Alfred Thayer Mahan, Theodore Roosevelt, Josiah Strong and the Development of a Rationale." PhD dissertation, Vanderbilt University, 1969.

Gilliam, Bates M. "The World of Captain Mahan." PhD dissertation, Princeton University, 1961.

Greene, Robert B. "Wisdom and Prudence: The Teachings of Admiral A. T. Mahan." PhD dissertation, Claremont Graduate School, 1979.

Griess, Thomas E. "Dennis Hart Mahan: West Point Professor and Advocate of Military Professionalism, 1830–1871." PhD dissertation, Duke University, 1969.

Schluter, Randall C. "Looking Outward for America: An Ideological Criticism of the Rhetoric of Captain Alfred Thayer Mahan, United States Navy, in American Magazines of the 1890s." PhD dissertation, University of Iowa, 1995.

Steepee, Jonathan L. "The Unity of Purpose in Admiral Alfred Thayer Mahan's Proposals for American Foreign Policy." PhD dissertation, New School for Social Research, 1977.

Index

abolitionism, 37, 39–40, 48, 141

Admiral Farragut (Mahan), 82, 109–10

Ambrose, Stephen E., 13, 47

American Church Institute for Negroes, 165, 166, 171, 193

"American Duties to her New Dependencies" (Mahan), 140

American Historical Association (AHA), 151–52, 186, 188

Ammen, Daniel, 80, 86

Angell, Norman, 174–75, 186

Angell-Mahan dispute, 174–75, 186

Anglicanism: ATM and, 54, 76–78, 81, 127, 184, 194; Colenso, 154; common prayer, 179–82; Episcopal comparison, 33; *The Guardian*, 171; High Church, 19, 33–34, 57, 70, 171, 204n71; liturgy, 19; Low Church, 18, 33–34, 98; Oxford Movement, 18; at USNA, 34; Woolverton and, 59, 63

Anglo-Catholicism, 19, 57, 69, 70, 78, 98

anti-imperialists, 144, 145, 159, 232n154

"The Apparent Decadence of the Church's Influence" (Mahan), 71–72, 160

arbitration: anti-arbitration, 140, 142, 160; arbitration treaties, 172–74, 185, 187; with Boers, 145; mandatory arbitration, 137, 139

Armaments and Arbitration (Mahan), 186

articles, ATM: on Boer War, 145; in *Churchman*, 160; collections of, 130;

on Hague Conference, 158; "Hawaii and Our Future Sea Power", 113–14; in *Leslie's Illustrated Weekly Newspaper*, 189; "Lessons of the War with Spain" (Mahan), 140; on moral aspects of war, 158; on naval officers, 147; on naval/diplomatic issues, 124; "The Peace Conference", 140, 141, 142; on prayer book revision, 178–79, 183–84; "Prayer Book Revision" (Mahan), 183–84; as reprints, 186; on Russo-Japanese War, 156; on social gospel movement, 138; on WWI, 189

Asami, K, 177–78

Ashe, Samuel A'Court, 29–30, 31, 34–38, 41, 52, 59, 65, 67–74, 78–79, 81, 85, 94–95, 126, 166

Asia/Asiatic race, 106, 146, 147, 156. *See also* China; Japan

Augustinian viewpoint, 138–39, 140, 158–59

Bailey, William, 22, 23

Blake, George, 30, 32, 35, 39–40

Britain: admiration for ATM, 191–92; arbitration treaties, 172; ATM's acceptance in, 112; ATM's admiration for, 103–4, 111, 140; ATM's celebrity status in, 115, 121; Boer War, 126, 145–46; church attendance, 123; comparisons, 113; interest in Sea Power, 106; London, 116, 186; naval supremacy of, 131; *Sea Power* reviews,

About the Author

Suzanne Geissler received her BA from Syracuse University. She holds master's degrees in history and theology from Rutgers University and Drew University, respectively, and she received her PhD in history from Syracuse University's Maxwell School of Citizenship and Public Affairs. She is professor of history at William Paterson University.